Analyzing Performance

Theater, Dance, and Film

Patrice Pavis   *Translated by David Williams*

The University of Michigan Press   *Ann Arbor*

English translation copyright © by the University of Michigan 2003
All rights reserved
Originally published in French as *L'Analyse des spectacles*
Copyright © by Editions Nathan 1996
Published in the United States of America by
The University of Michigan Press
Manufactured in the United States of America
⊗ Printed on acid-free paper

2006   2005   2004   2003   4   3   2   1

A CIP catalog record for this book is available from the British Library.

Library of Congress Cataloging-in-Publication Data

Pavis, Patrice, 1947–
      [Analyse des spectacles. English]
      Analyzing performance : theater, dance, and film / by Patrice
Pavis ; translated by David Williams.
            p.   cm.
      Includes bibliographical references and index.
      ISBN 0-472-09689-3 (Cloth : alk. paper) — ISBN 0-472-06689-7
(pbk. : alk. paper)
      1. Performing arts.   2. Performing arts—Semiotics.
3. Performing arts—Philosophy.   I. Title.
PN1584 .P3813   2003
791—dc21   2002005533

Grateful acknowledgment is given to the French Ministry of Culture
for support in the publication of this book.

These pages are dedicated, with great thanks,
to my colleagues and students, whose comments,
questions, and criticisms have helped me progress
in the analysis of performances.

Special thanks to David Williams.

Contents

Introduction

The task of performance analysis is enormously demanding, so much so that it is perhaps beyond the skills of any one person. Effectively it requires one to take into account the complexity and range of types of performance, using a series of available methods—some more tried and tested than others—or even inventing other methodologies better suited to one's particular project and objectives. The spectator nowadays, whether she is amateur or professional (i.e., a critic or an academic), is confronted with the most diverse kinds of performance without a repertoire of universally recognized and proven methods of analysis at her disposal. Existing analyses are rather discreet as to the means and methods they employ, as if the reception and interpretation of performances went without saying. The mapping of the various aspects of performance and their organization, however, is not at all self-evident; still less so their interrelations within the mise-en-scène itself, and the ways in which these elements are recomposed in the minds of the spectator. This study of performance analysis aims to clarify the array of different perspectives, and to provide simple and effective tools for the reception and analysis of a performance. First of all, therefore, an attempt must be made to clarify the principal techniques of "analysis" (a term to which we shall return).

It is thus with the utmost humility and, above all, caution that we should approach the field of performance; for it is both a minefield containing the most contradictory theories and the most insidious methodological suspicions, and a fallow field that has as yet failed to develop a satisfactory method of universal application. In order to assess the current situation and future possibilities for the analysis of mise-en-scène, therefore, we have to run the risk of treading on the odd mine *(mine en scène)*. This book aims to provide nonspecialist theatergoers with some guidelines and keys for analysis.

If such a bold undertaking is to succeed, in one way we would need to begin again from scratch, by putting ourselves inside the skin of a theater lover. We would need to forget everything that has already been written in the fields of semiology, the aesthetics of reception, hermeneutics, or phenomenology, so as to apply these knowledges more effectively and intuitively to the description and interpretation of live performance; but this would be as thankless as it is impossible. A pragmatic approach is made all the more delicate given that there are obviously no fixed rules nor evidence to determine whether a production has been "adequately" described and understood, or whether the many theories and contradictory observations have served only to impede a "simple and clear" view of the performance.

In addition to this multiplicity of methods and points of view, there is the extreme diversity of contemporary performances. It is no longer possible to group them all together under a single category, even those as broad as *performing arts, stage arts,* or *live performance.* Text-based theater (the staging of a preexisting text), physical theater, dance, mime, opera, *Tanztheater* (dance-theater), and performance art are all implicated; all are artistically and aesthetically produced forms of performance, and not simply "Organized Human Performance Behavior."[1] Mise-en-scène is no longer conceived here as the transposition of a text from page to stage, but rather as a stage production in which an *author* (the director) has had complete *authority* and *authorization* to give form and meaning to the performance as a whole. This author, it must be stressed, is not necessarily a concrete individual (such as a director or choreographer); rather it is a partial (in both senses of the word), reduced "subject" of limited responsibility informing every aspect of the process of producing the mise-en-scène, making artistic and technical decisions—without these decisions being reducible to intentions that would only need to be reconstituted, once the performance has been shown in its finished form, for the fidelity of their realization to be tested. In fact, analysis does not have to speculate about such decisions and intentions; it bases itself on the end product of working processes, however incomplete and disorganized it may be.

Performance analysis as discussed here should be distinguished from historical reconstruction. An analyst is present at a performance; she has a direct experience of it live, whereas a historian is forced to reconstruct performances from secondary documents and accounts. The analyst provides an account for a listener or reader who has (usually, but not necessarily) seen the same production. So analysis, in the strict sense, can only occur if the analyst has personally witnessed a live performance, in real time and in a real place, unfiltered by the distorting mediations of recordings or secondary accounts. In this way, analysis differs from the *reconstruction* of past performances.

The forms of these analyses and the discourses in which they are inscribed are extremely varied: spontaneous commentaries by spectators, specialist critical reviews in both print and electronic media, questionnaires drawn up after periods of reflection of differing lengths, sound or audiovisual recordings, written or oral descriptions of sign systems by conscientious semiologists, poetic or philosophical meditations inspired by a performance, and so on. The list of such discursive modes is open-ended, and their combination frequent. It is not a question of finding *the* right method of analysis (which, as one might expect, does not exist as such), but rather of reflecting on the merits of each approach, examining what each reveals about the object being analyzed—in other words, a pluralism of methods and questionings, which is the exact opposite of a postmodern relativism . . . We shall return to this point.

The structure of this book reflects my concern to provide nonexpert theatergoers and theater lovers with an outline of the current state of research (part 1). I will then go on to consider the principal components of performance in a more detailed way, drawing on diverse methods of investigation (part 2), before shifting the focus toward reception (part 3) in order to reconstruct the spectator's dramaturgical readings of a given performance, her conscious and unconscious reactions, as well as the sociological and anthropological dimensions of her perspectives and expectations. Each component of performance deserves to be examined both in itself and in relation to the others; each requires its own investigative tools, thus making a general theory of mise-en-scène highly improbable. Therefore specific methods suitable for examining the functioning of each component in a systematic way will be proposed. At the same time, an overview of a mise-en-scène as a whole remains of primary importance, without lapsing back into the kind of critical impressionism of which theater people seem rather fond. To avoid this ultimately reductive, albeit elegant, impressionism, a few detours will be taken to encourage the spectator to regain confidence in her own gaze, a confidence she should never have lost.

Part 1
The Conditions
of Analysis

1

The State of Current Research

Review of Research

Before Semiology: Dramaturgical Analysis

Obviously, performance analysis does not simply date from the age of structuralism and semiology. Any spectator commenting on a performance analyzes it ipso facto; for she selects, names, prioritizes, and employs particular elements, establishing links between them, extending and exploring some at the expense of others. In discussing a performance verbally, the spectator is not obliged to verbalize the unsayable; instead she endeavors to find points of reference. Description is usually layered on top of a telling of the story (the plot or *fabula*), or at least the narration of the most remarkable events on stage; this facilitates a broad overview of the materials used, a natural segmentation of the performance and a highlighting of potent moments from the mise-en-scène.

The tradition of dramaturgical analysis goes back to Diderot and Lessing (*De la poésie dramatique*, 1758; *Die Hamburgische Dramaturgie, 1767*), in whose work we find remarkable descriptions of acting and stage effects. Brecht, therefore, simply returned to a tradition already long established in Germany, that of the *Dramaturg* (the director's literary and theatrical advisor, now called the dramaturge). He offers dramaturgical analyses of the theater of his time and of his own productions, which are also very revealing in terms of the general conception of mise-en-scène. In France, dramaturgical analysis is the approach of critical theorists such as Roland Barthes or Bernard Dort. Their analyses always stem from a production's ideological and aesthetic mechanisms. Up until the 1960s, this mode of description dominated all others through its breadth of vision, its precision, and the compromise it managed to find between meticulously detailed observation and an interpretative overview. With no interest in an illusory exhaustiveness, and often without even being conscious of its participatory role in the description of a performance, dramaturgical analysis offers an initial synthetic approach to performance; it avoids a fragmented perception of a performance by underlining its lines of force.

The following chapter will show that we have at our disposal all sorts of other tools with which to take stock of a performance; it would be to our benefit to find links between these different methods and to increase our sources of information. It would be helpful to start by discussing the possibilities of a semiology of performance—at present both a well-established "science" and a research area in the process of undergoing significant structural changes.

Analysis and Semiology

The accepted term *performance analysis* is perhaps not the most felicitous. To analyze means to dismantle, fragment, segment a performance's continuum into fine slices or tiny units, to produce more of a "butchered" effect—a *mise en pièces*—than an overall understanding of (and through) a mise-en-scène. However, the spectator needs to perceive and thus describe the totality, or at least an ensemble, of systems that are themselves already structured and organized, that is, what is understood nowadays by the term *mise-en-scène*. In this respect, it would not make much sense to speak of an *analysis* of a mise-en-scène, since mise-en-scène is by definition a *synthetic* system of options and organizing principles, and not the concrete and empirical object of future analysis (unlike the performance). Mise-en-scène is an abstract theoretical concept, a more or less homogeneous network of choices and constraints sometimes designated by the terms *metatext*[1] or *performance text (testo spettacolare)*.[2] The *metatext* is an unwritten text comprising the various choices of a mise-en-scène that the director has consciously or unconsciously made during the rehearsal process, choices that are apparent in the final product. (Sometimes they can be located in the production book, if the need arises, although this record of a performance is not the same thing as the metatext.) The performance text is the mise-en-scène considered not as an empirical object, but as an abstract system, an organized ensemble of signs. These kinds of *text*—in the semiological and etymological sense of fabric/texture and network—provide a key to possible ways of reading performance, although they must not be confused with the empirical object: the performance in all its materiality and the particular context of its enunciation. The analysis of the performance—whether it involves dramaturgical analysis or simply a description of fragments or details—necessarily entails an understanding of its mise-en-scène, which regroups and systematically organizes the different materials of the empirical object the performance itself constitutes. In this respect, it seems easier—and perhaps more productive for the mind—to suggest some general hypotheses on the ways in which a mise-en-scène functions, rather than providing exhaustive and so-called objective descriptions of the heterogeneous aspects of performance. Obviously, such hypotheses are only worth as much as the person who proposes them, that is, the spectator/analyst in search of an understanding of the overall functioning of the mise-en-scène. They have neither the apparent objectivity of empirical observation, nor the absolute universality of abstract theory; they negotiate a space between detailed yet fragmentary description and general, unverifiable theory, between formless signifiers and polysemic signifieds.

Moreover, one should determine for whom the analysis is intended, its aim and the spirit in which it is undertaken. It seems to have two primary functions: reportage and reconstruction.

Two Types of Analysis

Analysis as reportage could have live radio sports reporting as its model; such an analysis would comment on the developments of a performance as it unfolds, as in a soccer match, indicating what is happening on stage between the "players," clarifying the strategies employed, recording the result, "goals" scored by opposing teams. This would entail dealing with the performance from within, in the heat of the action: reproducing the detail and impact of events, directly experiencing everything that moves the spectator at the actual moment of performance, determining its *punctum*,[3] the ways in which the spectator is emotionally and cognitively implicated in the dynamics of the acting, the ripples of meaning and sensations generated by the multiplicity and simultaneity of signs.

Ideally, reportage-analysis of this kind should be carried out during the performance; the spectator-analyst would react immediately, only becoming conscious of her reactions just after they have been expressed; she would note the "emotional punctuation" of the mise-en-scène and of her reactions to it. Although this practice remains uncommon in performance, apart from medical studies observing subjects' physiological changes or basic psychological reactions, nevertheless such reporting can cut to the heart of the matter, locating and observing in situ the spectator's dynamic, live reactions to events on stage. Most traces of these reactions are lost, however; for in Western culture, theater spectators (or at least adult spectators), particularly with text-based theater, are barely authorized to express impressions, reactions, and perceptions openly; they are expected to wait until the end of the performance to express them. Therefore an important part of these immediate impressions is lost forever, or at least buried away beneath memories and rationalizations of past emotions a posteriori. One of the tasks of performance analysis should be to witness when and how such emotions emerge, and the ways in which they influence the construction of meaning(s). Insofar as it is immediate and spontaneous, dramatic criticism sometimes retains an invaluable trace of initial impressions when it manages to account for a performance as a metaphor of those primary impressions.

Analysis as reconstruction, on the other hand, is a specialty of a Western culture inclined to conserve and store documents and to maintain historical monuments. On this level, it relates to historical reconstructions of past productions. Always effected *post festum,* it collects pieces of evidence, relics, or documents pertaining to a performance, as well as artists' statements of their intentions written during the performance's preparation and mechanical recordings made from every vantage point and in all possible forms (sound tape, video, film, CD-ROM, digital imaging). Such a *studium*[4] is endless, but the difficulty—as we shall see in chapter 2—is in studying all these documents in such a way as to restore a proportion of the audience's aesthetic experience. For any performance, whether it occurred yesterday or in ancient Greece, is lost for ever; and we can no longer have an aesthetic experience of it, nor have access to its living materiality. From that point on, we must settle for a mediated and abstract relationship with the aesthetic object and aesthetic experience. Such a relationship no longer allows us to evaluate objective, aesthetic data; at best, it permits some understanding of its creators' intentions and their impact on an audience.

Whether we are dealing with a production that has actually been witnessed by the person describing it or a reconstruction of a past performance, in reality we can only ever hope to restore some of its main principles and not the authentic event. Once these primary principles are established, the performance text becomes an object of knowledge, a theoretical object substituted for the empirical object the performance itself once was. However useful and important the articulation of such principles, intentions, or effects may be, they still do not constitute an analysis of the performance; they serve rather as a theoretical framework that the analyst will employ, if the need arises, so as to detail certain aspects of the performance.

Analysis as reconstruction is particularly concerned with the study of a performance's contexts; its aim is to understand the nature and extent of these contexts. These may comprise the venue or the audience for a given performance, that audience's expectations, its sociocultural composition; it may also include the concrete circumstances of the performance, the specificities of its physical location. Obviously it is not easy to restore these contexts and the modes of behavior that engendered them. Richard Schechner's notion of "restoration of behaviour" enables us to imagine and "restore" the behavior of actors and other artists involved in performance of various different kinds. But these contexts and behaviors are extremely variable, potentially infinite, and ultimately immeasurable.

> Even if human memory can be improved upon by the use of film or exact notation, a performance always happens within several contexts, and these are not easily controllable. The social circumstances change.[5]

Considered in terms of either restored behavior (Schechner), sociocultural codes, or *social context*,[6] these contexts place us in a semiological—or more precisely, sociosemiotic—perspective. Obviously this is not the only existing methodology for the analysis of performances, but it does already offer a range of analytic techniques that we should take on board. Rather than giving a standard exposition of these theories, already familiar through the work of Kowzan, Ubersfeld, Elam, and De Marinis, an overall critical review will be offered here, if only to determine what has been acquired and learned from semiology (even though this may seem self-evident today). I will evaluate the early stages of semiology, its debates and debits, in the hope of moving beyond certain dogmatic prejudices, which are mentioned here so as not to succumb to them a second time.

Semiology: Development and Crisis

In the 1960s and 1970s the structural analysis of narrative was applied to the most diverse of literary and artistic fields: fairy tales, comic strips, film, the plastic arts, and so on. Theater, in the form of both text and mise-en-scène, did not escape such systematization; the first theoretical works published sought to test the hypothesis of a theatrical sign.[7] A semiology of literature and theater was intended to offer a means of moving beyond the impressionist relativism of so-called traditional criticism, with its primary interest in texts rather than live performance. In reaction to the somewhat vague discourse of dramatic criticism, semiology sometimes believed it had found a universal model in cybernetics and information theory; however, this model often remains trapped in a linear construction of communication. It leads to an extremely naive conception of information in a theater context: encoded by the director, then decoded by the spectator, as if it were simply a matter of transmitting a message as efficiently as possible! Semiology is not a matter of accessing codes common to author, actors, director, and subsequently spectators who are supposed to decipher mechanically any signals directed their way. This caricature never had much purchase in later analyses inspired by semiology, despite a persistent and rather malicious tendency to attribute it to a particularly narrow and two-dimensional conception of semiology.

Theater semiology was able to establish itself as the dominant academic discourse of the 1970s partly because theater (sensitive after Artaud) had felt a need to be treated as an autonomous language in its own right, and not as a subbranch of literature. Its primary concern was thus to start from the stage, its significant moments or scenic units, and to examine the text in the context of its enunciation on stage. The net result of a radical separation of text from stage and dramaturgical analysis from "theatrical language" was that a semiology of the text became somewhat neglected, or even disqualified. But nowadays the dramatic text is making a remarkable comeback; theater is no longer conceived exclusively as performance space, but once again, albeit in a wholly different way, as textual practice. Talk of theatricality is once again in the air, but theatricality as found in text[8] and language.[9] We need to take into account this return to the staging of text (see chapter 7) and to a pragmatics of the stage in which the text is both spoken and withheld or retracted.

The rise of semiology in the human sciences coincided with the critique, usually Marxist, of so-called bourgeois ideology. Barthes best exemplified this alliance between linguistics and sociology:

> It seemed to me (around 1954) that a science of signs might stimulate social criticism, and that Sartre, Brecht, and Saussure could concur in this project. It was a question, in short, of understanding (or of describing) how a society produces stereotypes, i.e. triumphs of artifice, which it then consumes as innate meanings, i.e. triumphs of Nature. Semiology (my semiology, at least) is generated by an intolerance of this mixture of bad faith and good conscience . . . which Brecht, in his attack upon it, called the Great Habit. *Language worked on by power:* that was the object of this first semiology.[10]

What has changed since the dazzle and optimism of the 1960s is the belief that semiology has a necessarily sociocritical perspective, and the confidence in a radical critique of ideology. Since the collapse of "socialist" empires and ideologies, semiology has often been accused of having compromised too closely with ideologues and "masters of meaning." All the more so nowadays when there seems to be scant interest in denouncing impostures of all kinds, and any established system, any discipline, any claim to be representative in theater tends to be dismissed out of hand. For many critics, nothing emerges from the ruins of ideology and of militant critical thinking, apart from a skeptical relativism and a vague meditation on "the end of history" and the futility of theory. Such perspectives are rather limited and ultimately pointless, as this book will try to show, since theoretical reflection endeavors to describe systematically and in detail a production's every component; such a lengthy task obviously requires considerable patience.

This task is all the more demanding given that postmodern criticism accuses semiology of camouflaging notions of intention and authority behind the concept of signification, to which postmodernism opposes the ideas of openness and nonrepresentation. In this way, the very model of the sign is called into question.

This misunderstanding is not a recent one, for semiology has always been accused of mechanically applying the linguistic model to fields other than literature, to social and artistic practices in particular. Since Saussure and Barthes, however, it should be clear that even if these other practices are based on the signifier/signified opposition, they cannot be reduced to a grid in which nonlinguistic signifiers are automatically translated into linguistic signifieds. Nothing obliges (nor allows, for that matter) spectators to translate into words the experience of contemplating a light, gestures, or music in order for that experience then to be integrated into the global meaning of the stage. Therefore the objection made by the Québecois theorist Rodrigue Villeneuve seems inappropriate: "What seems to be difficult to accept," he writes, "is this general attitude, apparent to varying degrees, that makes us confine everything that is not linguistic translation of the stage object to an indefinable zone."[11] Semiology, even Saussurean semiology, is not obsessed with the desire to *describe* everything—which would be impossible in any case—and still less with translating everything into words.

There are, in fact, several questions mixed in with this critique of the sign. Of course the Saussurean model of the sign is binary (signifier/signified), and not ternary like Peirce's model (sign, object, interpretant).[12] It enables theater to be conceived of as an ensemble of signifiers that only assume their meanings as a series of differences. As for the possible signifieds arising from these series of differences, it is possible to link them with those of other semiological systems borrowed from the referent (or real world), and thus to include this world in our consciousness as a series of semiological systems already preformed and preconstructed by culture and language. Thanks to Saussure, therefore, we can grasp meaning as the construction of a signification, rather than naively, as the communication of a signification already existing in the world.

On the other hand, once we perceive the materiality of performance (the signifiers, in Saussurean terms), there is nothing to prevent us from locating ourselves in the prelinguistic, "just prior to language," of apprehending "the body in the mind."[13] After all, this is what we actually do when we watch a dance, a gesture, or any signifier not yet contaminated or transcribed through language. Another question is how to connect these prelinguistic impressions with the other elements of a performance, in particular linguistic and narrative elements. Later on (chapter 4), I will examine whether it is possible to effect this connection in ways other than through a binary semiology, and whether or not the gaze or desire the spectator brings to performance is always channeled, directed, *vectorized* by signs.

There are many other misunderstandings about this initial semiology that need clarification. Those that have been described above are easy to dispel; but this early phase of semiology contains a number of other limitations that we must endeavor to overcome by imagining other possible solutions.

Limitations of Classical Semiology

Minimal Units

Theater performance cannot be dismantled and segmented, like natural languages, into a limited series of units or phonemes whose full combinative range would generate all possible scenarios. So it is inconceivable to transpose the linguistic model of phonemes and morphemes into the sphere of what is known metaphorically, since Artaud, as "theater language." It is no use trying to locate, and isolate from the continuum of performance, minimal units defined in terms of the smallest distinguishable elements in time and space. Such an exhaustively detailed mapping is only of interest if it includes indications that help us understand performance; otherwise it fails to explain the functioning of signs. The minimal unit can no longer be conceived of as the philosopher's stone, taking a performance apart as if by magic.

Categories of Signs

Nor does analysis need to concern itself with establishing a repertoire or systems of signs to constitute and apply to any performance. Such a system does not exist, and an enumeration of signs or kinds of signs proves nothing—whether it be a semiotic typology of signs[14] or a classification of performance. So there is no point in drawing up a "hit list" of the categories of signs used in any (Western, text-based) performance, categories the analyst would have to order by recording the frequency of their occurrence. The categorizations of Kowzan,[15] Elam, or Fischer-Lichte[16] each include the same components occurring in "standard" Western theater performance, in particular those of illusionist and bourgeois realist theater. Unfortunately, these subdivisions serve to delimit and fix performance, rather than shedding any fresh light on it. They force us to think in ready-made, outdated categories that any avant-garde, or indeed any mise-en-scène, systematically calls into question. For instance, the way in which these categories effect a radical separation between human systems (animate) and object systems (inanimate) is no longer relevant in current theater practice. The human body is sometimes treated as inert material (Butoh dance); and an object can replace and signify a human presence (an item of clothing, for example, or a prop closely associated with a particular person). That is why these old categories will not be used in this current work, even though they form part of a Western cultural heritage and there are some difficulties in bypassing them completely when discussing theater.

Such categories stem from a European theater tradition that is classical, or indeed antiquated, whose aesthetics and division of labor no longer have much in common with current practice. I propose to replace them here with transverse systems and categories that sit astride several of the old categories—such as the system of chronotopes (see chapter 5 for a definition), the system of vectorization, and other lateral tools enabling us to move beyond a fragmented vision of performance.

New Departures

A "Dissemiotics"?

More recent endeavors have tried to separate themselves off from the earlier semiological work, which was overly taxonomic and fragmenting, by drawing on the hermeneutic and pragmatic German tradition (Wekwerth, Paul) or on phenomenology (Ingarden, Derrida, Carlson, States, Garner). Usually, here, the aim has been to go beyond Saussurean binarism and the "closure of representation"[17] by proposing a generalized "dissemiotics" and a "theatre of energies"[18] in place of a theater of signs. Lyotard, the most articulate representative of this tendency, in his essay "La dent, la paume" ("The Tooth, the Palm") (1973), has produced a radical critique of the sign from Brecht to Artaud; but his criticism of theater as "lieutenancy" (*lieutenance*: "taking/holding place") and as representation, and his proposal of an "energetic theatre," unfortunately remain rather underdeveloped and interrogative:

> The business of an energetic theatre . . . is neither to suggest that such and such means such and such, nor to say it, as Brecht wanted. Its business is to produce the highest intensity (through excess or lack of energy) of what is there, without intention. That is my question: is this possible, and if so, how?[19]

Lyotard's *dissemiotics*, it seems, is even less possible and feasible than semiotics, but its merit is in its destabilizing of the notion of the sign, or at least the fixed sign, as linked to language and taking the place of the materiality of performance. This is what *phenomenology* also sets out to do, criticizing the segmentation of performance into signs and thus of its semiological function. In phenomenology, perception of the performance event is global, making all semiological segmentation absurd. The problem with semiotics is that, by treating theater as a system of codes, it necessarily dissects the perceptual impression that theater makes on the spectator. As Merleau-Ponty has said, "it is impossible . . . to decompose a perception, to make it into a collection of sensations, because in it the whole is prior to the parts."[20] Here is the source of reactions against analysis, and the beginnings of a globalizing phase where the aim is to find syntheses rather than reading grids.

Global Understanding and Vectorization

In the 1980s, these various critiques of classical semiological analysis led to a globalizing phase in which performance was conceived as a series of syntheses or frameworks. Mise-en-scène, in the structuralist sense of the term, became the key notion in a new theory able to synthesize acting options, dramaturgical choices, and a performance's lines of force. Instead of dismantling perception into its component parts, classifying sensations, multiplying meanings, and thus arbitrarily segmenting the signifier so as to translate it into possible signifieds, here signifiers are conceived as anticipating possible signifieds; and the notion of individualized signs is reworked to establish series of signs grouped according to a process one might call *vectorization*. Vectorization is, at the same time, a methodological, mnemotechnical, and dramaturgical means of linking networks of signs. It consists of associating and connecting signs that form parts of networks, within which each sign only has meaning through the dynamic that relates it to other signs. Let us imagine that, as in Chekhov's *The Seagull,* a gun appears on a wall; the spectator tries to relate it to other indices, and at the moment it disappears and she hears a gunshot, she has no doubt that the depressed and suicidal hero has just put an end to his life. Such networks are weblike threads holding a production together, preventing it from total fragmentation.

Globalization of this kind is not free of risk, however, since it encourages analysis to set off in search of a sort of secret "key" or code to the mise-en-scène; in this context mise-en-scène is conceived in a centered, concentrated form, a conception that excludes performance practices based on decentering, arbitrariness, or chance. To avoid this overly coherent closure of mise-en-scène and its analysis, it should be made clear that mise-en-scène—its production as well as its reception—never comes ready-made and complete. Rather one has to outline the hypothesis, albeit a fragile one, of a certain vectorization: signs or moments in performance exist in relations of tension, interconnected through networks of meaning that make the dynamic interaction of the signs relevant. One can only describe the primary trajectories of a dramaturgy and the principal stage options, including those pragmatic decisions that appear to deviate from the production's general guiding impulses and lines of force. Since it is impossible (or boring, or irrelevant) to be exhaustive, it is useful to place signs and vectors within an overall guiding schema that is in constant evolution; in this way, one avoids being swamped by insignificant details. It would be better to reconstruct a network, with its orientations and through lines, than to be left with a disorganized mass of surplus material or useless recorded documents. The description of a performance always negotiates the space between a totalizing demand for synthesis and an empirical individualization, between order and chaos, abstraction and materiality.

The Experience of Materiality

This materiality is concretely experienced by the spectator when she perceives its particular materials and forms, provided she remains on the side of the signifier—in other words, that she resists the temptation to immediately translate everything into signifieds. Whether in relation to the corporeal presence of the actor, the grain of his voice, music, a color, or a rhythm, at first the spectator is immersed in an aesthetic experience of the material event. She does not have to reduce this experience to words; instead she can savor "the erotic in the theater process"[21] without trying to reduce the performance to its component signs, as, according to Bert States, semiotics sometimes does:

> What is disturbing, if anything, about semiotics is not its narrowness, but its almost imperialistic confidence in its product: that is, its implicit belief that you have exhausted a thing's interest when you have explained how it works as a sign.[22]

It is worth bearing this objection in mind; performance as representation should be conceived in terms of both materiality and potential signification; it should never be reduced to an abstract and fixed sign. When confronted with a gesture, a space, or a piece of music, the spectator should endeavor to appreciate its materiality for *as long as possible. At first* she will be touched, astonished, or silenced by these things that offer themselves to her, before *later on* they become completely integrated into the rest of the performance and evaporate into an immaterial signified. But sooner or later, the spectator's desire is bound to be vectorized; the arrow will inevitably reach its target, transforming the object of desire into a signified. Paradoxically, therefore, reading the signs in a performance means resisting their sublimation: the question is, for how long?

Desublimation

Coming to grips—"body to body"—with a performance's materiality should therefore be taken literally: the analyst (who is, after all, human) returns to the "body" of the performance, moving beyond the kind of sublimation that any use of signs represents; she allows herself to absorb fully the aesthetic experience and the material elements offered to her on stage. She desperately tries to overcome the "blindness many semiologists show toward the material force of aesthetic signifiers";[23] she remains aware of the "phenomenon of nonintentionality, of libidinal investment in events, of the sensual materiality of signifiers, which make it impossible to ignore the corporeality of things, structures, and living creatures through which signifiers are produced in the theater."[24] To experience aesthetically a circus, a piece of performance art, or any production using a diversity of materials, one must allow oneself to be "impressed" by their materiality, and not seek to give them a meaning. This is something children do quite naturally, as do those who watch a performance from a cultural tradition other than their own.

The current trend in performance analysis thus involves a return to the concrete, material realities of the stage, a desublimated return to the body of the performance. This tendency breaks with the abstract idea of mise-en-scène as sublimation of the stage body, as idealized abstract schema. In later chapters focusing on the components of performance, we shall see how this materiality can be revealed in detail, and the ways in which one can trace the vectorization that organizes this materiality in *space-time-action*. Suffice it to point out here that it is possible to "track" the trajectory and energy in any movement or utterance, to come very close to the breath, rhythm, and voice/way *(voix/voie)* of the performed text. This "logic of sensation" (Deleuze), this movement that moves the text along and "moves" the spectator, this displacement of affect and attention can only be apprehended and comprehended if we refrain from resublimating them into a univocal written trace, reduced to a signified or a secret code.

Nevertheless, this insistence on the material aspect of signs is always carried out within the structured framework of the organized, channeled event that a performance is—in other words, in accordance with a certain vectorization. Semiotization and desemiotization are, therefore, antithetical, but also complementary operations of a work of art and an aesthetic experience of it. This needs to be recognized when we come to evaluate the different methods of investigating performance. As we have seen, there is a twofold requirement when describing performance: on the one hand, we must return to the body of the performance; but on the other, we must step back and trace its contours and itineraries from the perspective of the desiring, observing subject. Such is the current state of analysis; the progress it has made is remarkable, but fresh developments are still needed. Semiology must take advantage of this age of suspicion into which it is drawn by its postmodern demon. Semiology is still faced with all sorts of methodological obstacles and unresolved questions that must at least be brought out into the open, even if they cannot be overcome; this volume will endeavor to tackle them systematically.

Unresolved Questions

However irritating and durable the limitations and unanswered questions of semiology may be, they reflect the difficulty of adapting analysis to performances that are constantly changing, resisting interpretation, and demanding new strategies.

Experience or Reconstruction?

Is a spectator's usual experience of seeing a performance only once sufficient for analysis? In principle it is, and this unique experience should be the golden rule when considering a performance that in itself is unique, its unfolding organized in terms of the ephemeral and the singular. However, there is a great temptation to cheat a little, multiplying one's experiences as a spectator by seeing a performance more than once, for example, or artificially reconstructing the performance using residual substitutes for the live event: photographs, audiovisual recordings, its creators' statements preceding the production (logs, preliminary plans and proposals, statements of intention or interviews). It is essential to distinguish carefully between, on the one hand, artists' intentions and public statements and, on the other, the artistic result, the final product presented to an audience— the only thing we should take into consideration here. One should make clear distinctions between the study of statements of intention (documents announcing a proposed project, commentaries, interviews, etc.); the paratext (or the array of texts produced around the dramatic text, notably stage directions); mechanical recordings of a performance (soundtrack, images, videos, or films); technical notation carried out after the performance, the semiological analysis of signs and networks of vectors, hermeneutic interpretation of the work, and critical discourse in the wake of the live event.

Analysis of the kind this book tries to practice certainly does not exclude the historical reconstruction of past performances and the range of disciplines that involves, but it is based above all on the unique, individual experience of the spectator present at a live event, an experience that theory endeavors to generalize in terms of a method of analysis.

Segmentation

Segmentation remains the core issue for performance analysis. If it is agreed that very little is to be gained by producing an "atomization" of a performance into minimal units, it is not yet clear what kinds of macro units to suggest. Unfortunately, the segmentation of performance is often still carried out in terms of the text, in accordance with its dramaturgical division into lines/dialogue, scenes, and acts; it is rarely based on observable units in the performance itself. A text-based segmentation, however, does not necessarily correspond to the dynamics of the performance. The latter has its own rhythmic frameworks, its moments of rupture or pause that provide the only appropriate reference points for any segmentation of the performance.

In reaction to this text-based segmentation (i.e., based on a structure suggested by the text), analysts have naturally looked for units based on the stage actions that constitute the performance. But here again, researchers do not always manage to resist the philological (or textocentric) temptation to reduce what occurs on stage to units marked by moments in the text where it is possible (or in their terms, *essential*) to record an actor's move. Such segmentation, which absolutely insists on movements and dramaturgical units coinciding at very precise moments anchored in the text, arbitrarily privileges one signifying system (visible, marked moves) and imposes a text-based segmentation on the rest of the performance. Instead, I propose a mode of segmentation based on the overall rhythm of the performance, the rhythm of physical actions and of the musical composition of the mise-en-scène—in other words, in accordance with the temporal

organization of its rhythmic frameworks. In brief, one should take into
account those sequences when text and stage move out of sync, paying particular attention to possible vectorization(s) in the mise-en-scène as a
whole.

Textual Concretization

In a similar logocentric way, there is (or was) a tendency to view a mise-en-
scène as the stage concretization of the preexisting dramatic text, something that ensues from a reading of the dramatic text to find its concrete
form in the mise-en-scène. With regard to classical works that have been
interpreted on many occasions, of course one can understand this need to
refer back to the text in order to compare the series of possible stage concretizations it has engendered.[25] But that again reflects a philological,
"scholastic" attitude (to use Lehmann's merciless term)[26] that aims to consider the stage solely from the perspective of the text—whereas in fact the
two areas are incommensurable. Performance analysis takes as its starting
point the fully realized, empirical object and does not attempt to go back to
what might have generated it. The stage should be considered an
autonomous field that, contrary to Ingarden's view, does not necessarily
concretize, realize, or destabilize a preexisting dramatic text; it is "an artistic practice that cannot be foreseen and predetermined from the perspective of the text."[27] I shall return to this relationship between text and performance if only to overcome this false opposition (see chapter 7).

The Status of the Text

At issue here is the status of the text in a production, what one might call
the "staged text" *(texte émis en scène)*. The words spoken by an actor (or any
other kind of stage utterance) must be analyzed in terms of the ways in
which they are inscribed and concretely produced on stage—colored by the
voice of the actor and the interpretation of the scene—and not in the ways
in which we would analyze them if we had read them in the published text.
Text and performance are no longer conceived as being in a causal relationship, but as two relatively independent spheres that do not always necessarily work together for the pleasure of illustration, redundancy, or commentary.

The Narratological Model

The analysis of theater performance can also have recourse to narratology, which serves to identify its various components and make explicit the narrative dynamics of the plot and the stage events. Here again, however, as with the segmentation of performance, a narratological model should not be based on the text alone, but also on stage events; it should be neither too universal nor too closely modeled on a particular case. Although narratology is particularly well developed for the analysis of narrative and of film, it has not been very productive in the field of theater; perhaps because theater, particularly Western theater, is often viewed in an all too unilateral way in terms of *mimesis* rather than *diegesis*. Instead of asking what is represented mimetically, we should consider what is recounted, how, by whom, and from which perspective.[28] Theater is not a world crammed with mimetic signs, but a narrative using signs. Some very lively research on the storyteller in theater[29] offers a timely reminder of the fact that an actor can also narrate, and that narratology would be of great use to dramaturgy.

A first step would be to arrange the different rhythms of stage systems, locating rhythmic frameworks and perceiving the overall rhythm that results. For those performances that tell a story in a figurative way, where the spectator is able to follow the sensory-motor logic of action and plot, it would be worth drawing on Stanislavsky's notions of physical action, through line of action, or superobjective. Later on, I will suggest a theory of vectors that group together and dynamize entire moments of a performance (see chapter 5 below). These vectorial figures themselves occur within the constrictive yet clarificatory frameworks of the oriented action: the *plot* (fable or *fabula*), and the ways in which it is presented chronologically in the *subject*—two Russian formalist notions that should be retrieved from the prop store![30]

The Question of Subjectivity

Semiology was set up as a means of avoiding an impressionistic discourse on performance. As a simple notation of signs, however, it automatically removed the spectator's subjective gaze—a gaze that is never neutral—focusing on the analyzed object by means of a conceptual and methodological apparatus. This fragile gaze, however, whether it be male or female, should never be totally eliminated; rather it should be considered in its relations with the stage and in particular the actor, if only to try to get an intuitive understanding of "the indefinable elements of acting, the obscure uprising of emotion."[31] But how can one grasp and record such emotional uprisings? At best, bearing in mind cinema's perspectives on theatrical reality, one could imagine that the analyst's gaze is comparable (albeit metaphorically) to that of film apparatus: point of view, distance, scales of shot, framings, connections, and free associations made through montage within a shot, and so on. In this way, theater analyses would benefit from the central elements of cinematographic language, which itself stems from a particular logic of the human gaze.

However, the subjective gaze of the (filmic or dramaturgical) lens constitutes not so much a fleeting impression mechanically apprehended, as a way for the spectator to experience *aesthesically* the moves of the perceived object, that is, of corporeally following the evolving movements of the actor-dancer and the overall dynamics of the performance. Like Eugenio Barba, I have in mind "those few spectators capable of following or accompanying the actor in the dance of thought-in-action."[32] In our view, such spectators should not be so rare; they should even be the general rule: theater lovers capable of feeling and understanding the sensations and movements of their own bodies, of perceiving "thought-in-action," the bodies of performers and performance as an *auto-bio-graphy* in its true sense—that is, as a writing of the body of/by the actor, and the spectator, a writing that inscribes itself in the scene (to be) described.

The Nonrepresentable

The stage event is not always easy to describe, because signs in current performance practice are often tiny, almost imperceptible, and invariably ambiguous, if not unreadable. Intonations, looks, gestures, restrained rather than explicit, constitute so many fleeting moments where meaning is suggested but scarcely externalized and difficult to read. How do we take account of signs that are barely materialized if not through intuition and a "body to body" relationship to the performance that enables sensory-motor perceptions? The rather unscientific and unsemiological term *energy* can be very useful in discerning such nonrepresentable phenomena; through their presence, movements, and phrasing, actors and dancers release an energy that strikes spectators forcibly. This quality makes all the difference and contributes to the overall aesthetic experience as well as to the elaboration of meaning. The nonrepresentable is essentially, but not exclusively, the invisible; and, in reaction to a hegemonic visual culture of the self-evident, one should try to identify the nonrepresentable as it exists in the areas of the auditory, of rhythm, of kinesthetic perceptions: in other words, over and above those all too obvious visual signs and units that are largely visible. For example, it is a question of reading bodies as one reads those of dancers:

> Literacy in dance begins with seeing, hearing, and feeling how the body moves. The reader of dances must learn to see and feel rhythm in movement, to comprehend the three-dimensionality of the body, to sense its anatomical capabilities and its relation to gravity, to identify the gestures and shapes made by the body, and even to reidentify them when they are performed by different dancers. This reader must also notice changes in the tensile qualities of movement—the dynamics and effort with which it is performed—and be able to trace the path of dancers from one part of the performance area to another.[33]

All such unanswered questions clearly demonstrate how theory and performance analysis, in trying to unlock every door, have moved away from a semiotics of communication and codes, and how minimally appropriate the semantic model of the sign and of levels of meaning is for contemporary mise-en-scène. On the other hand, we are already beginning to outline a more flexible model for the ways in which signs and their vectors function, if signifiers are not sublimated into immaterial signifieds and the guiding trajectories of vectors are clearly indicated; and I will return to this in the following chapters. The vectorization of desire—the desire of the body of the performance, as much as that of the spectator—becomes a possible model for analysis once we are able to conceive of vectorization as that which organizes the performance; we must open it up to contradictory perspectives rather than confining it to definitive immutability.

In order for this tentatively outlined model to develop further, the conditions for analysis and the appropriate theoretical spheres for it to prosper need to be specified.

The Renewal of Theory

The fundamental question of analysis is to know why and for whom it is being undertaken, and which method would be the most suitable. Reviews in the print or electronic media are addressed to a wide audience of people wishing to be informed or advised, whereas a semiological account, which requires more time for reflection and a more sophisticated conceptual apparatus, is almost always addressed to other theater theorists and intellectuals, to colleagues entrenched in the same rather prudent, studious, or fetishistic relationship with the stage. Theater practitioners are rarely users of analysis, either out of fear of being exposed, of vague misgivings about theory or some deep-seated anti-intellectualism, or of disinterest, lack of time or curiosity. The problem is not how to make them interested in our theories, but rather—all modesty aside—how our theories will influence their practice in the same way that their practice has given rise to our theories. To this tragic misunderstanding one might add the fact that research is nearly always carried out in isolation by and for a group of specialists working within the same critical tradition, often unaware of the other traditions that exist. It is common knowledge that there is practically no exchange between French semiology, Dutch empiricism, Swedish audience/reception studies, English pragmatism, German hermeneutics, or Italian historiography. Alas, poor Erasmus.

In spite of the rather discouraging list of unanswered questions and obstacles above, it seems that analysis, "twenty years on," could start over again on more solid ground if it were to draw on the existing range of well-established, sophisticated disciplines, such as sociology and anthropology, which have usually been developed in areas far removed from particular instances of text or performance. I will limit myself here to listing five fields of research, as a sort of reminder; each of them is most effectively applied in specific analyses, examples of which are to be found in later chapters of this book.

Production-Reception Theory

For an analysis that wishes to attend to the final product of a mise-en-scène as well as to the roots of its elaboration, one needs to invent a theory that will account for both production and reception, a theory that is neither partial nor unilateral—as studies of literary and stage creation, or the aesthetics of reception, have tended to be. In the latter, for example, everything is focused around readings of a work relativized by a series of successive audiences. Our task is to imagine a model combining an aesthetics of production and reception, studying their dialectical interaction—in other words, assessing both a production's anticipated reception and the relationship between the production and the spectator's activity in the process of reception.[34]

There is indeed a danger, as Hans-Thies Lehmann points out, in simply transferring the problems connected to production into the realm of reception, naively expecting the spectator to resolve them all with a wave of her magic wand, as if she were endowed with theoretical omnipotence. Production-reception theory invariably attempts to divide the creation of forms and signs evenly between productive and receptive instances; it assumes that one cannot ignore the other, that in fact they work artfully in tandem, generating strategies and pathways of varying degrees of practicality. This conception of production-reception promotes an interactive strategy of productive and receptive instances that we should seek to produce as creators and to receive as spectators. Such a strategy prevents us from slipping back into the debate about the intentionality of the artist-producer and the subjectivity of the spectator-receiver. It reminds us that the answer lies in neither one nor the other, but in their mutual seduction (as opposed to reduction): a seduction familiar to those cultures in contact with others through intercultural exchange, and something to which they surrender without hesitation but not without pleasure.

Similarly, it hardly seems useful to reintroduce the subjectivity/objectivity polarity simply to locate subjectivity on the side of the artist and the spectator, and objectivity on the side of the work-object. Of course it is the subject who analyzes and evaluates; but to say that analysis is subjective is not only banal, it also presupposes the existence of an objectivity on which everyone might finally agree: the common, enduring reference—the object finally caught in the flight of desire.

Sociosemiotics

Another area that should be developed is that of a semiology that is attentive to ideological questions, in the ways in which signs are anchored and constituted in a social, economic, and cultural context. Empirical studies of audiences have (or should have) understood that one cannot neglect the study of the cognitive, emotional, and semiological mechanisms used by the spectator to create meanings—a spectator who is therefore involved hermeneutically in the construction of such meanings.[35] Is a semiocognitive approach compatible with a sociological and ideological approach?

This is the central question explicitly posed by a method such as sociosemi- otics. Sociosemiotics differs both from reception theory, with its roots in German *Rezeptionsästhetik,* and American reader-response criticism. Both of these approaches unfortunately neglect the ideological plurality of the reader or spectator; for they presuppose an individual, isolated, "ideal" reader rather than someone at an intersection of ideological and cultural tensions and contradictions, the subject as dynamic nexus that reflects conflicting tendencies and groups (see chapter 9).

Between Sociosemiotics and Cultural Anthropology

Over the last few years, sociosemiotics has evolved toward a cultural anthropology that encompasses the cultural, relational dimensions of per- formance. The development of an intercultural theater in recent years (Brook, Grotowski, Barba) has accelerated the challenge to purely linguis- tic and semiotic tools for analysis. An intercultural semiotics invites us to relativize our choices, priorities, and habits in the analysis of performance. For example, it warns us against our obsession to describe a visible and readable space, to seek out and quantitatively process information and redundancies, to valorize all that deviates from the norm and shows origi- nality. Such semiotics may cure us of our "deafness" toward the phenom- ena of hearing, voice, time, and rhythm, and of our inability to follow sev- eral parallel actions simultaneously and to evaluate the actor's energy. Rather than renouncing our Western cultural habits in a demagogic way, quite simply we need to acknowledge the degree to which our ethno- or Eurocentric gaze influences and often distorts our perceptions, and how much we would gain by changing our perspectives and analytical tools from time to time.[36]

Phenomenology

The basis of phenomenological thought[37] is the idea that any phenomenal, perceived experience has a form or gestalt that is the sum of a range of orga- nized, defined wholes detached from a (back)ground. The spectator's per- ception tends to look for the most balanced, simple, and regular form, and to distinguish different ensembles with contours that are clearly defined, hierarchically ordered, but nonetheless globally perceived by the human eye and understanding.

> Perception is fundamentally a constructive act, rather than a receptive or simply analytical act. . . . A truly satisfying theory of mental processes can only exist, however, if we find an equally important place for theories of motivation, personality, and social interaction. Would it be risky to suggest that, when people watch a performance, they are looking almost continuously for points of recognition, for causal connections between events?[38]

Phenomenology provides an image of stage processes that is a theory of action and, at the same time, a theory of the perceiver's appropriation of the performance: "Theater doesn't happen to someone, someone makes theater 'happen' to them."[39] Whether in the context of conceptual thought, looking at a painting or watching a performance, the human eye and mind are active and not merely recording:

> To think is thus to test out, to operate, to transform—on the condition that this activity is regulated by an experimental control that admits only the most "worked-out" phenomena, more likely produced by the apparatus than recorded by it.[40]

Similarly, the spectator produces more and more of her own perceptions and the connections between them, which she doesn't simply record. The phenomenological perspective offers a valuable invitation to move interactively through the mazes of performance and meaning.

Theory of Vectors

To some degree, moreover, one must "follow the arrows" on such itineraries, for our movement is channeled by the arrows of desire, which seek but do not find. It is also oriented by the traces of an itinerary through the performance relating to vectors that, as we shall see in the chapter on the actor, organize and dynamize the performance as a whole. Once the components of a performance and ways of exploring them have been detailed (part 2), this view of an open yet coherent network will enable us to accept the necessary renewal of theory while retaining the general framework of vectorization. Semiology remains a discipline—in the sense of a series of ethical and methodological guidelines—to which we quite naturally turn in order to observe the ways in which theater performance functions. However it should be enriched—without losing any of its rigor, if possible—by studying the mechanisms of need (sociology) and desire (psychoanalysis) from the perspective of an anthropology of the actor and the spectator.

2

The Tools of Analysis

After our appraisal of current research in performance analysis, and before going on to study their principal components in depth, it would be useful to list the instruments at the disposal of the spectator-analysts that enable them to launch themselves into their work, whether it be "reconstitutive" or simply reflexive, on the mise-en-scène they have just attended.

These tools are numerous and diverse, but their effective use is subtle and tricky, and one has to adapt to circumstances. Therefore, a wide array is proposed here simply in order to allow each user to draw upon them in ways that reflect their needs at that particular time.

Verbal Description

Isn't the most simple method of analyzing a performance for spectators to discuss it between themselves minutes, hours, or days afterward? And in fact this is how spectators quite naturally proceed, without scientific pretension, as if to prolong the pleasure of the event, to verify that they have, if not understood, at least experienced comparable things. Certainly nobody would find fault with this "automatic" verbalization; although those that take part are sometimes reluctant to translate their images and emotions into words, and though language, whether spoken or written, risks fixing the stage event. "The memory of experience lived as theatre, once translated into sentences that last, risks becoming petrified into pages that cannot be penetrated."[1]

Verbalization goes against an art aesthetic that tries to preserve the *figural* character of stage presentation,[2] that is, its irreducibility to words. Certain elements endeavor to bypass language in order to latch on to the visual and rhythmic dimensions of the stage. More often than not, however, verbalization occurs through a description of greater or lesser thoroughness of the stage actions. Now, there is a long tradition of description, and it is primarily applicable to a narrative genre that describes a space and a static situation.

In the analysis of the novel, description is defined as "a sequence organized around a *spatial referent* (rather than a temporal one, as in the narration of events), producing the *state* of an object, a place, or a character (the portrait)."[3] From this point of view description is only partially applicable to performance, which is tied to a temporal series of events in which visible and active characters take part. Nevertheless, description can go some way to conveying the experience of a performance to someone who has not witnessed it.

> To describe always entails a given subject's selecting the properties of an individual in the world for another subject; thus it is an act of signification dependent upon pragmatic conditions.[4]

In describing a performance, we choose certain properties that we deem noteworthy for others. We do not try to register everything for ourselves; we evaluate what will interest both our companions and us. Any descriptive analysis is effected in accordance with the production of meaning intended for an external observer, as if it were a matter of having to convince them of the pertinence of one's observations.

In addition, there are other principles of description that are just as valid for performance:

- *Temporal markers* are indispensable for description *(first . . . then . . . finally)*: performance analysis requires them to respect a minimal chronology and to remind us of the order in which actions unfold and signs pass by.
- *Spatial organizers* enable the describer to orient herself in front of the object: faced with the action on stage, sometimes the spectator is induced to shift positions, which relativizes the adopted perspective.
- The "*units* that our experience of the world structures in more or less systematic networks"[5] could lead us back, within the performance, to preexisting and recurrent categories—for example, the professional bodies involved in the mise-en-scène (scenographer, costume designer,

makeup artist, musician, etc.). They will be more productive, however, if they start instead from the structure of the material and the systematics it suggests—for example, the vectorizations that one draws from material, or from one element to another.

■ *Aspectualization*—the division and classification of elements that compose the objects—thus depends more on the reading and vectorization we make of the performance than on the ready-made categories of professional bodies. It stems from the whole formed by the work and its segmentation into parts, relating its diverse components both temporally (chronologically) and spatially (topographically).

■ The *narrative and evaluative orientation* of all description applies to a described performance; it is always described to prove a thesis, to propose a value judgment to an implicit interlocutor.

Rather than as a description of a static object, one can conceive of performance analysis as a narrative *account,* a way of articulating a past event. While it may lack the authority of a written text, it constitutes a more general form of documentation of what happened, and provides us with several accounts: of the plot, of the events, of an archaeology, and of an anthropology that interrogates a culture buried in the sediments of history.

Taking Notes

Should one suggest to the apprentice-spectator and the troubled theater specialist that they take notes during a performance? Definitely not, but if they insist on doing so, we will venture to give them the following advice.

Should one write or draw? The writing of linguistic notes during a performance obliges the writer to shatter its charm in order to rationalize in writing. Ultimately one's vision of and commentary on the performance will be affected, and it will prove very difficult not to filter subsequent responses through the lens of one's initial impressions. On the other hand, unless she has invented a system of notation comparable to those of music and dance, the spectator will be forced to resort to language if she wishes to record a fleeting detail in the mise-en-scène.

Drawing—or rather scribbling in the dark—translates a much more primary reaction; it traces an outline, a movement, an angle in the scenography, without yet verbalizing the perception; therefore it retains a gestural and kinesic quality that will provide invaluable information later on.

Whether written or drawn, this kind of "emergency notation" will be able to register the connective continuities, breaks, and transitions that punctuate the performance. It is always evocative, as well as illuminating, to trace graphically the contours of a performance, its trajectories and lines of force—all images that lead us toward *vectorization.* In place of details, one looks for the general trajectory, the texture: in other words, the performance's score. Once trained and accustomed to "see" the score in terms of the categories of accumulation/displacement/rupture/shift, spectators will only require a few strokes to capture their prey.

As soon as the performance ends, spectators are already in search of a past experience both *in spite of* and *as a result of* writing. At what moment does one write about the mise-en-scène? Formerly journalists had to produce their copy in the hours immediately after the final curtain fell; it is said that certain critics were never able to see the fifth act of *Hamlet,* as they had to deliver their reviews before the final duel! Nowadays historians can have as much time as they need to bear witness to what they have just seen; but the longer they delay, the more the performance's *punctum* will escape them, as will those details that comprise the very flesh of the stage presentation.

The only imperative of this kind of critical writing is to provide the illusion of bringing a past event back to life through writing in the present. Therefore one either takes notes from the perspective of a future finished text that may be read by others, or as reference material for the critic after the event, when memories have faded. In the following section, I will suggest a questionnaire that should be seen as a reminder or memo rather than as a prescriptive way of thinking; it requires the critic to reconstitute the overall system(s) of a mise-en-scène—a type of theorizing one might characterize as academic *(universitaire),* that is, connected to the universal as much as to the parasitic.

Questionnaires

In order to try to be systematic and comprehensive—as much as one can—various questionnaires can be offered to spectators. Three examples are given here: those of Anne Ubersfeld, André Helbo,[6] and Patrice Pavis.[7] Brief comments will be made with regard to the first two; the third one has already been widely discussed, and this book as a whole strives to respond to these discussions in a detailed manner.

Ubersfeld's Questionnaire

1. Material carriers
   a. How does the performance make itself known, or not? Identifying marks, subscriptions, press reactions, publicity, and posters
   b. How does the performance locate itself in (urban) space? Locality, target audience, assumed desires, architecture, relationship to the everyday
   c. How does the performance locate itself in relation to historicity? Exploitation/rejection/disclosure of a tradition, a disposition, an order
2. Access
   a. How did you choose the play?
   b. Where and how did you find the tickets? Have they made a hole in your budget?
3. Communication
   a. Social function of the performance: construction of convention, of illusion (role of the foyer, the interval, the postperformance, the rehearsals)
   b. Role of the performance contract: Is one dimension of the performance privileged? A shared knowledge, the presence/body of the actor/group, emotion/stimulation, noncommunication, noncognitive
4. Reception
   a. How did you perceive/understand/interpret the performance project?
   b. Was the audience involved as a whole?

From the outset Anne Ubersfeld insists on the material foundation of the performance (1) by grouping publicity (1a), geographical inscription (1b), and relations to history (1c). The difficulty is in connecting these three levels conceptually.

The question of desire (choice of play) is crudely posed (2a), as is its relation to economics (2b). Psychoanalysis and sociology are called to the rescue, but will they respond to the call?

The link to theatrical aims is made in terms of communication, whereas one could imagine the performance to be an "end point without end": an object to be constituted through the spectator's desire, as much as something to be communicated in accordance with a clearly established performance contract (3b). Moreover the "dimensions" of the performance are particularly muddled, so much so that a spectator would have great difficulty distinguishing emotion, cognition, and stimulation—let alone the (plural) functions of the performance: "social," of course, but also ritual, cultural, therapeutic, metaphysical, and so on.

The notion of "performance project" (4a) is central in Western mise-en-scène, which implies collective decisions and an aesthetic coherence; it is wholly inappropriate for Asian traditions that recuperate a preset secular practice through repetition, confirmation, and minute displacement. Ubersfeld's final question (4b) is intended to determine whether the audience has been divided (as Brecht wanted) or if it reacted "as one" in the psychological and cultural performance.

Helbo's Questionnaire

1. The stage space
   a. Its form and the form of the theater?
   a. Its nature (mimetic-ludic)?
   b. Coordinates of the space (open-closed, height-depth, vast-reduced, empty-occupied)?
   c. Relationship between onstage and offstage?
   d. What is the "aesthetic" (colors, forms, "style," cultural references)?
2. Objects
   a. Origin? Material?
   b. Number? Polyvalence?
   c. Use?
   d. Rhetorical-symbolic functioning?
3. Actors
   a. Number of actors?
   b. Relationship between character and actor? Type-individuation?
   c. Appearance, age, sex, body movements, voice and diction, costume?
   d. Social aspects of the actor: background, roles already performed, company membership?
4. The drama
   a. Which genre?
   b. The plot?
   c. The mode of exchange?
   d. The role of improvisation and the aleatory?

5. The director's work
    a. How does he develop the fiction (fictionalization)?
    b. What kinds of referent does he choose (historical, conte\
       fantastic . . .)?
    c. How does he manage segmentation into units? Does he p\
       continuity or discontinuity?
    d. Is there a predominance of the visual or of the auditory (word,
       music)?

The majority of Helbo's points of enquiry relate to the concrete and visual elements of a performance. They privilege space, while neglecting temporality and rhythm. Although the descriptions seem to be easy, their aesthetic evaluation (1) creates all sorts of other difficulties.

The notion of the object (2), as practical as it is vague, leads to a neorhetoric; as we shall see, its symbolic functioning can be clarified through the use of vectors and the metaphor/metonymy polarity.

As far as the actors are concerned (3), the problem is that they are not state documents but both concrete and abstract constructors of meaning. This construction does not result from an accumulation of properties, but from what the mise-en-scène brings into play, the logic of which one should have grasped already.

In terms of the drama, one will find it very difficult to dissociate action, narrative structure (4b), and the actantial model (4c); and improvisation and chance are by their very nature unpredictable.

On the other hand, the essential questions are asked of the director's work (5), in particular its strategic place between fiction (5a) and reality (5b), and its way of grading and proportioning the senses—the five senses of human beings and the thousand senses of the realized work.

Pavis's Questionnaire

Elaborated during the 1980s through extensive contact with different productions (essentially Western and Parisian), a first version of this questionnaire was published in *Voix et images de la scène*.[8] A final variant, which takes into account objections raised and the evolution of theater production, is offered here.

1. General characteristics of the mise-en-scène
    a. What holds the elements of the performance together (relationship between systems of staging)

    b. Coherence or incoherence of the mise-en-scène: on what is it based?

    c. Place of the mise-en-scène in the cultural and aesthetic context

    d. What is it that disturbs you in this production? Which moments are strong, weak, or boring? How is it placed in the current production?

2. Scenography

    a. Spatial forms: urban, architectural, scenic, gestural, etc.

    b. Relationship between audience space and acting space

    c. Principles of structuring/organizing space

        1. Dramaturgical function of the stage space and its occupation

        2. Relationship between onstage and offstage

        3. Connections between the space utilized and the fiction of the staged dramatic text

        4. Relationship between what is shown and what is concealed

        5. How does the scenography evolve? To what do its transformations correspond?

    d. Systems of colors, forms, materials: their connotations

3. Lighting system

Nature, connections to the fiction, performance, the actor. Effects on the reception of the performance

4. Objects

Nature, function, material, relationship to the space and the body, system of their usage

5. Costumes, makeup, masks

Function, system, relationship to the body

6. Actors' performances

    a. Physical description of the actors (bodily movements, facial expression, makeup); changes in their appearance

    b. Assumed kinesthesia of actors, induced kinesthesia of observers

    c. Construction of character: actor/role relationship

    d. Relationship between the actor and the group: movements, ensemble relations, trajectories

    e. Relationship between text and body

    f. Voice: qualities, effects produced, relations to diction and song

    g. Status of the performer: past, professional situation, etc.

7. Function of music, noise, silence

    a. Nature and characteristics: relationship to plot, diction

    b. At what moments does it intervene? Repercussions for the rest of the performance

8. Rhythm of the performance
    a. Rhythm of various signifying systems (exchanges of dialogue, lighting, costumes, systems of gesture). Connection between real duration and lived duration
    b. The overall rhythm of the performance: continuous or discontinuous rhythm, changes of system, connection with the mise-en-scène
9. Reading the plot through the mise-en-scène
    a. What story is being told? Summarize it. Does the mise-en-scène recount the same story as the text?
    b. What dramaturgical choices? Coherence or incoherence of reading?
    c. What are the ambiguities in the text, and how are they clarified in the mise-en-scène?
    d. How is the plot structured?
    e. How is the plot constructed by actors and staging?
    f. What is the genre of dramatic text according to this mise-en-scène?
    g. Other options for possible mise-en-scènes
10. The text in performance
    a. Choice of version for staging: what are the modifications?
    b. Characteristics of the translation (where appropriate). Translation, adaptation, rewriting or original writing?
    c. Role given to the dramatic text in the mise-en-scène?
    d. Relationships between text and image, between ear and eye
11. The spectator
    a. Within what theater institution does the production take place?
    b. What expectations did you have of the performance (text, director, actors)?
    c. What presuppositions are necessary to appreciate the performance?
    d. How did the audience react?
    e. Role of the spectator in the production of meaning. Does the performance encourage a univocal or plural reading?
    f. What images, scenes, themes caught your attention and remain with you?
    g. How is the spectator's attention manipulated by the mise-en-scène?
12. How to record (photograph or film) the performance? How to retain memories of it? What escapes notation?

13. What cannot be put into signs (semiotized)?
    a. What didn't make sense in your reading of the mise-en-scène?
    b. What was not reducible to signs and meaning (and why)?
14. Final assessment
    a. Are there any particular problems that need examining?
    b. Any comments, further categories required for this production
       and for the questionnaire

Supplementary Documents

Whereas a questionnaire requires the spectators to take sides, there are objective elements that accompany a production to which spectators can refer before or after attending a performance. These include programs, production and promptbooks, publicity paratexts, press releases, and photographs.

Programs

Nowadays programs often contain much more than the names of directors and actors; their ambition goes beyond the requirements of minimal information, and they encroach upon the understanding of spectators. Indeed spectators themselves can refer, either just before the performance or at home, to a collection of critical materials devoted to the work, its author, and its historical contexts. Therefore reception will be prepared (should one say facilitated?) through an imposed understanding of the background, or through a summary of the plot, or even through the director's reflections on the work being staged.

For the analysis of performance, which actually remains the only reality that counts in this context, one must take into account these imposed "keys" and at the same time the overall structure that is being explored. One's enquiries may try to determine how much time spectators devote to reading the program before and after the performance, what elements they retain from it, and in what way these elements have been instrumental in their interpretation of the work. This will necessitate reassessing the precise limits of the work, its context, and the indeterminate threshold separating the work from the so-called outside world.

Programs provide the following kinds of information:

- Intertexts for the play and the performance: texts and artistic sources to which the mise-en-scène refers more or less directly, either through avowed borrowings or chosen affinities that have or could have inspired the director
- Outlines of discussions that preceded the production: interviews with artists or star performers during rehearsals, statements of intent given to collaborators, actors, the theater administration, or the press, texts by the performance's creators specially prepared for the program
- References to other productions of the work, or by the same director
- Extracts from scholarly studies of the play
- Textual selections from the play, in particular from the author's stage directions/staging proposals—or the entire play text
- Any other residual traces of the performance that are conducive to suggesting its splendor and originality: photographs, extracts, commentaries, etc.

Production Books

One must distinguish between programs and production books or logs; although not normally accessible to the average spectator, the latter are sometimes prepared by a theater or artistic team for a variety of reasons—but without intent to influence a future reader. Obviously the Berliner Ensemble's *Regiebücher* (documentation prepared by Brecht in the wake of each mise-en-scène intended for the use of future directors of his plays), the production logs of Stanislavsky, Reinhardt, Copeau, or the notebooks of Beckett, are all brilliant exceptions that prove the rule of production as ephemeral and traceless. In such cases, the production book not only accompanies the mise-en-scène, it is also its key, even indeed its substitute: Craig and Stanislavsky both prepared books on works that were never subsequently realized. The precision and intelligence of these documents are such that they almost dispense with the stage work and become creations on their own, much more than simply summaries, sketches, or commentaries. When researchers also have at their disposal documents on the realization of a performance (recordings, first-hand accounts, personal memories), sometimes they tend to consider their work to be finished, superfluous, as if such documents speak for themselves.

Press Releases

The press release comprises a document that often precedes the final completion of a production; it is prepared by a publicist with the aim of preparing the audience and persuading journalists to come to press previews. Comprising compiled details of various kinds, photocopied documents or unpublished notes by the artists involved, the press release would rather seduce ("come and see me") than convince ("this is what is said"). For major productions drawing on substantial budgets, press releases will provide journalists, community groups, and teachers with information that they must respond to, and that the press will have no hesitation in using systematically in its articles.

The Publicity Paratext

The paratext of a mise-en-scène, which should not be confused with the paratext of the dramatic text (stage directions, didascalia), comprises everything that a spectator might have read in the press about the production: announcements, interviews, the previews just prior to the premiere, any other print or electronic media publicity. However much one resists the brain-death induced by exposure to advertisements, one never emerges entirely unscathed—even in theater.

Photographs

The interest of photographs for performance analysts is evident, since they are the tangible trace of what was; while it does not necessarily engender an understanding of the photographed object, this trace does convey a perspective on a work of art, a way of seeing it.

Photographic documentation relieves the commentator's memory of some of its burden, providing reference points to anchor a verbal description, ensuring that the reporting is achieved with a certain method. In fact, anchoring of this kind is indispensable for a photograph to assume meaning:

> By itself, a photograph says nothing. It has to be made to signify and therefore placed in a sort of relationship of actualization with other elements related to the representation (remains, traces, description, text . . .).[9]

Making photographs signify is therefore the analyst's task; they are considered as much documents as autonomous works of art. The analyst strives to "de-aestheticize" artistic photographs by bringing their documentary dimension into relief, and at the same time to appreciate their photographic aesthetic so as to imagine what this vision reveals about the reproduced object.

What are the possible benefits of studying photographic documentation?

■ Identification of spaces, objects, attitudes, that is, of anything that can be fixed by the eye of the lens
■ The precision brought to a detail or a fleeting moment scarcely perceptible to the naked eye
■ The recognition of bilateral relations between, for example, the space and physical movements, properties and space, lighting and makeup, etc.
■ Reporting a range of theatrical activity around and outside the performance itself (Agnès Varda on Vilar, Roger Pic on the Théâtre National Populaire or on Brecht,[10] Josué on Dasté, and so on)

Video

Video reproduces the real time and general movement of a performance. It constitutes the most complete medium on the level of bringing together the greatest amount of information—in particular, in terms of the correspondence between systems of signs and between image and sound. Even when filmed with a single camera from a fixed position, a video recording is a testimony that effectively restores the thickness of signs; it allows an observer to grasp a sense of the performance style, and to keep sequences and the use of different materials fresh in the memory. Video is frequently used by directors to restage a revived production, to ensure effective promotion, to sell the performance to potential venues, or to retain a trace of the event itself.

Computer and Compact Disc

Computers are not only used to store records of transactions; nowadays they can be used to prepare a document that will be both a reconstruction and a detailed study of a production.

A CD-ROM can replay images and scroll texts; it can concentrate on particular details, compare a scene in different productions, provide information on a particular historical point, even create virtual mise-en-scènes combining scenography, acting, voice, lighting, and so on. In his work for the International Shakespeare Globe Centre, Larry Friedlander foresees educational projects that bring together on one computer screen different multimedia versions of a play; one would have the possibility of staging more recent scenes within the existing programs, playing with one's favorite actors, acting with them. Such innocent games know no limits, as long as one does not ask questions as to what use they are and how they participate in the production of meaning. For there is an ever increasing gap between the scientific technology of data and the subjective hermeneutics of interpretation. We are no longer managing to make connections between these two orders, all the more so given the unwillingness shown by so many analysts to risk the slightest interpretative intervention, paralyzed as they are by the possibilities of technology and the multiplicity of methods. In recording everything, we end up not knowing what to think.

An archaeology of theater knowledge is of particular interest here; it resists technologies of reproduction, and instead looks within actors and their archaeologies for the possibility of disengaging and reconstituting the past. For, as the conceiver of this approach notes, "archaeology is not just excavation (analysis). It must, in some way, synthesize (reconstruct, represent, simulate) the past."[11]

The Archaeology of Theater Knowledge

Theater Archaeology

Mike Pearson, one of the directors of the Welsh company Brith Gof, proposes an archaeology that reveals traces, scars, the cracks and breaks in representation. The objectives of his theater archaeology are

1. To find useful ways of describing what is/was going on in performance.
2. To achieve a synthesis of the narratives of the watchers and the watched.
3. To attempt reconstructions as text and as second-order performance. This is a creative process in the present and not a speculation on past meaning or intention.[12]

Reconstruction here entails new performance, rather than abstract analysis. Its particular interest is in dis-covering space, time, overall structure and its component details. For Pearson, structure corresponds to what we call *score/underscore*, whereas detail is the *style* attributable to a director or group, its trademark, what we will call the *ideologeme* of a performance (chapter 9) and the *overall discourse* of a mise-en-scène, or even its *style.*

Second-order performance has become a means of replaying/re-creating/(re)inventing a performance that has already taken place; patched up and revived, its value is in itself; it constitutes a living analysis/synthesis that implies the involvement of all technical and human means to (re)create an event. The distinction between old performance and new reconstruction, between original creation and reworked revival, tends to blur, as do the distinctions between analysis and synthesis, and theory and practice.

The Living Archive

Actors archive past roles within themselves; they maintain them, replay them, consult and compare them, relate them to past and present experience. The pupils of Decroux are capable of reperforming an exercise they worked on with their teacher twenty years before, for it has been remembered corporeally and can be reactivated with sufficient physical training. Such astonishing feats are also accomplished by the actors of Barba and Grotowski, or those of other creators who base their work on the "in-corporation" of physical scores of an extreme precision (e.g., those of Robert Wilson, Mike Pearson, or Pina Bausch). During work demonstrations, such actors sometimes return to fragments of their major roles in the past, allowing us access to the living archive of performances in which they have participated; the fragments they offer seem to have been snatched from the depths of theatrical memory. And it is this living memory of theater that is much the most precious, a treasure that escapes mediated recordings, and is of vital concern to the living memories of spectators: "In the age of electronic memory, of film and reproducibility, theatre performance appeals to living memory, which is not a museum but metamorphosis."[13]

So living reconstructions can take the form of enacted revival, of training conceived as the daily writing of a sort of physical journal in the actor, of a work demonstration, of a metaperformance or second-order performance: in short, of an archaeology that is "another way of telling."[14]

The Mediatized Body of the Spectator

In this account of the tools of analysis, shouldn't a special place be given to the mediatized body of the spectator? For the body as an instrument is becoming influenced by technological media; it has incorporated and internalized certain rules regarding the functioning of these media. The conjunction of different kinds of media and the ways in which they have become part of live performance work naturally lead to an examination of their *intermediality*: in other words, the exchanges of processes specific to media, traces of which can be found in the performances—traces we propose to analyze here. Theater often problematizes and questions dominant perceptual models, primarily constituted through the influence of media. In reality, this is not a new phenomenon:

> Modernist art began to question current models of perception. Contemporary art continues in this direction with its analysis of advertising and other forms of media, which all too often nowadays occupy the place left vacant by nature in our experience of the world. In such an environment, it is legitimate for art history to examine (with all the necessary precautions, of course) everything in its historical materials that relates to models of perception and mediation.[15]

In the case of theater, one must examine the impact of these models of perception and mediation on both the actor and the spectator: in what ways has the body been reached and refashioned by new technologies? Have they become the "prosthetic gods" Freud described in *Civilization and Its Discontents*?

> By means of all his tools [motorized machines, spectacles, telescope, microscope, camera, gramophone, telephone, writing . . .], man makes his own organs more perfect—both the motor and the sensory—or else removes the obstacles in the way of their activity. . . . Man has become a god by means of artificial limbs, so to speak, quite magnificent when equipped with all his accessory organs; but they do not grow on him and they still give him trouble at times.[16]

New Technologies, New Bodies?

Have our senses become superfluous? Are our eyes and ears replaceable or interchangeable? Are we about to be substituted by machines? As human beings at the beginning of the new millennium, these are some of the questions we constantly ask, more or less mechanically, of the body and brain we comprise. It is not so much a matter of a "brain drain" as of a dematerialization of the body, sometimes associated with a compensatory process of renaturalizing performance.

One can assess the degree to which daily exposure to a range of media—from the telephone to television, encompassing cinema, video, photograph, computers, even writing—influences our ways of perceiving and conceptualizing reality; furthermore, we perceive performance reality quite differently from twenty, fifty, or a hundred years ago. The impact of these mutations is not so much physiological as neurocultural; our perceptual habits have changed, all the more so given the ways in which means of producing and receiving theater have evolved. This can be demonstrated by comparing and contrasting two types of performance: first, literary performance, centered on the text and *theatrical* meaning; and second, performance linked to *electronic sound,* decentered and disconnected from mimetic reality. The distinctions between the two may best clarify the changes in our ways of perceiving the world (see table on p. 48).

Although rather brief and blunt, this comparison at least shows that reality and its mise-en-scène require us to change our ways of looking, and indeed our bodies, in order for us to be able to perceive them adequately.

The same bodily metamorphosis works on the actor, whose physical presence is not always the rule any more. This is no longer exclusively a matter for the film(ed) actor, for whom "the loss brought about by this transposition above all impacts on the heterogeneity of densities and corporeal registers with which live art plays."[17] It also concerns the actor endeavoring to control a virtual body; for "with the ever improving speed of computer operations, it is our hope that actors will soon be able to animate in real time, and with their own bodies, entirely synthesized, virtual bodies or bodies 'borrowed' from other people."[18] The physical transmutation is already well advanced.

At the risk of confusing their real bodies and their virtual bodies, of being as present as they are absent, the actors of the near future are in search of other bodies and, in particular, other conceptions of the body. "With this stage in knowledge and technology corresponds a desire for a renewed body, fantasized differently, a source of rejuvenated gestures and emotions; it is not impossible for another body to be born out of the sea of numbers."[19]

The consequences for analysis are considerable, since the mediatized

Theater	Electronic Sound
■ The "textual" text offers a correlation of systems of signs resulting in an overall whole, which may be understood by everyone. ■ Voice and body are correlated; the voice is solidly anchored in the body, just as sound and images are integrated.	■ Electronic sound does not seek to correlate its components; performances are often put together track by track, as in the editing of different tracks for a film.
■ The receiver is reassured by a binarism between signifier and signified; one refers to the other unambiguously.	■ A new kinesthesia is set up, producing a new corporeal synthesis in spectators; this goes against their habitual system of reference, which is based on the alliance of time, space, and body.
■ The work produced, just like its receiver, remains a centered and unified subject. All of the different kinds of perception are drawn together into a stable core: the structure of the work and the unified consciousness of the observer.	■ The subject is fractured and decentered; it is open to a range of different voices, and therefore we are obliged to look and listen in different ways.

body—the actor's as much as the spectator's—is now accessible through an awareness of the media that have (de)formed it. Such ways of thinking about the media relate to the psychophysical constitution of the spectator as much as to the *intermedial* composition of the performance within which the various kinds of media meet. Hence the importance of devising a theory of intermediality in order to analyze contemporary productions that are supposedly "theatrical."

Intermediality

I do not propose to undertake a comparative study here of the principal forms of media (cinema, video, radio, theater); studies of this kind have already been made elsewhere.[20] Modeled on the expression and methodology of intertextuality, *intermediality*

> does not mean the addition of different media concepts, nor the act of placing discrete works in relation to particular forms of media, but rather the integration of aesthetic concepts from different media into a new context.[21]

I understand by intermediality that "there are variable mediated relations between media, and that their function stems partly from the historical evolution of these relations"; and I presuppose "the fact that one medium contains within it the structures and possibilities of another or several other media."[22]

When applied to theater, the search for intermediality in a mise-en-scène involves determining the impact of different, specific kinds of media on its various components. For example, one might focus on filmic narrative structures, on dramatic writing that employs a dramaturgy of short, abrupt, and interrupted sequences, or on the influence of cinematic lighting on stage practice. One should avoid a comparative stylistics of "media essences" (traits deemed to be specific to one medium), for this would only compare commonplaces attributed to the fixed essences of different media forms. On the contrary, I propose to examine the ways in which media (not usually an integral part of stage work) are integrated into the materials of a performance; the historically verified properties of the source media will be used to look at the ways in which they take on wholly different dimensions in this new context.

In the three historical examples that follow, one can observe the impact of cinema on three different performance forms; these examples legitimize our discussion of an *incorporation of media* into live performance.

Incorporating Media into Live Performance

Meyerhold's theater aesthetic was influenced by Russian and Soviet cinema, in particular the films of his former actor Eisenstein; however, he never borrowed directly from film aesthetics. As Uwe Richterich rightly suggests:

> Meyerhold was not interested in the simple use of cinema as a means of extending the technical possibilities of theater, but in the incorporation of the *aesthetic* implications of the filmic gaze.[23]

Although there were few screens and stage projections in Meyerhold's the-ater, nevertheless the mise-en-scène and the acting employed the tech-niques of cinematic montage, notably the "montage of attractions."

Decroux, despite the homage he paid to Chaplin, did not draw his inspi-ration from silent movies; however, in *Paroles sur le mime*,[24] he refers explicitly to "two opposing movements" that characterize two ways of moving in mime: the *saccadé* (jerky) and the *fondu* (sustained, or "dis-solved" in the filmic sense).[25] In fact these terms and techniques are best illustrated in cinema, with reference to fast editing and the dissolve or slow motion. A mime will be able to execute the actions most effectively by thinking of these different ways of structuring film rhythms; familiarity with their realization on screen will help inspire the physical movements. Similarly the notions of close-up and montage find a gestural equivalent in the mobilization/immobilization of a part of the body and in the fragmen-tation of the body where each segment is used in turn. The opposition between the glance and the gaze has often been theorized, notably by Samuel Beckett in *Film*:

> The *glance* is an external perspective, that of the camera or the editing, which introduces a break from shot to shot and a discontinuity between one shot and another. Such glances of *haptic* vision aggress their object, and introduce a *staccato* that is reflected in the spatial-temporal disconti-nuity of shots. . . . In contrast, the contemplation of objects [the *gaze*] occurs in a legato, panoramic movement that travels seamlessly over the external world. As a result, this world becomes all the more stable and global, and it preexists being seen; objects and space seem to be already there, awaiting a look, an EYE/I focused on them, as if these objects were constantly available for viewing.[26]

Pina Bausch, along with a significant proportion of so-called postmodern dance practitioners, uses compositional processes in her choreography that one might rather expect to find in the aesthetics of film or video: the frag-mentation of gesture, the repetition of a sequence, close-up and focusing effects, dissolves, looks at the camera, narrative ellipsis, accelerated montage. It is as if her choreographic approach is filtered through a way of seeing that is mediatized by the camera or the editing suites of cinema or video.

The Unfortunate Landing

In Heiner Goebbels's performance produced at Nanterre in March 1993, a certain number of musical, textual, and scenographic objects were assembled following a "method" that reveals a new use of media. It was as if the traditional way of using stage materials had been displaced.

Texts by Conrad, Müller, and Ponge are recited and cited rather than acted by André Wilms. The montage is not only thematic (it was about a forest), but also grammatical: extracts from Joseph Conrad's *Journal of the Congo* are in the first person; Heiner Müller's narrative *Heracles 2 or the Hydra* places on stage a character described in the third person; Ponge's poem on a pine forest is like an objective description, without an implied subject in the narration, in accordance with the principles of a pseudo-scientificity. These three modes of discourse cover the full range of linguistic means of describing or writing about a forest. One sees the speaker and the human being gradually efface themselves in terms of presence, in order to create a self-sufficient language that restricts itself to defining its own terms ("A forty-year-old forest is called . . .").

Moreover, this language, "carried" rather than embodied by the actor, disappears in an omnipresent musical and scenic environment. The music is produced live from very diverse locations; the electric guitar and trombone players move around, as do the singer and the African kora player. There is an acoustic and symbolic struggle between these different musics and the words of the actor. Intermediality is most strongly thematized in a joust (more so than a test of strength) between Western technological music, with considerable means at its disposal, and the singing voice of griots accompanied by the kora, an instrument in traditional African music. Through an ironic inversion of signs and technologies, the daxophone is an instrument invented to reproduce the sounds of forest animals; natural cries can only be imitated by complicated technology, but a technology that is also closely related to the old technique of the musical saw. This new "coupling" between human and machine here entails the machine reproducing exactly what the bodies or voices of humans or animals produce without any difficulty.

Whereas there is a separate development in the visual media, a continuous jumble of new techniques and new effects, here is an acoustic space in which to listen to all of the different sound sources, its meaning residing in the contrast between unadorned voice and sophisticated technology.

The result is an imaginary shooting/recording/perception in a neutralized, open, multimedia space: a studio or workshop space where one shifts from one source to another, without really knowing what might emerge as a result. The impression is of a temporality measured "in miles," as if it were an interminable rehearsal or an improvisation in which one moved from studio to studio.

Such an environment brings the different media into the foreground, rather than trying to integrate them, as if the "landing" referred to in the title of Goebbels's production were above all technological; questions are produced, stockpiled, classified, the terrain is occupied and controlled. The only possible interaction of different media is dramaturgical, as the series of texts produces a logical plot in three time measures: colonialist intervention, violence, primitivist prejudices as traces in language.

The ideological message of the performance, what we will call its *ideologeme* (chapter 9), could be summarized in this way: the white man invades the black man's forest; the outcome of this landing is unfortunate (rather than "disastrous"),[27] which is to say that it does not succeed. This ideologeme, quite obvious on the level of narrative content, is open at the formal level; the interartistic, the intercultural, and the intermedial are all open—in other words, they do not impose a hierarchy, a result, an ideological itinerary or discourse. Although the musical technology and the African singing are very different, they find common ground in their capacity to listen and tolerate in reciprocal ways.

Intermediality is only one way, the most recently theorized perhaps, of notating and analyzing a performance. There is no lack of investigative tools, as we have confirmed, but none of them is universal, and nothing occurs automatically, whatever the tools used; one should be wary of falling into the "technologist's" illusion, which would have us believe that ultimately the machine will record and explain everything.[28]

Despite the ever increasing speed of informatization, including those of our own bodies, reflexes, and ideas, one may prefer to distance oneself from purely mechanical instruments of notation, and to place more trust in memory and intuition: in short, to take some hermeneutic risks instead of contenting oneself with electronic certainties. Indeed it is my wish in this volume to propose a dialogue with stage work, a questioning rather than a questionnaire, with the intent of encouraging disoriented spectators, whether experienced or inexperienced. Perhaps an archaeology of performance, based on anthropological thinking (outlined in chapter 10 below), might be in a position to renew the approach to performance, without falling prey to the vertigo of detail and quantification. This is why systems of notation and recording must retain their purely instrumental function. What really counts is the incorporation of performances within ourselves, and an archaeology of the living that will perhaps help us bring them to light and to life.

Part 2

The Components of the Stage

3
The Actor

Performance analysis should begin with the description of the actor; for the actor is at the center of mise-en-scène and tends to be a focal point drawing together the other elements of a production. At the same time, however, this is one of the most difficult elements of performance to grasp. Therefore, if we are to analyze acting, first a theory of the actor should be proposed.

The Work of the Actor

Approach through a Theory of the Emotions

What do we need to describe the actor's work? Must our starting point be in a theory of the emotions, as the history of modern acting, from Diderot to Stanislavsky and Strasberg, would seem to suggest? When applied to theater, such a theory of the emotions would only be valid for a very specific kind of actor: those involved in the theater of psychological mimesis and in the tradition of a rhetoric of passions. But we do need a theory of signification and of global mise-en-scène, in which the mimetic representation of feelings is only one aspect among many. Alongside the emotions, which are in any case enormously difficult to decipher and record, actor-dancers can be characterized through a range of other parameters that lack the fragility of the emotions, and are much easier to focus upon: kinesthesic sensations, awareness of the axis and body weight, of bodily structures and the location of their partners in space-time.

In theater, actors' emotions do not need to be real or lived; they must above all be visible, legible, and in compliance with the conventions relating to the representation of feelings. Sometimes the conventions are those of the current theory of psychological verisimilitude, sometimes those of an acting tradition that has codified feelings and their representation. The emotional expressivity of human beings encapsulates the range of behavioral traits through which emotion is revealed (smiles, tears, facial expressions, attitudes, postures, etc.). In theater, it is transposed into a series of standardized and codified emotions that represent identifiable behaviors that, in turn, generate the psychological and dramatic situations that constitute the framework of the performance. In theater, emotions are always manifested by means of a rhetoric of the body and of gestures in which emotional expression is systematized, or even codified. The greater the degree to which emotions are translated into attitudes or physical actions, the greater their freedom from the psychological subtleties of the unspeakable and of suggestion.

On its own, a theory of the emotions is insufficient if we are to describe the work of a dancer or an actor; we require an entirely different theoretical frame that goes far beyond that of psychology. Indeed, once one extends the study of actors to include performances from outside Europe, one soon leaves the psychological theory of emotions behind, a theory that is at best applicable to theater forms that seek to imitate human behavior (particularly verbal behavior) in a mimetic way, as in naturalistic mise-en-scène.

A Global Theory of the Actor?

Is a theory of the actor possible? It is far from certain, for although we think we know what the actor's task consists of, we still have great difficulty in describing and understanding what it really involves—in other words, understanding it not only with one's eyes, but also, as Zeami suggested, with one's spirit. The only thing we can say is that the actor seems to speak and act, not in his own name, but on behalf of the character he imitates or pretends to be. But how does he go about it? How does he realize these actions? And what meanings does he produce for the spectator? Any theory that claimed to account for the full range of meaning-producing activities involved in acting would be overambitious and rash; for the actions of an actor are comparable to those of human beings in normal situations, but with the additional parameter of the fiction, the "as if" of performance. The actor is at the very heart of the theatrical event; he is the living connection between the author's text (dialogue and stage directions), the director's instructions, and the spectators' attentive perceptions; and he is the immediate point of access for any description of performance.

Paradoxically, it would be easier to establish a theory of the actor by not limiting it to Western actors alone, and including the actor-singer-dancers of non-European traditions and cultures. For in these traditions, the actor's practical knowledge is much more technical, that is, easier to describe, and strictly limited to codified, reproducible forms that owe nothing to improvisation or free expression. They have little in common with actors from the Western psychological tradition, who have not acquired a similar array of gestural, vocal, musical, and choreographic techniques, and are instead restricted to a specific genre: the theater of spoken text. The primary concern of such Western actors seems to be to create the illusion of embodying an individual; the roles they assume require them to intervene in a story as protagonists of the action. Hence the difficulty of describing Western acting, whose conventions endeavor to deny or erase themselves. This also accounts for the added difficulty of outlining a theory of its practices from the observer's point of view (spectator and/or theoretician), rather than from that of the performer's subjective experience. What do actors do on stage? How do they prepare themselves for their artistic activities? How do they convey to spectators a series of orientations or impulses in terms of meaning? It is not our intention here to offer a history of the actor through the ages (although such an undertaking is still to be realized); instead I will confine myself to sketching out a methodology for an analysis of contemporary Western actors, bearing in mind how important it is not to restrict one's conception of them to naturalistic or Method actors inspired by Stanislavsky and Strasberg.[1] In fact, actors do not necessarily imitate "real people"; they can suggest actions by using certain conventions or through verbal or gestural narrative means.

First one needs to establish *when* a human being *starts* to be perceived as an actor in an acting situation, and what his specific features are at that time. An actor is constituted as actor from the moment a spectator (i.e., an outside observer) watches him and considers him to be "extracted" or "removed" from the surrounding reality, and to be the bearer of a situation, a role, an activity that is fictional, or at least distinct from the spectator's own reference reality. However, it is not enough for an observer to decide that a particular person is playing a role and is therefore an actor (which would be what Augusto Boal calls "invisible theater"). It is also necessary for the person observed to be aware of the fact that he is performing a role for the observer, thus clearly defining the theatrical situation. Once the convention has been established, nothing the observed person does or says is taken at face value; instead it is read as a fictional action that only acquires meaning and truth within the possible world that observer and observed agree to inhabit. In defining acting as a *fictional convention* in this way, one enters the world of Western actors who pretend to be someone else. On the other hand, Asian performers (actor-singer-dancer) produce the real actions of singing, dancing, or reciting in terms of *themselves as performers;* they make no attempt to pretend to be someone else in the spectators' eyes.

The term *performer,* as opposed to *actor,* is being used increasingly here so as to insist on the action accomplished by the actor, rather than the mimetic representation of a role. For it is above all the performer who is physically and psychically present in front of the spectators.

Components and Stages of the Actor's Work

Western actors—and more precisely those in the psychological tradition—establish a role systematically. They "compose" a vocal and gestural score into which is inscribed the behavioral, verbal, and extraverbal signs that provide spectators with the illusion that they are confronted with a real person. Not only do actors lend their body, appearance, voice, and emotions, they also pass themselves off—at least as far as naturalistic actors are concerned—as actual people, identical with those we mix with everyday: people with whom we can identify, since they create in us impressions of a similarity with what we know of our own character, our own experiences of the world, of emotions, and of moral and philosophical values. We forget very quickly that we are in the process of tricking ourselves by constructing a whole from a few bits of information; we overlook the actor's technique so as to identify with the character, and we immerse ourselves in the universe he represents. Yet the actor performs very precise work, and one is not always aware of its complexities. Nor is it easy to distinguish between *work on oneself* and *work on the role,* as Stanislavsky and Strasberg do. Work on oneself—essentially work on the emotions and on the external aspect of the actor—is at the center of their writings. However, work on the role, which involves dramaturgical reflection, remains rather neglected, and always comes after a psychological preparation. Work on the role should not begin until the actors have acquired the technical means to realize their intentions. In reality, it is more a matter of a constant movement between self and role, between actor and character. The actor's work on self includes techniques for relaxation, concentration, and sensory and affective memory, as well as vocal and physical training: in short, everything that precedes the figuration of a role.

The Indices of Presence

The actor's first task, which is not strictly speaking a "task" as such, is to be *present*, located here and now for an audience, a human being presented "live" and without any intermediaries. It is often said that great actors have *presence*, a God-given gift that sets them apart from other merely hardworking actors. Perhaps so. But doesn't any actor in front of an audience by definition manifest an inalienable presence? One of the hallmarks of theater actors is that they are perceived "first" as material presence, as real "objects" belonging to the outside world; only "subsequently" are they imagined within a fictional universe, as if they were not there on stage in front of the audience, but in the court of Louis XIV, for example (in the case of Molière's *Misanthrope*). So theater actors have a dual status: they are both real, present people *and* at the same time imaginary, absent characters, or at least located on "another stage." Describing this ambiguous presence is one of the most difficult tasks, for the indices of presence resist any objective pinning down, and the "mystical body" of the actor both makes itself available and takes itself back. This explains all those mystificatory discourses regarding the presence of particular actors, discourses that are in reality normative ("that actor is good, that one isn't").[2]

Relationship to the Role

The actor's second task is to *stay in character;* for the naturalistic actor this means sustaining it, never breaking the illusion that he really *is* this complex person in whose existence we are required to believe. This demands constant concentration and attention, regardless of the personal convictions the actor may have about being the character, or the techniques used to create an external image of the character. In fact actors can either identify with their roles by using a range of autosuggestion techniques, or mislead external observers by pretending to be someone else, or distance themselves from the role, quoting it, mocking it, leaving it, and returning to it at will. Whatever they do, they must remain in control of their chosen codification and the acting conventions they have accepted. Therefore descriptions of acting require us to observe and justify the evolution of the nature of the connection between actor and character.

Diction

The diction of a potential text is only one particular instance of this behavioral strategy. Sometimes it is delivered believably and convincingly, in accordance with the requirements of mimesis and the particular patterns of speech of the action's setting. Sometimes diction is disconnected from any mimeticism, and is organized into a phonological, rhetorical, or prosodic system with its own rules; in such cases, there is no attempt to produce reality effects by copying authentic speech patterns.

The Actor in the Mise-en-Scène

Through their command of behavior and diction, actors imagine possible *situations of enunciation* in which both their text and their actions assume meaning. In most cases, these situations are only suggested with a few indicative clues or signs that clarify the scene and the role. It is the responsibility of the director, as well as of the actors, to decide which of these indications are to be chosen. Only the actors know (more or less) the scale of their gestural, facial, or vocal signs, whether the spectators are able to perceive them, and what meanings they are likely to attribute to them. The composition and exposure of these signs must be sufficiently clear for them to be perceived, and subtle enough for them to be nuanced or ambiguous. In this sense, any theory of the actor needs to be part of a theory of mise-en-scène and, in more general terms, of theatrical reception and the production of meaning. The work of actors on themselves, and in particular on their emotions, only has meaning in the light of the gaze of the other (i.e., the spectator); and the spectator must be capable of reading the physically visible indices of the character proposed by the actor.

Managing and Reading the Emotions

Actors know how to manage their emotions, as well as how to make them readable. They are under no obligation actually to experience the feelings of their characters, and even if a significant part of their training, in the wake of Stanislavsky and Strasberg, consists of cultivating sensory and emotional memory, so as to be able to recover promptly and effectively a psychological state suggested by the dramatic situation, this is only one option among many—the most "Western," but not necessarily the most interesting. Moreover, even actors trained in Stanislavsky's "System" or Strasberg's

"Method" do not exploit their own feelings as such to perform a character, unlike the Roman actor Polus, who used the ashes of his own son to perform the role of Electra bearing Orestes' funeral urn. It is just as important for actors to know how to feign their emotions and reproduce them from cold, if only to avoid having to depend on spontaneity; for as Lee Strasberg remarks, "The basic problem of the actor's craft is the unreliability of spontaneous emotion."[3] More than an internal command of the emotions, ultimately what is most crucial for actors is the *readability* of the emotions they interpret for the spectator. It is not necessary for them to relive the same type of emotions as in reality; there is no need for them to give themselves up to an almost "involuntary" expression of their emotions. In fact, in particular styles of acting the emotions are sometimes codified, listed, and cataloged: for example, melodramatic acting of the nineteenth century, the rhetorical attitudes of classical tragedy, or in non-European traditions (such as Indian Odissi dance). Some Western mimes (Etienne Decroux, Marcel Marceau, Jacques Lecoq) have tried to codify the emotions through particular kinds of movement or attitude. According to Lecoq, for example, "Every emotional state shares a common movement: pride grows, jealousy moves in an oblique direction and conceals itself, shame stoops, vanity turns round and round."[4]

In contemporary practice, from Meyerhold and Artaud to Grotowski and Barba, the actor immediately lets emotions be read, which are already translated into physical actions; when read, the sum of these actions constitutes the "plot." Here the emotions are no longer sudden, fleeting disturbances, a detour in the trajectory of everyday life for the actor, as they are in affective reality. Instead they are movements produced, physical and mental *motions* that motivate the actors within the dynamics of their performing, in the space-time-action of the story in which they are implicated. So for actors as much as for spectators and theorists, it is preferable to start from the processes of forming and codifying emotional content, rather than indulging in deep introspection as to what actors may or may not feel. Indeed it is much easier to observe what the actor *makes* of his role, what he *does* with it, how he creates it and where he stands in relation to it. For the actor is

> a poet who writes in the sand. . . . Like a writer, he draws on himself, on his memories, the raw material of his art, to compose a story in accordance with the fictional character proposed by the text. A master of games of illusion and deception, he adds and subtracts, offers and withdraws; he sculpts his moving body and changing voice in the air.[5]

In contemporary theater practice, therefore, performers do not always refer back to an actual person, to an individual comprising a whole, or to a series of emotions. They no longer produce meanings through simple transposition and imitation. They construct meanings from isolated elements in different parts of the body (while neutralizing the rest of it): hands mime an entire action; only a mouth is lit, totally excluding the rest of the body (in Beckett's *Not I*); the voice of a storyteller offers narratives, while he slips in and out of a number of different roles.

Just as in psychoanalysis the subject is conceived as being full of "holes," intermittent, of "limited responsibility," contemporary performers are no longer required to imitate inalienable individuals. They are no longer *simulators,* but *stimulators;* they perform their own inadequacies, absences, and multiplicities. Nor are they required any more to represent a character or an action in a broadly mimetic manner, as a replica of reality. Ultimately, they have been reconstituted in their prenaturalistic form. They can suggest reality through a series of conventions that will be picked up and identified by spectators. Unlike actors, *performers* do not play roles; they act in their own names.

At the same time it is rare, if not impossible, for actors to be entirely consumed in their roles, to the point of forgetting they are artists representing characters, and thus constructing artifacts. Even Stanislavskian actors do not lead the spectators to forget that the actors are only acting, that they are engaged in a fiction and constructing a role, rather than an actual creature like some sort of Frankenstein. On the stage, actors never allow themselves to lose sight of the fact that they are artist-producers. For the production of a performance is part of that performance and of the spectator's pleasure; as spectators, we are always aware that we are at the theater watching an actor, in other words an artist, an artificially constructed being.

Identification or Distance

Actors often attempt to identify with their roles; dozens of tiny tricks are used to help them persuade themselves that they *are* the characters the text describes and that they have to embody for external onlookers. They pretend to believe that their characters are "whole" beings, identical to those in reality. In fact, they are composed of small indicative signs that both performers and spectators need to supplement and complete in order to produce the illusion of a person. On the other hand, sometimes actors indicate through a break in their acting that they are not taken in by this process, and that they are able to bring to bear their own personal perspectives on the character they are supposed to represent.

Methods for the Analysis of Acting

To counterbalance the metaphysical, even mystical, vision of the actor (and all the mystifying discourse that goes with it, in particular in journalistic writing on actors' lives), and to go beyond the futile debate about "reliving" or "pretending," there is nothing better than dry technical analyses of acting. Given that analytic tools in this area remain underdeveloped, I will restrict myself to outlining some possible directions for future research.

Historic and Aesthetic Categories

Each historical period tends to develop a normative aesthetic that defines itself in contrast to those preceding it, and puts forward a series of rather cut-and-dried criteria. Therefore it is tempting to describe in terms of acting styles: romantic, naturalistic, symbolist, realist, expressionist, epic, and so on. Modern spectators often have a rudimentary historical grid at their disposal that helps them to identify acting styles: "naturalistic," for example, or Brechtian, Artaudian, Method, Grotowskian. In this way, particular historical moments and schools of acting are compared to very approximate aesthetic categories. The advantage of this kind of categorization is that the study of the actor is not removed from its aesthetic or sociological contexts. Naturalistic actors at the time of Zola or Antoine, for example, would be described in terms of a theory of environment or milieu, an aesthetic of verisimilitude and of real facts, conforming with determinist and naturalist ideology and aesthetics. However, such analyses often remain rather superficial, or even tautological; a naturalistic actor, we are often told, is one who evolves within a naturalistic universe. Tautologies of this kind fail to throw any light on the specificities of naturalistic gestures or the devices of psychological acting.

It would be more valuable to explore the hypothesis of a cultural model that distinguishes in space and time between different ways of conceiving of the body and of participating in different modes of signification.

Semiological Descriptions

Semiological descriptions are concerned with all components of acting: the physical and gestural, the voice, the rhythm of diction, movements. It is

precisely the determination of these components and thus their segmentation into systems that is the main issue, and it is not self-evident, for in the
raw material there is no such segmentation nor an objective, universal
typology. Each area tends to resort to existing sectional semiologies in
order to identify its major organizational principles. The challenge, however, is in not fragmenting the actor's performance into overly narrow specialist units, thereby losing sight of the overall nature of its signification. A
particular gestural action is only meaningful in relation to a particular
movement, a type of diction or a rhythm, not to mention the other elements of the staging and the scenography of which it is one part. Therefore
one must try to develop a process of segmentation and units that preserve
coherence and wholeness. Instead of separating gesture from text, or gesture from voice, I will endeavor to identify macrosequences (within which
diverse elements come together, reinforcing or distancing each other), by
forming a coherent and pertinent whole that may in turn be combined with
other wholes.

The actor could also be considered to be the creator of a montage (in the
filmic sense of the word), since he composes his role from fragments: psychological and behavioral signs for naturalistic acting, which in spite of
everything ultimately produces the illusion of a totality; particular
moments from an improvisation or a physical sequence endlessly
reworked, flattened out, cut up, and pasted back together for a montage of
physical actions in the work of Meyerhold, Grotowski, or Barba. An analysis of an acting sequence can only occur if one takes into consideration the
totality of the performance. It must be resituated in the narrative structure
that reveals the dynamics of the action and the linear organization of its
motifs. In this way, it reconnects with performance analysis. It is possible,
for example, to distinguish several major kinds of vector within the gestural, vocal, and semantic work of the actor. A vector is defined as a force
and a movement from a particular point of origin toward a point of arrival;
the vector goes from one point to another, following the direction of this
line. There are four major types of vector:

1. *Accumulators* condense or accumulate several signs;
2. *Connectors* link two elements in a sequence in terms of dynamics;
3. *Cutters* provoke a break in the narrative, gestural, vocal rhythm, signal-
   ing the moment at which meaning "changes direction" (and meaning);
4. *Shifters* allow movement from one level of meaning to another, or from
   the enunciative situation to the utterances.

These vectors constitute a very rough framework for the actor's work, although of course it is much more subtle and labile than this, comprising a myriad of microacts with infinite nuances of voice and gesture. Nevertheless, they are indispensable for actors to be both coherent and "legible," and to both orient and amplify the rest of the performance.

In reality, the actor is only meaningful in relation to his partners on stage; therefore one must notice how he is in relation to the others, whether his acting is individualized, personal, or wholly typical of the group, the ways in which he is implicated in the overall blocking. But how is one to describe a gesture discursively without it losing all specificity, volume, intensity, and vibrant relationship with the rest of the performance? The actor's work is only comprehensible when seen within the overall context of the mise-en-scène, where it actively contributes to the elaboration of the meaning of the whole performance. There is no point in recording its every detail if one fails to recognize the implications and repercussions of this work throughout the performance.

A Pragmatics of Body Work

A description of the actor requires an even more technical approach if one is to grasp the variety of corporeal work carried out. Let us begin with a pragmatics of body work as outlined by Michel Bernard;[6] he details these seven elements:

1. The *range and diversification of the field of bodily visibility* (nudity, masking, distortion, etc.): that is, of the body's iconicity
2. The *orientation or arrangement of bodily surfaces* in relation to the stage space and the audience (front, back, profile, three-quarters, etc.)
3. *Postures,* that is, the ways in which the body is integrated in relation to the floor, and in wider terms, the ways in which bodily gravitation is managed or controlled (verticality, obliquity, horizontality . . .)
4. *Attitudes,* that is, the configuration of somatic, segmental positions in relation to the surroundings (hand, forearm, arm, trunk/head, foot, leg)
5. *Movements,* or the dynamics of ways in which stage space is occupied
6. Facial expressions in terms of the visible expressivity of the body (facial and gestural expressions), in actions that may be useful or superfluous; and consequently the visible expressivity of the sum of movements noted
7. *Vocality,* that is, *audible body expressivity* and/or its substitutes and complements (natural or artificial organic sounds made with the fingers, feet, mouth, etc.)

Bernard's seven reference points, a means of describing and comparing different uses of the body, enable a precise description of the actor's corporeality. One might add two further points: the *effects of the body* and the *spectator's proprioception.*

8. *The effects of the body.* The actor's body is not simply a transmitter of signs, a semaphore tuned to throw out signals in the direction of spectators; it produces effects on the spectator's body, whether they are called energy, vectors of desire, pulsional flux, intensity, or rhythm. As we will see later on in our analysis of *Ulrike Meinhof,* such effects are much more immediate and productive than a long explanation of gestural signs, patiently encoded then decoded, aimed at the "average" spectator-semiologist. Hence Bernard Dort's remark: actors are the antisemiologists par excellence, since they destroy, rather than construct, the signs of a mise-en-scène.[7]

9. *The spectator's proprioception.* This is no longer directly a question of something belonging exclusively to the actor, but rather of the spectator's internal perception of the body of the other—the sensations, impulses, and movements that the spectator perceives externally and internalizes.

"Techniques of the Body": Toward an Anthropology of the Actor
All the descriptions of semiology and pragmatics pave the way for an anthropology of the actor, a discipline still to be invented; in the most concrete ways possible, it would ask particular questions of actors and their bodies, questions that performance analysis should address systematically to any and every mise-en-scène.

1. What kind of body does the actor have at his disposal even before taking on a role? In what ways is this body already impregnated by the surrounding culture, and how is that culture implicated in the process of signification for both role and acting? How does the actor's body "dilate" the actor's presence, as well as the spectator's perception?[8]

2. What does the body show, and what does it hide? What does any culture, from San Francisco to Riyadh, agree to reveal to us of its anatomy? What does it choose to display, and what to conceal? And from what perspectives?

3. Who "pulls the strings" of the body? Is it manipulated like a marionette, or does it give itself its own instructions, from within? Where is the "pilot"?

4. Is the body centered in on itself, drawing any physical manifestation

from an operational center from which everything stems and to which everything returns? Or is it decentered, located on the periphery of itself, of primary importance for what is no longer only at the periphery?

5. In one's surrounding cultural milieu, what is a controlled body or an "unchained" (explosive) body deemed to be? What would be experienced as a slow rhythm, or a fast rhythm? In what ways would the slowing down or speeding up of an action change the perspective of spectators, appealing to their unconscious or provoking their exhilaration?

6. How does the speaking and performing body of the actor invite the spectator to "take part in the dance," to adapt synchronistically and bring communicational behaviors into convergence?

7. How is the body of the actor/actress experienced? Visually? Kinetically, in perceiving movement? Haptically, in performing movement? If from a distance or internally, as a result of what kind of kinetic or aesthesic event? How do their bodies impact on the body memory of the spectators, on their motivity and proprioception?

8. In short, to return to Eugenio Barba's question, do actors change bodies when they leave everyday life for stage presence and its free expenditure of energy? In what ways is the actor, for spectators, always a "dancing stranger" (Barba)?

Now that this framework of an anthropology of the actor has been set, we still have to examine some of the ways in which acting can form the focus of an analysis. In the following section, I will analyze the gestural system in *The Miser* and in *Ulrike Meinhof.*

Explanation of Gesture or Vectorization of Desire?

Different Perspectives on Gesture

With the analysis of acting, as we have just seen, the theoretical question immediately arises of what aspect to study and which categories or units to use in describing it. What exactly do we want to examine in focusing on an actor or actress? Various perspectives, aspects, and discourses are available for analysis, and we must be careful to distinguish between them:

■ *The actor/actress* in the broad sense, and his/her place in the performance

- *The body,* and the philosophical problem of its figuration in theater: its "corporeity"
- *The acting:* how the actor *acts*[9] in the performance, the style of acting adopted (naturalistic, realist, symbolist, etc.)
- *Gestures and their systems,* gestuality: ways of focusing attention on the use of the body, in particular the upper and lower limbs: poses, postures, movements, linked sequences of movement
- *Nonverbal communication,* or what actors "say" with their bodies, knowingly or unwittingly
- *Interactional coordination,* or "the set of phenomena of synchronization, tuning, and maintenance,"[10] that is, the ways in which gesture is linked to the word on stage, from the point of view of both actor and spectator
- *The postural-mimo-gestural chain,* which is "continuous in time and three-dimensional in space";[11] it assembles the set of physical data before establishing their links to speech activity.

All these perspectives and areas of study already exist, and any analysis of acting must tailor them to its specific concerns. In view of the complexity of theoretical phenomena that arise here, and the desolate state of current research on the actor, I propose here to perform a simple analysis of two short extracts from two separate works, with a focus on the work of the actors: Louis de Funès in his film *L'Avare* (*The Miser,* 1979), and Regine Fritschi in *Ulrike Meinhof* (1990), a piece of "choreographic theater" by Johann Kresnik.[12] The two examples are quite different, since one accompanies and illustrates Molière's "unalterable" text, while the other "dances" the imaginary life of the (in)famous Red Army Faction "terrorist." The "explanation of gestures" focuses on the "postural-mimo-gestural chain"; it considers this to be a system that, although it cannot be isolated and extracted from the performance as a whole, is at least coherent and analyzable in terms of its constituent parts. Beginning with an appreciation or explanation of gestures (*explication de gestes,* as one speaks of an *explication de texte*), I intend to establish empirically some typical ways in which gesture functions in theater. I will freely use theories of gesture in everyday life, where it has nothing (yet) to do with art, in order to examine how an actor uses gestural behaviors in building a character. In opposition to this semiological analysis of gesture in a mimetic system of communication, an "energetics" (Lyotard) of a "silent" but suffering body will be proposed. The question is to determine whether such a binary alternative in fact exists, and whether semiological communication should continue to be viewed in opposition to an energy-based system divested of any mimesis or referential signs.

Before turning to the detail of these analyses of gestuality, one should bear in mind that gestural systems comprise only one element of performance, arbitrarily isolated from the rest of the mise-en-scène. It is always the overall context of a scene and the spectator's gaze that overdetermine the gesture. Furthermore, one must be wary of simply describing gestures externally, only using visible indices that are little more than the apparent surface of behavior; such signs are only legible within an aesthetic of mimetic verisimilitude. In other words theories borrowed from nonverbal communication should be viewed as only one means, and not an end, of clarifying an aesthetic system, that is, an artificially constructed poetics.

Explanation of Gesture: *The Miser*

The first example chosen comes from act 3, scene 1 of *The Miser,* starting with Harpagon's speech to Valère and Master Jacques (the segments here numbered from 1 to 64, the end of the scene). In this approach, we distinguish between speech *(S)*, gesture *(G)*, and theoretical commentary *(T)* on the use of gesture. In this explanation of gesture, an attempt will be made to trace the trajectory of the verbal-postural-mimo-gestural chain in order to identify, as concretely as possible, some of the devices and techniques employed in the staging.

S1a. *Harpagon* (added text): "All right everyone, off you go!"
G. This addition to the original text (whose signified would be: "Everyone leave, except you two") can be inferred from the gestural situation as its immediate verbalization. The gesture extends the signified of the word ("leave").
T. There is a continuity between body and word; the postural-mimo-gestural chain is continuous; what is seen and what is understood blend smoothly. The redundancy and imbrication of information ensure a uniform reading of the message, in particular the direction of the movement, and the separation between what is included and what is left out of the conversation.

S1b. *Harpagon:* "Now then, Master Jacques, come along."
G. Harpagon draws his two hands, fingers together, parallel to each other, from the outside toward his chest; this indicates the deictic movement of approaching.

T. What typology of gesture would be best suited to the study of Western theater (in which speech is primary and accompanied by gesture)? Rimé's typology[13] distinguishes three main functions of gesture in social interaction:

1. Ideational gestures
   —markers
   —ideographic
2. Figurative gestures
   —iconic (pictographic, kinetographic, spatial)
   —pantomimic
3. Evocative gestures
   —deictic
   —symbolic (emblematic)

As it occurs here, the gesture is evocative-deictic; it refers back to the object of speech ("Come here") by inscribing it in the deictic situation[14] it wishes to generate; it points the conversation in the direction that matters to the speaker-gesticulator. This typology corresponds only in part to those of theorists of mime or physical theater; Lecoq, for instance, distinguishes the following three categories:

> Gestures of action tend to involve the act of the body itself; gestures of expression tend to involve a person's feelings and states of mind; gestures of indication punctuate speech, preceding, prolonging, or replacing it.[15]

Lecoq's classification artificially separates mimetic *action* from modalizing or emotional *expression,* while *indication* may be ideational, figurative, or evocative—either at the same time, or in turns.

> S2. *Master Jacques:* "Do you want to speak to your cook or your coachman, sir? I'm both the one and the other."
> G. In contrast to the agitation of Harpagon/de Funès, Master Jacques/Galabru presents a placid, mollifying, slightly overweight body; his hands open up toward Harpagon in a sign of request and offering.
> T. A gesture, particularly an actor's gesture, is only readable in relation to the gesture of another person; hence the importance of theories of *gestus* (Benjamin, Brecht) that examine the way in which social determinations and hierarchical relationships are inscribed in exchanges of looks, relations between body masses, differences in attitudes.

S3. *Harpagon:* "I want both."
S4. *Master Jacques:* "But which d'you want first?"
S5. *Harpagon:* "The cook."
S6. *Master Jacques:* "Just a minute, then, if you don't mind."
G. As in verbal dialogue, the sequence of gestural interaction should not be broken down into autonomous units, but analyzed as a whole; however, this does not rule out commenting on the various gestural moments of interaction:

- **S3.** Harpagon's nervousness produces a slight shrug of the shoulders; this gesture is passed on to his arms, forearms and hands.
- **S4.** Master Jacques's naive calm is conveyed through a smug, self-assured immobility, hence Harpagon's gestural and verbal irritation in S5.
- **S5.** Harpagon's trunk leans forward as if his entire body, and not only his gaze or his hands, wanted to launch itself into the discussion. In contrast, Valère remains motionless, standing in an expectant position, his chest solidly rooted within Harpagon's sphere of influence; meanwhile his eyes look straight ahead (into space-off, in the direction of Master Jacques), as if to avert any possible intrusion by the cook.

T. An overall understanding of the dramatic situation enables us to assign a bodily and gestural identity to each actor-character based on his type and function, which one could describe (impressionistically) in the following way:

- Louis de Funès/Harpagon: short, thin, wiry, agitated, volatile
- Michel Galabru/Master Jacques: tall, sturdy, jovial, slow, self-assured
- Hervé Bellon/Valère: tall, stiff, tense, elegant, oratorical

A rhetoric of passions, with an entire repertoire of typical attitudes and gestures, is quickly established, each resorting to his favorite gestural scenario. The characters are individualized on the basis of their temperament and their area of expertise: the miser Harpagon as manipulator, the valet as beast of burden, Valère as watchful aristocrat. The system of functional types in classical European dramaturgy or in the traditional arts of Asia is based on such properties, which are always defined in terms of a morphological type and a specific way of representing and moving the body and the character.

S7. *Harpagon:* "What the deuce is the meaning of this ceremony?"
G. The parallelism and difference in attitudes and expectations are marked by quite different indications: Valère, with his arms crossed, waits expectantly, deliberating with his body already tensed in anticipation of the possible sequence of events; Harpagon, his hands (not visible) on the table, locates himself squarely in the immediacy of the situation.
T. Any study of gestures is comparative; their system and rules are established in the contrast between the various protagonists. Interaction is not necessarily direct, but is sometimes parallel and relative. The *gestus* concentrates different temporalities in the body.

S8. *Master Jacques:* "At your service now, sir."
G. Master Jacques leaves the axis of the shot, moves to one side with the camera framing him toward the left, then returns to the same place, adjusting his hat. He reestablishes eye contact with Harpagon. The naturalness of this recentering (to which Jacques is apparently accustomed, given the diversity of his duties) is conveyed in the naturalness of his intonation, which suggests communication can be reestablished without the slightest difficulty as soon as eye contact and professional role are reestablished.
T. The perception of gesture and movement depends on framing, in the broadest sense of the word: not only the framing of the camera but, more fundamentally, that of the observer's gaze. The actor himself fixes the coordinates of his movements and largely controls the focalization/defocalization effects induced in the spectator.

S9. *Harpagon:* "I am committed to giving a supper tonight, Master Jacques."
G. On the word "supper," which closes the sentence [in the French original] with an emphasis provoked by the fact that this news is an unforeseen surprise, de Funès lowers his head as if to put himself at the same level as Galabru (Master Jacques); without actually saying as much, a suggestion of a nod implores the miraculous help of the cook.
T. Here the gesture follows, and simultaneously reveals, the utterance; it contributes to the dynamic of the interaction, and serves as "cognitive facilitation"—as an ideational gesture that acts as a marker—as if to anchor speech and gesture more effectively in a single, easily decipherable situation.

S10. *Master Jacques:* "Wonders never cease!"
G. Harpagon's gestural insistence in S9 is such that Jacques follows his interlocutor with his head, as if in agreement; at the same time he is holding his breath, since he knows what a miser his master is.

T. Here we see the facial and bodily attitude of the character modeling itself on his interlocutor's; the interaction develops in synchrony, between the reply to the other and the future riposte prepared for by the half-serious, half-ironic line S10, "Wonders never cease!" Cinema is particularly well suited to capturing the interlocutor's fleeting but distinct reaction, through intercutting short reaction shots.

S11. *Harpagon:* "Now, tell me, can you give us something good?"
G. The mimo-gestural chain divides the question into two parts. The first enunciates the master's feigned complicity with his valet ("tell me," "us"). The gestures mime this enforced rapprochement—Harpagon leans slightly toward his valet. The second part of the connection ("something good") extends the last word considerably, with no apparent reason, except perhaps as a gesture of uneasiness.
T. When verbal insistence (stressed intonation placed on a word) is particularly marked, the body is forced to follow and present a sequence whose duration and intensity are greater than the norm. Here the facial expression indicates the unusual length of the syllable, and the chest accompanies the utterance with a falling movement; its expressive force, clearly exaggerated in comparison with the norm, becomes a very strong signal of the aestheticization of gesture and of the actor's gestural signature, within which one of the gestures of his repertoire can be recognized.

S12. *Master Jacques:* "Yes, if you give me plenty of money."
G. The intonation and force of the facial attitude—namely, the attention drawn to self-enunciation through rollings of the eyes and Galabru's "puffed-up frog" effect—allows the rather old-fashioned-sounding word *bien* [in the French original] to be eliminated, without its omission being noticed.
T. Gesture, particularly when it accompanies an intonation, always tends to simplify archaic discourse by naturalizing it, by drawing attention to the essential or comprehensible elements of the verbal message. Placed in a position "overhanging" the text, as it were, intonational gesture clarifies, erases, and deforms the text at will. Not only does it control and oversignify the text, but it also regulates hearing and reception. Gesture has an immediacy and contemporaneity, linked to the deixis of its production, that takes primacy over the text's semantics; its semantics require a mental "step backward" and a slight time delay in order to be properly appreciated. In addition, the style of this mise-en-scène is so strongly centered around the immediacy of reception that textual detail is sometimes sacrificed in favor of the story and popular comic effect.

S13. *Harpagon:* "What the devil! It's always money. It seems to be all they can say. Money! Money! Money! It's the one word they know. Money! They are always talking of money. They can never do anything without money."

G. The first truly acute crisis of choleric avarice becomes apparent in this "money" monologue. The same word, repeated verbally and gesturally with obsessional rhythmic force, structures Harpagon the miser's fit. The archaic expression [in the French original] *épée de chevet* ("customary argument") is pronounced, but almost inaudibly—rhythmically rather than phonically, for it is virtually concealed by Harpagon's frantic arm-whirling.

T. Even the most archaic of texts is susceptible to being taken over by a predominant situation, as soon as gesture lends it a helping hand. In an aesthetic of verisimilitude (to which this mass-audience film belongs), the body acts as though it were creating the text at the moment of its utterance; it naturalizes it, and only retains the framework needed to construct a tangible situation.

S14. *Valère:* "I never heard such a fatuous answer. As if there's anything in providing good food if you have plenty of money. It's the easiest thing in the world. Any fool can do that much. The man who is really good at his job can put on a good meal without spending money."

G. This is a long speech; and from "As if there's anything . . ." the film frames Master Jacques's indignant reaction. Valère's gestures appear just as they are: a rhetorical construction erected exclusively for Harpagon the miser's benefit. The latter, in some ways defeated on his own turf—that of economy—can only add, "There you are," and open his hands in approval of Valère's speech.

T. The same gestures, in this instance oratorical and noble as befitting a vigorous plea, can sometimes seem vibrant and sincere, sometimes (as here) hollow and false. Their veracity therefore depends on an understanding of the situation (we see Valère watching Harpagon out of the corner of his eye to gauge the effect of his ruse). Ultimately it is a matter of determining whether the codes ("strings") of the rhetoric should be visible or not in order to reveal the character's fabrication. Only a knowledge of the context, and incidentally of certain indicative signs effected by the mise-en-scène, provide information on the gestural key to an entire sequence and on the value that should be attributed to the gestures. Whatever the case, there is always a codification of gesture that is more or less readable and subject to an index of truth or falsehood.

S15. *Master Jacques:* "Put on a good meal without spending money!"
S16. *Valère:* "Yes."

G. The quotation of the other's speech is accompanied here by a vocal and mimic effect of parody, that is, an exaggerated repetition of the words and gesture quoted. With Galabru, it is facial expression, particularly the way his eyes almost seem to pop out of their sockets that relays and amplifies the reported speech. Bellon/Valère's noble and "distinguished" rhetoric is repeated parodically in a "popular" mode, with a great expenditure of energy to block the trunk, puff up the features, and wave the arms in all directions.

T. Gesture can quote, parody, or mock other gestures, drawing on them to critique and oppose them. In the phenomenon known as "echoing,"[16] the interlocutor repeats his partner's facial and gestural expressions. Here, in Master Jacques's outraged repetition, echoing becomes amplification. Similarly, we see Harpagon approve Valère's speech with a gesture ("There you are": a deixis both verbal and gestural). He relives it and sees himself in Valère, giving the impression of pouring himself into his steward's thought and body; he straightens his torso, punctuates the speech with an approving "There you are." It is as if the gesture were rewriting ("regesticulating") earlier utterances by imposing its own modality and tension, which may be taken up in turn by the next "speaker." An intergestuality of this kind serves as a guiding thread for the entire sequence.

S17. *Master Jacques:* "Upon my word, Mr. Steward, I would like you to show how it's done. You had better take on my job as cook, since it seems you want to be managing everything."
G. Master Jacques gets easily worked up, his anger culminating in his accusation that Valère is a *factoton* [in the French original]: that is, a jack-of-all-trades, dogsbody; he punctuates his accusation with an ideational gesture of the marker kind.
T. This kind of gesture suggests more than it actually says. It is linked to

the verbal ambiguity of an element of speech that the gesture tries to clarify, or at least to signal. It intervenes "in sentences of verbal ambiguity, by placing stress on a specific element of speech, which has the effect of diminishing the degree of ambiguity."[17]

S18. *Harpagon:* "Be quiet! Just tell us what we shall need."
G. Harpagon brushes aside the valet's protests with a backhanded sweep of his forearm; the gesture is both evocative-symbolic (mimicking the elimination of an partner and of words deemed to be superfluous) and ideational-ideographic, in that it marks the progression of thought, shifting very rapidly from an order (to be quiet) to an interested question (what shall we need?).

S19. *Master Jacques:* "Ask Mr Steward there. He is the man who can put on a meal without spending money."
G/T. The valet continues in the same vein as in S15. The parodied rhetoric is increasingly caricatural; the level of agitation increases.

S20. *Harpagon:* "Hey! I want an answer from you."
G. The archaic word "Haye" [in the French original] is replaced, or can simply be covered up, by the sound of a fist banging the table—just as a chairperson calls a meeting back to order with their gavel.
T. The body covers language, but the inverse is less often true. The body creates the situation and produces an effect of immediacy that is corporeal, event-based, and psychological. However, the body can be effaced by the diction of a text, particularly an archaic-sounding classical text, causing an effect of mental slowing-down and obliging the listener to decipher the enigma or the language. An actor like de Funès works the contrast between a furious expenditure of gesture and an economy of means. As Valère Novarina remarks, de Funès was "an athlete of expenditure, and a masterly controller of energy; between two paroxysmal

crises, his exemplary sobriety and the purity of his acting were reminiscent of Helene Weigel."[18]

S21. *Master Jacques:* "How many will you be at table?"

Harpagon (added): "Sssh!"

Master Jacques (whispering): "How many will you be at table?"

G. This additional stage business allows Galabru and his character to show off their virtuosity and the impeccable control of emotions and delivery. Everything is played, even anger. A gesture from the master is sufficient to make the valet change his tone of voice; hands held parallel to the ground mimic the idea of "containing oneself" and produce a pacifying effect in themselves, like the gestures of an animal tamer calming a wild beast.

S22. *Harpagon:* "We shall be eight or ten, but reckon on eight. Provide for eight and there's always plenty for ten."

G. His right hand sweeps though the air from the outside inward, in the conventional codified gesture that means "just take care of it for me; that's enough; it really doesn't matter."

T. Any gesture occurs within a series of gestures; some of them are often repeated several times, allowing the gesticulator to allude to a kind of model or prototype gesture that he quotes and varies according to the inspiration of the moment.

S24. *Master Jacques:* "Right. You need to provide four sorts of soup and five main courses: soups, entrées . . ."
G. Master Jacques takes rather perverse pleasure in counting out the dishes on his fingers, all the while maintaining eye contact with Harpagon, as if to excuse himself for the obviousness of the list. There is a contrast and difference in bodily orientation between the gestural persuasion of the hands counting off the dishes and the intimidation of the gaze focused on Harpagon. The announcement of each dish is accompanied by a head movement from Harpagon—an echoing effect, as if he were trying to avoid blows that strike his body and make it react. In the end he collapses under the "blows," and his astonishment produces a series of wide-eyed stares at different levels of intensity, as if he was moving up a series of gestural "notches" or "rungs" that mark the progression of the narrative or the argument.
T. Ideational marking structures this enumeration by representing schematically the volume of dishes listed (therefore the gestures are also figurative-pictographic). The attention of those in dialogue here is then focused on the series and the volume of dishes evoked in mime.

S25. *Harpagon:* "The devil! You are not feeding the whole town."
G. The vocal gesture of insistent emphasis is on the final syllable of *entière* [in the French original]—"whole"; its final syllable is lengthened in a very marked way.
T. The stress is as much vocal (intonational) as gestural (attitudinal). It is marked by features common to body and voice: intonational lengthening, lowering of the trunk, holding the vocal gesture and the attitude way beyond the norm.

S31–32–33. *Valère:* "Do you want them to burst themselves? . . . *One should eat to live and not live to eat.*"
G/T. The same gestural technique as in S14. At the end of Valère's speech, a religious choir is suddenly heard intoning a Te Deum. Moved by a mystical illumination on hearing this maxim of economy, the miser Harpagon lifts his arms toward the heavens as if to thank God. This religious figuration appears as an incongruous citation right in the middle of the domestic dispute. With his eyes, the cook searches for the cause of this mystical outburst. He takes the question "Do you hear that?" (S36) as an allusion to the music he cannot hear. The religious

gestures come across as a facile imitation of paintings of mystics (one thinks of El Greco). A low-angle shot—which is pure Eisenstein—even blurs de Funès's frail outline, as if to better parody his sudden conversion.

In this way, the same body constantly changes its corporeity, that is, the context where it is employed and deployed: physical or clinical body (body use and technique), fictive body (of the actor), mystical body (in this section of the film), and so on.

S42. *Harpagon:* "We must have things people don't go in for much these days, things which soon fill them up—some good thick stew with dumplings and chestnuts. Have plenty of that."
G. Harpagon mimes the scene, reducing it to a performance of the eater, repeating the terms of the menu through sonic and facial onomatopoeia. With his cheeks blown out, the repetition of the "p" in "pâté en pot" [in the French original] as a filling consonant constitutes a mimic facial drama—as well as a psychodrama for Harpagon, who imagines the force-feeding of his guests by replaying it in his own body.
T. This sequence illustrates Marcel Jousse's hypothesis that onomatopoeia and gestuality are the primary means of communicating experience before the appearance of verbal language. Jousse suggests that what he calls the *mimeme,* the "reverberation of the characteristic or transitory gesture of the object in the human complex,"[19] enables human beings to construct their earliest expressions, their miming, even before language. In order to do so, they replay within themselves what they have received, which shapes them internally as they process their interactions with reality. Harpagon has only to replay these chewing and swallowing movements to become as sated as his guests, fed only by the sound of his voice: a somewhat Christ-like gestuality that serves as Communion for the entire household.

S43. *Valère:* "You may rely on me."
G. In absolute contrast to Harpagon's agitated mimo-drama, Valère manages to insert a pause after a tense exchange; it punctuates the sequence with a very aristocratic attitude and a vocal inflection that calms the acting.
T. Sometimes gesture works primarily through the art of structuring interaction, bringing it to an end or punctuating it. These pauses or culminating points are all the more useful in that they help the dramaturgical "breath" of an entire sequence; they mark the turning points of the action, and summarize the situation and the *gestus* of the protagonists. Walter Benjamin remarked, with reference to Brecht, that "the actor must be able to space his gestures as the typographer spaces his words."[20] This is a general rule of nonverbal communication: gesture helps to structure the flow of words. "It can be assumed," writes Klaus Scherer, "that the segmentation of verbal flow with nonverbal behaviors during encoding also helps the comprehension of listeners during the decoding process."[21]

S44–56 (summary). Master Jacques is now playing the role of the coachman. His horses are so thin that they are no more than silhouettes drawn on the wall; this introduces another register, that of the graphic representation of gesture. The horses, being the referent of the speech, are amusingly illustrated in a drawing that represents them in the stable. Harpagon and Jacques behave as though the horses were "real." The coachman's attachment brings him closer to his animals, which in turn allows the two men to be brought closer together; this is reflected in a tighter twin-shot framing both of them. A moment of relative calm in which Harpagon is no longer the monster disfigured by avarice, but a poet of lyrical exaggeration.

S57. *Master Jacques:* "I can't stand flatterers, master, and I can see that everything he does, all his everlasting prying into the bread and the wine and the wood and the salt and the candles is nothing but back-scratching, all done to curry favour with you. That's bad enough, but on top of it all I have to put up with hearing what folk say about you and, after all, I have a soft spot for you, in spite of myself. Next to my horses I think more of you than anybody else."
G. Master Jacques structures the rhythm of his speech with his hand, particularly when he enumerates the objects of Valère's "prying." These gestures help him organize his fury, and create an image of the vexations he has had to endure, the frequency of their occurrence and their range; they "structure the speech rhythmically and accentuate vocal

intonation, without seeming to be at all concerned with the verbal content per se."[22] By pointing vaguely in the direction of the object that is virtually present, the gestures set up an imaginary scene where the action could have taken place. There is no doubt that the scansion is also a way of giving a hiding at a distance; the steward witnesses his own chastisement.

S58. *Harpagon:* "Would you mind telling me what people say about me?"

G. Harpagon's line is delivered on a completely different auditory and visual level—in confidence and in a low voice, and at a very slow corporeal pace.

T. This slowing of effects and gestures miniaturizes the scene; it produces a change in scale and in the visual and auditory level, which requires the spectator to focalize quite differently. Evaluating a gestural system first of all implies that the frame, the scale, and the particular kinds of units employed to make it function have been decided. One must choose the right gestural key for a sequence; the actor modifies it when he wants, guided in the process by the overall strategy of the mise-en-scène.

S59. *Master Jacques:* "Yes, master—if I could be sure it wouldn't annoy you."

S60. *Harpagon:* "Not in the least."

G. De Funès massages his temples, softens and tempers his image; he composes an appropriate physiognomy manually, manipulating both his features and his character. At the same time, he displays this process of construction.

T. Actors always compose their faces and characters, but most of the time they conceal the process of manufacture. Unlike in everyday life, in theater the spectator is attentive to the construction of character; and this elaboration is not preliminary to the theatrical act, but an integral part of it. Even a naturalistic actor methodically builds his "gestural text," and a spectator with a well-trained eye will be able to make out the "strings" attached to the character and the actor's tricks. The mise-en-scène can choose either to conceal these "strings" or to bring them out.

S62. *Harpagon:* "On the contrary, I shall enjoy it. I like to know what people are saying about me."

G. Harpagon multiplies his facial signs to reassure his "informer." The more intimate and personal communication wishes to be, the more subtle and discreet the facial signals become. Harpagon's expression, and the message of encouragement and confidence it conveys, privatizes the use of the body; its subtlety necessitates an increased physical closeness with the other; it also indicates a change of register in nonverbal communication. Before Master Jacques confides in his master (in S63), Harpagon waves his steward away with a hand gesture, a sequence that is repeated even more violently by the valet; then he invites Master Jacques to sit beside him, in other words to share a common private space. They sit down beside each other, as if confrontation were giving way to consultation, and an "amicable" way of looking in the same direction. At the end of this short gestural parenthesis, Harpagon makes a gesture within a gesture; he invites Jacques to swing his legs to the same rhythm as him, thereby suggesting an equality and equivalence of status. This parenthesis in the authoritarian system of hierarchical proxemic relations does not fool anybody, not even the valet who only obeys reluctantly.

Master Jacques's long confiding speech (S63: "I'll tell you straight then . . .") can be read primarily in the reflection it produces in Harpagon's face. All his involuntary reactions to Jacques's description are registered as uncontrollable grimaces and nervous tics that Jacques does not notice, so preoccupied is he in amassing and enumerating the proof of his master's stinginess. De Funès's art lies in seeming to produce uncontrolled signs, to react to Jacques's arguments as if in spite of himself. It is the lack of "interactional coordination," the fact that the valet is not "plugged in" to his master's reactions, that creates the comic effect; Jacques notices neither Harpagon's grimaces, nor the moment when he rolls up his sleeves. This minute time-lag or gap is characteristic not only of the comic, but also of gesture in theater that is only pertinent if it is already projecting us into the next action, preparing the opposite gesture. This is similar to what Lecoq calls the *l'appel*, "the call" (in the tradition of Stanislavsky, Meyerhold, and Decroux):

> In the greatest displacement of an object or of oneself (throwing, jumping), before the gesture of action per se one creates a gesture in the opposite direction; this serves to define the direction, to locate support for it, to concentrate the force of its propulsion. This is the "call" of effort, its impetus, its élan.[23]

The "call" has as much to do with one's own gesture as with that of the other. Often two parallel series of gestures only assume meaning when compared through the spectator's *linking* and *laughing* gaze. On one hand there is Jacques, the overly sincere simpleton who bangs out his definitions ("a miser, a skinflint, and a niggardly old usurer"); on the other there is Harpagon, progressively rolling up his sleeves, his features reacting to each fresh accusation. The absence of "interactional coordination" is a source of misunderstanding between the characters, but it produces a comic effect for the spectator.

Jacques's hammering out of certain terms prevails as a means of rhythming the text and of structuring the argument. The actor's body "works" thought iconically and exerts a structuring influence on verbal memorization or production through its rhythmic (spatiotemporal) characteristics. In the case of a preexisting dramatic text that the actor must appropriate for himself, he locates himself within a spatiotemporal framework (most often miming a dramatic situation) by placing himself (as enunciator), the lines of his speeches and the reference points of the spoken-gestural chain. He is helped, more or less consciously and systematically, by the bodily positions he adopts; these help him fix his text (in space and in his memory), and constitute what I will call his "underscore" (see "The Actor's Score and Underscore" below).

S64. *Harpagon:* "And you are a silly, rascally, scoundrelly, impudent rogue!"

G. Harpagon sets off in pursuit of Master Jacques, grabs a stick, and beats him. The blows are announced and illustrated by a series of disorderly movements that show the pursuit and the protestations of the valet.

T. The blows with the stick clearly reveal the dual dimension of gesture; they are both real (i.e., authentically and painfully delivered) and fictive (i.e., entirely manufactured). The real blow is received *aesthesically* by the spectator, as an effect that is physically experienced, in the same way as a circus or dance performance. The fictive blow is perceived *aesthetically* in an imaginary framework. We can imagine that Harpagon, as a character, puts a certain amount of energy into his blows. What matters is their value as sign, for we know full well that the blows are not really delivered forcefully, or that the actor playing Jacques is wearing a padded costume to absorb them. Within the fiction, the differences will be clearly perceived. In the following scene of this film adaptation, for example, Valère is much more brutal than Harpagon; he shows no hesitation in beating Jacques vigorously, whereas, to judge by the feebleness of his punches, the miser is not so callous.

In theater, gesture is caught in the polarity of the real and the fictive, just as the actor's body is both a human being and the imitation of a human being. Every now and then, a school or theory of gesture seeks to establish a system of equivalences between aesthesic sensations and aesthetic (or psychological) meanings. Countless treatises on rhetoric set out the ideal codification of a passion in a given pose or facial expression. In some ways this is what de Funès does here; although his movements are defined by convention, in accordance with the received norms of Western culture (rather than of any anthropological universality); and the passions thus evoked are the most primitive ones. For instance, how does one illustrate a passion as complex as avarice?

De Funès's art consists of somatizing this passion or character trait; he makes it physically visible by inventing certain attitudes and simple movements that re-create it instantaneously, particular buffooneries that belong only to him. De Funès oscillates between *retention* (of information, goods, gold assimilated as fecal matter from which he cannot bear to be separated) and *explosions* of rage, whenever there is a threat of expenditure, which leave him beside himself; at that point, the emaciated body spends itself instead of the wallet. The semiotics of avarice limits this passion to a few pertinent traits, and reduces the acting to gestural leitmotifs (rage: clenched fists that appear to strike a table; cunning: smooth face and soft voice, etc.).

Body and gesture are there to manipulate the six great universal emotions, based on a limited repertoire of buffooneries, "trademarks" belonging to the actor: thinness, crooked legs, incisive gestures, sudden explosions, aquiline profile, a bird of prey's ruffled plumage. No attempt is made to internalize, "justify" (Stanislavsky), or psychologize all these physical marks. On the contrary, all emotion is reduced to a concrete and virtuosic use of the body. Beyond Harpagon's apparently disorderly *gesticulatio,* we find a refinement of gesture, an elaboration of *gestus:* irrationality of gesture, reason of *gestus,* writes Jean-Claude Schmid,[24] in connection with gesture in the classical age. De Funès conflates everything into a *gestus* of anger and cunning; "retain and explode" is his motto.

The explanation of gesture derives a good number of its techniques from nonverbal communication in daily life, but they are employed with a concentration and a stylization proper to theater processes. The more a performance is mimetic in relation to the real (human gestural behavior), the more the techniques are purely and simply reused and quoted. In this sense, description does not escape the sign and the communication of a more or less latent signification. Therefore it would be appropriate to modify the type of analysis for a performance that is not based on the mimesis of a communication, as in dance or dance-theater; this is what is proposed below with the example of *Ulrike Meinhof.* But first this explanation of gesture will be concluded by shifting the focus from the area of *gestuality* toward that of an *anthropology of corporeity.* The descriptions generated by semiology, pragmatics, or linguistics all pave the way for an anthropology of the actor, which is still to be invented; it will ask the most concrete questions possible of actors and their bodies. With reference to *The Miser,* I will answer the questions asked by any anthropology of gesture.

1. De Funès has a restless, agile body, a model of the (in)famous little Frenchman, highly strung and short-tempered, the "Saint-Tropez policeman" type who is always quick to react. His mobility and dynamic "attack" easily dilate his slender silhouette and presence; at the center of the acting throughout, he covers considerable ground.

2. Dressed in a black frock coat and a kind of loose overall that allows him to cavort freely, his costume is somber, sinister, and unembellished, rather like the *prozodiejda* worn by Meyerhold's actors on stage. Such "degree zero" costuming neutralizes characterizations and facilitates performing.

3. De Funès is the organizer of his own fits of rage and outbursts. Of course, he is carried away by his passion, but he controls its every aberration. In this "economizimg machine," one can hear almost all of the marching orders.

4. A one-man band who manipulates his entire world, ruling it with a rod of iron, Harpagon the miser is utterly self-centered until, "beside himself" in the grip of rage, he flies "off the rails" and loses all control. From then on, nothing returns to him—a tragic predicament for a miser—and he launches himself into all sorts of peripheral adventures. His waving arms and hands bear witness to this useless expenditure.

5. So he flies into a rage, but there is nothing exceptional in the rapidity of his movements; and as spectators we become accustomed to his sudden accelerations followed by calmer and more reflective moments. These lulls make the spectators reflect; they encourage us to nuance our negative judgments of Harpagon, as if they were being subjected to alternating hot and cold "showers."

6. The spectators are invited to follow this furious movement, to go along with it by synchronizing their own reactions with those of Harpagon. The hold of this likable, larger-than-life "ham" is such that one cannot be detached, and his fits of avarice seem to follow a logical and reassuring course. The acting and mise-en-scène are placed entirely at the ser-

vice of an immediate legibility of motivations and actions. Body and movement do everything possible to naturalize and convey a text that is sometimes archaic or literary. Gesture doubles speech to the point of creating a homogeneous verbal-postural-mimo-gestural chain in which every element expresses and replaces every other.

7. The body of the actor de Funès is sometimes experienced visually, when we observe his crises, sometimes aesthesically and haptically, like a kind of whirlwind that blows hot and cold. The effects of gestural caricature are less useful for a (wholly banal) characterization of the miser than for a kinesthetic experience of rapacity and constant motion. The corporeal memory of this film is composed of a continuous movement interspersed with paroxysmal moments and facial convulsions: moments of crisis that invariably culminate in virtuosity, and in which the spectator's proprioception and sensory motivity are quite often solicited.

8. In this way, the actor gives the impression of changing bodies, or at least of supplementing and extending his own body. Throughout, de Funès remains the dancing fool who makes the spectator dance too, with a great deal of pleasure.

The Figural

Such an explanation of gesture is only possible in the classical example of a preexisting dramatic text being embodied by an actor who imitates everyday behavior, and therefore necessarily assumes the characteristics of the postural-mimo-gestural chain of nonverbal communication. But what about a dance or dance-theater performance, in which gestures do not work in conjunction with a text or a story? In the extract I have selected from Johan Kresnik's *Ulrike Meinhof* (the last five minutes of the performance), we are in the presence of a group of characters, the prisoners, who are being mistreated by their guards. The meaning of the sequence is clear (a series of humiliations and tortures), but it is much more difficult to arrive at an analysis that can account for the quality and intensity of the gestures. First, because the gestures are "repressed," held in, unspectacular, and difficult to observe—and their source is not in the stereotypical codification of emotions; and second, because the action is discontinuous, confined to events that are intense but brief; finally, and above all, because they do not comprise a mimetic representation of real situations. Therefore, a means must be found to account for the aesthesic events of this choreography, other than through the techniques of semiological gestural analysis inspired by nonverbal communication. The logic of the signified and the relation to a canonical text, as in the case of *The Miser*, are no longer sufficient. One has to question, to experience the "flavor" of the signifier and "the logic of sensation" (Deleuze): a sensory and kinesthetic logic that slips through the grasp of any semiological notation of an external object, or at least supplements it.

I shall seek the help of thinkers who, like Jean-François Lyotard, mistrust all communication through signs and all semiology, and instead propose an "energetic" model of artistic effect on the observer. In his *Discours, figure*,[25] Lyotard makes a clear distinction between the *discursive*, which belongs to the order of the sign and linguistics, and the *figural*, which is a libidinal event irreducible to language. Indeed, gesture in *Ulrike Meinhof* does not seem to be reducible to a sequence of emotions or words. It consists of a series of isolated events: events that are thematically oriented in the direction of the signified "torture" if we focus on semantics and the syntax of the signs, but impulsive, drive-ridden events that follow one another at very heterogeneous moments and intensities.

These particularly intense moments could be called "figural" insofar as their translation (which is always possible) into a linguistic signified, a discourse, by no means exhausts their meaning and function. The moment when Ulrike Meinhof cuts off her tongue with a knife given to her by the guards does signify her enforced political suicide and her being reduced to silence; but it is also a much more complex figure, a theater of cruelty that represents nothing other than this very "energetic" action—action, or dreamwork, or stage work—which the spectator and the analyst must decipher with great difficulty. In this way, what can be read and deciphered using the techniques of semiology or vector theory can also be integrated into a circuit of energy. This process does not rule out aberrant or random decipherings: political or unconscious readings. For instance, we see Ulrike Meinhof mutilated and reduced to inaction against the backdrop of the demolished Berlin Wall. Should a connection be made between the two political messages? Could the wall only collapse in the East once terrorism had been stamped out in the West? Such a reading is unverifiable, but possible. It is not so much the conjunction and concordance of signs that produces meaning (as in classical semiology), as the circuit of energy we think we perceive within and between them. The mise-en-scène does not always provide the clue to this circuit, for such a clue needs to be rooted in visible, fixed signs. The vectorization of certain elements of the performance necessarily produces surprises, possibilities that must be accepted or ruled out.

How could an energetic theater "produce the greatest intensity (by excess or by lack of energy) of what is there, without intention"?[26] What is there, in these martyred bodies, is not there without intention; the political message is clear—too clear, some would say. At another level, however, that of the spectator's psychic investments in these scenes of torture, nothing is certain any more. If we consider these bodies and gestures as a dream that has been worked out and must be made to work, everything becomes open to the gaze of the interpreter.

Vectorization of Desire and Gesture Work: The Example of *Ulrike Meinhof*

I shall draw on the four operational processes of dreamwork identified by Freud: condensation, displacement, consideration of figurability, and secondary revision.[27] An example from each category will suffice to observe how gesture and its mise-en-scène constitute the theater of this dreamwork/stage work. Our hypothesis is that mise-en-scène is always, to one degree or another, a staging of the unconscious.

Condensation
The music shifts between the national anthem *Deutschland, Deutschland über Alles* and an opening ceremony for the Olympic Games. What exactly is the victory being celebrated here? That of the fall of the Berlin Wall? Of West German democracy? Or of the antiterrorist police? The musical montage leads seamlessly from one motif to the other. The resulting music is triumphant, sure of itself, ecumenical. This polarity of the object being celebrated recurs in the receptacle that presides over Ulrike's labors: both the eternal Olympic flame, and an allusion to the arson instigated by the Red Army Faction in Frankfurt. In the same spirit of concentration and condensation of effects, in the final tableau there are three parallel planes superimposed over each other; this construction of a layered perspective provides a possible clue to the tableau of mutilated bodies. In the foreground, Ulrike is flattened, reduced to a yellowed photograph from the mass circulation press; in the middle ground, a second Ulrike—also fixed, but like an official statue—displays her mutilation; in the background, the wall with a hole punched through it, with the prisoners writhing in the debris at its foot—the hole opens onto yet another reconstruction, in the East, open to violence. This is an instance of what Lyotard calls the *matrix-*

figure, a place that "belongs simultaneously to the space of the text, the space of the mise-en-scène, and the space of the stage";[28] these three planes are superimposed for our visual perspective, constraining us to a "figuration" of what could have been reduced, rather innocuously, to a parallel series of signs.

Condensation sometimes operates through accumulation-superimposition-interference of signs by means of accumulator vectors, and sometimes through shifting from one to the other by means of a system of equivalences and substitutions (metaphorical shifting).

Displacement

In displacement, one element is replaced with another, not through similarity, but through connection or spatiotemporal contiguity. "Displacement (Freud's *Verschiebung* or *Entstellung*) is an energetic process, a transfer of energy that Freud said is economic; the libido invests a particular region of the body's surface."[29] Let us return to our earlier example: the body, crushed and on display, compressed and reduced to the thickness of a newspaper photograph, refers by displacement to the *press:* a press that crushes the bodies of the recalcitrant, the media that tracks down, denounces, and finally shelves criminal matters. The body is displaced from the living to the inert, from burning actuality to archive. The displacement is effected in every direction. Just as "the erotic-morbid body can function in all directions,"[30] Ulrike's body circulates, is connected and displaced on at least three different planes (in the sequence analyzed): first, that of matters shelved, of museum monsters preserved and displayed in bottles; second, that of current events that are still raw and bleeding; and finally, in the background, that of the opening up of the wall, and the continuation or end of the (hi)story. Each plane displaces the next; like body wounds, the scenes are open enough to promote multiple and reversible connections between the *membra disjecta* of the performance (see fig. 6).

Displacement sometimes occurs as a visible element that displaces another; the connection is apparent, and the displacement thus seems part of a temporal or causal linkage (connector vector). Sometimes it occurs as a rupturing movement, a break that brings a series to an abrupt end and moves on to another without any transition (cutter vector).

Consideration of Figurability

Considering the figurability *(Darstellbarkeit)* of a dream means observing the ways in which "desire . . . takes words literally; the literal meaning is the

Fig. 6. Johan Kresnik's *Ulrike Meinhof.* (Photograph by Jörg Landsberg.)

figure. . . . The *Rücksicht auf Darstellbarkeit* is this arrangement of an initial text that, in Freud's eyes, pursues two ends: to illustrate this text, but also to *replace* certain parts of it with figures."[31] In the case of the dream, as in that of the stage or the body of the actress, we are confronted with figures that represent the initial text based on its figurations, its images proper to representation.[32] We will try to find out what *body model* this initial text implies, that is, what conception of corporeity is presupposed by the concrete representation of the bodies. For the sake of brevity, let us say that here the body represents both metaphorically and metonymically a prosthesis of state violence. The body of the different Ulrike is controlled, acted upon, operated by machines of torture that manipulate it from the outside: the mobile stage frame, the giant sugar tongs, the operating table, and the display case strip the body of all autonomy, decentering, and emptying it. The dominant figure is that of this prosthesis that penetrates human flesh and forces it to comply with its laws, through all sorts of harassing interventions that include remote-controlled suicide and, in the final image of the performance, placing the body in the prison of a translucent coffin.

Secondary Revision
The secondary revision or elaboration of a dream consists of turning it into a daydream *(Tagtraum)*, removing any appearance of absurdity and ordering it in a way that conforms with the laws of intelligibility. It imposes articulate language on material that bears no trace of reasonable thought.

Transposed to the area of stage work, secondary revision endeavors to transform this stage material into a rational language, that is, a verbal commentary. Such an undertaking is not without risk, since such a transformation reduces the figural to a discourse that focuses too strongly on linguistic signification; in strict terms, therefore, it risks *dis-figuring* actress and stage. Any overly symbolic or political reading would run the risk of such a disfiguring; so the severing of the tongue is neither merely a castration nor a banal gagging of the individual. Secondary revision seeks to impose such perspectives. Without denying the pertinence of such interpretations, it is more a matter of *figuring* something else concealed behind this shock action. It is Kresnik's strength to be very mimetic and political in his apparent message while *at the same time* working with affect, looking not so much for the meaning of the gesture, as for its aesthesic sensations, and for the gesture's deep origin: why does Ulrike make this gesture of cruelty? how does her body prepare itself through immobility and the uncontrollable affect of the transition to the act? Of course Ulrike is manipulated, remote-controlled, "suicided" by her guards, and therefore by the historical referent; but her body is danced, processed, moved, experienced very differently, as an event with its own rhythm and its own eventlike energy.

Unlike *The Miser,* it is not the meaning and mimetic fictionalization of the actor that counts, but the intensity, the corporeal effect produced on the spectator, the bodily silences and screams. At the same time, this body is transfigured to become a mystical, ceremonial, almost Christ-like body, symbolizing the situation of the prisoner who is almost "crucified." Instead of a representative, mimetic treatment of movement, which was quite sufficient in *The Miser,* here we are confronted with and subjected to fluctuations of intensity, and to kinesthetic and aesthesic demands: a range of physical and emotional manipulations that is in no way fictional.

This is apparent in sequences such as the one in which Ulrike cuts off her tongue with a knife. There is no need for a semiological reading of the signs here, which could only be banal. On the other hand, our gaze must evaluate the tension of the body, the rhythm of the fatal gesture, the figuration of suffering, the authenticity of the act, the effect produced by its cruelty.

Everything is in the levels or intensities of movement and effort. Before this act, Ulrike is motionless, facing the spectator, her back to the wall, totally relaxed. The decision to act is taken in a split second; its execution is rapid but controlled. Her face stays at the same level, barely grimacing; blood spurts from her mouth; then we see the bloody severed tongue, held out in her left hand as an offering, without excessive ostentation; the hand holding the knife returns to its previous position. Nowhere in the immobility of her body and the fixity of her gaze is there any representation of individual suffering, only the impact of her gaze and the mutilated body: only the place where "the libido invests a particular region of the body's surface (which turns inwards to its 'internal organs' also)";[33] where "a libidinal drive, a search for intensiveness, a desire for *potency*"[34] is produced, "a flux in motion, a displaceability, and a kind of effectiveness by means of affects, which belong to libidinal economy."[35] At the very instant it is accomplished, the sacrificial act refers to nothing beyond itself. The spectator does not identify with the character (Kresnik's aim is not to convince us of "terrorist" arguments), but with the physical sensations of the performer's mutilated body.

But how is one to read all these libidinal displacements? How can one make a secondary elaboration of them? The question is to know whether vector theory is able to bring out these fluctuations of intensity while maintaining a classical semiology of signs and their principal functions: accumulation, connection, rupture, shifting. Our hypothesis would be that signs and intensities are not mutually exclusive, and that, on the contrary, they are in fact based on each other; there can be no semiotic perception of a sequence without release of its energetic force, and vice versa. The net result of this is that the semiotics of gesture and the energetics of corporeal drives are not at all mutually exclusive; instead they complement each other in what I will call the *semiotization of desire* or *vectorization*.

To convince ourselves of this, let us take as an example the final sequence of *Ulrike Meinhof*, and examine the four main types of vectors of signification *and* intensity. They are arranged according to the polarity of displacement and condensation elaborated by Freud: two categories corresponding to the opposition between metonymy and metaphor, which can be subdivided into simple connection (through proximity or accumulation) and complex connection (through rupture or transfer).

Displacement	Condensation
2. Connector-vectors 3. Cutter-vectors	1. Accumulator-vectors 4. Shifter-vectors

In the sequence we are examining, each of these four categories could be given a title characterizing the operation effected by signs and affects at the same time:

1. The mutilated woman
2. The sufferings of young Ulrike
3. The end of a revolt
4. The victims of the victory of the nation

One can imagine an itinerary that leads us from one category to the next:

1. *The mutilated woman.* We can see a nonstructured accumulation of these sufferings and ill-treatment. This accumulation becomes rather wearing and restricts the message to a redundant affirmation. Once again here one can either hold fast to those signifiers that are immediately transformable into a single signified ("torture"), or let oneself be carried away by the unfurling wave, largely musical in nature, of the crescendo of terror and mutilation.
2. *The sufferings of young Ulrike.* Everything is connected in such a way that the spectator follows, step by step, the course of the single action: the ill-treatment inflicted on the prisoner. The connection is largely narrative, and so articulated around a series of signifieds that are rooted in a series of indications of suffering. The connection also implicates the signifiers that are conceived in such a way that they are linked together in accordance with an inexorable causal logic.

3. *The end of a revolt.* Nevertheless the accumulation and crescendo are periodically interrupted, and in rather a brutal fashion—through changes in shot, and in particular through the pauses at the end of a series. For example, at the end of the film, the image of Ulrike, crushed between the two glass panes of the cage, freezes and is transformed into a yellowing photograph that gives way to the German flag. When the principle of connection and accumulation is suddenly called into question, the story can only come to a grinding halt.
4. *The victims of the victory of the nation.* The end of the revolt and the physical destruction of the terrorists then shift directly to the triumph of the reunified nation, the collapse of the wall and the end of History.

Ulrike's suffering and mutilated body *represents,* that is, *figures* and *replaces,* another body: the regenerated political body of the triumphant nation, a body from beyond the stage where all the allusions converge. The mutilation is both the sign of this ideological discourse and the simulation of a true violence done to oneself. Kresnik's choreographic theater owes its potency to this intimate mix of the fictional and the authentic, the historical and the individual, representation and performance.

A comparison of these two examples easily convinces us that an analysis of an actor's gestures must be carefully adapted to its object, and that there is no all-embracing, universal methodology. The distinctions are based on whether the gestures represent a mimetic action or not, whether they accompany the reading and diction of a text (as in *The Miser*), or are presented as a body that is danced, rhythmed, energetic (as in *Ulrike Meinhof*). In *The Miser,* we are faced with a profusion of signs and cultural allusions, a hyperlanguage: "a hypersophisticated language of the body that is based on cultural, anthropological, pictorial, literary, or other references, which must be decoded to release their meanings and their 'flavor.'"[36] In *Ulrike Meinhof,* the body "speaks" of itself, but without making precise allusions, without being reducible to a story or a spoken language. What we have here is a "prelanguage": "a language previous to speech, more primitive and more direct, that speaks directly to the senses and the kinesthetics of the spectator's body, without the mediating filter of the intellect."[37] The body is a sort of medium through which uncontrolled flows pass; it is traversed at the same time by cultural phenomena and unconscious desires. It would be dangerous, however, to set up a radical opposition between hyperverbal and preverbal gestural systems. We have seen how *The Miser* has moments (although they are rare) of kinesthesia cut off from language (the beating scene), while *Ulrike Meinhof* is also very mimetic in relation to historical and political reality. Self-mutilation is as much a political parable, an allusion to history, as a moment of physical sensation provoked directly in the spectator, abstracting all symbolic signification. The divisive cleavage to be avoided, as Philippe Henry emphasizes in relation to the analysis of gestural works, is one that establishes "a sort of split or rupture between the suggestion of a fictive universe and the presentation of an event that has its own rhythmic and energetic qualities."[38] That is why our analyses examine the narrativity of gesture as well as bodily affects and their possible vectorization; the explanation of gesture must go hand in hand with a semiotization of desire, that is, a vectorization.

Although I have attempted to avoid a split of this kind, at the same time it is clear that one should not remain on the surface of gestures, and that one must understand both their origin and their spirit. Gesture relates to the body, but also to the world. The body sometimes appears restricted and enclosed within the mise-en-scène (as in *The Miser*, for instance); sometimes it seems expanded, exploded, bursting the parameters that surround it on the stage, dynamizing the mise-en-scène as a whole and in perpetual tension with it. Sometimes the study of the actor's body and gestures becomes dissolved in the overall "body" of the stage; the vectors and flows of intensity circulate at this price. On a stage where it is displayed, the actor's body leaves its narrow limits, stretching to fill the confines of the space seen and experienced by the spectator. It becomes emblematic of the question of meaning and the sign, and forces us to reassess categories that have been deemed to be mutually exclusive in the past (dance, theater, speech, song, etc.); in this way, it is inscribed in the "rainbow" of the arts of the body.

The dual example of *The Miser* and *Ulrike Meinhof* invites us to reconsider entrenched oppositions between a classical semiology of the sign and a poststructuralist energetics that refuses the sign and is prompt to evoke "flows of desire," or a signifying practice at the discretion of the spectator. Gestural systems (and more generally performance as a whole) cannot be described as an object without direction, without vectorization—as an object through which pass uncontrolled flows of desire. Inversely, vectorization, explanation, and the gestural connections proposed by mise-en-scène are susceptible to being interrupted and contradicted at every moment by the gaze and attention of the spectator. Therefore, there is a necessary compromise between explanation of signs and energetic event, a compromise that we have called *semiotization of desire* or *vectorization.*

The Actor's Score and Underscore

Definitions

Performance analysis tends to privilege the viewpoint of an external observer describing a performance's visible and audible signs. The actor is not excluded from this observation, but usually it is the external elements that are described best without too much attention being paid to the link between the performer and the rest of the production. The actor is observed like a strange animal, cataloged like a new book, dismantled like a disposable object, transfixed like an exotic butterfly. The actor is subjected to *partition* in two senses of the word: dissection into various zones (gestures, facial expressions, voice, gaze, etc.), and reduction to a kind of musical score recording the signs he emits or that seem to be perceptible in him—or rather *on* him, for here too the viewpoint is largely external and superficial. But is it sufficient in performance analysis to stay on the level of a superficial description of the actor's score? Shouldn't our interest be in the *underscore,* that is, what is hidden beneath the score as well as what precedes it, supports it, perhaps even constitutes it, like the submerged part of an iceberg whose visible tip is only the ice-cold superficial appearance of the performer?

This notion of underscore should be somewhat clarified. The neologism is modeled on the term *subtext,* which is now considered too closely associated with a psychological, text-based model of theater (as Stanislavsky interpreted it in his productions of Chekhov). *Score* is preferable to *text,* because score is not limited to the linguistic text; it also includes all perceptible performance signs. Indeed this notion of score was used explicitly by Stanislavsky, who considered it to be desired outcome of the preparation of all artists, according to the author's *superobjective:*

> If one could retain every phase of the work of all participants in the production, one would obtain a sort of orchestral score for the entire play. Everyone involved would have to play the notes of their role very pre-

cisely. Then all those taking part in the production would be able to play the poet's superobjective together—provided that they complement each other harmoniously.[39]

The underscore would then be the submerged solid mass on which the actor supports himself in order to appear and sustain himself on stage, that is, everything on which his acting is based. It is the sum of situational factors (situations of enunciation) and of technical and artistic know-how on which the actor leans in order to realize his score.

Two Types of Score

One should distinguish two types of score: a preparatory score, and a final score. The *preparatory score* is constituted in the course of rehearsals through a series of choices that are concretized in a basic structure that evolves continuously. The *final score* is that of the "finished" performance, or at least that of the performance presented to an audience; it fixes (more or less) the choice of signs and actions presented on stage; it corresponds, in another terminology, to the notion of *performance text (testo spettacolare)*. From our perspective in this context, that of performance analysis, the term *final score* is used in full knowledge of the fact that in itself it is never finished, and that it carries traces of the preparatory score.

Score and Underscore: Synthesis of Their Components

The Unknown, or My Personal Life
A first set of definitions concerns the performer's intimate sense of self: the secret self, and those private experiences on which the concrete moments of creativity are based: a whole series of personal, lived experiences that actors use for their roles, and that feed their performances, without it ever being fully known how they are used and how far they go.

Beneath and Behind
By definition, the underscore is located *underneath* the actor's visible, material score; unlike the score, it is not visible, perceptible; it cannot be assimilated into any concretely realized sign. It is the idea behind the

action, the ground of the score, an associational or imaginal network, the invisible body of the action. Whether it is *underneath* or *behind* or *alongside* the score, the underscore underlies and supports the visible aspect of the actor: his/her score; it carries it, precedes it, and gives rise to it. In this sense it is much more than a provisional and arbitrary support, much more than a formless glacial mass; it is the soil in which the actor flowers. In fact it is both ice and soil at once. For on one hand the actor's underscore is carved from the same translucent block as his score; there is no radical difference between it and what the actor shows; the difference between the hidden and the manifest is purely relative, and merely depends on the water level. On the other hand the actor needs to put down roots in terrain different from his own, which will nourish them by providing them with the raw materials, minerals, and vitamins necessary for their formation and growth. Ice or soil, slippery or boggy ground, the underscore is in fact what holds an actor up, what he leans on. Ultimately it is the actor himself, since everything he does can only come from his own physical and mental resources.

Overall Structure

Instead of searching for the essence or the hidden thread of the underscore, it might be more productive to consider the form of its presentation, and to look for an overall structure: that is, the relationship of each particular action or moment to the meaning of the whole, or a series of reference points or landmarks where actor and spectator can draw breath and verify their understanding.

Reference Points, Support Points

The actor orients and supports himself on a series of points that construct the configuration and framework of his performance. These support, or leaning points sustain his emotional and kinesthetic memory, his "thinking body." They are personal and unique to each actor and have no absolute value in themselves. They are very often deceptions, sites of indeterminacy, tricks to memorize mentally and physically the trajectory of a role and the actor's chronotopic situation. They exceed the boundaries of the individual and implicate the group. Indeed it is the group and the space-time of its scenic situation that produce the actor's kinesthetic inscription within the performance, orienting and localizing them by means of an invisible series of signals, reference points, and stimuli. Step by step, actors set up safety rails to guide their trajectories, according to different support and reference points that are both physical and emotional.

Preparatory Work

This kind of construction is the object of lengthy preparatory work, about which we know little, although we can readily imagine its importance. Does this work constitute part of a semiology of acting, and of an analysis of performance? In the classical sense of a semiology of a concrete and realized representation, it certainly does not; but shouldn't we introduce into the description of the actor's performance some consideration of the influence of the actor's tradition and acculturation on the future scoring of his role? In his own time Stanislavsky was already insisting on the importance of the actor's "work on himself," then "on the role." A fortiori, for a style of acting acquired through years of training and acculturation, it is important to observe the degree to which the sediments of time, culture, and body techniques are already built up within an actor's body before he even walks on stage.

Cultural Presuppositions

Underscore, however, is not simply a structure controlled by the individual actor in search of his score; it is constituted by the performer's cultural norms and models of behavior and reflects the imprints of culture on him.

Synthesis: The System of the Underscore

The system of the underscore brings the following principles to light:

- Underscore does seek to identify what is hidden in the actor's preparation, what exists before its expression becomes visible and fixed in the performance score; nonetheless it is already infiltrated and formed by the surrounding culture.
- The underscore is more or less fixed and immutable, in proportions not necessarily symmetrical with those of the corresponding score. A carefully elaborated and articulated underscore does not necessarily entail a score with identical qualities.
- It is clear that the underscore is constructed from the actor's perspective; but the actor remains aware of what the future spectator's perceptions will be, at least as far as the performance score is concerned. On this level, the spectator participates in its creation and validation.

These principles enable us to propose the following definition:

Underscore: Guiding schema of a kinesthetic and emotional nature, articulated through the actor's own points of reference and support; it is created and represented by the actor with the help of the director, but it can
only be made manifest through the mind and body of the spectator.

Putting the Body Back into the Mind

Conceived in this way, the notion of underscore could become a crossroads
between the genealogical approach to the actor's work (in the course of
rehearsals and in tandem with the director) and the descriptive approach to
the end result of the performance as received by the spectator. It would
breathe new life into a performance analysis too unilaterally based on the
observation of results and insufficiently attentive to the processes of preparation and inculturation that have sedimented on the object of the analysis.
It would correct the simplifying view that assimilates it to the inner life of
the actor, in opposition to the actor's external appearance, the character.
One would then perceive the process of mixing and filtering that occurs in
the passage underscore to score, a process Peter Brook has described rather
elegantly:

> The actor first looks to his customary baggage to understand the charac-
> ter; then, convinced that the character is at every level richer, greater,
> more extraordinary than himself, he endeavors to bring to light all that
> he harbors in a virtual state, deep down, those things that are not usually
> expressed and of which he is not aware, so that bit by bit these under-
> ground springs may find their way through the mud and reach the sur-
> face.[40]

The semantic theory of meaning and language is indeed not far away
from this process of mixing and filtering the actor's body and soul, in the
movement of underscore to score. In *The Body in the Mind,* Mark Johnson
shows how much the imagination and the body are present in the formation of meaning and reason. Our knowledge of the world is possible by
means of *image schemata,* which organize our perception and can be found
in the most abstract of forms:

> An image schema is a recurring, dynamic pattern of our perceptual inter-
> actions and motor programs that gives coherence and structure to our
> experience. . . . Experientially based, imaginative structures of this image-

schematic sort are integral to meaning and rationality. . . . Image schemata have a certain kinaesthetic character—they are not tied to any single perceptual modality, though our visual schemata seem to predominate.[41]

In the same way, as we have seen, the actor readily attaches himself to the safety rail of a visual or visualizable trajectory. As a basis for his underscore and then his score, he looks for what precedes language; and for him, meaning is based in the body and its physical states. For the actor, as for the semanticist, the goal, in Johnson's words, is to "put the body back in the mind," to regain the "preconceptual and non-propositional"; for as human beings or actors, "we are never separated from our bodies and from forces and energies acting upon us to give rise to our understanding (as our 'being-in-the-world')."[42]

The underscore is this combination of kinesthetic and verbal experience: in other words, this body ready to express itself (verbally and gesturally), "preexpressive," yet already infiltrated by culture and therefore also, at least partially, by language.

Toward an Aesthesic of Actor and Spectator

The question of the underscore brings us ineluctably back to the spectator's perception. Her response to the performance—particularly to the work of actors or dancers—is kinesthetic and in some ways symmetrical with their trajectory. Dance researchers have known this for a long time, describing the reception of movement in dance as a "kinaesthetic response" to the dancer:

> Any movement, no matter how far removed from normal experience, still conveys an impression which is related to normal experience. There is a kinetic response to normal experience. There is a kinaesthetic response in the body of the spectator which to some extent reproduces in him the experience of the dancer; if the dancer performs some movement without the motivation of inner compulsion, the spectator will experience no inner responsiveness.[43]

Meyerhold, in his series of biomechanical exercises, also wanted to test the effect on the partner and the spectator, to measure their kinesthetic response. Barba too observes the dilated body of the performer and, in

doing so, "dilates the cenaesthetic perception of the spectator by constructing a new architecture of muscular tonus that pays no heed to the economy
and functioning of daily behavior."[44] This is a response phenomenon that
is a means of making sense of the world through a bodily reaction that is
not yet infiltrated by language. Theater people therefore formulate a theory
that harks back to Marcel Jousse's anthropology of gesture, which studies
the origin of gestures and their role in our knowledge of reality:

> Man only knows that which he receives into himself and replays. This is
> our mechanism of knowledge through our gestures of rejection. . . . The
> Anthropos is an interactionally mimic animal, which is to say that only
> man is able to make his interactions with outside reality intelligible.[45]

So the spectator would be the actor's ultimate addressee; for she replays
the actor's score by taking into her mind and body the underscore she
thinks she reads in the actor, and that she ends up sharing with him. In this
sense, perhaps it would be wise to reassess those overconfident Eurocentric
oppositions that would have us believe that anthropologically and quintes-
sentially the theater always separates the tactile from the visual. According
to Darko Suvin, for example, there is no interactive feedback between stage
and audience:

> How is the feedback between stage and audience possible? It is rooted in
> the anthropologically basic and constitutive theatre fact: that the specta-
> tors' pragmatic position is specifically one cut off from tactility; they may
> look but not touch. The Possible World in theatre is centrally constituted
> by the resulting *basic split between visual and tactile space* experienced by
> the audience.[46]

At best this would only apply to classical bourgeois spectatorial practices
(the spectator hunched in a red velvet armchair at a respectable distance
from the stage). However, many other kinds of performance require an
ambulatory, and above all *kinesthetic,* participation by the spectator—
which basically means any performance in which one reacts to the human
body: dance, mime, in fact any genre in which the human body is displayed.
Instead of universalizing this alleged separation between the visual and the
tactile—which is, moreover, contested nowadays by psychology and
semantics, as we have seen with Johnson—and instead of adopting the
sedentary model of distant spectators seated in front of the stage (a model

that takes refuge in a purely visual and theoretical notion of an overall perspective), it would be more judicious to take into account the spectator's
aesthesic perception. For we need to observe the ways in which the spectator reacts physically to the score, and to what it implies in terms of underscore and the condition of the actor in the world. Semiological description
of actors and their scores therefore need to integrate the aesthesic perspectives of the spectator, and evaluate how conscious the spectator is of her
own corporeal and tactile presence. By evaluating the actor's underscore in
corporeal terms, by touching through eye contact rather than hand contact,
by modeling her own bodily schema on the actor's, the spectator learns to
see anew, and to question the received model of corporeity: classical
panoptic vision or fragmentation, vision as continuous movement or stac-
cato glances, video effects that provoke physical sensations in the observer.
Theater, that "realm of ocular and infantile identifications,"[47] invites the
spectator to bridge the apparent separation between the visual and tactile
with her own body.

The Example of *Terzirek*

Let us take as an example *Terzirek,* a video-film by the Théâtre du Mouvement (1992). Shot in a desert, the film is about the appearance of human life
on earth; it shows creatures barely identifiable as human beings gradually
being transformed into apes. The spectator very quickly recognizes that
these are actors miming the movements of these animals. The film provides
us with the possibility of an original aesthesic experience.

An Underscore That Can Be Recognized by the Spectator

Using the categories identified above, I will attempt to reconstruct and
sketch the underscore of the humanoid creatures emerging from the sand.

1. Mystery and the unknown characterize this film whose narrative is
    based on an enigma, a search for the identity of forms in movement.
    For the spectators, it is somewhat as if the unknown in their lives—pre-
    vious or internal—were emerging from the sand and becoming ever
    more identifiable. The evolution of this animated desert seems to sug-
    gest (through a topos as old as the world) that the actor must undergo

incessant transformations and give rise to new signs, to avoid becoming tiresome to the spectator. Moreover, according to Bert States, it is "our unconscious demand that there be something constantly *emergent* in the actor's performance."[48]

2. Underneath, under the sand, under the bag, under the appearance of stone or desert crusaders, are in fact concealed human beings (women and/or men) whose motivity remain quite human whatever their efforts to suggest the motivity of a scorpion, a headless phantom, a darting lizard, or a monkey walking on all fours. The difficulty for the dancers is in not giving away the human quality of their movement, while still suggesting that humanity will finally emerge from these archaic shapes.

3. The multiplicity of shots in the film reinforces the idea that each actant passes through the same phases, and that the orientation and meaning of the sequence (the evolution of the species) happens globally, with each image confirming, then extending beyond the others. Each dancer's progress is based on reference points identical to those of their partners—reference points clearly established for the type of movement, using the characteristic detail of each evolutionary phase of the animal species (see fig. 8).

4. The reference points operate quite naturally as points of support accompanying the humanization process of the desert animals. These reference points constitute a framework for the physical attitudes of the dancers, their bodily positions, and as markers in the course of the fiction. Every element of their gestural work is *justified* (in Stanislavsky's sense); that is to say, it occurs as the result of a logic of movement and a clear actantial situation. As States confirms, gesture is indeed "any form of expressiveness in which the actor's body is justified."[49]

5. To judge by the athleticism and muscularity of their bodies in the "monkey-walk" sequence, their *preparation* may have been like that of a classical mime capable of suggesting a great deal with very little. Their mastery is far from perfect; the monkeys show off their muscles, their feet are visible underneath the silhouettes that are supposed to glide by themselves, a swimming-in-sand sequence is somewhat laborious; and yet their gestures possess a quality of great restraint. In short, there is more than a hint of Decroux in the air. "One must be able to only mobilize what one wants to mobilize," Decroux suggested, "whether a single specific organ, or several."[50] The body is able to use only that part required for the particular movement; invisible feet (for they are concealed by the sacks) produce the movement while the rest of the body remains immobile, as if it glided miraculously over the surface of the dunes.

Fig. 8. Théâtre du mouvement, *Terzirek,* 1992. *Above,* the emergence of
humanity from the desert sands. *Below,* the monkey-walk sequence.
(Photographs by Claire Heggen and Yves Marc.)

6. The cultural presuppositions are easily recognizable. The genealogy of life, the evolution of animal species, the humanization of the ape: all commonplaces for which mime has a particular fondness, and which the spectator identifies without difficulty. The implicit encyclopedia is made up of almost conventional gestures to signify, life, movement, quest.

The Aesthesic Experience of the Spectator

The spectator's aesthesic experience is primarily linked to the narrative and rhythmic structure of the film and its music; tracks, shapes, and sounds emerge from the silence, infinity and entombing vastness of the desert. This model of appearance and identification underpins the entire story.

1. *Overcoming the separation between visual and tactile.* By its very nature, the film does of course prevent the audience from tactile contact with the performance. However the choice and composition of shots of the sand, the ridges of dunes, the flow of grains and the archaic columns all suggest the tactile materiality of this inviolate landscape.

2. *Counterbodies.* The shots of the desert suggest the genesis of movement and life. The emergence of bodies from the sand, the transformation from mineral death to animal life, liberate and activate our fears of being buried. Heads turning on their axes, detaching themselves from their trunks, hurtling down the side of a dune, are being subjected to antinatural movements; these are physically painful for the receivers, producing within them an anxiety about fragmentation and violently upsetting their bodily schemata.

3. *The trace of an irreversible trajectory.* Ultimately all these signs and affects, strongly and strictly vectorized in the same direction like a desire channeled by forms, trace a global trajectory, which ultimately each animal, as well as by the general story-line of this parable, takes up and adopts (reminiscent of Decroux's mimo-drama *Passage des hommes sur la terre*). We follow the traces of this parable, orienting ourselves by means of strong, clear moments in this account of the humanization of creatures—as if the underscore manifests itself most clearly when it breaks through the visible surface of the score of each dancer, and more generally, of the whole film.

It has to be admitted that the description and analysis of the actor/actress is much more complex than it appears at first sight, precisely because seeing and visibility are not sufficient in themselves. One must get used to perceiving the invisible behind the visible, the underscore behind the score, the other behind oneself, and oneself behind the other.

Description even encompasses the spectator's gaze, for she is not only the *other* to the performers, but also the *same*. She shares the same space-time, which she not only fits into but also institutes; she relives in her own body and soul the torments as the actor/character, who both exists out there in front of her and dwells within her as her image and body schema.

The underscore thus becomes the invisible (which does not mean unreal) terrain—the meeting place of the actor's work, before and during the performance, and the spectator; both are invited to enlarge their field of analysis beyond the visible and immediate.

In this way, they can perceive what the actor does and, at the same time, what this action of making visible and audible means in depth. First they must *read* the score, then *live* all it implies at a deeper level.

In performance analysis, the notion of underscore challenges many dogmatic assumptions about the analysis of the visible, of action, of the functions and meanings of signs. It allows actors to become the pivots of the production, not limiting them to mere presence as human bodies and extending their influence to the whole production of which the underscore/score becomes a scaled-down model.

The underscore is useful both to actors (to orient themselves in their roles and their scores) and to spectators, who rely on it to describe and understand the performance. For both parties, it becomes a sort of modeling of their entire experience, from the process of elaborating a role to its reception by spectators. The underscore is what is left when everything else has been forgotten.

In a certain sense, the underscore is the Trojan horse that introduces into the heart of performance analysis the subjective testimonies of actors, their biographies, their ways of articulating the performance and their own experiences. In this way the "sacrosanct" principle that used to pertain—of analyzing work without listening to what its creators have to say about it—becomes relativized from the moment when the articulations of performers are no longer deemed to be incommunicable or personal. Thus we are able to understand something of how a role is constructed, and of how the testimony of an actor can become what Julia Varley, a performer with the Odin Teatret, calls an "autohistoriography."

Theatrical Analysis, Filmic Analysis: The Example of *Marat/Sade*

To bring this overview of an analysis of the actor to a close, performers in theater and dance will be compared. First, this will entail some comparison of theatrical and filmic analysis.

Conditions of Analysis

The conditions for analysis of *Marat/Sade*[51] are simplified if one examines the video version recorded from German television, with the original English text of the performance and the German subtitles, which are in fact Weiss's original text. This video recording, easy to access and consult, makes a supposedly exhaustive account unnecessary. A scene-by-scene description by David R. Jones already exists,[52] although he does not specify whether it refers to the stage performance or the film. The methodological goal of our analysis here is to focus on the comparative description of stage performance and film.

The Analyst's Gaze

In this case, the director of the film is also the director of the theater production; his gaze, both in the wake of, and different from, that of the theater maker, is bound to account to some degree for what went on in the theater version. The film was shot in a two-week period, just after the Royal Shakespeare Company's final performances in New York, with the same cast, in a studio containing a largely faithful reconstruction of the original set. Peter Brook felt obliged to "keep as close as possible to the stage version, which was rehearsed and ready," and thus

> to see if a purely cinematic language could be found that would take us away from the deadliness of the filmed play and capture another, purely cinematic excitement. . . . In the end, I think I managed to capture a highly subjective view of the action and only afterwards did I realize that it was in such subjectivity that the real difference between film and theatre lay.[53]

One can imagine the difficulty of having this (filmic) subjectivity emerge from the stage subjectivity, from the point of view of production (since

Brook neither specifies nor clarifies his choices) and of reception (because no clues as to the theatrical mise-en-scène remain). So it is very difficult to establish the status of this film. On the one hand, it is not a recording of the stage event intended to document the theater performance. Its discourse is sufficiently elaborate and autonomous to obliterate all trace of what the original theater performance may have been like—and we have no access to it in any case—since the performance is re-played especially for the cameras in the absence of the theater audience's gaze. On the other hand, however, the camera openly states that it is using material that has already been worked and shaped, and comes straight from Brook's theater workshop. As film director, Brook ensures that the characteristic attributes of his theater work at that time are retained: speed, intensity, and immediacy of acting, a combination of moments of Artaudian cruelty and Brechtian distancing, constant shifts in tempo, alternating violence and lyricism. Brook recaptures all of these elements in his film, but inserts them into a particular filmic discourse by modifying imperceptibly the "pro-filmic" theatrical elements, which comes as no surprise since here too the point of view creates the object and destroys it at the very moment it is about to grasp it:

> During the filming, I analyzed shot by shot making deft little changes, modifying the approach so that the action would be more intimate, more convincing for the camera. I realized that the cinematic staging was improvised; we progressed very quickly as we worked, employing an entirely cinematic language of close-ups, long shots, in order to give a living and very subjective impression of the play.[54]

Both a "film film" and a "theater film," *Marat/Sade* can be analyzed in terms of either genre. In the "theater film," the camera moves toward its object, trying to capture it; in the "film film," the object is placed in relation to the camera. *Marat/Sade* alternates between being a film with its own techniques and documentation of a theater performance. However, the degree to which the hallmarks of the theatrical acting style are taken on and relayed through specifically filmic devices is remarkable.

Filmic Devices

Filmic Cutting (*découpage*)
The film is cut in accordance with the order of presentation of sequences and speeches as they occur in the English translation of the text. The edit-

ing seems to obey a requirement for actions to be clarified. The vectorization of the shots (the directionality that emerges from the way they are
arranged) cannot be ignored; all the materials are subject to this overdeter-
mination.

However, one must immediately add that the découpage is itself dictated
by a narratological structure that goes beyond and subsumes the minimal
units constituted by the shots. As a result it borrows its subdivisions from
Brook's reading of the story when he directed the theater production; its
shape emerges from the pro-filmic theatrical elements captured by Brook's
dancing cameras. The paradox is apparent: the filmic découpage, however
inescapable it may be, is only really readable with reference to a narrative
logic that has already taken shape in the story within the text and in the pro-
filmic elements given form by the stage space and the acting. An analysis of
the film should proceed via this dual perspective: strictly filmic *and* largely
narratological. Thus one should start with the units of individual shots, then
progress toward larger units within the narratological and dramaturgical
structure. Besides, spectators understand this straight away, as soon as they
realize that the herald plays a role that is both filmic and narratological
because he introduces and concludes most of the tableaux, and resituates
actions within the Sadean logic of this mise-en-scène, entering and leaving
the frame of the shot as if to further fragment and connect the film's shots
and the episodes' story. (See "Commentary on Photographs" below.)

Rhythmical Discrepancies

Despite the determining schema of narratological segmentation that, as we
have just seen, in-forms and makes available the film's division into shots
by totalizing it once more, the rhythm of the film is essentially imbued with
the filmic découpage. The découpage and rhythm are all the more notice-
able because they contrast sharply with the other rhythms contained in the
pro-filmic components, above all the gestural and spatial rhythms of the
actors and the verbal rhythms of the diction (the phrasing of the text); the
latter is, in part, grafted on to the actors' bodily rhythms. In the case of pro-
filmic elements already stylized by theatrical performance (as is the case
with *Marat/Sade*), one films—and thus "rhythms"—material that possesses its own segmentation, which, at least in principle, has not been
devised with a view to future filming. It is this double, even triple rhythming that characterizes the overall rhythm of the film, in which the discrepancies, parallelisms, and differences between the various rhythms become
pertinent.

In addition, there is a dual and contradictory movement in the diction of the *Marat/Sade* actors. Each actor treats his or her character in his or her own way, seeking out the vocal *gestus* that best corresponds to the illness and role in question; but the Royal Shakespeare Company actors share a general style of acting and delivery that makes their characters less individualized and contributes to a homogenized phrasing. The same is true of Weiss as of Shakespeare:

> In verse which is properly spoken, each character play his own rhythm—as personal as his own handwriting, but what often happens in Shakespeare is that everyone shares a generalized rhythm that passes impersonally from one to the other.[55]

This impersonal, prosodic generalization is reinforced by the homogeneity imposed by the rhythm of the editing, which tends to make all of the profilmic rhythms conform to its own.

Units of the Filmic Narrative

The filmic narrative is structured around units and types of shot, some examples of which are given here (sequence shot, scale of shots).

1. The *sequence shot* makes generous sweeps of the stage space, promotes a mapping of places and protagonists, and takes the spectator inside the space, in particular here the "cage" within which the patients are contained; in addition, it helps narrativize the plot. It constitutes a whole, a sequence in the technical sense that establishes relations between the actants, or between actants and places, and often provides the illusion of a theater stage (as in the very first sequence shot of the film, which takes us into the hospital/prison world). When the text is spoken as a voice-off—when the herald introduces the prisoners (scene 4), for example—the image seems to follow the text; it duplicates it, but also generates, through changes in focal length and focus, a kind of editing within the shot, a hierarchy of enunciations, a display of power relations. When Jacques Roux is introduced, for instance, we see him first from the front in close-up, with the herald over his right shoulder; then he turns his head slowly toward his left, and just manages to open his mouth to speak before being immediately interrupted by a gesture from Coulmier, the asylum director; with a shift in focal length and focal point, Coulmier miraculously comes into view over Roux's left shoulder, reducing him to silence. The dramaturgy of this scene is visible in the evolving relations between the three spaces and the three actants.

2. The *scale of the shots* plays an important part in indicating changes of fictional regime and varying the spectator's emotional distance from the action. Three kinds of shot recur systematically:

- The *group shot,* when the actors in Sade's performance are supposed to lead the action: for example, "We want revolution now . . ." or the pantomimed copulation in scene 30. These group shots allow us to view the overall space and suggest a theater stage by making the actantial configuration and dynamics of the group clearly readable. Contrary to the conventions of filmed theater, this kind of shot is not used at the beginning of the film to establish spatial relations; here it is used after the group has been introduced in a series of individual portraits and has emerged as a collective force. The group shot also serves to punctuate a sequence by drawing from it an overall visual summary: for example, the end of scene 11, "Death's Triumph."
- The *medium shot* brings together a smaller group of two or three characters involved in a single action: for example, the chorus of four singers, or the characters activated by the herald. In this subscene, the actors appear to enter freely when moving into the shot frame: for example, Charlotte Corday's arrivals at Marat's door, mimed by the herald.
- The *close-up* tracks down patients or prisoners, trying to extract their secrets from them, and providing us with an impressive gallery of portraits. By framing their faces in close-up, the camera heightens the sense of authenticity in these scenes; it both underlines the reality effects of psychology and brings the spectator closer to the human reality of the hospital or of the prison.

Pulsations

The interplay between these three types of shots creates a dynamic by alternating stronger and weaker moments in the narrative framework. The result is a "pulsation" based on the accumulation of energy and violence, vocal or visual dramatic intensity, which leads to an explosion: a patient's breakdown, an intervention by Coulmier, outbursts from Roux or Marat. Each explosion ends with a return to calm: a cold shower, the straitjacket, repressive control, or perhaps a rare lyrical moment of song and listening. Then the tension resumes, the contradictions build up again, until another explosion takes place, and so on. The actors' energies are thus controlled, channeled, and accompanied by the filmic discourse.

A similar pulsation governs the alternation of crowd scenes with music and song and calmer individual scenes devoted to the discussion of ideas.

This cycle provides a structure for the pulsation, building to a crescendo that culminates in a paroxysm of violence with the final revolt of the inmates. The film ends abruptly with a blackout and the sound of a gong, thus denying any possible release of tension or any conclusion.

Transition
These abrupt changes in intensity are usually produced within a single scene. Transitions between the scenes are effected by the herald as intermediary, either through a direct intervention addressed to the camera or through a voice-off. A final group shot summarizes and punctuates one phase of the action.

All of these filmic devices—découpage, scale of shots, rhythmic discontinuities—inscribe the pro-filmic theatrical elements (or what is left of them) within a discourse with a strong filmic identity, which never gives the impression of being filmed theater. Once again one can verify André Bazin's remark that "the more cinema tries to be faithful to the text and its theatrical demands, the more it needs to explore and extend its own language."[56] In this *Marat/Sade*, all the filmic processes are at the service of theatricality.

Theatrical Devices

Address to the Camera
Whether explicit and extravagantly exaggerated (as with the herald), or confidential and discreet (Sade or Marat), direct address to the camera opens up the fourth wall, breaks the illusion of a self-enclosed performance and exposes the realist convention by pushing theatricality to an extreme.

Opening Up Space
The herald, who effects transitions, beginnings, and encounters, is often responsible for opening up spaces in the narrative; he uses his staff as a magic wand to create narrative spaces and to interconnect words and things. Through deictic gesture or his roving gaze, the space is transformed into a ludic and convention-driven place to be filled with acting and actors.

Scenography
The same heterogeneous regime operates for the stage space. Sometimes the camera makes us inhabit the interior as if we ourselves were confined

there; sometimes it shows us this enclosed area in perspective, from afar, over the heads of spectators in the diegetic audience, or through the bars that delineate an intangible boundary. In both cases, we perceive nothing outside this frame, no adjacent space to which we and the prisoners could escape; we are all in the same situation—hermetically sealed in a world without exits that is pathological, prisonlike, ludic, and formal. The pro-filmic elements have been abstracted, reduced, stylized, and this has trans-formed the actual place into "another place" (*ein anderer Schauplatz:* Freud), a symbolic site in the imaginary. The classic no-way-out situation reduces the many actions to the major figures of alienation, imprisonment, and madness. There is no attempt here to inject a cinematic force into the-ater; we can see that the place filmed is a theater set and not a hypothetical asylum in Charenton. The stage space is equated by the film spectator with a stage architecture, that is, "a place that is materially sealed, delimited, cir-cumscribed, in which the only 'discoveries' are those of our consenting imaginations."[57] The lighting is also somewhat artificial and theatrical: a pale, milky light that blurs contours rather than accentuating them; often backlit, it maintains a certain homogeneity, as if all the scenes were viewed through the tinted glass of an aquarium.

Diction

In this space that is closed or ironically opened up to the camera, the main protagonists (apart from the chorus of patients imprisoned within their alienation) adopt a slow, "presentational" diction, a mode of delivery shaped by the rhetorical convention of long classical monologues recited on stage. The text of Geoffrey Skelton's translation is perfectly in tune with the gestural, vocal, and musical rhythms adopted. It is musicalized, steeped in the rhythms of music and prosody; sometimes opened out toward the camera, sometimes folded in around the alienated actor, malleable like some very supple material, it marks all of the acting options. The German subtitles relaying Weiss's original text enable the spectator-reader to verify the accuracy of the translation while concentrating on the phrasing and plasticity of the English melodic line. It is as if the text is carried along on a stage dynamic, particularly through the effects of attraction and repulsion of the performers in front of the camera.

Fictional Status

These effects of theatricality and interpellation are all the more notable for being alternated with moments that appear to have been extracted from a documentary on madness and incarceration. The progression of the story and the film editing have the effect of constantly varying the fictional status of the performance. Documentary moments from a report in a hospital environment, delivered in present time, are alternated with a historical reconstruction of the life of Marat as performed by the detainees of 1808. Spectators must continually adapt their gaze to the period and the stage reality, which oscillates between a raw hospital documentary and the staging of fictions played by apprentice performers.

Two Kinds of Vision

The body model and the determination of its representative density are established on the basis of a type of vision that corresponds to a very precise camera placement.

Vision from a distance, rather cold and clinical, corresponds to the bodies of the patients (and the patient body); these shots in the film are instantaneous, often fixed portraits. This is the contemplative vision of the gaze.[58] The body of the histrionic actors or of the prisoners, on the other hand, are usually approached by means of a haptic vision, in which an avid gaze and camera, passed over the entire body, realizes the act of perception, the glance. Here the mobile cameras aggress and pierce the object to be photographed through a scopic vision in which "gesture as movement is offered up to view."[59] They "wrestle" with their object, as does the theater spectator who invests in those elements of the stage on which she has chosen to focus. In the ideological debates (between Marat and Sade, and particularly with Marat and Roux), the exchanges seem to be located in relation to a fixed and "preexisting" camera toward which they direct their eyes and their bodies, taking "us" as witnesses: a camera that breathes in and comments upon the agitation on stage. The reportage analysis proposed in this volume must include the spectator's reactions to the filmic language; here it should describe how she is torn between different bodily schemata, between distance and involvement, panoramic vision and haptic visual intervention. Brook appears to have conveyed perfectly, through filmic means, this indeterminacy of meaning and the ideological contradictions that the play discusses:

Weiss forces us to relate opposites and face contradictions. He leaves us raw. He searches for a meaning instead of defining one and puts the responsibility of finding the answers back where it properly belongs. Off the dramatist and onto ourselves.[60]

This increased responsibility of the spectator and her gaze perhaps distances us from an objective description of the mise-en-scène, but it does not exempt us from studying actors and the way in which we receive and (re)constitute their acting. To describe acting is to evaluate the body-to-body relationship to which we give ourselves with the actor and the stage, with the further possibility of using the camera and its gaze as substitute for our bodies. It should be easier to study the actor in this way, but is this really the case?

Studying the Actor

Paradoxically, the film actor has only been examined in rather a sketchy fashion in semiology, narratology, or enunciation theory. It is true, as Christian Metz and Marc Vernet contend,[61] that an analysis of acting requires one to leave aside semiological, narrative, and enunciative structures. Actors can then be extracted from the filmic discourse by reconstituting them in the pro-filmic, without one worrying too much about the forms, in order to "meet" the actors directly. Even though the processes of film actors remain relatively unfamiliar to us (and given the fact that the preservation of their images on film does not help our study in the least, contrary to what we might expect), the "theater film," that is, the film dealing with theater, can help us understand more of the actor's work.

What does this mean for *Marat/Sade,* and how could we use it as a plan for the study of acting?

Fictional Status
The aim is to determine the framework within which we perceive actors, and the status of truth or fiction we accord them. For example, the acting of the patients is most "natural" and pathetic (i.e., loaded with reality effects) when they try to play a role. On the other hand, the acting of the "organizers" (Coulmier, Sade, the herald, the four singers) is "presentational"; it foregrounds theatrical conventions. One could rank the characters by their degree of self-awareness and of theatricality displayed in descending order, as follows: the herald, the four singers, Coulmier, Sade, Duperret, Marat, Corday, the other patients.

Authenticity/Theatricality Dialectic
Brook alternates (rather than opposes) effects of authenticity and effects of theatricality. The emphasis on acting and convention reinforces the authen-

ticity of the situation (patients condemned to act); the recourse to natural-ism in the portrayal of madness leads to scenes of pure convention. A single actress, such as the one who plays the role of Simone, can at the same time create an "ill" character who is unnervingly true to life (gaze, bodily attitude, rhythm) and perform theatrical actions determined by convention (opening the fictional door to Corday). Naturalism and convention alternate inces-santly. This endless cycle explains the characters' ability to "change bodies," and provokes a physical and psychic discomfort in spectators, a feeling that is reinforced by the constant changes of perspective, type of shot, and fram-ing. The spectator is always aware that a theater event is being recorded; the highly mobile cameras effect a reportage analysis that latches on to the event, moves toward it, finds ways to film it by observing the actors, and thus pre-serves part of the spontaneity of the theatrical event. Therefore the analysis of the film proposed here looks more to reportage analysis than reconstruc-tion analysis for inspiration. The result is a heightening of theatricality in the film. We are always aware of the fact that this is theater, that both setting and protagonists are "false"—in other words, that they are aesthetic objects and not photographs of reality.

Relationship with the Camera

The authenticity/theatricality polarity, which is in fact characteristic of Brook's productions, is borne out in the actor/camera relationship. The more frequent and insistent the camera's gaze, the more hypertheatrical the acting; the more the camera has to go in search of an actor who pretends not be aware of it, and to exist without it, the more naturalistic and docu-mentary the acting seems (portraits of a lunatic, a prisoner or an amateur actor).

The System of Types of Acting

The system of types of acting is all the more easy to elucidate if the theatri-cal pro-filmic remains readable and integral, not shredded by a dominant filmic discourse. Indeed, theatricality and the effects of theater are easy to perceive because the structure of the story, the diegetic music, and the sys-tematic wholeness of the acting are all perfectly conserved, for the pro-filmic elements (the theater play) unites them in a closed system of con-ventions. In the same way, the story and dramatic structures (actions, space, time) hold up remarkably well, like a sort of *basso continuo*, or unin-terrupted sound-track (or "story-track") that cannot be broken down into its component parts.

The analysis of a theater film draws much of its inspiration from the categories of dramaturgy; it need not be technical, precise, driven by a shot-by-shot filmic analysis. The découpage of a theater film is not tied purely and simply to the narrative structure of the film; it is based in part on its reference to dramatic and theatrical structures, and is much more flexible in terms of the determination of its units and segmentation. Inversely, one can see the truth of the old adage used by film people that the more formally and specifically refined a film is, the less need there is for actors who know how to act in front of a camera. According to Alfred Hitchcock, for example, "the best film actors are those who know best how to do nothing."[62]

In reality, both on screen and on stage, actors do a great deal; but we are ill equipped to describe their skills—particularly when we hesitate between a filmic analysis obsessed with specifically filmic devices, and a dramaturgical, theatrical analysis that lacks verifiable points of reference.

Formal analysis and the typology of vectors are not confined to the instances listed here. The vectors mobilize all of the materials, connecting signifiers in various networks rather than merely translating them into signifieds. Moreover, they are not incompatible with a sociosemiotic approach to the play or film; in fact they call for a theory of ideology and invite research into ideologemes.[63]

Ideologeme of the Undecidable

The ideologeme that appears to surface most frequently in *Marat/Sade* is that of the undecidability of the debates. As soon as one attempts to clarify the philosophy of Sade, Marat, or Roux, one is confronted with insoluble contradictions; points of view are relativized and cancel each other out. This is all the more so given that the play-within-the-play is Sade's construction; he has others say what he was chosen for them to say, and what Coulmier, his benevolent boss, is able to tolerate. Even Coulmier's protestations have the effect of interventions provoked by Sade or rehearsed in advance by a crony rather than a true opponent. The origins of the words are obscured by the imbrication of discourses and a clouding of the subjects' identities. The undecidable nature of the polemical debates reflects an ideologeme of the alienated, introspective subject, who can neither be set free by others nor free herself; such subjects are prey to a psychic, political, and artistic dead-end within which they are condemned to (re)play the past, and to be played and played upon by the authorities.

Peter Brook transposes this ideologeme of entrapment, of mental, political, theatrical, and artistic alienation, to the formal level of the filmic discourse. He treats the protagonists in an equitable way (scale and duration of shot, focus) and isolates the debaters rather than showing their exchanges of ideas. While maintaining a strict equilibrium and status quo between Marat and Sade, Brook seems to privilege the ambiguous role of the herald. Is he really ill, like the others? He does not appear to be, although he listens to his master quite distractedly. On the other hand, he organizes the performance not only through speech, as Weiss's text suggests, but also through his control of the framing of images and tempo. Brook appears to make use of him as an ironic double charged with organizing the show, emphasizing important points in the story, connecting events and characters. Ultimately the impression of undecidability is reinforced to breaking point at the film's climax: the sudden interruption of the film, and of the prisoners' revolt, with a blackout and the sound of a gong. The final outcome of the revolt remains uncertain; is it an uncontrolled outburst of madness, of fiction over reality, of agitation over public order or brutal check? Although Weiss's text tends to suggest repression by Coulmier, Brook chooses indeterminacy. Is it a game that degenerates and falls apart, or absolute control over all revolt? "We must choose," as the herald says. All the film's threads, the vectors and their tensions, the speeches and their contradictions, converge upon this unlocalizable place of indeterminacy, where the thematic and formal networks find a precarious balance and meaning has just enough time to take hold.

Commentary on Photographs

In the absence of the temporal dimension, it is not possible to offer a full vectorial analysis. Film stills require us to grasp the fixed image of a photographic moment and augment it with what will occur immediately after the instant recorded. In this image, the framing sets up a whole network of gazes and hierarchies between different groups or individual figures on stage:

- In the background, the audience of patients with the enraged madman and Duperret on the right-hand edge.
- In the foreground, Sade, waiting, his gaze reflective and introspective.
- In the middle, crouching, with her back turned, Charlotte Corday.

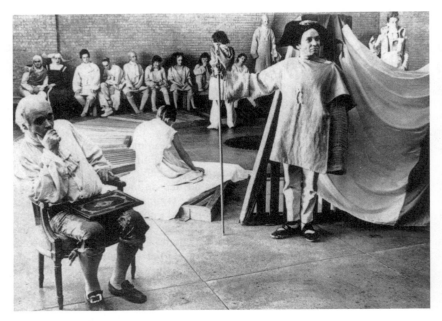

Fig. 9. The direction of meaning. Film still from Peter Weiss's *Marat/Sade* (United Artists, 1967), directed by Peter Brook, with Sade (Patrick Magee) and the herald Michael Williams (*right*).

■ Standing to the right, staring out toward the audience, the herald, the master of ceremonies who introduces the performances.

These different groups are connected through a system of vectors:

The *accumulators* function from the outset in terms of redundancy or repetition of the same signified or signifier. For example, on the bench in the background, each actor uses and varies the same body positions, creating the same impression of prostration. Accumulation of these positions leads to variations, moreover: the madman and Duperret, both standing, ready to participate in the action. Even when deprived of its duration, the scene enables us to imagine the accumulation of actions on stage.

The *connectors* link the groups by organizing an action and a narrative between them, above all through a system of gazes:

- The introspective gaze of the patients, the accumulation of which results in a half-distracted, half-interested gaze directed toward the center of the stage.
- The absent/present gaze of Sade, already turning his back on the reality that he is staging.
- The absent gaze of Corday, imperturbable until later on when she is given the weapon for the crime (see fig. 10).
- The seemingly circular and connecting gaze of the herald, who is responsible for making the performance happen; he is the stage manager, drawing together all the strings of the "inert puppet" that the play-within-the-play is.

The *cutters* also need time to intervene, but as one can see in figure 9, they also serve to divide up and distinguish the different groups and their interactions.

The *shifters* enable a gradual passage from one level of meaning, or from one "world," to another—for example, from one kind of alienation to another:

- The patients: mental and physical illness (mental alienation).
- The herald: theatrical *bouffonnerie* (alienation effect and distanciation).
- Sade: philosophical reflection (political alienation).
- Coulmier and us (off-screen): aesthetic-political manipulation (political-theatrical alienation).

With this system of four main vector types, many points of access to the scene are possible: various circuits and trajectories are set in motion, and they intersect, converge, and separate. The point of access and circuit chosen nevertheless occur in terms of a hierarchy determined by Peter Brook's mise-en-scène. In this context the vectorization, such as one can read it in the spatial configurations of the groups, clearly outlines a circuit that goes from the patients at the back, toward Sade (via Corday), and from Sade toward the herald.

We can mobilize our reading of this fixed scene in the performance by both taking part and taking sides in the trajectory between the various groups on stage; meaning is produced at the culmination of a vectorization trajectory. The moment when Sade gives Charlotte the dagger intended to kill Marat is a *punctum*, in Barthes's sense: the primary detail of a photograph that "pricks"[64] us and imposes its meaning upon us. In

Fig. 10. The *punctum doloris*. Film still from *Marat/Sade*, with Sade and Charlotte Corday (Glenda Jackson).

this case, the *punctum* is a dagger, foregrounded here through a zoom focus effect in the protagonists' gazes; Sade's and Corday's eyes both converge in/on the dagger.

The four main modes of vectorization are apparent here:

- The *connectors* relate to the gazes—Sade's oblique and distant gaze, and Corday's direct and fascinated gaze; they intersect and coincide in one place and at one time, but their end is different. Sade pursues a still distant goal by manipulating the dagger and its user; Corday already lives and sees Marat's death scene.
- The clarity of the connections, the intersecting looks and the actions they envisage make the use of *totalizer-accumulators* unnecessary.
- In spite of the sharpened weapon, neither is there any need for *cutters,* since we move smoothly and continuously from one gaze and one object symbolism to another.
- The same object lends itself to shifting and the transition from one action to another (Sade's delivery of the weapon, Corday's future execution of the murder). It also ensures the passage between denotative use of the implement and its symbolic value (sexual, ritual, political) in the course of the play. Organized in this way, connection, accumulation, sectioning, and symbolization converge in order to produce meaning in this scene—the *deixis,* which consists of signs made with the hand, the gaze, the crisscrossing of vectors (all of which only has meaning in the situation of the moment). This deixis is concrete (handover of the knife) and at the same time abstract (phantasmal evocation of the future murderous use of the weapon).

The following close-up (fig. 11) shows three of the four singers surrounding Marat, his apathy contrasting with the liveliness of the clowns. The interweaving of gazes and the difference between Marat's facial expression and those of the singers are symptomatic of a multiperspectivism, and of the impossibility of reducing the conflicts to a central given, as if the vectorization was blocked at this point. The connections do not lead to any accumulation and do not motivate a shift from one level to another. A complete study of vectorization should therefore compare the "representative densities" of various elements of the stage, and in particular of the actors' faces.

In this film still, one can immediately distinguish between a ludic, theatricalized, fictional corporeality, that of the singers, and a clinical, naturalistic, referential corporeality, that of the patient playing Marat. These two attitudes contrast with each other in terms of their rhythm, concentration, and the

Fig. 11. The difference of representative densities. Film still from *Marat/Sade,* with Marat (Ian Richardson, *center*) and members of the chorus.

tension in facial expressions. Their density is palpably different: Marat's face is empty, immobile, wan, and introverted; those of the singers are expressive, mobile, colorful, and extroverted. The difference in their faces is kinesthetic and corporeal, rather than psychological. It is not so much a question of the spectator identifying (with) the face, as of experiencing its kinesthesia and its physical effects. The density of an element increases when it is integrated as part of a greater number of vectorizations, and when it occurs at the intersection of vectorizations and trajectories of meaning.

The Rainbow of Bodily Arts: Mime, Dance, Theater, Dance-Theater

In order to summarize and synthesize our analyses thus far, in this section I will compare the use of the body in different performing arts.

"Between dancer and mime there is always treachery,"[65] Étienne Decroux suggests; and, one might add, "it's because of theater." For if dancers and mimes do not know how to meet on common ground, perhaps it is because they fail to find an area of shared understanding in theater. I will, however, refrain from some abstract comparison of the "essences" of these three genres, for it is clear that contemporary stage practices move from one to another with great ease, borrowing from each of them. Indeed contemporary practices suggest a rainbow of bodily arts, in which one shifts imperceptibly from one color in the spectrum to another, adopting a lateral, cross-disciplinary itinerary that scoffs at the old compartmentalized distinctions.

So as to avoid an abstract comparison of essences, I will examine the ways of describing mime, dance, and theater (and to round things off, *Tanztheater,* or dance-theater). I will not take specific examples, for lack of space, but the work of the following figures will be in the back of my mind: Étienne Decroux (mime), Karin Saporta (dance), Patrice Chéreau (theater), and Pina Bausch *(Tanztheater).*

Mapping the Trajectory

The Mime Artist

As the etymology of the word suggests, mimes imitate their object, although the imitation does not have to be direct and faithful to the original. It is based on a codification of gesture and character; it establishes and fixes points through which the mime must pass in a gestural sequence, producing distilled outlines of gestures that are recognizable and thus repeatable: "For, among many other things, our art is this: always purifying: then, if necessary, enlarging. Purifying and enlarging what? Everything we do in life, when we are not dancing."[66] The mime's body arranges, organizes, and maps his trajectory, thus paving the way for the movement of the spectator's gaze.

The Dancer

Dancers do not have to imitate an action or tell a story. Their trajectory is more difficult to trace, since it is not structured according to narrative logic. On the other hand, the intensity and direction of movement are much easier to perceive than its content or meaning. "Dancers can only work by bringing into play a body vector which does not define itself in terms of its structure, but in terms of the ways in which it organizes intensity."[67] Expending everything at their disposal, dancers' bodies give themselves over to a "knowledge of the uncontrolled" (Saporta).

The Theater Actor

Theater actors adopt an intermediary position between mimes and dancers. On the one hand, they base their gestures and words on codifications; on the other, they tend to deny them, to efface their structural reference points and mask the conventional construction of their characters. The theater body is subjected to a perpetual denial; it is displayed in its materiality and at the same time takes refuge in its fictionality.

The Actor-Dancer of Tanztheater

Tanztheater performers waver between two types of gestuality that they perform alternately: danced gesture and mimetic gesture. Actor-dancers' bodies convey this uncertainty as to their grounding to the spectator; they change strategies continually. Sometimes they allow their impulsion to come from muscular movement, sometimes they imitate and codify the world they represent. The movement choreography doubles up with a mise-en-scène (use of space, settings, text, and narrative construction) that usually belongs to theater.

Vectorization

Once this initial mapping of trajectories has been realized, we can examine the types of itinerary and vectorization that occur between the components of each of these areas. Vectorization is the dynamic momentum created in a narrative or chronology between the various parts of a stage work: the itinerary of meaning through the labyrinth of signs, the ordering of the performance.

The Mime

Mimes subject their bodies and gestuality to a fanatically precise vectorization that makes their itinerary readable and prevents any deviation from their "straight and narrow" path (or at least tends to delimit its effect). The vectorization in this case is certainly chronological, but it is usually translated visually and spatially. Thus it is easy to trace, repeat, and objectivize.

The Dancer
On the other hand, dancers—at least those involved in so-called postmodern dance—flout the conventions of any narrative or mimetic vectorization; this may suggest that they are subject only to their own impulses and desires, and that their bodies are free of any control, linearity, or any ensemble concern. The difficulty, for dancers as well as for spectators, is to decide what is to be seen as marked with the arrow of desire.

The Theater Actor
The theater actor and, a fortiori, the actor-dancer are split between linear vectorization and drives that cannot be channeled. They shift the rules of the game constantly by alternating between mimetic desire and drive-ridden flux.

The Spectatorial Gaze

Vectorization is evidently of concern to the actor-dancer, but it requires the spectator's gaze in order for it to be affirmed and confirmed. The nature of this gaze changes according to the genre and the grid for reading or desire it demands.

The Mime
The classical mime (e.g., Decroux) captures the spectator's gaze in order to get it to follow a clearly perceived and only minimally modifiable trajectory. The spectator identifies (with) the gestural technique, more so than the character and his/her emotions. The spectator's body is usually inscribed without ambiguity in the trajectory perceived and the mode of codification. The spectator's task is to identify the mimed object and to grasp how this object is signified.

The Dancer
Dancers attract the spectator's body as a whole; the spectators launch themselves headlong into the swirling arabesques of the movement. Without the safety net of a clearly established narrative, the "danced" spectator (i.e., the spectator touched by the grace of the dance) is at the mercy of the dance's flux, unable to avoid being touched by the energetic intensity of the dancing body. The dancer's perception is connected to the bodily image of the

observer, which is above all motorial and kinesthetic; for it is neither narrative nor codified, tied neither to the linear unfolding of meaning or story, nor to the deciphering of figurative contents.

The Theater Actor

Theater actors present a theatrical representation of the action, a fictional world delivered as a whole, but nonetheless subject to a certain narrative logic. The spectator's body and mind continually shift between the interior and the exterior. Sometimes spectators perceive themselves internally, by identifying with the object; sometimes they perceive the other externally as a "foreign" body. There is an ongoing denial of the reality of the perceived.

The Actor-Dancer

Actor-dancers simply amplify and accentuate the pendular movement of this denial. They invite the spectators the tread a line between distanced fiction and lived performance, either drawing them into the movement or, at other moments, grounding them in a fiction that merges with their own knowledge of reality.

So the status of gesture varies from genre to genre, although as one predominates the influences of others are not excluded:

- *Fiction* for theater, in which the body always also represents something other than its being-here
- *Doubled fiction* for mime, in which the body designates its object as a construction effected by the miming body
- *Friction* of the dancing body, with everything that surrounds or impinges upon it provoking immediate "combustion" through simple contact, as well as through the observer's identification with the movement and the bodily schemata
- *F(r)iction* between representation/performance and event in *Tanztheater*

Furthermore one might add:

- *Fusion* for opera and its multiple art forms combined in the work as a whole, its components sustaining each other by fusing with each other
- And *micturition,* as it were, for the incontinent outpouring of images on film, video, and in virtual synthetic spaces

Types of Analysis

A particular kind of analysis corresponds with each kind of trajectory and spectatorial gaze, although it is desirable to combine all these analyses when one is dealing with contemporary gestural/physical work.

For mime, one should endeavor to determine the quasi-geometric rules that control the processes of codification, refinement, and "amplification" in gesture and body. An understanding of the gestural system is crucial, for it allows both spectator and analyst to read the mime's performance by looking beyond its physical reality. Description presents no insurmountable difficulties once the rules for the transposition and codification of the real have been clearly established.

For dance, analysis should attempt to orient itself, neither through the laws of transposition from the real nor the points through which the gestural trajectory passes, but rather through the "aimless finality" (Kant) of the movement itself, the vectorial force of the body in movement and of the dancers as a whole. Spectators (or perhaps more accurately *spectactors,* since it is a question of them moving through the body and the gaze, rather than just watching) can only "decode" in the moment: not by recording signs and their sequences, but by becoming involved through the intermediary of their bodily schemata and their motivity, accompanying the dancers on their routes through the choreography. What remains of our loves, of our choreographies? A few intersections of desire. When choreographic analysis restricts itself to listing, notating, or tracing movements, it is bound to remain superficial; in the case of mime and theater, however, the identical residual materials would produce useful cartographies of the gestural and stage score.

For theater, in fact, these residues of analysis—performance score, composition of the role, scenographic points of reference, etc.—constitute first-hand documents that are informative in terms of the production of meaning. For meaning is essentially interconnected with the representation of a fictional world that can be distinguished from the actual, event-based world of the stage. Furthermore, theatrical analysis remains very dependent upon narrativity and the establishment of story.

The other "genres" also require special treatment, combining different aspects of the above: that is, *f(r)ictional* for dance, *fractional* for film, *fusional* for opera.

Opera, despite the richness and diversity of its signs and sources, does not really lend itself to analytic dissection and an enumeration of its component materials. Already materially influenced by musical and gestural rhythm, it is a fusion, combining, and blending of elements that seem to be in opposition: word and music, space and time, voice and body, process and stasis. From Wagner to semiotics, it has become quite commonplace to look for correspondences and fusional modes operative between the elements of opera. This facility for lateral connection and generalized fusion demands an analysis that resists a radical separation of the elements of musical drama.

As far as cinema is concerned, despite the incontinent flow of film (its *micturition*), it can be characterized above all in terms of the *fractional* and *fusional* aspects of its cutting structures (its découpage): cuts, collages, moments of breaking or rupture, its modes of construction that are willfully fragmentary, elliptical, and contrapuntal.

4

Voice, Music, Rhythm

Even more difficult to analyze than gestuality, the actor's voice (primarily the spoken voice) cannot be dissociated from his body of which it an extension, nor from the linguistic text it embodies or at least conveys. It seems useful to discuss voice in conjunction with music, sound, and rhythm. It should be remembered, however, that the entire acoustic universe, however coherent it may be, only becomes apparent in the time-space of the stage actions (chapter 5) and in relation to all the other elements of the performance (chapter 6).

The Voice

The Vocal Apparatus

An analysis of the voice requires an extensive knowledge of the vocal apparatus,[1] which comprises the respiratory system, the larynx, and the resonator cavities. Each of these three components could be the focus of a very precise physiological description, but in the context of an analysis of actors' voices, our primary concern is with the particular effects produced by each organ.

The Respiratory System
Through the abdominal muscles (notably the diaphragm) and the internal intercostals, the respiratory system is responsible for breathing in and out. In the analysis of sound, one must describe the physical work of breathing,

measure efforts and energies employed, determine whether respiration (inhalation or exhalation) is clearly audible and what sensations and emotions it carries, and evaluate the corporeality that breath brings to our awareness and experience. A text and its articulations, in conjunction with the scenic continuum, seem to be structured to some degree by the taking of breaths:

> To convey and re-create an author's thought with maximum precision, the actor must break up the text into energetic vectors connected to his breath and dictated by the syntax.[2]

Understanding and analyzing a text and a scene first of all entails recognizing blocks of speech, using their intervals as rest points en route, and following actors in their thought and breath. These respiratory "contours" can be notated and used as a score within which all sorts of nuances appear.

> With truly great actors, one cannot distinguish the verbal trajectory from the feeling. The alliance between technique and expressivity is perfect. One can no longer tell whether the feeling gives rise to the verbal trajectory or the verbal trajectory gives rise to the feeling.[3]

The Larynx

The larynx is the organ that produces variations in pitch, and these can be divided up into registers. In the lower register (known as the "chest" register), the vocal chords are slightly elongated, whereas in the upper register ("head") or falsetto voice, they are significantly tensed. An experienced listener will be able to recognize the five principal registers and record their effects: chest voice (lower register), falsetto, combined voice, bass, whistle. One should not confuse the registers with the modes of emission:

- Registers: ultralow, low, medium low, medium, upper medium, high-pitched, super-high-pitched.
- Modes of emission: chest voice (ultralow, low, medium low), combined voice (medium), head voice (women) or falsetto voice (men).

The Resonators

The resonators are constituted by the cavities that laryngeal sound has to traverse in order to reach the open air: pharynx, oral cavity, nasopharynx, nasal fossae. It is possible for a trained listener to discern the body parts upon which resonators depend: jaws, tongue, pharyngeal muscle, larynx, soft palate, lips. The physical quality of the voice will thus be an information source of primary importance in preventing the reduction of spoken language to abstract semantics, and instead emphasizing its physical production and the corporeal impression conveyed to the spectator (or, perhaps more accurately, the *spectauditor*).

The much more complex question of the singing voice will have to be left to one side here. Suffice it to say that it is regrettable that no training exists for spoken voice that is as precise as those that exist for singing:

> The difficulty of singing training stems from the fact that one has to abstract the automatisms used in speech to acquire new and extremely complex neuromuscular coordinations, without any visual or tactile help such as those used in training for other musical instruments. In addition to this difficulty, there is the constant search for a delicate balance between the aesthetic of the sound and the intelligibility of the sung text.[4]

Objective Factors

Various acoustic parameters of the voice can be objectively measured with sonographic technology and, in the case of spoken or sung voice, can become the object of scientific analysis.

The average *frequency* for each individual—their "usual speech fundamental"—is used to evaluate variations while speaking, as expressed in melody and inflection. For languages in which tonal variations and melodic differences have a semantic value, it will be crucial for the listener to spot them and take them into account so as to understand the meaning of a phrase. Knowledge of the intonational organization of a language, perception of its melodies—of affirmation, interrogation, doubt, and so on—will provide precise indications as to a character's state, although individual variations among speakers are always considerable and thus not directly attributable to differences between characters. Inflection, which Artaud called an "undercurrent of impressions, connections and affinities beneath language,"[5] is a rich source of information; furthermore, it often transcends any objective framework and possesses individual and cultural connotations. The tone of a voice is what makes it high- or low-pitched, and is attributable to variations in pitch. Intensity characterizes the power or weakness of the voice, while timbre concerns the vocal quality: bright or dark, blank, husky, hollow, deep or soft.

Vocal *intensity* stems from the pressure of pulmonary air over the vocal chords and their resistance. It is a pertinent factor that depends on a subject's anatomy/physiology, their habits and vocal education. Individual and cultural variations are perceptible, as are significant variations for the interpretation of a role in terms of the listener's implicit theory of the emotions. The expression of emotions is connected to changes in intensity that tend to find their appropriate codification; one will sense anger, for example, in a greater degree of intensity and vocal tension. On stage, an actor must place and project his voice, that is, adapt and engage resonators in such a way that they amplify the larynx. If actors simply increased the intensity of their voices, they would wear themselves out and fail to make it to the end of the performance.

Timbre is the result of shaping laryngeal sound in the resonator cavities; vocal timbre varies with each individual. In order to further refine analysis of the voice, one needs to appreciate the modulation of timbre and the reasons for changes. Timbre or vocal *color* relates to a notion of correspondence between colors and sounds or vowels, as in Rimbaud's poem *Voyelles:* that is, a connection with tactile sensations. This is linked to Roland Barthes's notion of the "grain of the voice." Register describes the pitch of a voice, its timbre, its color.

Given this list of objective factors—frequency, intensity, timbre—it is probably the properties of delivery that are most relevant theater performance. In particular, in our analysis of elocution:

- Continuity/discontinuity of verbal flow
- Caesuras and pauses: length, place, function
- The speed of elocution in relation to the cultural and individual norm of the listener
- Accentuation, contouring, and effacement of the voice

Interpretation of these factors is not always self-evident, and it produces subjective vocal particulars. Individual speakers thus appropriate and use language to situate themselves in the world.

Subjective Factors

The subjective factors are the most numerous, difficult to understand, and, above all, decisive in the analysis of voices, actors, and mise-en-scènes.

The Betrayal of Feelings

All vocal activity produced on stage inevitably reveals an emotional state that sometimes, but not always, is accompanied by and codified through a vocal action: moans, screams, tears, surprise, laughter. The voice is colored, in an indelible way, by the emotions it expresses and at the same time generates; it betrays and transposes the speaker's involuntary and unconscious states. This fact is persuasively illustrated simply by comparing the voice with voices that have been treated electronically;[6] they obey quite different rules. It is no longer feasible to gather information on the sex, identity, and psychological state of the speaker, for such details are distanced by the resynthesizing of their voice. It is now possible to change a speaker's sex live by modifying their original voice by a few half-tones, making it stronger, warmer, or weaker. In this way, the voice—apparently the most human, direct, and authentic of elements—can be disconnected from the body and channeled through loudspeakers. What is important in such vocal manipulation is not to describe the scientific protocols of the experiment, but rather to explain the dramatic repercussions of technological intervention.

The Projection of Self

A speaker acts on his interlocutor through his voice, by varying its intensity, tonality, delivery, and paralinguistic gestures. "It is through the voice that consciousness opens itself to the unconscious, and one opens oneself both to oneself and to others."[7] The vocal projection that results from this is doubly necessary on stage since actors must make themselves heard not only by their partners on stage, but above all by the audience. Therefore, it is difficult to distinguish between what relates to techniques of projection as stage convention to deliver the text "properly" and what belongs to the vocal technique of the character, revealing his psychological and social nature. From a Stanislavskian perspective, actors must both feel and possess the art of modifying the parameters of their own voices in order to establish their characters more fully. Their task is to discover not only a character's bodily attitudes, gestuality, facial expression, and "psychological gesture" (Michael Chekhov), but also the character's vocal identity. In addition, they must develop their ability to touch the listener directly by means of effects and affects that go beyond the semantic communication of information, and use the corporeal materiality of the voice and its unforeseeable (i.e., indescribable) effects. Thus, for Antonin Artaud:

Whereas most people resist the subtleties of a speech, with its intellectual dynamics and subtleties forever escaping them, they will be unable to resist the effects of physical surprise, the dynamism of cries and violent gestures, the full gamut of startling effects.[8]

Listening to voices on stage constitutes an experience that can sometimes provoke an affective discharge, reminding us of particular people, living or deceased. In this sense, performance analysis is also a psychoanalysis telling us as much about ourselves as the perceived object of our study.

The Grain of the Voice

According to Roland Barthes, "the 'grain' is the body in the voice as it sings":[9] in other words its materiality, its bodily tessitura (range), its roughness and rawness, its physicality and uniqueness (and sometimes also its "eunuch-ness"). What delights and exasperates us is precisely that which is most important in the actor's bodily manifestation; this is also what is most difficult for the spectator to describe, for the effect produced is so powerful, unconscious, and nonverbalizable. In theater, an actor's words (and not only a singer's melody) are always to some degree *en-chanted*, constituted by an affect-body that colors it vividly. "Song constitutes the artistic form in which the affect-body most prevails over the word-code."[10]

Paradoxically, it is once again technology, the microphone in this instance, that most effectively enables the bodily, drive-ridden dimension of the voice to be revealed:

> We who always arrive *after the event,* who lack *animality,* now quite suddenly have at our disposal electronic technology that will give new impetus, not to our knowledge of the voice, but to our *lived voices.*[11]

The analyst's task is to account for this "lived" quality, not to restrict the focus to the rational, semantic aspect of information conveyed, but to reveal the drive-ridden, unconscious dimension of voices, to show how actors deal with this alliance between the rational and the pulsional, how they deliberately allow their corporeality to "overflow" and impact; for it always says more than the intentional signs of the character. This is why analysis should always remain attentive to the language-voice-body nexus in the actor, observing their intimate interrelations.

From One Semiology to Another

Indeed the voice always says more than the signified of the character (its identity in the fiction). The voice does not simply convey a message or characterize the state of a fictional character, for it is also a signifier (a corporeal materiality) that is open and irreducible to a univocal signification: a trace inscribed into the flesh of the listener who cannot escape it. Here I propose, therefore, to abandon a classical semiology that locates the voice merely as a signified of the character,[12] in favor of a Barthesian semiology. Fischer-Lichte's classical semiology, for example, is only interested in the communicative function of language and the voice, for "the actor's voice always functions as a sign," and "as the sign of particular corporeal and/or psychological attributes of the character."[13] Barthesian semiology, on the other hand, is sensitive to the "grain of the voice":

> Semiology would consequently be that labor which collects the impurity of language, the waste of linguistics, the immediate corruption of the message: nothing less than the desires, the fears, the appearances, the intimidations, the advances, the blandishments, the protests, the excuses, the aggressions, the various kinds of music out of which active language is made.[14]

This "labor" of semiology is essential for a study of the actor, if one wishes to grasp the impurity of the text and the corporeality of the naked voice, which is cut from the same material as the body of the speaker. In this way, one's descriptive accounts will avoid separating comments on the voice from those on the actor's corporeality; in the same way that one can discern whether a voice on the telephone is smiling, one should be able to sense the body that conveys and is conveyed by the voice.

Materiality and Theatricalization of the Voice

Yet how does one analyze this materiality of the voice?

- The semantic "thickness" of the voice: its corporeality, sensuality, and musicality are so powerful that they eclipse the meaning of the text.
- The formal perfection of pronunciation, the spatialization of the phrase, the sense of rhythm have the effect of an oratorio: one can almost draw the outlines of the trajectory and polyphony of the voice, one discovers the "landscape" of the text.
- Words in incantation: they are "construed in an incantatory, truly mag-

ical sense . . . not only for their meaning, but for their forms, their sensual radiation."[15]

■ According to Fonagy, language is based on bodily actions, and the pronunciation of certain consonants requires an energy related to the anal-
sadistic drive: some trace of this anal energy is perhaps recognizable in
the "mouthing" and "spitting out" of text and in mimo-dramas of the
face and body. Thus we can perceive vocal energy's trajectory and its
physical, visual marking of the body of the actor and the stage.

All of these phenomena are wholly concrete and can be the focus of a systematic mapping. They emerge from what is often called the theatricalization of the voice, both its externalization and its spatialization. Indeed,
according to Barthes, this is the very definition of theater: "The written text
is from the first carried along by the externality of bodies . . . the utterance
immediately explodes into substances."[16] Theatricalization always entails
an exaggeration of vocal mechanisms in relation to the norm: sung decla-
mation, hypercorrect pronunciation with all phonetic liaisons and allitera-
tions, that is, ludic visualization of the melodic schema.

Dramaturgical Analysis of Vocal Changes
What is essential in performance analysis is not to find a technical
definition of the voice; it is to understand the dramaturgical value of vocal
effects, to differentiate the full range of voices, and to sense how speakers
change voice according to their interlocutors and what these variations signify.

Cultural Factors

As well as objective factors connected to human physiology, and subjective
factors prone to individual variations, vocal analysis should take into
account cultural constraints. These make the evaluation of voices virtually
impossible if one is not familiar with the relevant cultural codes. Among
the Dogon people, for example, the griot is able to use six to eight different
voices. Western actors are trained to change their voices continually,
according to the person they are addressing. The criteria for appreciating
the voice vary considerably from one culture to another. A falsetto voice,
deemed to be somewhat odd in Europe, may on the other hand be considered normal in North Africa. No universal emotional coding for vocal
expression exists. So for example in India, an alto timbre will express sad-

ness, and a low timbre happiness, which is quite the reverse of European coding. The use of timbres is extremely varied: head or falsetto voice in Beijing Opera *(Jingju)* and Vietnamese *Hat tuông;* deep, guttural voice in Japanese No, where the actor-singer modifies the diction of phonemes in everyday language. Even the manner of crying and laughing is peculiar to each tradition; Vietnamese *Hat tuông,* for example, has twenty-nine ways of laughing, each reflecting a very precise vocal technique rather than a distinct emotional situation. The variety of breathing techniques and bodily techniques that result are just as impressive. Therefore all aspects of performance analysis, and most notably those concerned with the human voice, should relativize their results from the outset by placing them in the light of a cultural tradition whose rules, norms, and their deviations one needs to know.[17] Descriptions should avoid any universalizing comments, in particular in the evaluation of vocal performance.

Analysis of the Actor's Voice

An analysis could use the mechanisms available in experimental phonetics and information technology to record and visualize the fundamental frequency of a voice, to study its variations in pitch and its melodic contours.[18]

In the absence of such sophisticated processes, an analysis of voice in theater will have to make do with these few simple observations:

- Diction is subject to modes: certain kinds of delivery—fast or slow, the encoding of easily recognizable emotions, the use of "foreign" accents— all depend on the contextual norm at that moment.
- The actor's voice is necessarily forced, even deformed by the necessity of talking in a loud voice and remaining audible.
- It is very informative to note the frequency of pauses, their duration, and their dramaturgical function: hesitation, respiration, emphasis, or construction of a recognizable rhetorical framework?
- The actor, who takes possession of a text that is not his own, although at the same time his inspiration in some ways, must organize and structure his breathing; he speaks (and lies) as he breathes—in "groups of breaths," the unit(y) of what is pronounced between two easily recognizable pauses. These groups include an ascending curve, the rising of the melodic line, and a declining line.
- The melody of a sentence, for actors and subsequently for spectators, is a means of clarifying the syntactic structure and thus the meaning of their text.

■ The voice brings to light the rhythmic frames of speech; in other words, it allows us to recognize "the mental trace of the primary rhythms within a speaker's utterance and the expectations of subsequent developments provoked by these primary rhythms."[19]

■ Ultimately, the voice is also a projection of the body into the text, a means of making the corporeal presence of the actor felt. Often it alternates between spoken word and song, or sung speech *(Sprechgesang)*.

■ Analyzing the voice also means examining the relationship between body and voice, the way in which an actor suddenly seems to embody a character. It also means listening to the voice in terms of how it seems to rise up from and ride on the text, at each turn in the sentence expressed.[20]

Music

Our aim here is not to examine music and its reception as such, but the ways in which it is used in mise-en-scène, how it serves the theatrical event. Only its dramaturgical function interests us here. The term *music* is employed in the widest possible sense here, as acoustic event—vocal, instrumental, sound effects, that is, everything audible on stage and in the auditorium.

> One should call *music* the set of all acoustic elements and sources: sounds, noises, environment, texts (spoken or sung), prerecorded music (channeled through loudspeakers), etc. Music should thus be understood in wider terms, as the *organized sum* (and where possible, deliberately so) of acoustic messages reaching the ears of the listener.[21]

Music is asemantic, or at least nonfigurative; unlike words, it does not represent the world. Located within a performance, it radiates, without us knowing precisely what it is that is given off. It influences our overall perception, but it is difficult to say exactly what meanings it gives rise to. It creates an atmosphere that makes us particularly receptive to the performance. It is as if the soul's light stirs inside us.

Music within the Performance

Semanticism of Music
Within a performance, music has an utterly unique status. As Wagner said, "Whereas other art forms say *it means,* music says *it is.*"[22] Whereas signs in

setting, actor, or speech refer to given things, music has no object; thus it can mean anything, its value being measured above all in terms of the effect it produces. Performance analysis should both account for references to particular objects in the world, and for acoustic material that contains no mimetic reference to the world.

Sources of Music

One should endeavor to determine where music comes from, how it is produced, and how it is dispersed in space. The location of loudspeakers in a variety of possible places on stage and in the auditorium creates acoustic contours, a computer-controlled "soundscape" that seems to move around within the space: for example, the soundscapes in Robert Wilson's productions (such as *Hamlet*, 1995), which are realized from countless "auditory points of view."

The analyst's first task is to establish how and where musical sources are produced. Is the music played live on stage by musicians (or actor-musicians), or has it been prerecorded and introduced on cue by technicians? The decision to make musical sources visible, or on the other hand to conceal them, has significant repercussions in determining the nature of dynamic relations between the music and the rest of the mise-en-scène, particularly the space and the acting. It is not only a matter of the emotional influence of the music on the theater performance, but also of the impact of the stage on the music and the ways in which it is perceived. This reciprocal influence, in which one element is strengthened, and sometimes destroyed, by another, should be the object of some critical evaluation. These phenomena of mutual reinforcement are little understood, because only rarely has there been any examination of what changes in the perception of a text, a space, a gesture when they are "accompanied" (or rather "animated") by a musical intervention (vocal, instrumental, or prerecorded), or even by a shift in the lighting state. The description of performance requires one to think of visual and acoustic phenomena together, to sense the effect one produces on the other and, if possible, to recognize which element is most affected by the music at a particular moment. In order to do this, one must consider whether the music only plays an ancillary role in relation to the performing, whether it simply remains isolated in short sequences, or whether it tends more toward an integrated form, as in musical theater, where music and performing are equal partners that complement each other and blossom into a new genre.[23]

For example, in Heiner Goebbels's *Oder die glücklose Landung (Or the*

Unfortunate Landing), performed at the Théâtre des Amandiers, Nanterre, in 1993, all the elements present in performance—the words of a character reciting the text, the traditional African music (kora and voice) or the electroacoustic music, the rectangular playing space beneath an enormous inverted cone from which sand flows—contribute to the figuration of an acoustic space and a spatialized sound within which each component is so perfectly integrated that it becomes difficult, and indeed fruitless, to isolate any one element to the detriment of others.[24]

The Effect of Music on the Spectator

The appreciation of music produced *stemming from*, or *in tandem with*, the visual elements of a production requires an ethnomusicological perspective attentive to modes of understanding music and its links with the other components of the performance.

In Western mise-en-scènes, and particularly in productions of classical texts, music's effect is that of accompaniment; it is always indirect, "incidental," and thus judged in terms of the degree to which it serves our understanding of the text and the acting.

In an African performance, on the other hand, one would not be able to detach artificially the music from the rest of the performance, from movement, dance, the rhythming of the text. In fact in most African languages no single word exists to translate our term *music*. The words used tend to designate "dance" as much as "music"; and in addition, they make no distinction between music and noise or sound.[25] In Africa, music is characterized in terms of movement: "For many Africans, the successful absorption of sequences of movements is an important criterion in the understanding of music."[26] Thus the conception and reception of music are not purely auditory as they are in the West, they are also motional. The movements of musicians occur in such a way that certain notes cannot otherwise be produced; the patterns and structures of movement impact upon the accenting and realization of the notes.

> In performance practice, spectators arranged around the event *hear* and *see* the "music" at the same time. They make movements, either internally (immobile presence, but accompanying the vibrations internally), or through motor participation directed externally.[27]

This ethnomusicological clarification invites a great degree of modesty in one's evaluation and comprehension of different forms of music and voice. It broadens a Western perspective by inviting us to observe the connections between "music" and other scenic systems, not only for other musical cultures, but for our own.

For vocal and musical performances that belong to cultures other than our own, it is appropriate for us to be aware of our chronic "deafness," of the listening customs and habits that we project on to the other culture(s).

> In certain areas, such as that of tonal systems, for example, listening habits are genuinely irreversible. When one has grown up from childhood within a particular tonal system, one always perceives tonal systems in relation to one's own system.[28]

Functions of Music in Western Mise-en-Scène

Often used in contemporary mise-en-scène, music fulfills numerous functions:

- The creation, illustration, and characterization of an atmosphere introduced by a musical theme, which can become a leitmotif; during these intervals, the listeners can pause for breath, orient themselves, and imagine what is to follow. Such music thus acts rather like a pain-relief medicine.
- Sometimes this atmosphere becomes an actual acoustic setting; a few notes serve to locate the action.
- Sometimes the music is simply a sound effect whose sole aim is to make a situation recognizable.
- It can also be a form of punctuation for a mise-en-scène, particularly during pauses in acting and scene changes.
- Sometimes music creates a counterpoint effect; examples range from Brechtian songs that comment ironically on the action, to the baroque music G. Bourdet placed between sequences in his production of Gorki's *The Lower Depths*.
- Adopting the approach of cinematographic technique, music can create a sequence of atmospheres and surroundings.
- It can also involve a production of action through musical means. Musical theater goes far beyond the ancillary function often attributed to music in theater; in this context the music becomes the focus of

attention, integrating theatricality for its own requirements (see, for example, the work of G. Aperghis and H. Goebbels).

Description must identify these functions and evaluate their impact on the overall performance. One must first list all musical interventions and their forms, noting the influence a sound has on an image and vice versa; second, track the vectorization these interventions suggest; and finally, evaluate the passage from one to the other, or from the acoustic to the visual. All these notations will form part of the musical score that is the mise-en-scène. Within the category of "music," one should encompass all sound, from prerecorded sound effects to sounds in the wings, or even unforeseen, parasitic sounds (in street theater, for example). All of them contribute to both the construction and destruction of atmosphere, and should be taken into account by the spectator/analyst.

Music in general, and particularly on stage, has a function that is sometimes integrative, sometimes disintegrative, both for the performance and for the "self" of the characters:

> The different moods evoked by music—joy, sorrow, anguish, desire, satisfaction, plenitude—can be related either to a continuity of the self (what one might call integrative music), or to a self that is fragmentary, exploded, shattered (what one might call disintegrative music).[29]

Rhythm

Voice and music are clearly rather difficult to analyze, notate, or interpret; imbricated in time, they seem almost immaterial, or at least nonvisualizable in terms of a spatial score. At the same time, they create precisely contoured structures and landscapes like mountain ranges, landscapes upon which the other elements of a production lean and are grounded, in particular space and acting.

Overall Rhythm and Specific Rhythms

The third element in this acoustic and temporal grouping, both containing and organizing them at the same time, is rhythm. Our concern here is not with the rhythm of a mise-en-scène in its entirety, which requires us to distinguish the different partial rhythms of each signifying system (any homogeneous and coherent set of signs, e.g., the lighting, costumes, diction, gestuality, etc.). The general rhythm of a mise-en-scène, the "electrical current"[30] that unifies the various components of a production, arranging them in time in the form of stage actions, becomes the overall system of the mise-en-scène, that is, what organizes speaking bodies moving in the time-space of a stage. Sometimes the metaphor of a performance's *musicality* is also used, in other words its "musical" organization in time. Nobody has described this temporal organization better than Meyerhold:

> One must teach actors to feel time on stage as musicians feel it. A performance organized in a musical way does not mean that music is played in it, or that people sing constantly behind the scenes; it means a performance with a precise rhythmic score, a performance in which *time* is rigorously structured.[31]

The particular rhythms of different scenic systems obey their own rules. Here are a few examples that might provides methods for analysis:

- *The word:* its enunciation allows us to understand it best in terms of binary effects—silence/word, speed of delivery/slowness, accentuation/nonaccentuation, varying contours/monotonal banality, tension/release.
- *Breath:* in a spoken text we can record the groupings of breaths, examining their length, their linkage, the syntactic and semantic organization of each group, the function of pauses: structuration of thought, recapitulative moment, semantic content.
- *Prosody:* according to Garcia-Martinez, rhythm needs to constitute rhythmic frames, "primary organizations of prosodic components (intensity, duration, pitch),"[32] which form the basis for the perception of changes of frame.

Rhythm and Tempo-Rhythm

Often used in a contrasting way by Stanislavsky, these two notions need to be distinguished carefully.

Tempo is invisible and internal; it determines the speed of a mise-en-scène (quick or slow); it shortens or prolongs action, accelerates or decelerates diction.

In terms of tempo, the spectator/analyst is able to note impressions of speed or slowness by determining the means that produce these impressions:

- Acceleration by means of overlapping lines (one utterance is not yet finished before the next one begins), repeated motifs, and the creation of automatic responses in the spectator's perception
- Deceleration by means of the absence of surprises, confirmation of the rhythmic frame, and repetition of the same information

Rhythm is not so much to do with changes in speed, as with changes in accentuation, in the perception of stressed or nonstressed moments. It refers to a rhythming of time within a defined duration, the linking of physical actions according to a precise schema, a "through line of action" related to a text's subtext (in Stanislavsky's terms) and to the actor's underscore. Rhythm is the sense and direction of time, of its elasticity in the hands of a director:

> A director must sense time without having to look at his watch. A performance alternates dynamic and static moments, and the dynamic are also of different kinds. This is why the gift of rhythm seems to me to be one of the most important prerequisites for a director.[33]

As far as rhythm is concerned, it is rather difficult to show which elements of a performance it attaches itself to. For example, the actor's body is the locus and support for several rhythmic systems that are not necessarily synchronized: diction, and the alternation of accented or nonaccented moments; movements and fixed attitudes; externalizing emotions and changes in intensity; the structuring of groups of breaths; the dis/appearance of visual contact through variations in lighting, and so on.

Rhythm can transform the textural construction of language by "spatializing" it, structuring it according to a rhythmic schema that is different from that of conventional semantics. It can become a drive-ridden, unconscious rhythm that reintroduces the body into language,

> an unconscious, pulsional, translinguistic rhythm, inscribed in the national language, but directing us, through it, to an-*other* stage. . . . This *other rhythmicity* bears witness to a more marked autonomy in relation to the system of the language, and refers to processes of displacement and condensation of an unconscious kind.[34]

Rhythm and the Subjective Duration of Performance

The most important rhythm in a mise-en-scène is that of the net result of all the sign systems, that of the performance as it unfolds. Who is actually responsible for this? There is no temporal equivalent for the scenographer in relation to space, no "tempographer" in charge of the performance's ordering, determining the rhythm with which it evolves, its pauses and shifts in speed. The director acts as a kind of tempographer for the performance; she controls its temporality and mediates between its propositions and our expectations.

The tempographer—or at least the director sensitive to the temporal structure of his creative work—controls vectorization in terms of its temporality (and thus not exclusively in terms of the space within which she can give *direction* to vectors and decide on connections/breaks). She chooses the moment at which two signs or vectors converge or shift from one to the other. She puts in place what Manuel Garcia-Martinez has called "rhythmic frames," the "mental trace of the rhythms of the initial moments that become points of reference for subsequent rhythmic development . . . the spectator's appropriation of the rhythm of the production's unfolding development, both memory of its development in the immediate past and expectation of a subsequent development."[35] In order to sense (rather than notate or trace graphically) the rhythmic order of a performance, one needs to invent a system that represents the imbrication of all of these rhythmic frames: the system of expectations it creates, the influence a particular rhythmic frame can exert on the perception of a system of signs. An appreciation of the shifting speeds of a sequence will thus depend upon the way in which the frame has been placed and systematized within the performance as a whole. Claude Régy's production of Gregory Motton's *La Voix de Satan (Satan's Voice)*, for example, adopts a rhythm that seems very slow; however, given the variations in the performance and the relative frequency of its shifts (the scenography gives the impression of a variety of effects), its rhythm seems to quicken movement and keep the spectator's attention in an alert state.

The analysis of voice, rhythm, and temporality poses major problems, and yet these elements often leave indelible traces in the spectator, traces that resist being measured and mapped. They crop up again when we deal with other, more visible sign systems (such as the actor, or the space) and the other material elements of performance; but none of these other systems has quite the same degree of subtlety and resonance as musical and vocal phenomena.

5
Space, Time, Action

Our analysis of performance thus far has concentrated on the very body of the performance: the physical presence of the actor. The actor's voice, the rhythm of his diction or gestuality have shown themselves to be much more difficult to evaluate, even though they are at the very heart of that elusive quality, "presence." One might expect space, action, and time to be more tangible elements of a performance, but the difficulty lies, not in describing them separately, but in observing how they interact. One does not exist without the other two, for dramaturgical space-time—the trinomial nexus space-time-action—constitutes one body by drawing the rest of the performance to it, like a magnet. Moreover, it is situated at the intersection between the concrete world of the stage (as materiality) and the fiction, imagined as a possible world. It comprises a concrete world and a possible world within which all the visual, acoustic, and textual elements of the stage are intermixed.

A simple triangle will clearly illustrate how the three points of the trinomial nexus are interdependent and necessarily defined in relation to each other.

If we were to consider each point on the triangle in itself, it would produce an art form other than theater:

- Without space, time would be pure duration: music, for instance.
- Without time, space would resemble that of painting or architecture.
- Without time and space, action cannot unfold.

The interconnectedness of a time and a space constitute what Bakhtin, in the context of the novel, called a *chronotope:* a unit in which temporal and

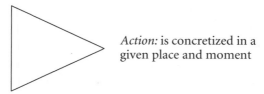

Time: manifests itself in a
visible manner in space

Action: is concretized in a
given place and moment

Space: is situated where the
action takes place, and unfolds
with a specific duration

spatial indices form an intelligible, concrete whole. When applied to theater, action and the actor's body are conceived as the amalgam of a space and a temporality. As Merleau-Ponty suggested,[1] the body is not only *in* space, it is made *of* this space and, one might add, of this time.

This space-time is both concrete (theater space and time of the performance) and abstract (fictional place and imaginary temporality). The action that results from this union is sometimes physical, sometimes imaginary. The space-time-action is thus perceived in the here-and-now as a concrete world and, "on an-other stage," as a possible imaginary world.

Let us risk a comparison with Freud for whom, according to Sami-Ali, the unconscious coordinates space, time, and body:

> In the unconscious, time is transformed into space and space into a corporeal unit. In the process of this transformation, the body, functioning as a schema of representation, acts as a mediator between time and space.[2]

This can be illustrated by another triangle, showing the routes from one angle to another. It remains to be established whether the homology of these two triangles is merely fortuitous, and whether the Freudian model can actually help us elucidate spatiotemporal relations within a performance.

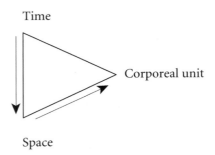

Before considering the spectator's experience of space-time, which is based on her reception of chronotopes, I will reflect on the conditions necessary for spatial experience, then of temporal experience.

Spatial Experience

Rather than a historical overview of the different types of stage that theater has used over the years, I propose to evoke the spatial experience of the spectator: the ways in which she experiences, reads, and evaluates the spaces she negotiates. Many excellent histories of scenography have been published,[3] but reference to them will not guarantee a valid understanding of the types of spaces used in contemporary mise-en-scène.

In theater as elsewhere, two possible kinds of spatial experience are available, and all theories of space seem to oscillate between them:

1. Space is conceived as an empty space to be filled as one fills a container or an environment that has to be controlled, filled, and made expressive. Artaud is one example typical of this conception: "I maintain the stage is a tangible, physical place that needs to be filled and it ought to be allowed to speak its own concrete language."[4]
2. Space is conceived as invisible, unlimited, and linked to its users, determined by their coordinates, movements, and trajectory: space as a substance not to be filled, but expanded and extended.

To these two antithetical conceptions of space correspond two very different modes of describing it: objective, external space and gestural space.

Objective, External Space

Objective, external space is the visible, often frontal space that can be filled and described. The following categories can be distinguished:

- ◼ *The theatrical site:* the building and its architecture, its relation to its urban location or the landscape; but also sites not intended for performance used for site-specific work, which are not transferable to a theater or some other place. In institutional theater contexts, one can examine the configuration of the various interior spaces (auditorium, stage, backstage areas, etc.) and exterior spaces (terrace, entrance to the foyer).
- ◼ *The stage space:* the area used by the actors and technical staff; the actual playing area and its extension into the wings, auditorium, and theater building as a whole.
- ◼ *Liminal space:* marks the separation (more or less clear, but always irremovable) between stage and auditorium, or between stage and backstage spaces. Liminality is more or less clearly demarcated, for example, by footlights, candles, the "circle of attention" traced mentally by actors to isolate themselves from the gaze of others.

These objective, measurable spaces are easily described; indeed they have been extensively throughout history. They reflect historically attested uses of the stage. Their imbrication, interaction, and the dynamics of their changes do not pose insurmountable problems for commentators either, provided, however, they do not rigidly fix all of its categories but accept transitions between them. An urban space can thus be transformed into a performance space, and a foyer or audience space can become an area for actors to negotiate. The hierarchy of spaces is able to be modified at any moment.

The important thing is to specify the point of view a description adopts: the place from where the performance is watched, what is only half seen, what is not seen at all, what others see from their perspectives. One must also note the parameters of the playing space as they evolve, the relative positioning of the actors in flexible spaces, the way in which the spatiotemporal frames that encompass all of the actions are established and dismantled.

In our efforts to understand spaces in the most flexible ways possible, it seems we are moving with increasing clarity toward the notion of gestural space.

Gestural Space

Gestural space is the space created by the presence, stage position, and movements of the performers: a space "projected" and outlined by actors, induced through their corporeality, an evolving space that can be expanded or reduced. One should pay particular attention to the following manifestations of gestural space:

- The *"ground"* actors cover with their movements; the "trail" left in the space in their wake, which marks their taking possession of the territory; this trail disappears when spectators shift their attention to some other element on stage.

  Example: in *Marat/Sade,* the patients' entrance into the prisonlike space of the bathhouse, the ways in which they stagger and circle around to get their bearings of this enclosed place; contrast this with Coulmier's assured, processional arrival, his way of inspecting his surroundings and immediately taking possession of them.

The *kinesthetic experience* of actors can be sensed in their perception of their own movement, body schema, gravitational axis, and tempo-rhythm. In theory all of this data is only available to actors, it belongs to them; but they transmit these qualities more or less voluntarily to the spectators.

  Example (Marat/Sade): a woman patient, vigorously supported by two "sisters," moves forward dragging one leg; she only partially controls her body, which has been straightened and made "docile" by the penitentiary institution. When she suddenly hands a bunch of flowers to Madame Coulmier, we also feel the unexpected, involuntary aggression in this gesture.

The *underscore,* the actors' support, providing them with reference points and orientation in space, the charged moments that facilitate their anchoring in space and time, also provides us with an itinerary and trajectory that are inscribed in space as much as space is inscribed in them.

  Example: in the expository opening sequence of *Marat/Sade,* gesturally one feels each performer's trajectory, each one a sort of "psychological gesture," to use Michael Chekhov's term: the patients' trajectory is circuitous and winding; the guards', percussive and interventionist; Coul-

mier's, self-assured and feline; the herald's, contradictory and schizo-
phrenic.

Proxemics[5] is a well-established discipline that analyzes the cultural coding
of spatial relations between individuals.

> *Example:* the young woman with the bouquet of flowers startles both
> Madame Coulmier and her daughter, for her gesture is an intrusion into
> the private sphere of social representation, and has not been preceded by
> the usual approach and compliments.

The *centrifugal space* of actors extends out from their bodies to the world
outside. The body is extended through the dynamics of movement. Sometimes props or costumes are used to extend the body; in a Bauhaus performance, for example, sticks were attached to a performer's limbs, to accentuate and amplify their positions; or the dancer Loie Fuller used her veil to
allow the trajectory and volume of her movements to be visualized. In a
performance context an actor's body is "dilated," to borrow Eugenio
Barba's image; in other words, it tends to express in the strongest possible
way the actor's physical attitudes, choices, and very presence. On the other
hand, framed space waiting to be filled is *centripetal;* it goes from the frame
to the individual, and focuses all movement in an area on stage.

Dramatic Space, Stage Space

Although dramatic space (the space mentioned in and symbolized by the
text) is not of central concern in performance analysis, and does not belong
to objective or gestural space, it is worthwhile saying something about it
here. The dramatic space, which comprises any indications as to the fictional
location, the characters, and the narrative, necessarily impacts upon the
stage space. In particular it creates interference between the iconicity of a
concrete space and the symbolism of language. The spectator-listener is no
longer in a position to distinguish between what she sees with her eyes and
what she perceives "in the mind's eye," to borrow Hamlet's phrase.

However, in the Western theater tradition, the distinction between language and stage is maintained at all costs: hence the separation between
dramatic literature and performance practice. This distinction constitutes a
primary exclusion of the body in favor of vision—the concrete vision of the

eye and, above all, the vision of fantasy, "in the mind's eye." Vision, at the root of the Greek word *theatron* ("seeing place"), suppresses the olfactory, gustatory, and tactile dimensions of the theatrical event. The visual is privileged at the expense of the gestural to such a degree that ultimately most Western performance theory universalizes the visual dimension, sometimes excluding, or at least devaluing, all other kinds of sensory experience. The theater theoretician Darko Suvin even perceives, in this separation of gaze from hand, an anthropological characteristic of all theater (although in so doing, in our opinion, he "pokes himself in the eye"):

> [Theater] is rooted in the anthropologically basic and constitutive theatre fact: that the spectators' pragmatic position is specifically one cut off from tactility; they may look but not touch. The Possible World in theatre is centrally constituted by the resulting *basic split between visual and tactile space* experienced by the audience.[6]

Suvin's thesis seems applicable to the Western tradition, but not at all to other performance practices that have not dismissed and devalued the body and touch. Moreover, and most importantly, in our hypothesis the spectators' gaze, even in the West, is also always "haptic" to some degree; the spectator touches with her eyes, her body is only immobile and passive in appearance, it imitates tactility and gestuality internally. Understanding can only occur if movements are re-played on an imaginary level, and bodily schemata are activated.

The consequence of such a hypothesis is that, in analyses of stage or gestural space, one should not radically separate visuality and gestuality, objective and gestural space; on the contrary, one should look out for units that participate in one or the other with indifference. Later on, we will see that chronotopes constitute spatiotemporal wholes that correspond with specific types of corporeality. I have already noted, in the example of the trajectory and ways of moving of groups entering the space in *Marat/Sade,* that each one embodies ("in-corporates") a very particular corporeal and chronotopic identity. Thus one might also talk of *bodied spaces.*[7]

Other Ways of Approaching Space

It would be more useful to talk of *other ways* of approaching, conceptualizing, and experiencing space, rather than of *other kinds* of space.

- *Textual space,* not to be confused with dramatic space (the way in which a text talks about space), is a metaphor for the enunciation of the text in space-time, a metaphor for its rhythmic architecture, "the pure configuration of masterpieces" that Copeau described.[8] It is the way in which the spectator inscribes the recitation of the text in space.
- *Internal space* (nothing to do with indoor rooms!) is the representation of a fantasy, a dream or waking dream evoked by the mise-en-scène, whose processes of displacement or condensation one can analyze. The stage becomes a derealized space where dream mechanisms can be represented, and into which spectators can project themselves. Such is the case in Japanese No theater, where the acting evokes a dream or fantasy; in plays where a character contemplates his internal world, which is represented by the stage (e.g., Arthur Adamov's *Si l'été revenait*); or at moments of visual evocation in a mise-en-scène.
- The *ergonomic space* of the actor,[9] that is, his working and living environment, includes a *proxemic* dimension (relations between people), a *haptic* dimension (ways of touching others and oneself), and a *kinesic* dimension (the movement of one's body).
- *Installation space:* descriptions of theatrical space should differentiate it from architectural space or an installation, in particular by taking into account the presence and movements of actors. Nevertheless it should be noted that sometimes theater does occupy a specific site or building, in a similar way to an installation; this must be borne in mind if we are to understand the diverse functionings of time-space.

Temporal Experience

All that has been suggested above in relation to space—the possibility of apprehending it either in terms of a measurable quantity to be filled, or in terms of a quality conveyed and controlled by the actor—also applies, mutatis mutandis, to time. In fact there are two types of temporal experience: one is objective, quantifiable, and external; the other is subjective, qualitative, and internal.

Objective, External Time

Objective, external time is time conceived as an external, measurable, and divisible given: the mathematical time of clocks, metronomes, and calendars. In theater, this kind of time is that of the duration of the performance; it is time controlled by and subject to the "straitjacket" of the mise-en-scène, with its reference points, regularities, and repetitions: a time that can be repeated every evening, due to a very precise and almost unmodifiable score. It is also the time of the dramaturgical framework with its obligatory transition points (exposition, buildup of the action, climax, resolution). This strictly controlled time is easy to notate and describe, particularly in terms of its relationships with the performance's "visible" signs. In fact, the performance is often timed—if only with the video counter—to map the appearance and disappearance of the various signs, and to determine the principles and regularities with which their repetition is organized in each given performance, as it goes back to what has been more or less fixed by the mise-en-scène.

This objective management of time, the quantifiable spatiality imposed as if from the outside by the composer, director, or actor, and the highlighting of the prosody of the text, its textual space and "eurhythmic gesture,"[10] are what characterize rhythm. Indeed rhythm is the "recurrence of the same,"[11] the recurrence of time frames or rhythmic accents at regular intervals.

In a mise-en-scène, the spectator recognizes the pattern of repetitions, leitmotifs, and the alternation between accented and nonaccented moments. Rhythm does not only concern music, voice, or temporal organization; it also relates to the mise-en-scène as a whole, which is the result of particular rhythms within each system of signs, especially visual signs. It is always instructive to trace the trajectories of the performance's overall score, for all of the different systems figure graphically within it, each with their own rhythmic structure. In this way, the coordination, parallelism, or redundancy of each different rhythm becomes clearly apparent, as do those moments that deviate from these structures when things move "out of sync."

Subjective, Internal Time

Subjective, internal time is peculiar to each individual; in theater, each spectator experiences the duration of a performance or sequence intuitively, without being able to measure them objectively. This impression of duration is not uniquely individual, however; it is also cultural, linked to the habits and expectations of an audience. This explains the difficulty, even impossibility, of evaluating the management of time in theatrical or musical performances beyond one's own cultural horizons.

For this subjective, somewhat Bergsonian duration, or when evaluating another culture's temporality, the scientific measuring of time is not what matters. What is important is to sense the variations in the flow of time, changes in speed, the length of pauses. This subjective, variable time is that of *tempo*, "the inscription of a relatively large number of units in a predetermined chronometric time."[12]

It is the actor's task to determine the tempo; actors mark their enunciation of text and role with their own stamp and internal tempo. Temporal analysis of acting will focus on recording the pauses, silences, and interruptions in the action, as well as mechanisms used to slow things down or speed them up: vocal delivery, movements, changes in tempo in relation to the cultural norm or a previously adopted system.

Dramatic Time, Stage Time

As with space, which comprises both the performance space (concrete space) and the represented space (imagined), one must distinguish between the time of a performance (or stage time) and the represented time (or dramatic time, that of reported events). For the spectator, there quickly comes a point where dramatic temporality and stage temporality (which also corresponds to the spectator's lived time during the performance) start to interpenetrate and mutually reinforce each other's credibility. However, the stage temporality remains the common reference point for both actors and spectators, attracting everything else like a magnet, including the dramatic time (i.e., that of the plot), and making all stage actions concrete and physical. In fact it is the stage enunciation itself—the fact of concretely using the stage, *hic et nunc*, with actors and other materials—which mobilizes and actualizes time in the physical actions on stage. One should therefore examine the ways in which temporality is mobilized and produced by the stage actions.

One might think that temporality is an innate frame for thought. In reality, it is produced in and through enunciation. . . . The present is really the source of time. It is this presence in the world that the act of enunciation alone makes possible, because, if one thinks about it, man has at his disposal no other means of living the "now" and of making it real than by introducing discourse into the world.[13]

In this context, "introducing discourse into the world" means configuring the stage and the theater apparatus to produce a duration, a plot, an action. Analysis endeavors to draw out the ways in which the signs used are inscribed within a temporality and a duration, how they structure the performance by establishing its framework (the score).

Another result of this convergence in the spectator of stage time and dramatic time, of objectivity and subjectivity, of quantifiable rhythm and subjective tempo, is the notion of *tempo-rhythm*, for which I am indebted to Stanislavsky. This umbrella term reconciles the objective regularity of measurable, "spatializable" time with the subjective variability of flexible time, as may be the case with duration in Bergson's sense of the word. The tempo-rhythm of a performance indicates the through line of action (objectivity of rhythm) and at the same time the unpredictable subtleties of the subtext, with its pauses and silences (subjectivity of tempo). In *Marat/Sade,* for example, the through line of continuous stage action is clearly outlined by the mise-en-scène and its "directorial" enunciators: Coulmier's manipulation, his mise-en-scène as imprisonment *(mise en prison);* Sade's mise-en-scène of the id; the herald's and chorus's mise-en-scène as critical framing making fun of proceedings *(mise en boîte)*—all of this creates a fully controlled narrative and scenic rhythm, a restrictive yet carefully defined framework. Within this rhythmic framework, however, the acting of the performer-patient-inmates is subject to individual variations in tempo, for which each of them seems to have retained control. The net effect of this rhythm and tempo is a film that has a very precise rhythmic structure, and yet dexterously handles those moments when the stage actions are infused with an extremely diverse range of tempi.

It is the task of analysis to evaluate the relations between constraints in rhythm and freedoms in tempo. An evaluation of the ways in which time is managed necessarily involves determining whether the performance describes a full temporal arc, relatively fixed and only divisible and structurable as a rhythm; or whether, on the contrary, time has been divided and reworked anew with each fragment, without a predetermined, overall, fixed rhythmic template. In the latter case, one could use Pina Bausch's choreography as an example: the structuring of its rhythms stems from isolated fragments, rather than harmonizing the performance as a controlled, fragmentable totality through the imposition of an aprioristic organization of time. The net result is a series of sequences each with their own tempo.

Temporality is not exclusively a matter of rhythm and tempo, and is not simply limited to the flow of time. It is constituted of *particular moments* (or privileged moments) in which time seems to come to a stop; and these are the moments that art theorists have endeavored to locate.

This was the case with Lessing's "fertile moment," which he discussed in relation to the static representation of an animated scene (in painting, sculpture or tableau vivant); it is this moment that also interested Brecht in his theory of *gestus,* and Barthes in his theories of the *third meaning* and of the *punctum.* It is the search for a quasi-mystical moment in which everything will become clear: the *ma* of Japanese Kabuki performers, the pause between two units of action where there is neither movement nor words, a dynamic stasis that results from their breath control; the *to* in Korean Tao, a dimension with neither beginning nor end, a moment and place that is "both unnameable and the mother of all things in the universe"; or, on a more mundane level, the moment when an actor captures the attention of his audience, the "propitious moment" according to Daniel Mesguich.

Spatiotemporal Experience: Chronotopes

I have just pointed out the difficulty of treating space and time as autonomous categories, and the necessity of combining the concrete enunciation and space and time on stage with the symbolization of dramatic space and time. By examining the connections between time and space in performance, I hope to avoid making partial, fragmented observations about particular details of a mise-en-scène's space and time. Instead my aim is to understand how a mise-en-scène organizes spatiotemporal "blocks" into a sequence of physical actions, usually embodied by an actor.

Bakhtin's Notion of the Chronotope

In borrowing the notion of chronotope from Mikhail Bakhtin, the aim here is even more ambitious than a simple spatiotemporal conjunction. I wish to determine whether this alliance can assume the dimensions of an artistic chronotope. According to Bakhtin, this is what the novel succeeds in doing: creating a figure or symbol using concrete data, finding a figure or image of the world that is as concrete as it is abstract, and that enables a spatial metaphorization and a temporal experience.

> In the literary artistic chronotope, spatial and temporal indicators are fused into one carefully thought-out, concrete whole. Time, as it were, thickens, takes on flesh, becomes artistically visible; likewise, space becomes charged and responsive to the movements in time, plot and history. . . . The indicators of time are discovered in space, while space is perceived and measured in terms of time.[14]

A primary instance would be, for example, an artistic chronotope that perfectly illustrates the Spanish picaresque novel; it enables the picaro, a popular hero, to move freely across every social stratum; time is concretized in space, and vice versa.

When analyzing individual stage works, it would certainly be difficult to find similar culturally codified images (although it might be easier to find examples within a given genre—medieval farce, classical French tragedy, European naturalism, etc.). Instead what emerges from a structural analysis of theater performance is rather a series of chronotopes in which the use of time and space produces a specific kind of corporeality. Let us take an example from the first few minutes of Brook's film of *Marat/Sade*.

In the opening shots, the camera shows the patients from behind; they are introduced into the performance area one by one. Space is created by the movement of the camera; the perspective is that of a spectator moving forward among the patients. The dominant chronotope is that of sensory experience that, whether we want to or not, draws us inexorably into the prison environment. The body represented is also our own, apprehended sometimes from the inside, sometimes from the outside; and disoriented by the absence of spatial markers, caught in the grip of an initiatory movement, it cannot avoid this descent into hell. This chronotope produces a *compassionate corporeality,* in the etymological sense of the word (com-passion).

Two or three wider shots of the bars that separate the stage from the auditorium capture the overall space in a frontal and distanced manner; the point of view is fixed, objective, external. The chronotope that fixes the space is that of a frontal, clinical, objective observation; it is as if the gaze is separated from the body. Here the corporeality is *scientific.*

The filmic narrative takes its course; now it is the turn of the amateur actors to assume their roles; several shots capture them as if by surprise while they put on their stage costumes. We watch their preparations, we are present at the very threshold of their becoming characters; we become aware of the *liminal* moment and place where acting begins. Here the dominant chronotope is that of liminality and the actor's denial of his role; sometimes himself, sometimes already in character, he is *alienated* in the etymological sense, that is, he belongs to another. This corporeality is *fictive* (or theatrical), in the sense of a continuous movement between representation and reality, illusion and disillusion.

These chronotopes of theatrical denial should not be confused with those of manipulation, the focus of a number of other shots: the manipulation *manu militari* of the guards, Coulmier's more subtle manipulation—he delivers a liberal speech as a camera movement brings the bars of the prison cage into view. The chronotope of these manipulated bodies is that of a critical distancing or alienation, and the corporeality is that of distanciation: the body displays and conceals, it says the opposite of what it seems to say.

Each of these four main types of chronotope thus produces an original model of corporeity, undoubtedly very "volatile," but nevertheless capable of adapting to new situations and of constantly renewing the spectator's psychological and kinesthetic experience.

Therefore four models of corporeality emerge: the experienced and experiencing body, the disciplined and punished body, the body whose identity changes according to convention, and the manipulated and alienated body.

An analysis of this sequence has helped us distinguish the dominant type of chronotope and corporeality within each shot. I have also endeavored to take into account the ways in which they are connected as a sequence and the strategy of their order of appearance. Just as each type of chronotope can be transposed into a specific model of corporeality for the characters and actors who embody them, spectators must also follow this evolution by continually changing their perspective and their corporeality; for it is with their own bodies that they must taste the spatial, temporal, and action-based experiences that unfold before them, and *within them*.

I shall give some examples of the ways in which these chronotopes are formed, noting how they articulate space, time, and action.

Fundamental Typology

The recipe for the preparation of chronotopes is simple: using the contrasting properties of space and time, mix and stir them together. One must simply be careful with the proportions:

Space	Time
open	infinite
closed	limited
large/wide	long
small	short
global	uninterrupted
fragmentary	interrupted
etc.	etc.

By combining at least two properties, we will obtain chronotopes that already exist in our experience and categorization of the world; for example:

▪ Open + infinite = open field, infinite plain
▪ Global + limited = an island

In an even more systematic way, we could obtain the four fundamental chronotopes show in the table, which are rather like the "primary colors" of performance.

1. large space fast tempo	**2.** large space slow tempo
3. small space fast tempo	**4.** small space slow tempo

One could give titles to these four fundamental chronotopes as follows:

1. "Megalomania": for example, the running "caracole"-style entrances of the performers in Ariane Mnouchkine's Shakespeare productions.
2. "World in slow-motion": for example, the slow-motion movements of performers in Robert Wilson's *Deafman Glance*.
3. "Excitability": for example, the commedia dell'arte scenes on the small stage in Renoir's *Le Carrosse d'Or*.
4. "Minimalism": for example, the concentration and immobility of the bodies of Butoh dancers.

It is worth noting that these categories exactly match those suggested by Michael Chekhov in his search for the *psychological gesture*.[15] Take the gestural action of "closing," for example, which Chekhov says can be executed

- quickly in a large space;
- slowly in a large space;
- quickly in a limited space;
- slowly in a limited space.

Performance analysis should begin by looking, within the continuum of the performance, for large blocks or groupings defined by the homogeneity of their chronotopes. The sequence of these chronotopes will provide the key to the mise-en-scène: its dynamic, logic, and physical effect on the spectator.

Integrating Different Kinds of Perception

The linking of chronotopes and the overall perception of their groupings confirm the difficulty of examining signs separately, and the need to gather fragmentary perceptions together in order to form more complete units like chronotopes. However, we should be aware of the distinctive and differentiated ways in which human beings perceive through their hearing, sight, touch, and mental introspection.

The smallest discrete units one can distinguish are those of hearing: changes of sound, the difference between phonemes, variations in rhythm can all be distinguished very precisely.

Mental introspection, the mental perception of groupings, occurs in much broader and more imprecise units; it is unreliable and difficult to verify.

Sight and touch are differentiated a little more precisely than mental introspection, but much less so than hearing. Most of the time they are dissociated (we look but we do not touch), thus eliminating the possibility of verification and cooperation between the sensory systems.

The integration of different kinds of perception within an overall schema must account for these differences and the consequences they have for the spectator's perception and memorization. From the perspective of mise-en-scène, what has been perceived in the clearest, most detailed manner is not necessarily what is most important, although it tends to become so for the perceiving subject.

Linking Chronotopes

The integration of various kinds of perception, particularly those of space and time, is not exclusively a punctual, "vertical" matter. It can also be realized in the narrative linking of scenes, in accordance with the logic of the plot. Therefore the plot is not a disjointed series of episodes and motifs; it constitutes a coherent pattern of chronotopes and corporealities. Thus the opening of *Marat/Sade,* as analyzed above, systematically establishes contradictions, conflicts, and the "rules of the game" by attributing to each type of shot a chronotopy, a corporeality, and a very specific set of tactics:

■ The introduction of the patients, with the impression that the spectator is part of the group, or at least inescapably implicated in their containment within the "cage" structure.
■ The establishment of different "fronts" and conflicts; the actors are seen from a distance, behind the bars, as if in a frontal, proscenium space that both imprisons them and at the same time denounces their incarceration.
■ Allusions to theatricality, to play-within-the-play, to distanciation/alienation.
■ The shift to another type of alienation, this time political; evidence of duplicity (Coulmier's, the warden-like sisters', the herald's) and manipulation through the camera's placement and points of focus.

This linking of different elements, which confronts us from the outset with wholly different acting techniques, strategies, and uses of the body, is facilitated by a very coherent vectorization that employs and applies the four main types of vector.

Chronotopes in the Network of Vectors

In this same sequence in *Marat/Sade,* one can note the following operations that clarify, orient, and vectorize the sequence as a whole:

■ *Accumulators:* the signs of sickness, incarceration, and prison multiply, not without some ambiguity and confusion. One must wait a little before shifting to other levels of reading that go beyond appearances.
■ *Connectors:* a number of indices are linked together to help identify the location, and specify the logic of the therapeutic-theatrical-repressive

processes in place. This series comprises whiteness of the walls/psyche-delic music/pallor of the faces/emptiness of the place/establishment of an acting configuration/police force rather than medical help/appear-ance of the "leaders" (Coulmier, Sade, the herald).

- ▪ The connection is soon diverted toward a series of clarifications that expose what lies behind appearances, by means of *shifter* indices that allow us to slip from one level to another: patients > the mentally ill > amateur actors > simulators > common-law prisoners > political pris-oners. On each occasion a detail in behavior, costuming, or the filmic mise-en-scène is sufficient to effect the transposition.

- ▪ *Cutters:* to finish a sequence and move on to a completely different one, the transition is sometimes very abrupt; for instance, during a change in the soundscape, we hear the sudden, realistic sound of a key in the lock of a prison door being opened by Coulmier, who has come to share the inmates' space with them.

Once all of these operative processes have been observed and notated, and the various hypotheses verified, the analyst of space and time, and the actions in which they are embodied, may feel the need to let things settle for a while. This can be achieved through the gentle pleasures of drawing: out-lining the trajectories of the movements of actors and objects, or of the overall score and broad rhythms of the mise-en-scène. Let us take the actors' movements as an example.

Displacement as Vectorization

Directors and stage technicians are very familiar with this graphic method of notating movements. Computer-assisted notation works in the same way, by schematizing the trajectories of movements.

Whatever the method of notation, the vectors outlined in the drawing indicate above all the form and pattern of the movement; its duration and timing; its speed and variations in intensity; the actors' locations in relation to each other in the stage space; the amount of force and energy used.

A vector is as much a trajectory inscribed in space as a temporal and rhythmic itinerary. In the same way as a chronotope, the vector no longer distinguishes between space and time. In this way time is vectorized, spa-tialized, folded and unfolded, concentrated and extended within the partic-ular space. Space itself "becomes body"; it is in-corporated, em-bodied.

Here are a few examples of such conversions:

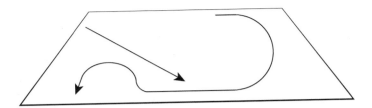

- A costume blows in the wind, inscribing the trajectory of its train in space, thus making the flow of time apparent.
- A set unfolds like a film, or a strip cartoon.
- A halting, trailing accent makes us aware of the speakers' relation to time.
- An action develops, stops as it is blocked, then starts again.

When movement is conceived as vectorization, the analyst-spectator is able to describe actors' actions, not in terms of psychological motivation, but rather in terms of physical tasks to be accomplished, energies to be expended, objects to be moved: that is, in *ergonomic* terms.

Rhythmic Vectorization and Its Representation

There is something utopian about drawing the score of a mise-en-scène, but perhaps it is a necessary utopia if we want to represent the performance as a whole by means of a system that integrates space, time, action, and corporeality, that is, *embodied* space and time, a system on to which all the other materials of performance can be grafted.

The different signifying systems compete in the performance, but they tend toward *synchronicity* and thus produce that single current of a performance that Honzl describes.[16]

If the different systems remain out of sync, a *polyrhythmic* phenomenon is produced, or, according to Honegger's definition, "a superimposition of different particular rhythms with mutual discrepancies between the rhythmic accents."[17]

Within each system, from the beginning of the performance, *rhythmic frames* are established; Garcia-Martinez describes these frames as "the mental trace of the rhythm in the initial moments that becomes a reference point for what develops subsequently."[18] This notion allows us to understand the management of time, and the subjective impression of duration and speed. It is connected to the notion of the chronotopic frame, vectorization, and Guido Hiss's *Sinnklammer* (bracketed unit of meaning).[19] In each of these different conceptions, "rhythm involves the segmentation of particular material in space and time; it is by nature noncognitive and inaccessible."[20]

The locating of such units or rhythms brings us directly to a way of notating a performance's score and underscore that is extremely useful for performance analysis. It also opens up the living trajectory for actors and the performance in general in terms of its score; this is what Mike Pearson defines in terms of *pattern,*

> the explicit structure of performance as sequence, route map, montage, set of rules. Also the juxtaposition of different orders of material, and different styles and techniques of performance. And as an unfolding of inciting incidents and their trajectories, ruptures (sudden shifts in direction), nodes (density of activity), thresholds (entrances), breaks (pauses), irrevocable acts (environmental change), and decay (destructions).[21]

Return to the Original Hypothesis

To conclude this section, let me return to the original hypothesis. I compared the triangle of the theater chronotope (time, space, action/corporeality) with the triangle of relations between time, space, and the unconscious as corporeal unit, following Sami-Ali's reading of Freud. I will use Dimiter Gottscheff's production of Büchner's *Woyzeck* at the Schauspielhaus in Düsseldorf in May 1994 (film version broadcast in French television) to test the hypotheses of psychoanalysis.

According to Freud, space and time in the human psyche differ in terms of the ways in which they are treated in the conscious, preconscious, and unconscious. "The time relation . . . is bound up with the work of the conscious system,"[22] whereas the unconscious bears no relation to time:

> However much the unconscious ignores the temporal order, it could not do without the spatial symbolic in order to express time and provide duration with its sensory figures. And, on the other hand, just as time is connected with the conscious, one is forced to conclude that the unconscious is timeless because it is spatial.[23]

If we apply this theory of dreams to performance analysis, we have to reconsider the relations between space and time, in terms of whether we think of them in a conscious, preconscious, or unconscious way.

Let me summarize using Sami-Ali's perspectives, and attempt to draw some conclusions for performance analysis:

- "Real time and space, conceived as two distinct structures, one reversible, the other irreversible, belong to the Cs [conscious] system." If we adopt the perspective of a director conscious of what she is doing, or of a spectator watching the stage in a conscious manner, we can in fact distinguish space and time as well as their particular modes of functioning.
- "The Pcs [preconscious] system is reflected in unstable space-time amalgamations within which space and time, halfway between the real and the imaginary, remain irreversible and reversible respectively, time acting on space and vice versa." In the act of creation, a director organizes her materials in space-time through the actors without really knowing whether she is guided by a sense of rhythm or by a vision of a space to be traversed or deployed; when directing actors, she may not consciously discriminate between asking them to vary their tempo or to (re)locate themselves spatially. Preconscious creativity is to be found in precisely this indiscriminate kind of amalgam. Similarly the spectator sometimes approaches stage analysis with a sweeping, scanning gaze, and sometimes through an intuitive grasp of duration and tempo, without really making a clear distinction between them.
- "In the Ucs [unconscious] system, time does not exist; only an imaginary space, i.e. corporeal space, exists; its reversibility serves as a model for the symbolic representation of time." One could represent a director's unconscious mechanisms while working on stage materials in terms of the production, within the "cauldron" of the stage space, of reversible actions; actions able to go back in time and in any direction, actions available for any possible kind of vectorization. "Space" is as much the actual stage space as the imaginary space, the "great theater of the world," a space that can be figured as a malleable body, manipulable in any way one wants. Let us now turn to the example of *Woyzeck*.

A Dissected *Woyzeck*

The play is performed on an entirely empty podium, open to spectators on three sides. When the actors are not performing, they are seated on simple chairs at the back of the stage, maintaining the illusion of their characters by continually repeating the sequence of gestures that best characterizes them. At the beginning and end of the performance, everyone is on stage, each obsessively repeating their own "psychological gesture" (Michael Chekhov) ad libitum. Woyzeck is not singled out in this universe; he is not the object of focused actions that could denounce his alienation and humiliation. He is either dismantled or reassembled in each of the other characters; they constitute a range of alter egos dispersed throughout the common space. There is nothing in the stage space nor the development of the scenes to locate the play in a particular place; time does not flow in a linear fashion; there is no intent to construct a plot with a beginning, middle, and end. The bare stage freely becomes any imaginary place; it changes its identity simply through the gestuality particular to one character taking the stage for a moment and becoming the focus of our attention. There is no temporal logic, no dramaticizing of the action; thus rather than coming as the climax to the action, the murder scene passes virtually unnoticed.

Space-time (as director Dimiter Gottscheff was able to "dream" it, and as it appears to us in actual perception or memory) is a kind of score on which is displayed a body broken up into its variants and compulsive repetitions; it is the body of Woyzeck, as if laid out and dissected in front of us, fragmented into its partners (alter egos rather than adversaries), a body dispersed in space-time as if it were on an operating table where the various organs of one and the same social body are exposed. This dissected, collective body is "reversible," insofar as the vectorization (of connection in particular) is left up to the spectator.

This approach in the mise-en-scène and its chronotopic organization seem to correspond perfectly to the way in which space, time, and body function for an analysis of conscious, preconscious, and unconscious mechanisms. Time, which has become cyclical and reversible, is that of the "dreadful fatalism of history" that Büchner wrote about. Cyclical, reversible, and imaginary, the appropriate time for the "reign of repetition,"[24] here it has been transformed into an autonomous anatomical space. The bodies of the performers and the body of the stage in its totality constitute much more than a set; they are the mediation between theatrical space (the figuration of Woyzeck's mental universe) and theatrical time (the horrifying, cyclical fatalism of the play's construction). These are not simply bodies that can be read semiotically; they are also phenomenological bodies, embodied bodies, as it were, which take hold of the spectator's body and unconscious like real, concrete bodies, once space and time have

Fig. 15. "A figuration that fuses time, space, and body within a performance of the unconscious": Dimiter Gottscheff's production of *Woyzeck*, Schauspielhaus, Düsseldorf, 1994. (Photograph by Sonja Rothweiler.)

been em-bodied by their presence on stage. In Gottscheff's mise-en-scène, corporeality and the corporeal unit are not sustained by a performance located within a concrete place and space, but through a figuration that fuses time, space, and body within a performance of the unconscious: in this instance, the fragmented unconscious of character, author, director, performer, and spectator.

This example, along with many others one could use to support the argument, confirms the importance of an integrated, "global" approach to the analysis of performance, and of space-time-action in particular. The following chapter, which focuses on other material elements within performance, will further confirm and reiterate this notion.

6

Other Material Elements of Performance

All the elements of performance that performance analysis proposes to examine are by definition *material;* they exist concretely on stage as material, as signifiers created by the makers of the production. Nevertheless, it could be said that some of them are, so to speak, more material than others: in other words, those that are not directly linked to the presence of actors, their voices, the space-time in which their actions evolve, nor to rhythm or music. The actors' central function, their magnetlike effect on their immediate surroundings and on the performance as a whole, has already been sufficiently emphasized here. It remains for us now to indicate how certain stage elements used as materials require their own particular approach, and how they form different signifying systems. However, any list one might propose will not be exhaustive, given that the processes of creating theater can always turn to new materials and signifying systems. The analyst's role is not to predict or prescribe the list of these elements, but to describe the main existing manifestations. Therefore, in this section, the focus will be on costumes, makeup, objects, and lighting.

Besides the priority given to the living person of the actor in our reception of theater, there is no absolute hierarchy, no imposition of an order that determines the ways in which the spectators apprehend the different signifying systems. At the most there is, as the Australian sociologist Maria Shevtsova remarks, the habit of Western spectators, when questioned about a production, usually to mention the acting first, and then, in decreasing order, "sets, costumes, lighting, pace, spatial configuration, choreography, music and atmosphere."[1] Evidently the chronology of our impressions as spectators is fundamental, but it can never be absolutely determined by rules. At most, one might suggest that spectators are struck first by what is visible and human, that is, by the acting, then by the more "intrusive" materials, such as the set or costumes, and finally by what perception itself allows: the lighting. Thus the material segmentation that we effect is rather arbitrary; and it would not be able to state the pertinence and exact number of stage systems to be distinguished within a performance.

Whether the devil is in the detail or not, the meaning of a performance and its analysis is surely in its details. An apparently innocuous fragment often turns out to be characteristic of the whole, and one must know how to recognize these "insignificant" details that regularly nestle in some of the material elements privileged in the performance. Each signifying system is valid in its own right, but it also constitutes a sonic echo, an amplifier with implications for the rest of the performance. This is why the detailed, fragmentary study of a particular material element often illuminates in a way that clarifies the work as a whole, or at least a good part of it; this element can then be inserted as part of an overall mosaic as smooth and shiny as the parquet in the Galerie des Glaces at Versailles.

This eulogy to detail should not make us forget the meaning of a performance's overall structure and its major units; for if they are to assume meaning, the material details we draw out in our analysis must be inscribed within a dynamic and a vectorization in which space, time, and action are closely interconnected: *an action takes place*. This will be borne in mind in the account of the minute material traces that come to light under the microscope through which I now propose to examine performance.

An initial possible mapping entails an evaluation of the proportion of each element within the mise-en-scène. This requires one not only to quantify the signifying systems, but also to conceive of their limits and points of contact. Each performance genre gives a particular weighting to these components, although obviously the proportions are flexible. For example, if one focuses on visual, material aspects in relation to their spatial support, one will obtain the approximate divisions shown in the table.

The proportions are unstable, and they vary in the course of a performance; but the relationships between the main structures and the divisions between components remain the same:

- In psychological theater, one must grasp the relationship between effacement of the body and overdevelopment of facial expression.
- In a Bauhaus "mechanical ballet," both the dancer's body and the space

System of Materials

Psychological Theater	Bauhaus Theater	Postmodern Dance
set	set	space
costume		
body	costume	costume
face		
makeup	body	body

in which he moves tend to be made to disappear by the costume; the set is reduced to a colored background, and the dancer's body is not supposed to be visible—although it sometimes betrays its presence (feet at the base of a bell-shaped costume, the human suppleness of a figure's articulation).

- In postmodern dance, one sees a neutralizing of materials other than the dancers' bodies, which move within a nonfigurative empty space.

The division of stage materials into signifying systems is arbitrary and the legacy of a critical tradition; it impedes theoretical reflection by requiring us to think in terms of fixed categories. From another perspective, however, our cultural habits of perception always determine our decisions to validate a particular detail or method of dividing performance. But who could lift themselves up and out of their own cultural "soil," and, besides, what for? For our perceptions and "objective" evaluations always bring us back to the same "ground." Therefore let us take three inherited categories (costume, makeup, object), and simply try to grasp their broad contours and internal organization.

Costumes

The Limits of Costume

It is not easy to pinpoint the precise point at which clothing begins, nor to distinguish costume from more localized elements like masks, wigs, hairpieces, jewelry, accessories/props, or makeup. Extracting the costume from an actor's overall outfit in his milieu is a delicate operation. Thus what one gains in the precision of analyses of clothing, one risks losing in the evaluation of its impact on the rest of the performance. Insofar as costume usually constitutes a spectator's initial contact with and first impression of an actor and his character, it is there that a description might begin.

Organizing Observations

Observations about costume are generally made in frames that go from the widest focus to the narrowest:

- The widest when one refers the costumes to the mise-en-scène, verifying whether they confirm or invalidate the other material givens of the performance, what the nature of the costume design is, and the ways in which the costumes selected are presented
- The narrowest when one describes how they are made, and when one tries to establish how performers invest and feel in them

Like any sign of performance, a costume is both a signifier (pure materiality) and a signified (element integrated into a system of meaning). In fact this is exactly how Roland Barthes conceives of "the good costume": it "must be material enough to signify and transparent enough not to turn its signs into parasites."[2]

The Functions of Theater Costumes

As a result of the thinking of Brecht and Barthes, we are much more familiar with the pathology of theater costumes than their semiology. The "diseases" of theater costume are so frequent and endemic that their categories are useful in the regular analysis of performance; whether it be archaeological, historical, or aestheticizing, the disease reveals a fundamental tendency of all mise-en-scène.

The major functions of costume are

- Characterization: social milieu, era, style, individual preferences
- Dramaturgical orientation for the circumstances of the action; the identification or disguise of a character

- Orienting the overall *gestus* of the performance, that is, the relationship between the performance, and the costumes in particular, and the social world: "Everything, in terms of costume, that blurs the clarity of this relationship, everything that contradicts, obscures or falsifies the social *gestus* of the performance, is bad; on the other hand, everything in the forms, colours, materials and their arrangement that helps the reading of this *gestus*, all of this is good."[3]

Costume and Body, Costume and Space

Costume and Body

A body is "worn" and "carried" by a costume as much as the costume is worn and carried by the body. Actors develop their character and refine their underscore while exploring their costume; one helps the other find its identity:

> A sleeve that is too wide or too narrow, too long or too short, can alter the stage projection of a character, and require from the actor a modification of his attitude; this then provokes subsequent inventions/constructions in terms of the costume; and so it goes on.[4]

A description of acting requires an understanding of the elements regulating gestuality and clothing. In manuals of rhetoric, from the sixteenth to nineteenth centuries, illustrations reproduce the pleated folds in tragedians' togas, which make a significant contribution to the characterization of attitude and emotion.

Or consider this portrait of the Butoh dancer Kazuo Ohno (fig. 16). Both his face and his dress present the same crumpled, fragile quality. The costume is an extension of the dancer's vulnerable body and of his "character," La Argentina; and, in a reciprocal way, the costuming allows us to see the body of the old man, as well as that of the great dancer to whom he pays homage.

As far as nudity is concerned, it does not constitute the degree zero of costuming; instead, this would be a costume that represents a degree zero through its familiarity and appropriateness to our values. Nudity can embrace a wide range of functions: erotic, aesthetic, "disturbing strangeness," and so on. The apparently naked body in figure 17 is lying along the top of a sort of menhir, a tomblike stone supported in a horizontal posi-

Fig. 16. Kazuo Ohno in *La Argentina*. (Photograph by Norman Price.)

Fig. 17. "The body as landscape." (Photograph by Norman Price.)

tion; the body looks as though it is just as mineral and inert as the stone that supports it and seems to have engendered it. The costume (or the body with its corpselike rigidity) dissolves into the surrounding environment; it simply serves to amplify the attitude of the body and the strange nature of the site.

Costume and Space

Costume often constitutes a kind of traveling scenography, a set reduced to a human scale that moves with the actor: a *décorcostume,* as the costume designer Claude Lemaire calls it.[5]

Certain forms of traditional Asian dance, such as Balinese dance or Beijing Opera, concentrate such a degree of richness into their *décorcostumes* that any characterizing of the stage space is rendered superfluous, and the space remains empty to accommodate the choreography and song more effectively.

It is important to note the absolute contrast between costume and space. The hypersignifying, codified costumes of Beijing Opera or of commedia dell'arte evolve within an empty space; the naked, "empty" body of a Butoh dancer, on the other hand, is perceived in a normal, "full" environment (rural or urban landscape).

With each element of a mise-en-scène there corresponds a signifying function for costume that analysis should endeavor to record systematically. Thus, in the space-time-action-light continuum:

- The costume fills up and constitutes a space, if only in the way in which it privileges the body in its movements.
- The costume "unfurls" to varying degrees, able to materialize an era, as well as a rhythm and a way of moving with the air currents.
- The costume participates in the action, always intimately connected to the skin of the actor, or transported in a kinetic volume; it is always worn by the performer, unless this "skin" is shed like an abandoned chrysalis.
- The costume receives light to varying degrees, thereby structuring and rhythming the changes in lighting intensity.

Performer's Costume, Character's Costume

Even before describing and interpreting the costumes in a performance, it is worth enquiring as to how they were elaborated. Do they stem from an immutable tradition that has fixed and regulated the use of costume, as in the majority of Asian acting and dance traditions? Or have they been created from scratch by a costume designer, in accordance with the particular demands of the play and the role, in order to serve an "original" mise-en-scène in the Western sense of the word?

In the first case, the costume is that of an actor-dancer (the performer); in determining what led to a particular cut, hue, or detail, one can only discuss historical factors.

In the second case, the costume is that which is appropriate for a particular character, within the fiction and given the characters' situations. As with acting, space, or mise-en-scène, one can thus discuss the *style of costumes:* classical, romantic, realistic, naturalistic, symbolist, epic, and so on.

Vectorization of Costumes

Any verbal description of costumes that reflects the nuances in the ways they are employed is useful; but it may be inadequate if it gets lost in details and prevents the "fashion system"[6] that regulates their use from coming to light. This is why I propose to classify them according to the typology of vectors that has already been explained above (see the table).

Axis of Metonymy	Axis of Metaphor
2. Connectors	1. Accumulators
3. Cutters	4. Shifters

Let us return to the example of Peter Weiss's *Marat/Sade* in the film version directed by Peter Brook in 1966, and examine the function of costumes in the mise-en-scène as a whole.

Costumes as Accumulator Vectors
In order to place the numerous characters in this play, the spectator needs to identify clearly defined groups of characters. The use of particular kinds of clothing thus implies a repetition, confirmation and accumulation of signs that enable differentiation, for example:

- The white garments or underclothes of the patients
- Highly theatricalized costumes, such as the outrageously colorful costuming of the four choral singers
- Evening dress for the Coulmier family (Empire style), and so on.

Costumes as Connector Vectors
Once these indicative signs have accumulated to a sufficient degree, spectators try to orient themselves in terms of the most marked oppositions, to read a costume in relation to others, and to understand the system of regularities that effect connections or disjunctions. In this context, it is not relevant, for example, to distinguish between patients, the alienated, common-law prisoners and political prisoners. On the other hand, clothing allows one to recognize the difference between prisoners and guards, or between the amateur actors directed by Sade and the members of Napoleonic society who have come to watch them. Connections are made bit by bit, a detail in one costume linking with another detail in another costume, or perhaps a state of costuming paving the way for what follows; in this way, the patients' entrance corresponds to the prisoners' attempted breakout at the end of the film. An experienced observer will recognize the

signs systematically inserted by the costume designer in order to facilitate narrative development and the perception of changes.

Costumes as Cutter Vectors

When abrupt changes in the action occur, one always notices some modification in the appearance of costumes. For example, when the Coulmier family appear in Empire-style formal dress, their image suddenly interrupts a series of portraits of patients dressed in rags; these portraits do not locate the action in a precise historical moment, but instead signify alienation in all its forms and in every era. The appearance of Sade, then of the singers, is similarly marked by a change in clothing.

Costumes as Shifter Vectors

The system correlating costumes is not only operative within the fiction, for it also ensures the transition from one fictional world to another. This is often the case when a costume contains a number of signs that facilitate the passage from one era to another. In general terms, for example, the costumes from revolutionary and Napoleonic times are transformed without any difficulty into allusions to all eras in which prisoners are incarcerated under the pretext of psychological and physical rehabilitation; the amnesiac or narcoleptic become instances of the alienated or convicts once their clothing has been filmed and presented with the prerequisite signs. Clothing and behavioral indices converge to ensure transitions, allusions, and parodies. In this context, therefore, it is not even necessary for the representatives of the law to be dressed as riot police (as they were in Roger Planchon's celebrated production of *Tartuffe*) for allusions to the conflict of the 1960s to become evident.

Naturally enough, costumes impact upon the bodies of actors and everything that surrounds them; they become part of the fundamental trinomial structure of performance (space-time-action) by bringing its movement to light. According to the designer Gischia, "On stage, the representative forms and colors of a character are in movement. They move around in a three-dimensional space in accordance with a rhythm that, when properly controlled, should possess the rigor and unity of a musical movement. The costume thus ceases to be a disguise and becomes an essential element of dramatic movement."

In a more certain and concrete way than any of performance's other signifying systems, the use of costumes is based on verifiable observations, on networks of strictly codified signs. This is why semiology's functionalist approach is particularly appropriate for the analysis of costumes. In theater, clothing is a natural shifter between the private, physical person of the actor and the character whose skin and attributes he assumes. A perfect double agent, a costume is worn by a real body to suggest a fictional character. Thus one can approach it from the perspective of the living organism of the actor and the performance, or from the perspective of the "fashion system" it conveys in the most precise way possible: as precisely as a marionette (which is much more reliable than human flesh and emotions). Theater costumes are in fact worn (or endured) by actors and conceived externally by costume designers and directors. Any description of costumes therefore requires a dual perspective from the spectator: existential ("how will the actor manage?") and at the same time structural ("what will s/he make of it in terms of the overall production of meaning?").

Makeup

Makeup and Cover-Up

A set applied to the body of an actor becomes a costume. A costume inscribed on an actor's skin becomes makeup. Makeup adorns the soul as much as the body of the wearer; hence its strategic importance for seduction in life, as for an actor on stage.

In theater, everything is "made up," or even covered up; the face and body always have something to hide, as if to make it more appealing to buyers.

Yet makeup is not an extension of the body, as masks, costumes, and props sometimes are. Nor is it a "technique of the body," one of the ways in which "men know how to use their bodies."[7] It is more of a filter, a film, a fine membrane attached to the face; nothing is closer to the actor's body, and nothing serves or betrays an actor more than this paper-thin coating.

Topology of the Face

When one tries to describe the makeup of actors, the first difficulty is in being able to read it in relation to the face that wears it. In one way, it is as difficult to distinguish between the actual features of a human face and the painting that reworks, masks, or transforms them, as it is to distinguish between the spontaneity of a facial expression and the "operatic machinery" that activates this apparently natural expression (to borrow Marivaux's image).

Physiognomists elaborated theories of emotions that can be read from the human face. Codified forms of theater, from farce to melodrama, use these practices extensively, and as spectators are already familiar with the acting codes, they have no difficulty in reading characters' motivations. Therefore it is important that spectators know how to recognize these mobilizations of facial expression, and that they have some conception of the topology of the face. Dumézil and Dagognet[8] (and Delsarte[9] before them) distinguish three zones that relate to different functions and emotions, and for which one might give the following examples from theater:

- The mouth and lower jaw are linked with the nutritive function. The greedy Arlequin draws much of his identity from this area.
- The gaze and cheeks are the site of the respiratory function, breath, and emotions. All actors know full well the importance of the right breath combined with a precisely placed gaze.
- The forehead is the place of contemplation and theory; reflexive monologues seem to focus attention in the forehead and the "higher" human functions.

Traces and Functions of Makeup

In interpreting makeup, I will try to describe not only its techniques and the lines it traces, but also to understand how it modifies, and even constitutes, the human body and the imaginary connected with it. One must evaluate the symbolic function it fulfills at particular moments in the processes of bringing the body into performance. This will allow us to focus here on a couple of recurrent scenarios.

Accentuation and Highlighting of Features

As a result of the distance from spectators, expressive facial characteristics tend to have to be enlarged in a way that makes them seem natural, even some way away from the stage. The perspective and scale of enlargement can be deformed, so the observer should remain aware of this acting convention, to which chamber theater or cinema is not subjected. Only makeup specialists will be able to appreciate what products have been used (and these are renewed very quickly as new products come on to the market, as with military equipment). The use of latex masks that reproduce the texture and elasticity of skin heightens the illusion. A thorough knowledge of lighting variations and effects is indispensable in determining the way in which facial art leaves nothing to chance. Depending on the aesthetic of the mise-en-scène, makeup either tends to reinforce the verisimilitude of situations (realistic or naturalistic use), reproducing the faces of characters mimetically; or, on the other hand, it may highlight its own devices and become an end in itself, a facial or bodily painting no longer at the service of other signs, but focusing our eyes on its own autonomous practice.

Autonomous Makeup Work

Once makeup no longer simply fulfills the banal task of highlighting and confirming the conventionally realistic features of a character, it forms an aesthetic system that only obeys its own rules. Such is the case with highly codified genres like Beijing Opera, which employs makeup that is both arbitrary and immutable. However, this is also part of certain European avant-garde practices, from the moment they declared war on naturalism in art. The various kinds of grotesque makeup used by Meyerhold's actors are still well known, for they opened up a new avenue for Western mise-en-scène by reproducing the theatricality of the acting forms, and by granting each component full power to develop according to the logic of its possibilities.

The difficulty for performance analysis is in evaluating the way in which makeup abandons its highlighting or embellishing functions so as to become *body art;* at this point, moreover, in order to found its own "republic," it risks abandoning the federation of art forms that constitute performance.

The Unconscious of Makeup

What is most difficult to evaluate—but also what is most important—is the effect makeup produces on the observer, and in particular on his unconscious. The highlighting or modifying of features can produce a seductive, terrifying, or comic effect, without one really knowing how. The spectator is implicated, not in some trivial decoding of information, but in a face-to-face situation in which what she reads engages her desire. On the painted and unpainted face of the other, I read my own thoughts and desires; I associate it with a scenography of hypersensitivity and a ceremony of seduction.

Any disguise or "dressing up," in terms of clothing or facially, heightens the sense of vertigo and the ambiguity of my own identity, whether it be a disguising of sex, age, or human nature (as opposed to animality). Thus, in Alfredo Arias's production of *Jeu de l'amour et du hasard,* in which Marivaux's elegant and eloquent protagonists were played by actors disguised as monkeys, the spectator no longer knew whom to identify with (see fig. 18).

Human gaze? Animal fright? Furry animal or bearded woman? In contemporary mise-en-scène, makeup often becomes much more than a disguise or a highlighting of existing features; it produces a vertigo that disables the possibility of any assured interpretation and definitive metamorphosis.

Protocols for Observing Makeup

How is one to analyze vertigo? So let us simply try to specify the experimental protocols that analysis could follow. First, it must determine the nature of the affect produced in the spectator, using psychoanalysis in particular. Then it can enable us to differentiate between perception in proximity and perception at a distance; the same makeup, seen from far away, will seem appropriate and mysterious, and from close up, theatrical and demystifying. One could call this "the Archimboldo effect":[10] from close up, the flowers (makeup) are visible in all their detail and materiality; from further away, the face made of flowers is now no more than a face represented in its entirety. Distancing and proximity are foundational elements of meaning; and it is the degree of distance that one attempts to evaluate when determining makeup.

Analysis makes both revealed and concealed traits emerge through the makeup: the traits of lines drawn by makeup pencils as well as character traits, the lines traced in the overall sketch the scene suggests. Spectators feel the atmosphere and emotional coloring produced by painted faces and bodies.

Objects

Identified Object, Unidentified Object

By "object" I mean anything that can be manipulated by the actor. This term tends to replace *prop,* which is too bound up with the idea of a sec-

Fig. 18. Makeup as "vertigo": Marivaux's *Le Jeu de l'amour et du hasard*, directed by Alfredo Arias. (Photograph by Marc Enguérand.)

ondary tool belonging to a character. Not only is the object not a prop or accessory, it is at the very heart of performance; it underpins the set, the actor, and all the plastic values of the performance:

> The object in this context refers to everything that figures on stage and is not the actor—props, sets, drapes and hangings, even costumes; by its nature on stage, the object constitutes a supple, manipulable, changing material, almost by definition.[11]

The same stage element can sometimes be treated as set or prop, or as plastic object, but the categorization is of decisive importance for understanding the performance.

Different Degrees of Objectivity

Without entering into a debate on the identity of objects, analysis can at least distinguish several types of object by locating them within a continuum that goes from materiality to spirituality, with the stage object *stricto sensu* only being shown and represented (see fig. 19).

In order to classify objects according to their degree of objectivity, a few possible examples of these categories will now be provided:

1. This first kind of object is actually a natural product, an element that is not man-made. For example, the sand in Peter Brook's production of the epic Indian poem *The Mahabharata,* or Brook's production of Shakespeare's *The Tempest.*
2. Nonfigurative forms could be cubes or items of working scenery, abstract forms that one cannot find as such in reality. For example, the inverted cone in Heiner Goebbels's *Oder die glücklose Landung* (see fig. 20).
3. Legible materiality refers to those objects within which one perceives individual materiality as well as a sense of belonging to a particular social group. For example, the objects or costumes in a Brechtian style of performance, such as the coarse, worn fabric of Mother Courage's clothing (see fig. 23).
4. Recycled found objects are borrowed from external reality and used in an aesthetic way within a new environment. For example, the oil drums manipulated by the Brith Gof actors in the group's performance of *Camlann* (see fig. 21).

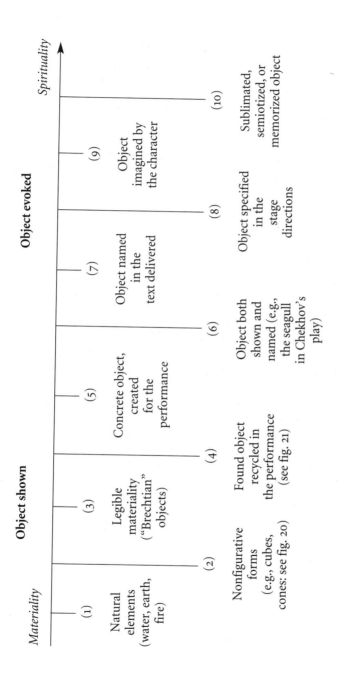

Fig. 19. Typology of objects in theater

Fig. 20. "Nonfigurative objects": the inverted cone in *Oder die glücklose Landung*, directed by Heiner Goebbels, scenography by Magdalena Jetelová (Nanterre, 1993). (Photograph by Marc Enguérand.)

5. Concrete objects created for the performance borrow the characteristics of real objects, but they are adapted for the requirements of the stage (new proportions, stylization, etc.).
6. Sometimes a real object is also named in the text, in such a way that one is able to perceive it concretely and conceive of it abstractly. For example, the seagull in Chekhov's play of the same name.

Fig. 21. "Recycled, found objects" and "components of a mobile scenography": *Camlann,* production by Brith Gof, 1993. (Photograph by Jens Koch.)

Once the object is evoked in words (categories 7 to 10 in fig. 19), it assumes a quite different status; here too, however, there are still various degrees of abstraction, as if the object gradually moves further and further away from concrete usage, to the point at which it is no more than an element of language stored in the memory.

Categories for Description

No ready-made categorization exists to account for the countless objects found on stage. At best one can describe the forms, enumerate the materials, and distinguish between utilitarian function and aesthetic usage.

Minds with a mathematical inclination will enjoy placing objects within different sets or groupings—sometimes distinct from each other, sometimes inclusive of each other, sometimes intersecting with each other. This kind of classification reveals the logic and system of objects within a mise-en-scène; it also allows them to be manipulated mentally. Above all, the "system of objects"[12] reveals their function in the performance and thus requires one to think about the mise-en-scène as a whole.

At the same time one must bear in mind the materiality of objects and consider what makes them objects in their own right (and not simply functional cogs in some anonymous mechanism). Analysis thus endeavors to convey the aesthetic experience felt by the spectator in relation to them, particularly in terms of the objects' materiality. This may be

- visual: wood fibers, texture of fabrics;
- olfactory: smell of forest, water, earth (Peter Stein's production of Gorki's *Summerfolk*);
- auditory: the resonance of oil drums rolled and struck *(Camlann)*.

Objects frequently border on other elements within the performance. The oil drums in *Camlann,* for example, are both mobile implements and the components of a mobile scenography (see fig. 21); or the sand in *Oder die glücklose Landung* is both raw material and artifact—giant hourglass, cement works, inverted pit shaft, tunnel, proscenium stage, bellows (see fig. 20).

Detailed records of objects intervening in a performance are only of interest if they are linked back to a unit being constructed, that is, to a vectorial dynamic that orients descriptions and accounts for the objects' metaphorical and metonymic usage. Therefore we return to the table of vectorizations, in this context examining which operations are effected by the spectator perceiving the object, and what kind of vectorial trajectory is thus constituted. Let us take the example of the inverted cone in Magdalena Jetelová's scenography for *Oder die glücklose Landung*, which lends itself to the four major types of vectorization.

1. The *accumulation* of different possible identities for the object produces successively, or at the same time, a funnel, a cement mixer, a truck tipper, etc. Each possible object condenses two or more significations,

Displacement	Condensation
2. Connector (pourer) 3. Cutter (observation post)	1. Accumulator (funnel, mixer, cone, etc.) 4. Shifter (machine for playing or for fixing meaning)

which it represents through a certain resemblance; for example, mixer = funnel + pourer.

2. A *connection* is established each time a new use for the object crops up, *displacing* its former use to a reserve of meaning. For example, the pourer for the heap of sand enables the sudden appearance of the explorer, his head bowed, imperturbably pursuing his monologue—it is as if he emerges from the top of a chimney or in an observation post. The comic effect of this object resides in the continual displacement of its enigmatic identity, and the metaphorical association it maintains with a new property.

3. When this displacement produces a strong sense of surprise, a rupture occurs in the metaphoric or metonymic chain; the new identity of the object breaks the thread of what has occurred beforehand, and necessitates a fresh start from new bases: for example, the appearance of the explorer in the opening at the top of the pourer, or the tilting of the cone on to one of its sides (see fig. 20).

4. Accumulation and displacement destabilize perception; the conical object is transformed into a playing machine, and it shifts to quite different levels of meaning; it changes from a ludic object to become a disturbing object, a war machine for photographing or erasing the virgin forest beneath the disastrous influence of the mad explorer.

In the same way as space, the object frequently comes to represent an integrative system, a focal point or parameter for the rest of the performance; the spectator appreciates it as reference point, a marker between two moments or spaces. In the case of the oil drums in *Camlann,* for example, the play of symmetry in these found objects used in a rough way structures the rectangular space, represents the two armies that are present, and clarifies the narrative (see fig. 21).

Lighting

Lighting occupies a crucial place in performance, since it brings it into existence visually, connecting and coloring all of the visual elements (space, scenography, costume, actor, makeup), endowing them with a particular atmosphere.

Technical Considerations

No other stage system has made as much technical progress in recent years as lighting has. Furthermore, the profession of lighting designer has become one of the essential roles in performance making since Vilar's popular theater experiences, and nowadays lighting designers assist directors from the earliest readings and rehearsals of a work. For the "average" spectator, there can be no question of keeping up to date with lighting's technological feats; nevertheless it would useful if she were at least sensitized to the dramaturgy of light. Rather than aiming for a technical knowledge of the lights used, it will be more helpful here to observe the location of lighting and the layout of light sources, noting where they are placed in relation to stage and actor: in front; laterally; behind ("backlighting"); at low level ("floor lighting"); horizontally; overhead.

Lighting and Color

It is the lighting that creates color. Therefore there must be some degree of consensual dialogue between set designer, costume designer, and lighting designer for chromatic choices not to override each other. Spectators are sensitive to the colors used: warm hues for a pleasant sensation; cold ones to produce feelings of sadness; middling tones to create a neutral, calm impression. The colorings chosen provoke emotions and sensations through the level of light (brightness) and the shade of gel placed in front of lights (color). Detailed observation of colors used should account for the effect produced on the observer, and of the emotional construction of the performance. Although the mental images produced may not be any more comprehensible to the observer, they will at least be more closely connected to the objective use of colors. Such images would also include musical listening, dreamlike or waking dream moments, as well as moments of drifting attention; for listening and dream also give rise to colors.

Dramaturgy of Light

When one attends a performance, one can always try to understand the lighting design as system, that is, the mise-en-scène of light, the production's particular way of bringing light and shadows to bear within the performance.

The type of light used needs to be established: whether it be natural sunlight or moonlight, or artificial light (currently capable of re-creating the conditions of natural light).

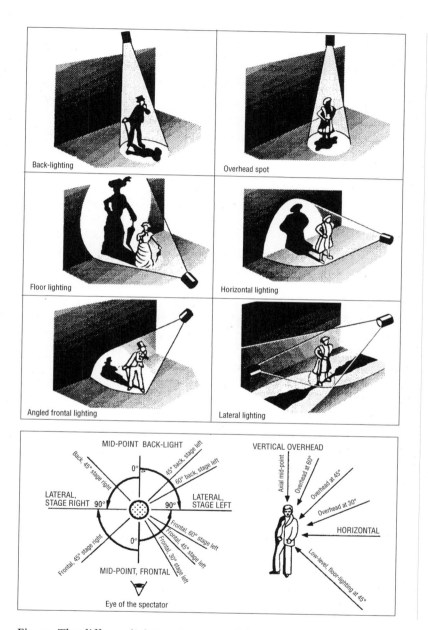

Fig. 22. The different lighting directions. From François Valentin, *Lumières pour le spectacle* (Paris: Librairie Théâtrale, 1988, 30–34).

One should signal the moments at which light intervenes in the performance as it unfolds, and with what kinds of effect.

The kinds of phenomena, whether fleeting or ongoing, that light has enabled us to perceive should also be evaluated: isolated effects or continuous changes of atmosphere, revelation of a feeling or overshadowing of an action, and so on.

One should ask oneself what the light illuminates as well as what it conceals, whether the mise-en-scène established light in order to place itself in the shadows or vice versa.

Light facilitates understanding. If a lit object is well contrasted, it will be clearly recognized. Light is responsible for the degree of comfort and discomfort in the act of listening, the more or less rational understanding of an event. When the bright, open wash of a Brecht or Jean Vilar production is replaced by the twilight stage of a Patrice Chéreau or André Engel production, it is as if the vision of the world has darkened. When Giorgio Strehler (and his lighting designer Guido Baroni) successfully reconcile the white Brechtian light of a dramaturgy that has nothing to hide, with the sensual, southern European light of an Italian Renaissance painting, lighting achieves a unique compromise between rationality and subjectivity.

Lighting and the Other Elements of the Performance

An appreciation of lighting entails an understanding of the ways in which light impacts upon the other components of the performance.

Scenography
Scenography either allows natural light to penetrate the space, or not. Artificial light allows one to choose to make an illusion out of a particular element of the set, or to make it disappear. Through changes in its direction, light can suggest the progression of a day: for example, in André Engel's production of *Le Misanthrope,* or Gildas Bourdet's *Britannicus.* The same technique can also be used to disorient the observer: for example, Chéreau's productions of Koltès's *Quai Ouest* or Marivaux's *La Fausse Suivante,* in which the actors projected enormous and disturbing shadows, their directions shifting with no concern for verisimilitude.

Costumes
Clothing receives light in a particularly immediate way; folds are emphasized, and colors are made visible and variable by the type of light and gel used.

Makeup

Makeup is amplified, positively or negatively. A pumpkin or orange hue
will bring out the complexion of the skin in an attractive way; green or blue,
on the other hand, will make skin look gray, giving it a particularly sinister
quality. Makeup is almost always a necessity under lighting.

The Actor

Every aspect of the actor is sometimes affected by light; his energy is
either heightened or muted. An actor's relationship with the spectators
is transparent, particularly with the lights on full, or disrupted if he is
blinded by a shaft of light or reduced to a voice in the shadowy gloom. If
an actor needs lighting in the same way that a plant needs water (as
Chéreau suggests), sometimes they can be victims of lighting that is violent, antagonistic toward them, as if it set out to destabilize or assault
them. An experienced external eye will be able to distinguish between an
aggression effected with the actors' "agreement," and an untimely intervention by a lighting designer who has failed to consult either the director or the actor.

In short, lighting allows the *dramaturgy* of a performance to be guided
and inscribed in time, particularly in terms of the temporal and narrative
articulation of the action.

Materiality and Dematerialization

To conclude our discussion of the range of material elements apparent in
performance, it is worth mentioning three human senses that seem to be
rather underused in theater: smell, touch, and taste.

Smell

The sense of smell comes into play as a result of what stems from what is
on stage as much as what is in the auditorium; a stage set composed of
natural elements (earth, trees, flowers) will be smelled by an audience
more accustomed to artificiality and pretence. Some years ago, the Russian symbolists (e.g., Balmont, whose *Trois Floraisons* Vachkévitch
directed) proposed olfactory performances. More recently, a number of
experiments have tried to produce olfactory performances using per-

fumes and other odors: for example, Dominique Borg in *De l'autre côté de l'Alice* (1988), and Dominique Paquet in *Patience du baobab* (1994). The activation of the sense of smell can unleash very potent emotions and memories, which may lead the spectator to identify strongly with the situations evoked.

An odor on stage is not fictional in kind; it constitutes a reality. This is why it hinders the processes of illusion and fictionalization, impeding the spectator with feelings experienced as very strong and personal. This accounts for the difficulty of treating olfactory signs as fictional elements, and of combining them with other sign systems. It also accounts for the extreme difficulty of using fragrances on stage, and of "reading" them as a theatrical sign in the same way as visual or auditory signs. Everything that can be smelled thus risks remaining at the level of pure materiality, resisting conversion into a meaning, a sign, or a dramaturgy.[13]

Touch

Although touch is absolutely integral to games, erotic or otherwise, it seems to have been banished from Western theater experiences that clearly separate actors and onlookers with, for example, footlights. Nonetheless, other forms of performance around the world have resorted to touch; and the avant-garde of the 1960s—happenings, or Schechner's environmental theater—provoked a quite different relationship to the body of the other by reinstating touch:

> As a result of the sense of touch, dramatic art is a fundamentally carnal, sensual act. Theater performance is a collective mixing, a true act of love, a sensual communion between two human groups. One opens itself up, the other touches and penetrates; the two become one, they consume each other. . . . As it essentially addresses the sense of touch, the art of theater is thus above all an Art of Sensation. It is the opposite of all intellectual preoccupation.[14]

Once she is touched not only by the art of theater, but by the body of the actor, the spectator radically modifies her approach to the performance; she breaks free of the cool analyses of the geometrical eye and enters a world of sensations, which are sometimes also accompanied by abstract reflections.

Taste

The sense of taste is rarely solicited in theater, unless it is in a figurative sense; in Sanskrit poetics, for example, the term *rasa* is used to designate flavor, the joyous awareness of the spectator, the feeling of "tasting" an aesthetic pleasure. In a number of experiments, actors have prepared a meal during the performance, then offered it to the audience once the fictional fare has been "consumed": for example, *Risotto,* produced by the Politecnico of Rome.

Of course, one could conceive of further materials other than those whose essential properties have been outlined here. One might also challenge the pertinence of their segmentation into different signifiers, although it should be noted that they are organized in accordance with a particular overall movement, that is, a vectorization. What is important, therefore, is not to enumerate signifiers exhaustively, but rather to perceive their dynamics using all five of our senses: their emergence, the ways in which they are linked as sequences and memorized, their ability to occupy the foreground or background and to establish correlations and alliances. Understanding vectorizations of this kind is the analyst's task in relation to any mise-en-scène, any manipulation of stage materials. The experience of the senses—*aesthesis*—is also the emotional participation of the spectator, the very fact of being there and allowing oneself to be transported for a moment.

7

Staging the Text

When a text is produced on stage, how is it received and interpreted by the spectator? This is a crucial issue for analysis of performance that still often uses texts. In the Western tradition, the dramatic text remains one of the essential components of performance. In theater it has long been assimilated as the primary component, with its performance on stage only accorded a subordinate, optional role. However, things changed radically with the recognition of the director's function, toward the end of the nineteenth century, when it was acknowledged that a director is capable (or culpable?) of marking a text produced on stage with the stamp of a personal vision. For the theater of mise-en-scène, therefore, it is quite logical to focus analysis on the performance as a whole, rather than considering the latter to be something derived exclusively from the text. Theater studies, and performance analysis in particular, are interested in performance as a whole, in everything that surrounds and exceeds the text in an overall event. One repercussion of this has been the reduction of the dramatic text to the status of a sort of cumbersome accessory, now left, rather contemptuously, at the disposal of philologists. So in the space of fifty years, there has been a shift from one extreme to the other: from philology to scenology.

Perhaps it is time to restore a little more equity and, if possible, subtlety. My aim here is not to return to a purely literary vision of theater, nor to engage in an endless discussion as to whether theater constitutes literature or performance. Instead I propose to reconsider the place of text in performance, and to distinguish between text as read off the page of a book and text as perceived in a mise-en-scène.

In the concern to review the principal elements of contemporary Western mise-en-scène, and to conceive of the most appropriate analytical methods for them, one should quite naturally reserve a select place for the dramatic text—without however prejudging its status *inside* the performance; here the text is conceived as being *within* the performance, rather than *above* or *beside* it. Most importantly, this chapter aims to suggest a viewpoint and a method that are adequate to evaluate the impact and function of text within performance. Commentaries on dramatic texts only rarely take into consideration the ways in which they are manifested: the individual reading of words in a book, or attendance at a live performance, in the course of which the text is perceived, most often delivered by the actors.

Staged Text, Articulated Text

Written Text, Enunciated Text

Before even being able to describe the devices through which a dramatic text is vocalized, embodied, and performed by actor and director, one must start by specifying the object of an analysis of a staged dramatic text. Two perspectives seem legitimate here:

- To examine the ways in which a (preexistent) text has been staged *(texte mis en scène)*;
- To observe the ways in which the text is articulated on stage *(texte émis en scène)*, how it is made audible and visible.

Study of the Mise-en-scène of a Text
This form of study is devoted to the genesis of a mise-en-scène, the preparatory phase before the final fine tuning of a performance: dramaturgical analysis to determine the time, place, and protagonists of the action; readings by the actors and director, involvement of the scenographer, costume designer, lighting designer; the trying out, activating, and rejecting of avenues opened up by possible readings; the exploration of vocalization, and the progressive establishment of the vocal and gestural score.

Study of the Articulation of a Text on Stage
This describes the way in which a text is delivered, enunciated, "emitted" on stage: a text produced, switched on, transmitted with all possible mean-

ing in all possible directions. The *articulated* text is already there, colored by a voice, a concrete vocal version of a text uttered that the spectator, or listener, does not need to activate with his own voice (as the reader of a written text does). The articulated text is already integrated into a mise-en-scène, it is already staged; for the actor, with the help of the other practitioners, has already vocalized it, ipso facto realizing a vocal mise-en-scène that makes the dramatic text the object of a performance. For the listener/spectator hearing and seeing the actor deliver her text, it is difficult to abstract from what is perceived and to read the dramatic text as if discovering it on paper, giving it life and voice through one's own reading. If by chance she already knows the text (it is a classic, for example), evidently she could compare the current mise-en-scène with her own former reading of the text; however, it will be difficult for her to preserve this former reading from the insistent particularities of the actor's vocalization in the present instance. Only an expert spectator will be in a position to reconstitute and distinguish between the current mise-en-scène and the reading she was able to make previously. (Similarly, one would not know how to distinguish which elements of a mise-en-scène stem from stage directions in the text and which are contributed by the mise-en-scène.)

These two forms of study and the perspectives they offer are obviously not incompatible, but only the study of text as articulated in a given mise-en-scène is of concern for performance analysis; the "average" spectator is not expected to know about the genesis of a performance. Nevertheless the process of a performance's genesis—the repetitions, adjustments, improvements, changes of mind made in the elaboration of a mise-en-scène—leaves indelible traces in the final product that will not escape the expert, although they may well go unnoticed by the audience in general. Performance analysis—or more precisely the classical analysis of Western performance, for it is a different matter for intercultural performance or performance from other cultures—is based on a final, more or less stabilized version of theater work, which is not concerned with exact reasons for artists' aesthetic choices and therefore does not need to try to locate their intentions. Another reason not to confuse a text that is read with a text that is performed . . .

Read Text, Performed Text

In order to analyze the true merits of a text, one must know how it presents itself to its receiver: is it read by the receiver, or is it performed by actors in front of the receiver? And what happens when the reading is staged, as is the case with contemporary performances that test the boundaries of performance and reading?

A *text that is read* has not been activated by a human (or synthetic) voice other than that of its author, who is not present to deliver it. It is activated in the act of its perception, but in an individual and silent manner. (It is only since the end of the Middle Ages that reading has been silent, and the individual has become the depositary of meaning, the subject internalizing laws and norms.)

A *text that is performed* and delivered by the actor is already served by a stage space and prosodic, visual, and gestural signs one can no longer abstract. Listening to this verbal copy of the text, seeing what kind of enunciatory situation is put in place, in turn producing a certain meaning for the text, the spectator receives a quite specific option (even though it's often rather illegible or incoherent) that closes interpretation to other options. On the other hand, the same spectator may be receptive to particular qualities of the dramatic text that would have perhaps escaped her in a reading.

The performed text is already divided up and distributed between various different speakers; the enunciatory situation has been specified in a nonambiguous way. The meaning of the situation immediately leaps out, dazzles the spectator just as we are blinded by evidence, even though the dispersal of the sources of enunciation discourages any clear and definitive synthesis.

The performed text is subdivided into a text that is *only heard* and a text that is heard and *seen* (i.e., performed, activated, staged). The text that is heard is that of a reading, what used to be called an "oratory recital." The listener has at her disposal information about its enunciation, its psychological interpretation; but she must imagine a performance context (as if they were hearing it on the radio). In the case of the text that is *seen*, this context has been materialized visually and scenically, and the spectator cannot avoid it; she watches what occurs there. For performance analysis, it is a matter of determining whether primarily to watch or to listen, whether one is inundated with visual signs or whether one should employ one's imagination solely by listening to the text: in short, whether one is attending a *drama* or listening to a *story*.

Comprehension of the Read Text

We need to return to the current state of our techniques for reading dramatic texts: an impossible undertaking in the context of this study. Despite the dispersal of the dramatic text into autonomous utterances, a multiplicity and apparent equality of the different perspectives, despite the rapid procession of words and the acoustic difficulty of hearing them, the reader/listener takes her bearings by forming units or ensembles. She goes toward the pre-text or post-text, in accordance with the operative processes that the phenomenology of reading calls *retention* or *protension*. Lost in the maze of utterances, she watches out for textual indications as to the "given circumstances," the motivations and superobjectives of characters. She makes full use of her ability to synthesize, to cross-check and to analyze dramaturgically; she has to establish who speaks, to whom, with what end in mind, where, and in what way the word gives rise to an action. She plays with the discontinuity of the word in theater by examining "what occurs between one utterance and another in an exchange, and what is at the heart of each reply. What kind of movement takes place to engender the shift from one position to the following position."[1] In so doing, she provides herself with the means to imagine, if not a concrete mise-en-scène, at least a dramatic situation within which the text necessarily assumes a meaning, since it is already divided up among speakers and structured as a sequence of conflictual situations.

Obviously all of these dramaturgical and textual processes remain valid for the study of the text in the context of a mise-en-scène; but this performance context adds on a series of particular treatments of verbal material (which will be described below). First one must clarify the relation between text and performance, thereby establishing their hierarchy and conflict.

Text and Performance

In order to elucidate these very complex interrelations, it is advisable to specify one's historical moment and cultural location; for the text is not always (far from it) the preexistent and fixed element that it is the stage's task to serve or illustrate—to put on stage *(mettre en scène)*, in the Western sense. In fact it is only since the beginning of the seventeenth century that the text has preceded performance, and that actors have placed themselves at the service of an author's text. Before that time, there was a close alliance between bodies and words, and actors improvised around familiar scenarios. From the time of Rotrou and Corneille, language begins to secure possession of bodies so as to incarnate the word of the author; and performance sometimes resembles the incarnation (and therefore also the servant) of a text deemed to be the source of everything. The fixing of texts and their infinite revivals—initially in accordance with a rhetoric of highly codified actions, then subsequently in accordance with a creativity connected to the irresistible emergence of a director—is a historical accident, which has managed to pass for a universal law, according to which the text supposedly precedes the stage in both temporal and statutory terms. This is the "textocentric" vision of theater that still holds sway to a large extent over theater theory; and it remains very difficult to move away from this predominant model, whatever the importance accorded to mise-en-scène and the nonverbal elements of performance.

"Textocentric" Vision of Mise-en-Scène

Returning to the framework of performance analysis, and performance containing a text (preexistent to the performance or not), one must once again consider the relations between text and performance; this then leads one to ask whether the performance issues from the text or not, and from the reading one might make of the text.

Now, this comparison or confrontation of text and performance is a deadly habit that encourages the thought that a mise-en-scène is an actualization, manifestation, or concretization of elements already contained within the text. Perhaps this is true from a diachronic perspective on a study of the mise-en-scène's genesis, following on from the director's own study of the dramatic text she intends to stage. However, it is not inevitably true from a synchronic perspective, since the spectator receives the text and extratextual signs at the same time, without one necessarily being anterior and superior to the other. Indeed it is possible to imagine a model of mise-en-scène elaborated without knowledge of the text, the text only being selected at the very last moment, once the mise-en-scène has been concluded; Robert Wilson and a number of other theater artists proceed in this way.

The problem is not one of knowing to an absolute degree which element is primary—the text or the stage—for clearly responses will vary depending on the historical moments envisaged. The problem is this: in a performance containing a text (which may have existed prior to the theater work or not, we don't know), how does one know whether one element stems from the other, and therefore requires the other in order to resolve itself, to determine its own forms?

In truth, it is rare to come across the thesis that suggests that the text stems from the stage space used and from the actors' performances; and yet it would be easy to show that the writing of texts is substantially influenced by the stage practices of an era, by what it can do theatrically.

Inversely, it is common to consider the mise-en-scène as issuing directly from the text; in other words, the stage actualizes elements contained within the text. Fundamentally, that is the actual meaning of "putting a text on stage" *(mettre en scène);* after reading the text, elements are extracted from it and are put on stage. So the text is conceived as a reserve, even as the depository of meaning; and the task of performance is to extract and express this meaning, just as one extracts (scenic) juice from a (textual) carrot.

This vision of the relation between text and performance is that of philologists—for whom the dramatic text is all and the stage a simple illustration, a rhetorical aspect to "season" the text—as well as of numerous theater theorists, including semiologists. I will restrict myself to a few quotations drawn from the latter:

- Anne Ubersfeld talks, for example, of "kernels of theatricality," "textual matrices of representativity," textual holes to be filled by the mise-en-scène.[2]
- Alessandro Serpieri is interested in the scenic virtuality of the dramatic text.[3]
- Erika Fischer-Lichte sees theory as "the systematic study of possible relations between the written text and performance";[4] according to her, performance should be understood as an interpretant for the possible significations of the drama that lies at its base.
- Keir Elam asks "in what ways are the dramatic text and the performance text related—what are the points of contact between them?"[5]
- Horst Turk dreams of finding "the articulation missing between the semiology of theater and the poetics of drama, which would yield results for each of them."[6]

All of these positions are philological insofar as the performance appeals to the authority of a text for its interpretation and its very existence. The text is not described in its scenic enunciation, that is, as stage practice, but as absolute and immutable reference, fulcrum of the mise-en-scène in its entirety. At the same time, the text is declared to be incomplete since it requires performance to acquire its meaning. These philological positions all have in common a normative and derivative vision of mise-en-scène according to which mise-en-scène should not be arbitrary, but should serve the text and justify itself as a correct reading of the dramatic text. It is presupposed that text and stage are bound together, that they have been conceived in terms of each other: the text with a view to a future mise-en-scène, or at least a given acting style; the stage envisaging what the text suggests as to how it should be performed in space.

"Stage-Centered" Vision of Mise-en-scène

To move on from these philological viewpoints, perhaps one needs the radicality of an aesthetician like Thies Lehmann for whom "mise-en-scène is an artistic practice that is strictly unforeseeable from the perspective of the text."[7] This radical position denies any causal connection between text and stage by granting mise-en-scène the sovereign power to decide on its aesthetic choices. And in fact this is precisely how many directors proceed, from Wilson to Grüber, from Mesguich to Heiner Müller. They prepare text, music, scenography, actors' performances in an autonomous way, and do not realize the final "mix" of these different aspects until the end of their process, in the same way one edits a film. In these examples, the text no longer enjoys an anterior or exclusive status; it is only one of a number of performance materials, and it neither centralizes nor organizes the nonverbal elements. On the other hand, Lehmann's thesis is virtually untenable in relation to mise-en-scènes of texts read and known in ways that are "inevitable," so to speak (such texts might be very well known, or simply based on characters and situations of which it would be difficult to be unaware); for spectators will not fail to interrogate the relation between artistic practice and text, even if only to ask themselves how the stage could ignore what the text suggests to us at a particular juncture.

In the case of a mise-en-scène in which an understanding of a text can still be discerned, I propose the following compromise (in relation to Lehmann's clear-cut affirmation). Mise-en-scène is not dictated by a reading of the text alone; however, readings do provide practitioners with suggestions for an experimental and progressive placement of enunciatory situations—in other words with a choice of "given circumstances" (Stanislavsky), which propose a perspective for an understanding of the text, activate a reading of it, and generate interpretations that a reader undoubtedly would not have foreseen, emerging from the intervention of actors and other artists involved in the stage practice.

Let us conclude, therefore, in favor of a compromise between a text-centered and a stage-centered position. There is no sense in wanting to tie mise-en-scène to the potential or incomplete elements of a text, even if one always ends up finding a textual indication on which to hang the mise-en-scène "legitimately." There is no "pre-mise-en-scène" already inscribed in the dramatic text, although the text can only be read by imagining the dramatic situations in which the action can unfold.

What are the implications of this for the analysis of a performance containing a dramatic text? To what should analysis be attentive?

- At all costs it should avoid comparing a mise-en-scène with the text that seems to be its source. The text is not some indisputable reference point to which analysis must return in order to analyze a performance.
- It must painstakingly separate what it knows of the written text, through previous knowledge "on the page," from what is discerned of the text as articulated on stage, and thus expressed in a very precise enunciatory situation that its first task is to describe.
- Therefore it is a question of separating one's thoughts on the study of written texts from that of stage practices involving texts.

A common tendency of contemporary mise-en-scène is to deny any link between texts and stage practices. Certain directors seek out texts that theoretically cannot be performed on a stage, or resist being performed. Heiner Müller even made this the criterion of a productive theater: "It's only when a text cannot be realized with the existing theater that it becomes productive and interesting for the theater."[8]

So today mise-en-scène is no longer the passage of a text to the stage; sometimes it is an installation, in other words a bringing together of diverse stage practices (lighting, plastic arts, improvisation), without the possibility of establishing a hierarchy between them, and without the text assuming the role of magnetic pole for the rest of the performance.

In that sense, it is the performing of a text that provides initial indications as to the text's meaning, and in particular the status one should accord it within the analyzed performance.

Status of the Staged Text

This question also concerns performance analysis, for it requires the spectator to establish the status of the text in a mise-en-scène.

Autonomy or Dependence of the Text

In order to establish the status of the dramatic text one perceives in a mise-en-scène, one must first establish whether it exists independently of the mise-en-scène, as a published or publishable text: in other words, as a legible or at least audible text existing in a form other than stage orality.

In the case of a classic or modern text, by definition this text exists independently of and anterior to its stage enunciation; therefore one can always reread it and compare this reading with that proposed by the mise-en-scène.

It is equally possible that the text of the play did not exist as a starting point, and that it was elaborated gradually in the course of rehearsals; or even that it was introduced right at the very end of rehearsals, even though the stage score had already been definitively fixed. So there is no sense in searching for a link between what is shown and what is said.

Finally, it is possible for a text not to acquire any semantic value; in other words, one is not in a position to read or hear it, it constitutes nothing more than verbal decor, a music comprised of sounds or words whose arrangement makes no sense. Such is the case, for example, with Robert Wilson's text for *The Golden Windows*. There is no point reading the script (although it has been published), for not only did it not exist during the creation of the mise-en-scène; above all it simply comprises vocal and rhythmic material to be used as a plastic element without any claim to semantic referentiality—so it would be quite fruitless to launch oneself into scholarly exegeses.

One thing is certain: our evaluation of the intrinsic value of a text evolves over time. What appears illegible to us today was perhaps legible formerly for an audience familiar with the relevant allusions and cultural practices (nineteenth-century vaudeville, for example); or it becomes legible with the passage of time, once an audience has the keys and rules to decipher it (e.g., Beckett's theater has become "classic," in the sense that it is now known and understood by most spectators). Therefore one must be very careful in determining a text's legibility, for it is always relative. It would be better to stick to the criterion of knowing whether or not a text is known to the audience, like the classic play, myth, or news item at the source of a mise-en-scène.

Specificity of the Dramatic Text

An examination of performances currently using texts clearly reveals that all sorts of texts are used on stage, and not only dramatic texts written for theater. So it seems out of the question to limit texts for the stage to a specific type of dramatic writing, or to talk of "the specific character of theater writing,"[9] as Vinaver does. Moreover, it does not seem possible to define this specifically dramatic writing in a transhistorical, universal manner. But the only thing one can affirm is that each historical moment, and each dramaturgical and stage practice corresponding with that moment, possesses its own criteria of dramaticity (way of setting up a conflict) and of theatricality (manner of using the stage). Consequently, instead of attempting a phenomenological, universal, and abstract definition of the specificity of dramatic writing, it would be more useful to deal with each particular case historically—in other words, by examining how a text has been conceived in terms of a certain practice of language and of the stage, and recognizing what dramaturgical processes are privileged. For performance analysis, it is advisable to determine what a particular stage practice enables us to understand of the text, what meanings it opens up or empties out. We know that every text, and the dramatic text in particular, metamorphoses in the course of history; it gives rise to a series of different interpretations, sometimes called *concretizations* (in reception theory).

Once these different concretizations have been outlined, along with the horizon of expectation of the reader/spectator and the historical framework, one is in a position to enumerate the specific properties of the dramatic writing in question.[10]

Consequently historical knowledge of the production and reception of a text paves the way for its dramaturgical analysis, for increased awareness of elements that affect text as much as stage, in particular

- The determination of action and actants
- The structures of space, time, rhythm
- The articulation and establishment of the plot

Dramaturgical analysis of text "at the origin" or "at the heart" of a mise-en-scène is the primary reflex of performance analysis; it clarifies and systematizes the majority of isolated perceptions and provides information on the way stage and text influence one another permanently.

Evidently dramaturgical analysis is applicable primarily to classical or figurative works, when a story is told through actions effected by characters. Nevertheless, even for texts devoid of plot, character, and mimetic representation, dramaturgical analysis has something to contribute—if only in elucidating the textual mechanisms or the language games at the surface of the word.

The relativity of the specificity of dramatic writing (and therefore its nonspecificity) problematizes any method of textual analysis that makes a claim to universality, connecting it with some mythical essence of the dramatic. Therefore analysis of performance containing text should start by specifying the "given circumstances" of the text, but without restricting them to psychological situations, as Stanislavsky advised. It should locate the text historically, at the moment of its production as well as that of its current use within the mise-en-scène, the moment of its inscription in a sociocultural context. Contrary to Michel Vinaver's assertion, one cannot read a dramatic text without imagining a concrete situation, which depends on the ideological conditions of that particular moment, nor without having at one's disposal a minimal amount of preexisting knowledge of the text and the mode of performance.[11]

This historicizing process also involves the text/performance interrelation, which one must be wary of approaching in the absolute, eternal terms of an immutable theory set in concrete. A few major historical references will be sufficient here:

- In the era of French classicism, that of Corneille, Racine, and beyond, up until about 1750, a rhetorical system regulated the relations between text and stage, using strictly codified postures and vocal inflections that were supposed to fix emotions. A performance consisted of respecting and reproducing this system.
- From 1750, with Diderot, and increasingly so until 1880, a demand for realism and a reclamation of authentic romantic emotions launched a broadside on classicism's gestural rhetoric; this tended to impose an individualized reading of the text, with gestural language and scenic interpretation breaking away from stereotypes.[12]
- After 1880, with the appearance of the role of director, increasingly the text seems to be a relative and variable element, tied to the historical context—as variable as the gaze of the reader/spectator (and consequently the director) can be. The text was now displaced in relation to a monolithic stage; it was decentered, even dispersed by psychoanalysis that announced the displacement of the subject. The mise-en-scène, assuming overall charge of the text to be interpreted, was supposed to bridge the historical, cultural, and hermeneutic distance between the text and its new audience.
- From 1880 to about 1960, mise-en-scène consolidated its position and coincided with the emergence and apogee of theatrical avant-gardes. Whatever the particular moment or current of practice, one witnessed a radical critique of the text in its pretension to rationality and universal-

ity. In place of the linguistic text, mise-en-scène sought to substitute a "language of the stage" (Artaud) or a "gestus" (Brecht)—the emanation of a visual mode of thought controlled by the mise-en-scène, which would put an end to logocentrism once and for all. According to the classical conception, that of Copeau for example, mise-en-scène constitutes "the outlining of a dramatic action. It is the ensemble of movements, gestures and attitudes, the concordance of physiognomies, voices and silences, the totality of the stage performance, emanating from a unique way of thinking that conceives, regulates and harmonizes it."[13] The director had gradually replaced the author as authority controlling the production of meaning and the stable signification of the text. In turn, it would not be long before the director was suspected of closing meaning down: of being an authoritarian subject whose authority neither the (ex-)author, nor the actor, nor the spectator would feel disposed to recognize for much longer. And this leads us directly to the negation of mise-en-scène, to "post–mise-en-scène."

■ Post–mise-en-scène (after 1960): in these times that no longer know how to describe themselves except to say that they are "postmodern," the director is now accused of being the one whose supposed systematicity and authoritarianism are harmful to the productivity of performance. Both stage and text are now no more than open "signifying practices" (which means one can get them to say whatever one wants, and that theory is nothing more than a game). The alternative is no longer (as it was formerly) between a text having a signified to transmit "faithfully" and a text one can use as building material; neither is it any longer between a *metaphorical* type of mise-en-scène (in which the stage metaphorizes the text's meaning) and a *scenographic* type (in which the only writing is that of the stage).[14] Instead, the alternative is now between the pretension to control overall meaning and the renunciation of all foreseeable meaning. In the latter case, in fact mise-en-scène is only an installation; all of its materials are installed in a space-time and are activated to the full extent of their possibilities, while spectators are quite content to observe fortuitous interactions and to see what happens and who wins.

This review of some historical stages still provides many models for contemporary performance, and so it seems useful to outline them, albeit all too briefly. In fact, they often coincide within one mise-en-scène, and seem to illustrate well the diversity of relations between stage and text. One should relativize these relations further by comparing them with completely different cultural contexts. Then it would become apparent that whereas Western culture and the most beautiful feather in its cap, the theatrical mise-en-scène of literary texts, consider the text as source or reference for a performance, it works otherwise in other cultures. In African culture, for example, it is quite appropriate to reconsider the dividing lines between text, movement, dance, and music. The text is no longer the focal point; it could be replaced or taken over by a completely different medium—for example, by talking drums conveying a text that white people cannot understand (in Soyinka's *Death and the King's Horseman*). But for Western mise-en-scène, text remains the one element that enables us to compare the major types of mise-en-scène.

Typologies of Mise-en-scène

In relation to contemporary mise-en-scène, it is very difficult to get one's bearings in the multiplicity of experiences. However, one can suggest a few typologies, in particular if one returns to the categories that emerged from the history of theater at the turn of the last century.

Historical Typology
These categories are well known and frequently used:

- *Naturalist* mise-en-scène: the actor's performance, scenography, diction, and rhythm all claim to provide a mimesis of the real; for example, Stanislavsky's productions of Chekhov's plays at the Moscow Arts Theatre.
- *Realist* mise-en-scène: the real is no longer rendered photographically, as in the preceding case, but is codified in an ensemble of signs that are deemed to be pertinent; mimesis is selective, critical, inclusive, and systematic; for example, the mise-en-scènes of Brecht, or of Planchon in the 1960s and 1970s.
- *Symbolist* mise-en-scène: the reality represented is the idealized essence of the real world; for example, Meyerhold's 1905 mise-en-scène for *The Death of Tintagiles*, and certain Robert Wilson productions.
- *Expressionist* mise-en-scène: particular aspects and features of reality are clearly emphasized, as if to express the personal attitude of the director; for example, the productions of Fritz Kortner or Matthias Langhoff.
- *Epic* mise-en-scène: it narrates by means of the actor, the scenography and the plot; for example, the work of Piscator and of Brecht in the past, and of actor-storytellers today.

■ *Theatricalized* mise-en-scène: instead of imitating the real, the signs of performance insist on play and fiction, and an acceptance of the theater as fiction and convention; for example, the mise-en-scènes of Meyerhold in the past, or of Vitez and Mesguich more recently.

Other aesthetics have also provided model performance forms, by setting up new stylistic categories and raising to an aesthetic and theoretical status particular historical characteristics arising from concrete circumstances.

The case of productions of so-called classic texts should be examined separately, for the relation to the classic text varies considerably.

Mise-en-Scènes of Classic Texts
This typology is based on the conception that a mise-en-scène stems, implicitly or explicitly, from the dramatic text: does the mise-en-scène attach itself to the letter of the text, to the story narrated, to the raw materials the text offers, to the multiple meanings it allows, to the rhetoric that animates it, or to the myth in which it takes root?

■ The *archaeological reconstruction* of a performance attempts to rediscover the text as it may have been presented (to the best of one's knowledge) when the play was first created. Such mise-en-scène is preoccupied with archaeological details only, without reevaluating the new relation between this rather questionable reconstruction and the contemporary spectator's horizon of expectation.
■ *Historicization* is the exact opposite of archaeological reconstruction. With little concern for the historical exactitude of performance conditions at the original creation of a work, it endeavors to relativize this perspective, and to rediscover in the narrative a (hi)story that concerns us directly, adapting situations, characters, and conflicts as required. In the 1950s and 1960s, this led to a "sociological" mise-en-scène in which the text was illuminated by all sorts of socioeconomic indications (Planchon, Strehler).
■ The *recuperation* of a text as raw material is the most radical method for dealing with the dramatic text. In contemporary practice, it bears a number of different names: actualization, modernization, adaptation, rewriting, and so on. It includes many working processes that not only modify the letter of the text, but insistently work at not being interested in the text, treating it as pretext for variations or rewritings; which makes this practice of recuperation unpredictable and untheorizable.
■ *The mise-en-scène of possible meanings* does not aim to reconstruct an

earlier type of performance or to adapt a play to our own times; instead it aims to open the text to a plurality of readings that contradict and are in dialogue with each other, refusing to be reduced to a final overall meaning. The plurality of possible meanings is achieved by means of a multiplication of enunciatory voices (actors, scenographer, musician, etc.), all of whom work for themselves; this multiplication stems from a refusal to hierarchize signs, to divide them up into major and minor systems, and ultimately from a desire to give rise to "an infinite number of interpretations."[15]

▪ *Vocalizing the text* avoids any aprioristic interpretation of a text, particularly in terms of a reading of situations, of characters' motivations, or of the world of the play, so as to focus on a rhetorical and vocal treatment of the linguistic text; it suggests actors approach their roles through a breath-based, rhythmic reading of the text. Systematized by Copeau and Jouvet, then Vitez, this reading technique starts resolutely from the text as respiratory trace of the author, hoping subsequently to tap into the text's meaning once the actors are able to convey it through their diction and the rhythmic structures of their vocalizations.

▪ *The return to myth* represents a negation of historicization, recuperation, and vocalization. It takes no interest in the dramaturgy of the text, its forms and codes, so as to go directly to the heart of the plot and of its founding myth.

These six categories rarely occur in a pure state; productions often combine several of the respective characteristics above, thus making any strict typology problematic. So we will have to content ourselves with major distinctions such as those suggested by Pavis or Lehmann.

Auto-, Ideo- and Intertextual Dimensions

Any *text* (in the semiological sense of the word) is defined by its autotextual, ideotextual, and intertextual dimensions.

Autotextual mise-en-scène endeavors not to go outside the boundaries of the stage, not to make reference to an external reality. This category includes "archaeological" mise-en-scènes, which reconstruct the performance conditions of a particular time and shut themselves off from modern perspectives, as well as mise-en-scènes that are hermetically closed around a director's choice or thesis; such productions do not tolerate any external perspective that might impact upon their orientation. This was the case with avant-garde mise-en-scènes, in particular symbolist work (Craig,

Appia); it is also the case with Robert Wilson. Such productions invent and isolate a coherent scenic universe, closed in upon itself in an autonomous aesthetic system.

Ideotextual mise-en-scène, inversely, opens itself up to the psychological or social world within which it is inscribed. It loses its texture and its autonomy in favor of ready-made knowledges and discourses: ideologies, explanations of the world, concrete references to social practices. All mise-enscène that alludes to social reality produces a subtextual or metatextual commentary—and this connects it back to the external world. Mise-enscènes that endeavor to engage with social reality belong to this category, that is, so-called Brechtian productions. This category also includes pedagogical plays, social parables, work that uses actual documentary material.

Intertextual mise-en-scène ensures a necessary mediation between the autotextuality of the first category and the ideological reference of the second. It relativizes mise-en-scène's desire for autonomy, locates itself within an ongoing series of interpretations, demarcating in a polemical way its differences from other solutions and other kinds of mise-en-scène. Often the mise-en-scène of a very well known classical text is necessarily intertextual, for it alludes to preceding productions, or at least to the major ways in which the enigma of that text has been resolved in the past. Vitez proceeded in this way in his productions of Molière, which invariably included possible allusions to one or more of its predecessors.

Metaphor, Scenography, Event

The final and most recent typology, another very general one, is that of Hans-Thies Lehmann (1989), which distinguishes between metaphorical, scenographic, and eventlike mise-en-scènes.

- *Metaphoric* mise-en-scène uses the stage as a metaphor of the dramatic text that it comments upon and illustrates by scenic means. Amateur directors often proceed in this way, using the stage as an illustration of how they have understood the text.
- *Scenographic* mise-en-scène constitutes an autonomous scenic writing; from Artaud to Wilson, it uses the stage as an entirely separate language. Signification is at the discretion of the observer, as simply the possibility of a synthesis.
- Mise-en-scène is *eventlike* when the stage is presented as an event that owes nothing to a reading of the text, but provides a configuration or an installation, a situation characterized by the copresence of production

and reception, of actors and spectators. Lehmann gives the example of a Viennese group, Angelus Novus, who produced a continuous reading of Homer's *Iliad* lasting twenty-two hours.

This typology relates fairly closely to that of Robert Abirached,[16] who also distinguishes three possible orders of mise-en-scène:

- Mise-en-scène wholly bound by and compliant with the text (Lehmann's "metaphoric")
- Mise-en-scène having an absolute autonomy and possessing its own scenic language (Lehmann's "scenographic")
- Mise-en-scène making use of texts, rather than being at their service (Lehmann's "eventlike")

Whatever typology one retains, the categories remain very general and at best only draw out a few indicatory properties or tendencies. They provide an initial orientation enabling a mise-en-scène to be placed within existing frameworks, although this may be dangerous if the particular mise-en-scène actually endeavors to occupy new territory. More often than not, this orientation goes hand in hand with a critical evaluation that one must differentiate from a straightforward semiological analysis; it is closer to dramatic criticism. Although it tends to be avoided by the deliberately functionalist and intellectualist approach of semiology, critical evaluation is nevertheless an integral component of critical theory as it is understood here.

Treatment of the Text in the Public Space of Performance

An analysis of the text as articulated on stage must concern itself in a concrete way with all of the processes that the text has been through, and continues to undergo, in the mise-en-scène, in terms of the manner in which it is treated through stage means.

Plasticity of the Text

Once a text is enunciated on stage, in whatever form, it is treated plastically, musically, gesturally; it has relinquished the abstraction and potentiality of the written text so as to be activated in performance. Colored by voice and gesture (in accordance with its "coloration"),[17] the text becomes texture; it is embodied by the actors, as if they are able to "physicalize" it, to absorb it, to breathe it in before breathing it out, to hold it within themselves or, on the contrary, to discharge it, to make it available to others or to retain it partly for themselves. Their approach is physical, before it is psychological and abstract:

> So a reading of a text by an actor in no way resembles a learning process outside of meaning in which psychology strives to make it comprehensible to us. The text *works*, it shifts in its texture; and it is transformed through the very fact that the body itself has meaning, and always keeps mobile the *directions* of meaning that constitute the *style* of the text. This is the way of temporality, for the body here neither acts nor speaks but is the site in which all creation originates.[18]

Here Fédida is talking about text in general, but his words are all the more valid for the dramatic text, which becomes *scenic* and *theatrical* as soon as mise-en-scène turns it into action.

The "Given Circumstances"

As soon as it has been enunciated, "articulated" on stage, the text brings to the fore what Stanislavsky called the "given circumstances," and what linguists call the situation of the enunciation. The text is distributed among different speakers; the mise-en-scène has clarified who speaks, to whom and why; paraverbal elements provide immediate information about the verbal message. The dispersal of the word into the various utterances of different characters, and therefore the multiplicity and apparent equivalence of different perspectives, can be disconcerting to the spectator. However, they oblige her to watch closely for indications as to the "given circumstances," to follow the characters' motivations and the superobjective of the play, to attempt a dramaturgical synthesis and to organize the scenic material around its major axes.

The division of text among different speakers plays on the discontinuity of the word in theater; it requires us to examine "what occurs between one utterance and another in an exchange, and what is at the heart of each reply. What kind of movement takes place to engender the shift from one position to the following position."[19] Mise-en-scène clarifies and specifies this transition from one position to another; analysis endeavors to redis-cover the logic according to which it occurs. Therefore, finding a text's meaning entails gathering information as to the ways in which the mise-en-scène secures and represents this logic. The work of the actor consists of complementing the work of the author: "The richer a text is, the poorer the actor's music must be; the poorer a text, the richer the actor's music."[20] It follows that analysis must evaluate the respective "riches" of text and per-formance and understand the system of their correlation. One must show what the text receives through the actor's performance, as well as what the performance reveals of the hidden richness of the text: something very difficult to describe, undoubtedly, since one must establish what the stage gives rise to in the text.

Reconstituting the System of Stage Enunciation

In order to describe what arises in the text, it is useful to reconstitute the system of stage enunciation; this is achieved by considering the factors in play and their hierarchical structure. This structure is never fixed, but as the mime artist Decroux noted, there is a scale of expressive factors, the word being the strongest of all:

> In the order of importance of the elements of expression, gesture comes last. First of all, there is the word as written and therefore read with the eyes; then there is diction; then the correct posture; finally, that leaves gesture.[21]

Any analysis should reconsider this hierarchy of word, diction (which is "a kind of mime, the vocal form of mime"), posture, and gesture. One must venture an evaluation of the proportionate amounts of text and gesture; a production's gestural strategy (which is ultimately what I understand by *mise-en-scène*) consists of either communicating or silencing a particular part or aspect of the text. It is always revealing to observe the gesture on which text is said, and its particular rhythm, once one realizes (with Decroux) that "a gesture deployed without acceleration, slowing down, or jerkiness, does not distract from the text."[22] It is instructive to examine the ways in which a mise-en-scène sets out the text as it unfolds: whether or not it allows spectators time to be transported by it, to immerse themselves in their own thought processes, to ponder, to draw closer or to withdraw, distancing themselves from the words.

Voicing the Text

The voice also provides valuable information for apprehending the emergence of meaning in the text. It should be the object of a psychological decoding (if it conveys situations drawn from ordinary communication); psychological analysis occurs quite naturally and provides information on the motivations of characters, particularly by means of analysis of paraverbal elements of communication. In addition, it gives a corporeal and material dimension to the text that is much more difficult to perceive than emotions and motivations. This materiality, the quality Barthes called "the grain of the voice," is the incarnation of the text in the body of the actors. An analysis of text delivered by actors requires a baring of their corporeal sensibility and an analysis of the effect produced on the spectator:

> Reciting or singing in front of others entails showing them something of one's body; it also means discovering, in a flash, a given diffuse sensibility of our body. . . . The voice is bodily *matter*—preobjective *element* (quite unlike the objectivity of our ocular relation to the person and their capacity to represent themselves).[23]

When the voice of an actor reaches us, the vocal mise-en-scène of the text has already occurred; the spectator receives a vocal copy of the text, so she does not have to activate it herself, as a reader does. It is this vocality, this concrete and personal signing of the message, that constitutes its originality and that analysis should endeavor to describe.

It is also useful to determine which of the resonators used are prioritized. It is a matter of sensing the part of the body from which words seem to arise, how the actor has controlled their emission and the ways in which their meaning and impact are affected by bodily postures. A standard diction exercise consists of corporeally displacing the point from which words emerge, varying one's posture, adjusting the meaning of words through the manner in which they are delivered; similarly spectators, receiving a text embodied by the actors, should try to imagine the impact of their physical enunciation on the production of meaning on stage and in the text.

Kinesthetic Factors of the Text

The text articulated on stage can be felt in its vibratory quality, as if the text were able to trace in space-time the trajectory of its directions and moves; its intonatory and rhetorical schema is immediately figurable; a word to the wise is enough. Analysis focuses especially on the following particularities:

- The intonatory schema of sentences and speeches
- The mimo-posturo-verbal sequence, that is, the way in which the message moves imperceptibly from body to posture, and to voice.
- An enunciation's logical and rhetorical points of support, the sum of which constitute the actor's underscore
- The coloration and origin of the voice; where does the voice come from? Does it emanate from deep in the body and the breath, organically supported by the body as a whole? Or is it in fact a voice "prompted" (Finter) from outside, artificially grafted on to a body extraneous to its source?
- The "carriage" of the text (in the way one talks of the "carriage" of a head); the ways in which the text is carried are examined

- by a voice, an intonation, extended by a gesture, as if from a rocket launcher, or on the other hand held back within the speaker, spoken as an aside;
- toward the exterior or toward the interior; the speaker endeavors to reach the other, or keeps the meaning to herself, she speaks without projection;
- by means of the modalization of what is said in all its possible nuances: affirmative/negative, dubitative/assertive; the numerous modalities that are of a physical or kinesthetic order, rather than decorative or psychological;
- as a vocal or corporeal punctuation; verbal and gestural phrases require stopping points, pauses for clarification and figuration of structural relief; these provide contrast.

Text and Paraverbal Signs

Text needs to be considered in the light of how one hears and feels it evolve through systems of nonlinguistic signs. One should examine the effects of interaction and correspondence[24] between two or more systems. One must ask why certain sign systems are traditionally (in productions of classic texts, for instance) at the service of others—as lighting and music are at the service of text and its maximal legibility in the case of the classics.[25] The desired effect is of insistence, confirmation, redundancy, or clarification.

Vectors of the Text

Texts have a distinct propensity to exploit their neighbors, to base themselves on them or amalgamate with them. For example, a text often relies on

- The conventional system of emotions and postures, that is, on the rhetoricization of the body (in the eighteenth century)
- The space, which structures and fixes the major reference points in outlining and establishing the score
- The general rhythmic pattern of the performance (in particular constituted by music, diction, the tempo-rhythm of physical actions)

Effects of Synchronization/Desynchronization

Between text and paraverbal elements, there is

- *synchronization* when each signifying system tends to coincide, in terms of its rhythm, with the others: a "symphonic" effect in which the part blends with the whole and reinforces its coherence;
- *desynchronization* when dissonances between rhythms are perceptible, particularly when one system is sufficiently strong not to assimilate with the others;
- an effect of *syncresis* when a sonic phenomenon and a visual phenomenon coincide. Syncresis, a word coined from the terms *synchronism* and *synthesis,* is "the irresistible and spontaneous conjunction or suture that is produced between a specific sonic phenomenon and a specific visual phenomenon when they occur at exactly the same time, in a way that is independent of all rational logic."[26] This is the case in cinema (the focus of Chion's description here), but also in theater when the text conjoins with a paraverbal phenomenon in an unexpected way: for example, when the repetition of a word or phrase (e.g., "le pauvre homme!" in *Tartuffe*) is the repeated signal to the speaker or his partners for some shared mimic action or stage business, for example, eyes raised to the sky (see chapter 4).

Double System for Perception/Codification/Memorization

The force (which is, above all, mnemotechnical) of these sudden conjunctures of text and paraverbal signs stems from a radical difference in nature between verbal and visual codes.

Visual codes are suitable for global, spatial, and synchronic information; several systems of visual signs can be perceived synchronically and synthetically in their spatial coexistence.

Verbal codes are subject to the spoken sequence, to an irreversible temporality; they are suitable not only for language and discourse, but also for the narrative structures of plot. Our perception of them is therefore successive, analytical, discriminatory, our memorization of them conceptual and abstract.

When a spectator "hears" a text articulated on stage, she is no longer in a position to dissociate it from her visual environment. So two kinds of codification and memorization come into play, with their different but complementary properties; as a result they consolidate the aesthetic experience and make analysis problematic insofar as it must dismantle what is one body.

Verbalization or Figurability?

In addition to the problem of analysis and of dissociating the verbal and the visual, a further difficulty lies in the difference between the mental decoding of visual signs into words and an ineffable aesthetic experience. According to psycholinguists,

> from childhood, a human being is . . . accustomed to *mentally* decoding *all* denominational (verbal) signs. A "percept" is only effected when one gives a name, mentally, to any perceived object.[27]

According to Simon Thorpe, when we leaf through a magazine full of images, we are able to "identify the majority of the images perceived, and also to find the verbal 'labels' necessary to describe them."[28]

But what about in theater? Evidently we are able to recognize all sorts of percepts on the stage that we could name. But this would be to confuse the stage with a fashion catalog, rather than attempting to bring these objects into relief by naming them systematically. In fact, we perceive all sorts of other materials that remain in the state of signifiers, forms and colors that disallow translation into words—the perception of which constitutes the spectator's aesthetic experience. The stage and its images, music and its sounds, text and its vocality all resist any figurative recognition; they remain in the order of what Lyotard designated as *figural*.[29] Much contemporary stage work, for example physical theater, discourages any verbalization, immersing the spectator within an ineffable experience. "Vectorization of desire" limits itself to referencing some of the transit points of the gaze and of spectatorial desire, without ever naming the proposed route or the zones it traverses. The unnameable is part of the plan.

The Text Treated Electronically

Nowadays, the text is not only processed by the actor's body, but also by the means afforded by electronic sound equipment. The voice can be "extracted" from the natural body of the actor, treated electroacoustically and reinserted into the body of the speaker with wholly different properties. In this way the relationship between body and word is destabilized, distorted, reworked, and yet maintained live. Processed in such a way, the text loses its stable identity, becoming a very plastic material that loses its central or primary position, and intertwines with other signs in the performance, thus becoming desublimated. Opening the way to all sorts of manipulations, the electronic text tends to abolish the distinction between language and music, between the arbitrariness of linguistic signs and the iconicity of visual signs, as well as between presence and absence, human being and object. The electronic text is infinitely manipulable; it can be reduplicated, extended spatially, its gaps filled with noises of all kinds, broken up and transmitted to various sources in the overall sound space of stage and auditorium.

Therefore it is the text/stage pairing, and above all the bonding of text and stage, that is challenged here. Not only must one get used to not deriving an entire performance from a text; one must also look closely at the ways in which a text *feels its way*, and sometimes gets lost and desperate, within the spatiotemporal elements of its configuration or installation on stage. The text creeps among these elements, resisting the fatal attraction of an actress's mimicry, of a place, or of an old story. It is a substance that insinuates itself everywhere, but that no longer commands or guarantees anything, a plastic material no closer to the source of meaning than any of the other stage components.

The principal difficulty of analyzing a text within a mise-en-scène is in not confusing the reading and the analysis we would make of it while reading, with reception and the impact it produces in the spectator. These are two different perspectives, which are obviously interconnected, but which must remain distinct. Between text and stage, union and uniformity are impossible:

> The union of text and stage, which is the primary aim of theater, in some ways goes against nature. It is only ever realized through compromises, partial and unstable balancing acts. Sometimes it is the stage that is subordinated to the text; a certain tradition in the West wants it that way. . . . Sometimes the text is submissive to the stage. . . ; such is the rule in all non-European traditions.[30]

Evidently it would be quite wrong to deprive ourselves, in the analysis of text in performance, of the range of procedures for textual analysis that literary theory has refined over the centuries. The methodology proposed by Vinaver and his collaborators can serve as a starting point, but it must of necessity be verified and completed through a historical approach to texts.[31]

Each new stage practice changes the ways in which the dramatic text is treated. The current tendency is to separate text and stage radically, not to make the stage into a metaphor of the text, or one the match of the other, but to disconnect listening and sight; text and stage are no longer consubstantial, they are dissociated. The stage is no longer the site of the text's enunciation and actualization; it is no longer its metaphor, but its absolute alterity. One sees this in the work of Heiner Müller or Robert Wilson, where everything is done to make the mise-en-scène totally "foreign" to the text. Or, for example, in Tadeusz Kantor's work, where the actor plays with the text like a cat with a ball of wool, pulling back from it or drawing closer to it, juggling with the phonetics of words, making signifiers vibrate: the actor as "a mill to grind the text." The text no longer has to be represented, staged, made explicit, nor even, as in Meyerhold, divorced from the plasticity of the stage; it is in an entirely different universe where the endeavor is (as in Kantor's Emballage Theatre) "to telescope the body of the text with the theatrical body."[32] Such telescoping problematizes all theory on the production of meaning and the relations between text and stage. At least until that time when the telescoping ends up repeating itself, and lays itself open to theory . . .

Part 3
The Conditions of Reception

8

Psychological and Psychoanalytical Approaches

Having surveyed the principal components of performance, and having undertaken the Herculean tasks of a spectator-analyst (more of a Sisyphus than an Oedipus), one might well hope to enjoy a brief respite to stop and take in the seven wonders of the performance world in one look. Unfortunately, this would mean we had failed to recognize the complexity of the undertaking; for the sum of these tasks falls a long way short of providing the key to their analysis. Therefore, we need to reflect on the attributes of reception and the overall methodology available to us for dealing in a coherent way with the mass of information gathered by the spectator—a method inspired by phenomenology, since its interest is in the way in which the spectator experiences "the world as it is lived, rather than the world as it is objectified, abstracted, and conceptualized."[1] It is a question of the way (or ways) of looking that the spectator brings to bear on the performance, in more or less conscious and extensive ways.

One can imagine the spectator at the epicenter of a scenic earthquake, endowed with three kinds of vision: psychological, sociological, and anthropological. These three perspectives are distinct but complementary, forming many concentric circles that widen individual and psychological perspectives endlessly, taking them toward a sociological vision and to an anthropology, where the stage work reconnects with the surrounding human reality of the spectator.

From out of this seismic catastrophe emerges our phenomenological project of describing reception in the light of the three principal perspectives on way(s) of looking: psychological, sociological (chapter 2), and finally anthropological (chapter 3). Each of these perspectives will distinguish certain details more or less clearly, the field of vision becoming increasingly peripheral and global as it gradually encompasses anthropology.

In venturing toward a phenomenology of performance perception, one locates oneself resolutely on the side of the spectator and the audience. The difficulty lies in distinguishing between these two instances, and in adapting for each of them an appropriate and differentiated set of conceptual tools. The audience is not simply the sum of spectators, it does not obey the same laws as individual psychology; and this authorizes our dealing separately with spectator and audience, through psychoanalysis and then sociology.

It should be stated at the outset that, in this context, one can do no more than sketch a psychology and a psychoanalysis of the spectator. These areas soon slip free from the theater specialist's vigilance; and I am simply interested here in the "reception" of a performance work, and not in theater's relation to the unconscious in general. Therefore I will confine myself to some core operative processes that could be directly accessible to the users of performances.

Gestalt Theory

Gestalt theory—"psychological theory that has particularly emphasized the aspects of configuration and, more generally, of totality in psychological life"[2]—provides a general framework that favors description/interpretation by the spectator. When applied to theatrical performance, it reminds us that analysis should focus on an ensemble of given aspects, not on isolated details. Indeed, as the Belgian theorist Carlos Tindemans states:

> Totality is different from the sum of its parts, and the essential quality of this view is that the perception of an event or an object cannot be predicted exactly by means of the knowledge acquired through the perception of different parts of the event or object.[3]

Tindemans judiciously suggests dividing the perception of performance into synthetic temporal blocks, for "we perceive all elements simultaneously as total segments of time, as synthetic scenic units." So we perceive a sequence of units, what Garcia-Martinez has called *rhythmic frames*, "the mental trace of the rhythms of initial moments that become the reference point for subsequent rhythmic development";[4] this is what is defined in this book as vectorizations of a performance, which construct meaning and rhythm as a sequence of *oriented* frames or segments. Tindemans conceives of these frames or segments as "interactive moments between the actors/characters that represent active and reactive currents of energy." This dynamic—whether one calls it focalization, interaction, or vectorization—engenders the movement of a work, its meaning as much as its rhythm. Spectators locate and reference it, experiencing it with increasing ease as they participate in its creation through their quality of listening and their reactions. Perception and reception therefore comprise an act of rhythmic construction of a work: "Theater doesn't happen to someone, they make theater 'happen' to them."[5] And yet the scenic material is already oriented, molded in a certain direction, that is, *vectorized*. This conception of vectorization is closely connected with Michel Chion's as adopted by him for cinema: "The dramatization of shots, the orientation towards a future, a goal, and the creation of a feeling of imminence and expectation. The shot goes somewhere, and it is oriented in time."[6]

This book thus proposes the hypothesis that all mise-en-scène is organized according to the operations and processes of vectorization, and that global signs exist—*signs of gestalt:* in other words, totalizing vectors that structure a mise-en-scène as a whole, to which all individual signifiers that spectators are able to recognize will be subordinated. These gestalt signs constitute the principal vectorization, the frame within which everything is legible—at least until a new vectorization emerges to efface what preceded it.

Above all, gestalt theory evaluates the cognitive processes of the spectator. However, spectators are not "simply" intellectuals, cerebral beings, computers with human faces; they are also participants, reactive and affective beings. A performance contains a wide range of stimulations, suggestions, elements intended to keep spectators alert or to move them—to make them participate in an event that they do not always face frontally, but that surrounds, seizes, and transports them.

Participation in the Event

The Effect Produced

Although rather difficult to evaluate, the effect produced on a spectator is at the very heart of participation in an event. Many contemporary performances are characterized by a plethora of very powerful sensory stimuli. In the Welsh group Brith Gof's *Camlann,* directed by Mike Pearson,[7] for example, the multiple stimuli that act directly on corporeal memory include the noise of empty oil drums, the disturbing darkness of the factory space, the acrid smell of smoke. Consequently, in order to measure the effect produced, one must be particularly sensitive to the performance as real, material action (and not as production of images, signs, and metaphors). The body of the actor, like that of the spectator, belongs to a real em-bodied being, rather than to some abstract "model" spectator. The spectator's tonal-postural modifications become of interest here; haptic, tactile, and olfactory perception, kinesthesia—all these senses that are often sterilized or anesthetized—are here reinstated.

Evaluation of the effect produced entails being able to feel the energetic charge of a work, and the discharge produced in the spectator:

> In order to judge a work of art, one must therefore activate this notion of energy: does this work touch us? does it create a disturbance in our sensibility, in our imaginary? does one feel strongly what it evokes?[8]

The analyst's task is to feel and to make felt a work's *aura* (that which makes it unique and unreproducible, above all mechanically). Artaud advised us to:

> return . . . to the active, inspired, plastic wellsprings of language, reuniting words with the physical moves from which they originated; the logical discursive side of words would disappear beneath their physical, affective side, that is to say that . . . words . . . would be understood from a sound angle or discerned in movements.[9]

This implies that observers, while knowing it to be a matter of artistic conventions, experience the affective feelings the work produces in them: "What [the artist] aims at is to awaken in us the same emotional attitude, the same mental constellation as that which in him produced the impetus to create."[10] When this state of passion is absent, one ponders possible analytical resistances to the work:

> So-called analytical resistances stem from emotional and/or sexual blocks; they will be triggered by works that bring into play sexuality, drives, phantasms (surrealism, for example), or by works that evoke the tragic, destruction, crisis, giving rise to anguish and despair.[11]

Such blocks frequently impede aesthetic experience. Hence the importance of elucidating the relational mechanisms between stage and spectator.

Relational and Interactive Theories

Often inspired by phenomenology, Merleau-Ponty's in particular, relational theories aim to clarify exchanges between stage and auditorium—rather than conceiving of such exchanges in terms of the emission of signs from stage to auditorium, or of a production of signs closed in on themselves. Allow us to illustrate these complex relational theories through a simple fable. The spectator, an "eagle" surveying the stage, notices tiny mice in the process of gnawing at the knots of all possible relations: actantial, thematic, formal. At such a great height, the eagle still takes himself to be the partner and mediator of entangled relations; he alone is able to perceive the knots in their entirety, but only because of the mice who pull at the threads and scurry about in all corners of the stage. The eagle fails to describe this scene objectively, for the mice move around incessantly. They are rather like the body of the actor that does not allow itself to be grasped, a sign returning the eagle's gaze: a phenomenological situation that requires us to conceive of the stage as a mirror sending back the observer's gaze.

> From the phenomenological point of view, the living body capable of returning the spectator's gaze presents a methodological dilemma for any theoretical model—like semiotics—that offers to describe performance in "objective" terms. Alone among the elements that constitute the stage's semiotic field, the body is the only sign that looks back.[12]

This return of the gaze by the body of the work, which is probably unique in the arts, obliges spectators to place themselves in front of the actor and the stage, and to identify with them or to distance themselves from them.

Identification and Distance

Mechanisms of Identification

Proximity to the stage event, or distance from it, are factors that spectators should be able to measure. But how can one succeed in this, given the allure and fascination of the stage event? How does one analyze reactions that touch us so intimately?

The spectator's identification with a character produces an increase in pleasure, that of experiencing events vicariously without the risk of actually being implicating in them. This relates to the phenomenon of denial ("It isn't me, although . . .") that Freud recognized within psychic life and works of art:

> The spectator knows quite well that actual heroic conduct . . . would be impossible for him without pains and sufferings and acute fears, which would almost cancel out the enjoyment. He knows moreover that he has only *one* life and that he might perhaps perish even in *a single* such struggle against adversity. Accordingly, his enjoyment is based on an illusion.[13]

Pleasure in danger and absence of genuine risk induce an identification in the course of which the lover of fiction enjoys seeing "psychopathological characters" represented on stage; for she then witnesses the mise-en-scène of drives that she would usually repress but now no longer needs to censure, given that they have become the object of scenic fictions. So she is able to enjoy the satisfaction of "someone other than herself . . . acting and suffering on the stage . . . after all it is only a game, which can threaten no damage to her personal security."[14]

Identification implicates the actor in relation to his/her role, as much as the spectator toward a character or an actor; this is what keeps us there. In the absence of an incontestable theory of the emotions, it is difficult to propose a typology of ways of identifying with another in the sphere of fiction. Nevertheless, literary history contains numerous attempts to define ways of reacting to tragic and comic situations (from fear and pity, to ironic and cruel superiority in relation to a ridiculous character).

Modalities of Identification

Hans-Robert Jauss has produced one of the best syntheses of the full range of these attempts in his account of aesthetic and hermeneutic literary *experience* (to borrow the German title of his book),[15] in which he places himself firmly on the side of receivers and their aesthetic pleasure. Jauss proposes a typology of modes of identification covering the full gamut of possible reactions, from simple associative participation to ironic distanciation.

Associative Identification

Its only end is to understand each point of view in order to establish the overall situation. It is what we do by listening to each of them in turn, and reconstructing their motivations.

Admirative Identification

We admire a character unreservedly—hero, saint, demigod, and so on; we are invited to imitate him/her.

Sympathetic Identification

The hero is meritorious, although imperfect; she presents herself in a human, accessible light, which provokes an identification through compassion and sentimentality.

Cathartic Identification

Beyond sympathy, it provokes a violent emotion and a "purgation of the passions," a catharsis, which arouses pity and fear toward a tragic figure, or on the other hand sarcastic mockery in relation to a ridiculous character.

Ironic Identification

It would be a contradiction in terms if irony did not allow a certain sympathy, in spite of everything, for an unfortunate hero or an antihero; our feeling of superiority is colored with a sensitization to the problems of the other. This leads us directly to the opposite of identification: a critical distance that Brecht christened *Verfremdungseffekt,* an effect of distanciation or, more precisely, of defamiliarization.

Distance

Critical distance always remains relative; if it pushes too far, the spectator loses all interest and leaves the theater. This distance is established by actors in relation to their role as well as by spectators in relation to a character.

As an example, let us take the moment in Brecht's play when Mother Courage hears the volley of offstage gunshots that kill her son Swiss Cheese. Her suffering is so intense that she can only express herself through an inaudible scream that never actually breaks out of her chest. This repressed scream distorts her entire body, throwing her head backward. Immediately afterward, Mother Courage shifts her position, dropping her head into her neck, then sinks into a chair as she shuts herself off from the outside world.

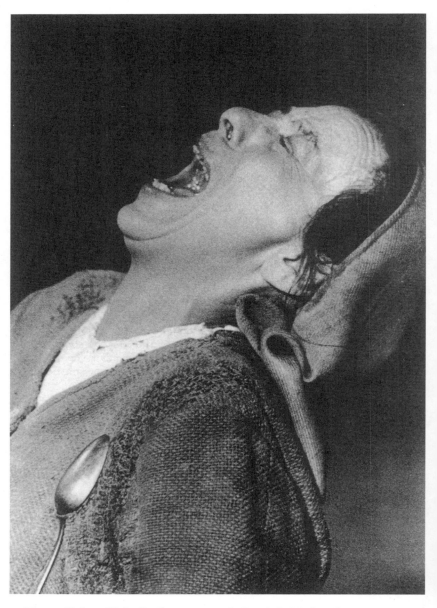

Fig. 23. Helene Weigel's silent scream, in Brecht's *Mother Courage*. (Photograph by Roger Pic.)

In just a few seconds, the spectator has to be able to move through this succession of Mother Courage's "hot" and "cold" emotions: moved to tears at moments, removed and critical toward this ambiguous character at others. Therefore in Brecht's dramaturgy, as in any performance placed at a distance, actors play "against the current of expressive conventions," and spectators "undertake a mental correction that preserves the rights of the performance."[16]

Beyond the Identification/Distance Binary: The Example of Butoh

The choice between identification and distance is not absolute, and each mode of reception sometimes occurs in a way other than the fiction/nonfiction dichotomy, based on a quasi-direct and physical relation to the body of the actor. Such is the case with the kinesthetic perception of movement and of an actor's body in pain. More so than any other genre, Butoh dance makes the spectator experience the fear of the displayed body. The next few photographs will provide an opportunity to reveal our own fears as polymorphous receivers.

The Fragmented Body

All that is left of a body in pain is the torso; the head and limbs in the shadows seem to have been severed. A fragmented body such as this, cut into bits and pieces, "regularly appears in dreams, when the notion of analysis touches upon a certain level of the aggressive disintegration of the individual."[17] One can do little other than identify its disconnected pieces in the morgue and feel an anxiety of fragmentation.

The Eyeless Face

Without a gaze, the eyes enucleated like a death mask, the face no longer possesses any living element with which an observer could identify. The disappearance of all emotion, the fixity of features, and the rigidity of postures disturb the gaze of the other to the point of destabilization. In the absence of psychological identification, with no possibility of imagining a hidden meaning or a defined situation, the face becomes an object bereft of soul and fear creeps in. So there is always a face-to-face encounter with the work: we examine its authenticity, its creator's investment, "the degree to

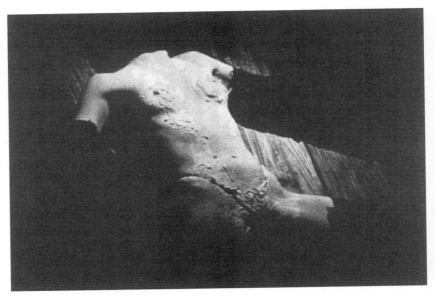

Fig. 24. The fragmented body. (Photograph by Norman Price.)

Fig. 25. The face without eyes. (Photograph by Norman Price.)

which desire is implicated, which enables one to say of a particular work that it is *charged,* inhabited, whereas another is disaffected, *fabricated.*"[18]

The body lying on the dolmen (see fig. 17), fixed in one position as if by rigor mortis, shows the same mineral appearance, and to such an extent that the eye takes a moment to distinguish the body from its support and to identify a human being. Scarcely able to distinguish between animate and inanimate, actor and setting, the spectator perceives a grotesque body, half-human, half-mineral; here it is no longer a matter of finding a place for the body in a landscape, but of perceiving the body itself as a landscape, subjected to the inclemencies of the weather.

Contagious Hanging
Because of its unusual and dangerous situation, the body in figure 26, hanging from a crane by its feet in a town center, attracts the attention of passers-by. Once again one hesitates: human flesh, or the marble of a statue in the process of being installed? Will this exquisite corpse come to life? We are placed in the position of occasional voyeurs aesthesically reliving the actor's movements, wavering between sadism and masochism: our sadism is reflected in our presence at this hanging; we become as masochistic as the actor as a result of a perception that is no longer aesthetic and distanced, but instead is *aesthesic,* corporeal, and contagious, like the plague evoked by Artaud. The reality of pain bursts into the work of art; body art shatters the conventions of performance and of psychological identification.

All of these unforeseen effects on the corporeal identity of the spectator revive traditional modes of identification, by providing increasingly physical bases and "a language of direct communication";[19] they displace the usual boundaries between body and spirit. In this way Butoh reveals a crisis of identification in Western art; and it provides a timely reminder of the fact that the theory of identification is not universal, at best only valid for the Western tradition, from Aristotle to Brecht, a fact that will become further apparent through consideration of the Indian treatise on the *rasas,* or aesthetic tastes.

The Taste of Identification

In Indian culture, Bharata's treatise the *Natya Shastra* (sixth century B.C.) employs the notion of *rasa,* or aesthetic taste. A *rasa* is a powerful and lasting emotion aroused by a transitory emotion of pleasure or pain. The *rasas*

Fig. 26. Contagious hanging. Senkei Juku, *Jomon Sho* ("Homage to Prehistory," 1982). (Photograph by Norman Price.)

(love, heroism, sadness, mirth, fear, disgust, anger, and wonder) constitute the "flavors" of a work. A spectator can taste them only if she has found freedom and detachment, overcome desire and egoism, and attained the requisite concentration and purity of spirit. "Thus through its Flavors, its Feelings, and its modes of movement, this Theater will be a source of teachings to all."

Masculine or Feminine Identification

Identification is bound to culture; is it also bound to sex? Is there an identification that is masculine *or* feminine? Let us be clear on this; sex is a matter of gender and not of biological determinism. For performance analysis, the question is to know whether to distinguish between a male and female gaze brought to bear on a mise-en-scène, and whether the individ-

Fig. 27. "A language of direct communication": La Fura dels Baus.
(Photograph by Jens Koch.)

ual process of spectating perceives it in terms of that individual's sex—and to what precise extent.

It does not seem very easy to determine the feminine or masculine characteristics of a mise-en-scène, without lapsing into painfully banal platitudes. On the other hand, it does not take long to understand whether a mise-en-scène sides with the viewpoint of women or of men. A production of a play like *Woyzeck* could choose to portray Marie as victim, or Woyzeck as sympathetic killer; in the same way (and whatever the thesis of the mise-en-scène), in the process of reception someone could choose to identify with Marie rather than Woyzeck.

What is important to recognize here is not femininity or masculinity per se, but their performative representation by the *actoress* (to borrow a term of Julian Beck's). For example, in Kazuo Ohno's magnificent evocation of La Argentina[20] (see fig. 16), there is no need for a spectator to wonder whether the performer is a woman or a transvestite; s/he observes the showing of certain feminine traits in the Spanish dancer and in Ohno's mother, without ever having to identify with them. Ohno's work to produce signs of femininity and his pursuit of the identity of feminine alterity are quite touching; and it is this quest the observer is invited to share.

Similarly, feminism explores the hypothesis of a sexual difference in the evaluative gaze spectators bring to bear on what they perceive. For feminism, the difference is evident; masculine spectators have supposedly seized upon, and profited from, a humanism that is constructed as "universal"— although it disregards the specificities of women's gazes and voices. Phallocratic humanism establishes an opposition between the universalizing transcendence of man and the natural immanence of woman. In the context of performance analysis, our task would be to determine whether a woman's body is more receptive, and/or receptive in different ways, than a man's. There is no known way of settling this.

However I would agree with feminists such as Irigaray, Kristeva, Cixous, or Grosz, who reject the conception of a body that is preexpressive, precultural, prelinguistic, or presocial. I share Elizabeth Grosz's evocation of "a body as social and discursive object, a body bound up in the order of desire, signification, and power," which contributes to "the production of knowledge systems, regimes of representation, cultural production, and socioeconomic exchange."[21] In addition, I subscribe to her suggestion for the need to develop "some kind of understanding of *embodied subjectivity,* of *psychic corporeality.*" These concepts seem to be related to Michael

Chekhov's notion of *psychological gesture*, which inspired much of chapter 5 above. If applied to the spectator, *psychic corporeality* could provide a productive basis for a concrete analysis of the activity of spectating. The measuring instruments for this activity are rather imprecise, however, and I will restrict myself to a few introductory remarks on the spectator's corporeality.

The Spectator's Body

The Concrete Situation

Quite simply, the concrete situation comprises the ways in which one's body is affected by the physical space it occupies: its comfort, discomfort, perspective, sight lines, and so on. There is a great difference between the plush armchairs of a private theater, a box in a proscenium arch theater, and an uncomfortable bench at the Théâtre du Soleil, the latter crammed with traumatized observers who must reckon themselves fortunate to have found a seat. The body is surrounded with successive environments and envelopes:

> The architecture of an auditorium—its scale, its ornamentation or bareness, its overall shape, the variety or uniformity of its seating, its rake in relation to the stage, its entrances and gangways, and of course its visual and auditory qualities, distances between seating and stage, and the various proxemic relations in broader terms—all are determining elements in which the body is directly implicated.[22]

It seems as though spectators are tied to their seats; they cannot intervene in what goes on in front of them. On the other hand, they seem to be able to move themselves (their "selves") freely around the stage by means of multiple identifications with characters. The motor system, however, only appears to have been neutralized; in reality, observers act and react physically to what they perceive.

Evidently these reactions depend upon the auditorium, which reflects a "mise-en-scène of social links."[23] The behavior and movements of spectators are regulated by rites of interaction.

> This ritual aspect inscribes a symbolics of faces and bodies, a suspension of the word, into a symbolics of space and time. In the auditorium, the

spectator is physically solicited. Whereas cinema develops a bracketing of corporeity, a suspension of the senses in favor of a rigid visual and auditory configuration that saturates the relation to space, creating a sort of hypnotic state that leaves the spectator quietly paralyzed, at the theater, inversely, it is difficult to forget the chair on which one sits, the presence of others at one's sides, in front and behind.[24]

The theater space constitutes a body; each spectator's body reverberates into those around it, and further afield—it has an effect on the stage and is sensed by the actors, whose performances will inevitably be affected, positively or negatively. Performance analysis should draw attention to the reactions of those present and evaluate their impact on the performance as it unfolds. These are not isolated moments, but constitute an entire structure of meaning, which intervenes in every aspect of reception.

Anthropology of the Spectator

The study of reception leads us to attempt an anthropology of the spectator's corporeity. The latter has evolved a great deal over time: today's dimensions, perceptual habits, faculty of attention are not those of two thousand years ago, not even of a century ago. The body of a Greek spectator, witnessing a trilogy of tragedies in the open air; the coiled body of someone in the honeycomb of boxes in a proscenium theater; the fragmented, disjointed body of someone perceiving sound through a loudspeaker, effecting a partial delocalization; a body plugged in to a cybernetic outfit, a VR suit—undoubtedly none of these function in the same way. The mediatized body of a postmodern spectator is subjected to entirely different treatment from the body of someone taking part in a medieval mystery play. The study of *spectators and their bodies*[25] will provide an indispensable foundation for studying authors and their works, their textuality included.

Pleasures of the Spectator

When it refocuses its attentions on the study of spectators' bodies, analysis of spectatorial pleasures is by no means limited to the cognitive sphere, nor to decoding significations tied to signs or words. Psychology teaches us that mental representation is located between perception and concept, and that one shifts smoothly from the sensory-motor sphere to the cognitive sphere.

The mental representation of movement is dependent upon the same mental structures as actual movement. To return to Barba's image, the dilated body of the actor "dilates the kinesthetic perception of the spectator by erecting a new architecture of muscular tonicities that do not respect the economy and fictionality of everyday behavior."[26]

The only limit to pleasure, the only "devil," is boredom, as Peter Brook reminds us at just the right moment.[27] But boredom is sometimes distilled by the spectator himself,

> the *deadly spectator*, who for special reasons enjoys a lack of intensity [in a mise-en-scène] and even a lack of entertainment, such as the scholar who emerges from routine performances of the classics smiling because nothing has distracted him from trying over and confirming his pet theories to himself, whilst reciting his favourite lines under his breath.[28]

Such kill-joy scholars, whom one cannot prevent from entering theaters, are still widespread; so it is quite legitimate to allow them to enter this book (or to remain in it!).

Nevertheless, the most sought-after theatrical pleasure remains that which, as in the lyric arts, is able to "communicate profound emotions . . . and is in fact a sort of reaction against those hyper-intellectual inquiries that characterize a great proportion of contemporary art."[29] Of course it is this spectator, immersed in feeling, who is the most difficult to get to talk and to analyze—and this is the one who interests us the most.

Dreamwork, Stage Work

Dream and Phantasm

In relation to dreamwork, psychoanalysis has at its disposal some precious tools, certain of which will be directly applicable in performance analysis and psychoanalytic interpretations of works of art, in this context theater performance. Freud proposes three types:

- Focus on the process of creation itself, but without ever being able to explain the mystery of the creative gift
- The relation between artist and creation, illuminating the unconscious problematic that has marked the work
- Analysis of the work without reference to its author[30]

The second and third of these are particularly pertinent to performance analysis—above all the examining of a mise-en-scène without reference to the director, about whom the "average" spectator knows little. One would like to be able to study stage production in a way similar to Lyotard's approach to painting after Cézanne; he envisages such painting as aiming "to produce on the canvas sorts of *analoga* for unconscious space itself, which can only arouse disquiet and rebellion."[31] This hypothesis suggests the stage as phantasm materialized by participants in the theatrical event— phantasm rather than dream, according to André Green:

> The texture of performance is not that of dream, and it may be tempting to compare it with phantasm. The latter owes a great deal to the reprise by the secondary processes of elements whose characteristics link them to the primary processes; these are then elaborated in a way comparable to the elaboration of the ceremonial, of the ordering of actions and dramatic movements, of the coherence of theatrical intrigue.[32]

Whether dream or phantasm, Green goes on, the figuration of mise-en-scène is to be "placed between dream and phantasm." This authorizes us to look closely at some of the processes of dream symbolization, and to play with "the double articulation of theatrical phantasm: that of the scene which occurs on stage, ostensibly privileged by the spectator; and that of the other scene which—despite the fact that everything is voiced in a loud and intelligible way, and is displayed in bright light—occurs in the spectator's domain, thanks to a mode of concatenation that obeys an unconscious logic."[33] We have already had an opportunity to appraise the pertinence of this double articulation for time and space, in chapter 5 above.

Consequently spectators are analysts confronted with enigmatic mechanisms comparable to dreams and phantasms, mechanisms whose latent content they have to decipher (rather than decode). Therefore one imagines that the authors and spectators of a performance, each in their own way, go through the same unconscious psychic processes; and one must now endeavor to reconstitute this "concatenation that obeys an unconscious logic," referred to above.

Which Unconscious Logic?

But what is the unconscious? Let me attempt a "theatrical" definition: the unconscious is like a radio chattering away, without anyone ever having switched it on. Instead of making works "speak," in the manner of semiotics (as conceived by Lyotard at least), a psychoanalytic approach conceives of the stage as a body that is libidinal, critical, mute, and impenetrable. Butoh's tormented bodies provided a particularly mute, if violent, example (see fig. 24).

What touches us, and leaves us stupefied in the face of this mute body is first the torso's fragmentation, the amputation of its head and limbs. This is castration anxiety, and the agitation that takes hold of our body schema; it is also our uncertainty as to the cause and the reality of this mutilation, our inability to understand our emotion: "Some rationalist, or perhaps analytic, faculty in me rebels against being moved by a thing without knowing why I am thus affected and what it is that affects me."[34] Interpreting Michelangelo's image of Moses, Freud writes that "precisely some of the grandest and most overwhelming creations of art are still unsolved riddles to our understanding. We admire them, we feel overawed by them, but we are unable to say what they represent to us."[35]

Confronted with this inert torso, or with *Hamlet,* a play that leaves us "in utter darkness as far as the character of the hero is concerned,"[36] we always perceive what is hidden or missing: the subtext behind the text, the corporeal subscore behind the visible score of the actor. Not only do we project ourselves and identify with this mysteriously "cut-up" character, but we also imagine what our role would be in the elliptical scenario suggested by text and stage.

Without pushing the analogy between dream (or phantasm) work and stage work too far, I propose to compare the psychic processes that lead from latent content to manifest content.

Processes of Stage Work

In considering the stage as the figuration of a dream or phantasm that is to be deciphered, we need to refer back to some of the operative processes in the construction of unconscious meaning. The Freudian categories *condensation* and *displacement* constitute the core framework in the functioning of scenic phantasm.

Condensation

Condensation is realized in two distinct and antithetical processes: *accumulation* and *shifting.*

Accumulation concerns both signifier and signified; by dint of their being repeated, materials ultimately combine to produce a third term that is wholly autonomous from the first two. In this phenomenon of metaphorization, two elements are located as partially intersecting equivalents. The Butoh dancer's torso (see fig. 24), for example, condenses quite distinct properties: human flesh or marble, life or death, man or woman. The resulting ambiguity and uncertainty confirm the metaphorical condensation of both signifiers and signifieds.

Shifting is much more than the simple passage from one signifier to another; it involves entire sequences, enabling movement from one plane or level of reading to another, or translation from one world to another. Shifting requires indices that are common to both worlds, or that at least facilitate their intercommunication. In relation to the Butoh torso, the shift could be the cultural interference or jamming of different contexts: Christ's descent from the cross, mutilated Greek statue, image of a war victim, and so on.

Displacement

Displacement manifests itself in two major forms: *connection* and *rupture*.

Connection occurs when one segment refers to another through its substitution or replacement by a part of the object referred to (metonymy). In his representation of La Argentina (see fig. 16), Kazuo Ohno does not imitate or "condense" the traits of a young or an old woman; he refers to the woman glimpsed long ago, now absent, through a play of the gaze, and a corporeal attitude that indicates a folding back in on himself (right hand) as much as an opening toward the other (taut left hand). His nostalgia for the deceased woman and youth is perceptible in what Ohno's aged body suggests through its own effacement. Connection through contiguity and/or concatenation is ensured through gestural signs, there is nothing magical or inexplicable about it; it regulates the coordination of body parts, as well as the link between the visible and the invisible: memory, phantasm, waking dream.

Rupture comprises a connection that is abruptly interrupted, obliging the observer to shift perspective immediately and to account for jumps in meaning. In the sequence danced by Kazuo Ohno, the sudden interventions of European symphonic music create a rupturing effect; they require an approach to the dance through a series of emotional tonalities and free associations. Ohno's disguise is never ambiguous or ridiculous; it is charged with the associations of ideas we perceive there, guided by thousands of metonymic signs.

Primary Processes, Secondary Processes
As is the case with dreams, analysts first confront the primary processes; these make available to them a scenic work that reveals a free and imaginative mode of thinking, for which the movement of signifiers does not submit to the weight of concepts; here meaning slides freely in unknown directions. Mise-en-scène is conceived as research and unconscious desire, as fulfillment of desire using the concrete means of the stage—bodies, space, light, time, rhythm—and the whole series of actions these means permit, without aprioristic intentionality. As an artist, the director does not try to express a previously known idea, but to create an aesthetic object with the means at hand, and to see what eventuates. The artist plays the game, allowing unconscious desires to filter into the working methods as a whole, behaving as a desiring subject and not as a speaking subject. Later on, the spectator will have to produce an account of this "dream"; so she will move on to the secondary processes. Nevertheless she will not reduce everything to language, to verbal communication; she will maintain the idea that mise-en-scène is the site where artists manifest their desire, without communicating in a univocal way what they have to *say*, which is precisely what cannot be *said*. Therefore one must distinguish two levels:

■ the pre-conscious and conscious level (which is *manifest*), in which one can discern signifiers and signifieds: in the example of Kazuo Ohno, one sees a man dressed and dancing as a woman;
■ the unconscious level (which is *latent*), in which one must venture a metaphorization or metonymization in order to make conjectures regarding the way in which motives are concealed.

In unconscious connective processes, the signifier/signified distinction is no longer operative, as it was on the manifest level; one can no longer rely on the preexistence or predominance of one or the other, as was the case with verbal connective processes. Now it is a matter of reconstructing what was at the origin of the desire, what has been repressed—substituted or displaced—by something visible. We should remember that, according to Freud, "images constitute . . . a very imperfect way of conveying conscious thought, and one can say that visual thought is much closer to unconscious processes than verbal thought, and is much older from a phylogenetic rather than an ontological point of view."[37]

The Example of Terzirek
In this performance by the Théâtre du Mouvement[38] (see fig. 8), the initial forms one discerns emerging from the sand resist immediate identification: are they mineral, vegetal, animal, human? The shifting of the sand on the dune reflects that of meaning, which does not attain an identifiable form and goes no further than the primary processes. Meanwhile, creatures gradually emerge from the desert; shapes start to stand up and out; we begin to modify our initial perceptions, as if this were a dream we do not know how to interpret, but which we endeavor to present in the form of a coherent scenario: the shapes become columns, then ancient statues, then crosses and desert combatants. What Freud calls the "taking into consideration of intelligibility" (or of "representability") helps us decipher the scene like a dream whose latent meaning begins to emerge, leading us step by step toward the secondary processes. From such a perspective, the buried figures that emerge in a very laborious way would be the disguised expression of a repressed desire, perhaps for a return to the bowels of the earth/mother. The civilizing process—a favorite theme of mime artists, as we know!—would consist of emerging from a hole, raising oneself up toward an ever greater autonomy, toward an anthropomorphism. Emergence from materiality, concrete forms, primary processes, so as to accede gradually to the signified, to meaning, symbolism, and language—such is the destiny mapped in the narrative of *Terzirek;* and this narrative is also emblematic of all interpretation, all sublimation.

Psychoanalysis applied to the interpretation of a mise-en-scène examines how the unconscious of the performance's creators is expressed by means of the *stage work,* and its way of both concealing meaning and bringing it to light. Psychoanalysis provides a stable framework to put in perspective the diverse observations that performance analysis has already generated. It encourages us to choose the ways in which we receive and deal with the images presented to us in performance. Fundamentally, we can choose between two strategies; either to give ourselves over to the pleasure principle, or to recognize the reality principle.

PLEASURE PRINCIPLE AND REALITY PRINCIPLE

Pleasure principle	Reality principle
1. *Literal meaning*	1. *Figural meaning*
The spectator is only interested in the literal meaning and the	The spectator tries to find the hidden or figural meaning; he

materiality of the performance, manipulating material without trying to interpret so as to discover a figural meaning. Like a pig that has been given too much jam, he wallows in the signifying matter.

looks for what all of this could mean; he translates all perceived material into signifieds.

For example, the Butoh torso (fig. 24) could be approached initially as form and matter, as experience and rough art of dismemberment.

For example, the Butoh torso is reminiscent of a mutilated or defaced Greek statue; it recalls Christ's descent from the cross as represented in Italian Renaissance painting.

2. Primary processes
We trust intuitive thinking, free associations, our spontaneous reactions. Inspired by dreamwork, we verify whether material has been treated in particular as condensation, or displacement, or association of incompatible ideas (oxymoron), or reflection on figurability.

2. Secondary processes
With Freud, we attempt to put the primary material in order, through linear and narrative thought, a logic of cause and effect, a sequencing of episodes, a referencing of categories used.

3. Affective thought and logical thought
The opposition of these two principles intersects with that made by Robert Musil between affective thought and logical thought:

> In any mind, beyond logical thought with its strict and elementary sense of order that reflects external structures, occurs an affective thought whose logic, if one can still speak of logic in this context, corresponds to the particularities of feelings, passions and humours; in such a way that the laws of these two modes of thinking are interrelated in roughly the same way as the laws of a saw-mill, where blocks of wood are squared and stacked for dispatch, and the much denser laws of the forest with its growth and its murmurs.[39]

4. Danger of the inexpressible and the unfocused
The spectator remains prisoner of free and unfocused association. He refuses to talk about the performance, the experience seems incommunicable. The object of

4. Danger of rationalization
The overly rationalist spectator loses the sense of the scenic event, its pulsional quality, the "primary mysterious and indescribable movement" Musil

desire remains external and	writes about. Reflection remains
untouchable; there is no	locked within the analyst, and the
felicitous analysis.	analyst within his reflection.

It would be best to avoid choosing between these two strategies and these two dangers, quite simply because logical thought and affective thought are "two modes of thought that get mixed up with each other,"[40] and because spectating, like any cultural activity, is a sublimation that overcomes this cleavage between pleasure and reality, play and work, eroticism of the object and autoreflection; for "the cultural object, or sublimation, is halfway between the narcissistic impulse and the erotic object position; it is a point of stabilization in the libido's fluctuation."[41]

A stabilized libido: one can see the importance of a psychoanalytic analysis in the evaluation of performances, although the complexity of the undertaking has already been glimpsed—in particular the epistemological difficulties of reconciling a general phenomenological inspiration, a technique of semiological description, biological considerations regarding perception, a symbolism of the unconscious, all with an attention equally sociological and anthropological. In fact one must insert this psychoanalytical perspective in the broader contexts of sociology and anthropology. For "culture demarcates the origin and horizon of the subject, marking sexuality and the unconscious with its seal, just as it is marked by them."[42] Spectator-subjects will not be satisfied for long with prediscursive experience and prereflexive immersion; guided by the demon of interpretation, they are certain to turn to a deciphering of secondary processes—and so they will need the blinking lights of sociology and anthropology.

9

The Sociological
Approach to
the Spectator

Despite its complexity, a psychoanalytical approach on its own remains inadequate for a full understanding of the perceiving subject, for it does not provide a sufficient account of the subject's inscription in the social fabric—starting with the audience within which she sits. A sociological perspective therefore endeavors to keep in mind the fact that the spectator is not only a desiring subject, but also an "unidentified seeing object" located within a more or less clearly identified audience.

Is it utopian to want to bring together around the spectator the questions and parameters generated by textual theory, sociology, and sociosemiotics? Of course, it all depends on the articulation of these knowledges and on how opportune it is to choose a particular aspect at a particular moment. The difficulty is in basing a theory of aesthetic experience on the spectator's point of view.

> Problems arise once the aesthetic experience—which is nothing other than a lived experience of a scientific kind—is declared to be the object of scientific research. These problems go right back to the successive legacies of aesthetics and hermeneutics.[1]

So before focusing on a sociology of performance, one should take into account these aesthetic and hermeneutic legacies; this will provide a timely opportunity for some initial frames of reference for dramaturgy.

Dramaturgy of the Spectator, or *Spectator in Spectaculo*

In search of a general treatise on the reading of texts, it wasn't long before I came across Umberto Eco's work, *Lector in fabula: Le rôle du lecteur ou la coopération interprétative dans les textes narratifs* (1979), which provides the best comprehensive study of interpretative mechanisms in the reading of narrative texts. This remarkable study is the first to integrate within an overall schema the full range of the parameters of the act of reading—psychological, ideological, and semiological. Evidently the task here consists of adapting this model to the analysis of performances (or, metaphorically speaking, to the "reading of performance texts"); for the analyst's task is to track down the *spectator in spectaculo*, rather than the *lector in fabula*. Furthermore, perhaps it is easier, and above all more legitimate, to study the spectator *within* the performance, since the former is concretely implicated in the latter. So I will discuss the "model-spectator" who receives the performance, and the range of cognitive and emotional mechanisms to which she is subjected, before considering the concrete "flesh and blood" spectator through a sociology of theater.

First, I will endeavor to transpose Eco's diagrammatic representation of the levels of textual cooperation[2] for theatrical performance, all the while ensuring that this transposition does justice to the stage event (see figs. 28 and 29).

Circumstances of Enunciation

The spectator-analyst considers a mise-en-scène as a collective of enunciators: the actor enunciates texts and displays signs, which in turn give rise to a flood of information regarding the choice of actors (casting), modes and styles of performing, options for the scenography, lighting, music, and so on. The cultural moment at which the performance occurs, the identity of the director and her associates, the ways of presenting the acting—all are indications providing starting points for observation. I have already signaled the importance of the paraverbal elements of acting, and of the necessity to understand the frames and "given circumstances"[3] within which they evolve.

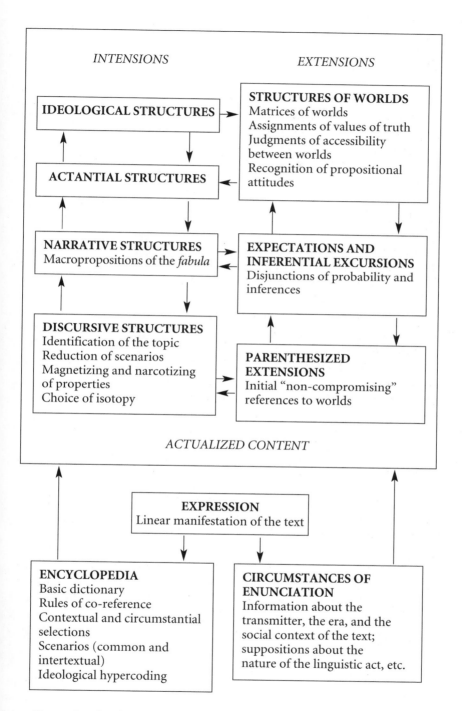

INTENSIONS   EXTENSIONS

IDEOLOGICAL STRUCTURES

STRUCTURES OF WORLDS
Matrices of worlds
Assignments of values of truth
Judgments of accessibility
between worlds
Recognition of propositional
attitudes

ACTANTIAL STRUCTURES

NARRATIVE STRUCTURES
Macropropositions of the *fabula*

**EXPECTATIONS AND
INFERENTIAL EXCURSIONS**
Disjunctions of probability and
inferences

DISCURSIVE STRUCTURES
Identification of the topic
Reduction of scenarios
Magnetizing and narcotizing
of properties
Choice of isotopy

**PARENTHESIZED
EXTENSIONS**
Initial "non-compromising"
references to worlds

ACTUALIZED CONTENT

EXPRESSION
Linear manifestation of the text

ENCYCLOPEDIA
Basic dictionary
Rules of co-reference
Contextual and circumstantial
selections
Scenarios (common and
intertextual)
Ideological hypercoding

**CIRCUMSTANCES OF
ENUNCIATION**
Information about the
transmitter, the era, and the
social context of the text;
suppositions about the
nature of the linguistic act, etc.

Fig. 28. Levels of textual cooperation. Umberto Eco, *Lector in fabula*
(Paris: Grasset, 1979), 88.

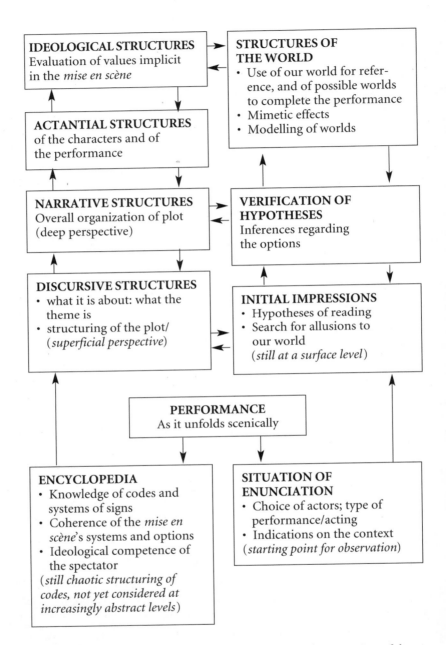

Fig. 29. Application of Eco's schema in figure 28 to the reception of dramatic text and of performance.

Initial Impressions

"Initial, noncompromising references to worlds" occur once "the reader is induced to mobilize referential indices"[4]—in other words, once the relation between the text and the reader's reality is tested by the reader. In the same way, in the case of performance, the spectator tests the indices that make reference to her own world, that create allusions to the surrounding reality. In this way, the spectator explores initial hypotheses for reading an overall mise-en-scène and the dramaturgy of the performance. Is the world represented in performance a possible world, a totally imaginary one? Or does it in fact borrow from our reality, and if so, what exactly is borrowed?

Encyclopedia/Knowledge of Codes

In order to appreciate a mise-en-scène, the spectator must know the principal rules of "theater language" and have at her disposal a "basic dictionary" allowing access to what happens on stage: knowing, for example, that a spotlight focused on an actor would signify that one must pay particular attention to this character, or to some aspect of their performance.

Corresponding to co-reference in a text is the coherence of signs, their vectorization, particularly through the effects of connectors. The spectator undoes the ambiguities of deictics and anaphoras; she fills moments devoid of meaning, secures connections, brings together disparate elements—in short, she ensures the coherence of the mise-en-scène's options.

Her knowledge of the context familiarizes her with other kinds of mise-en-scènes or performance styles. Her ideological competence enables her to understand the fictional situations presented to her.

Discursive Structures: Theme, Plot, and Subject

Discursive structures are at the surface of a text, visible to "the naked eye"; one can easily discern the organization of the plot, its nodal points, twists and turns, resolutions, the physical actions from which it is constructed. The same can be said of performance, with this one difference: in performance, all signifying systems—and not only the text—contribute to the plot. The spectator's first task is to reconstruct a narrative thread, a plot, by means of the signs onstage, and to outline its *subject* (in the sense used by the Russian formalists, who contrasted subject with *fable,* or plot). In the case of a production of a classic text, the spectator will observe the choices made in either foregrounding or effacing a particular episode and will establish the plot that is privileged and elaborated by this particular mise-en-scène; this will lead her directly to reflection on the narrative structure of the plot.

Narrative Structures: The Plot

At this point the action is examined at the deep level of its narrative organization, its *fabula:* "the fundamental schema of narration, the logic of actions and the syntax of the characters, the course of events ordered temporally."[5]

The plot provides the key to dramaturgy and reveals how a mise-en-scène is put together, how it is anchored in space-time and subjected to dramaturgical choices. The plot is constructed from a sequence of physical actions. These actions invariably comprise an agent (the acting subject), their intention, the possible world in which it occurs, its movement (where it is directed), its cause, and its ultimate aim. An analysis that successfully identifies these components will provide a description based on a deep interpretation of the stage action.

Actantial Structures: The Characters' Action

Going deeper by a notch (and thereby moving away from the surface), one comes to the actantial structures that regulate the heart of the action and the "subsoil" of the performance. Of course, none of us is obliged to fill in conscientiously the different categories and divisions of the actantial models proposed by Propp, Greimas, or Ubersfeld; but each of us organizes the indices of our reading by integrating them within an overall action, and bringing into relief the active forces that come into conflict in the reconstituted plot.

Pragmatic Verification of Hypotheses

In order to reconstitute the plot and grasp the narrative logic of the performance, the spectator must continuously leave this fictional world and verify the text's propositions with reference to the laws of her own world. "In order to make predictions which have any probability of satisfying the course of the story, the reader leaves the text."[6]

This exit from the text is well known to actors who, heedful of Stanislavsky's advice, invariably ask themselves: "What would I do if . . . ?" It is important for the spectator to verify whether her reading hypotheses are corroborated, or whether they need some adjustment. The spectator compares them with the structures of the world.

Structures of the World: Effects of Mimesis

This comparison is carried out through a modeling of the possible worlds proposed by the fiction, and of the world—or worlds—the audience inhabits. In the arts of fiction, since the stage has the unique property of showing the possible world of the dramatic universe through ostension and mimeticism, a term-by-term comparison with the real world (or something deemed to be thus by the spectator) inevitably asserts itself. The effects of recognition are multiple, and mimetic illusion frequent; the spectator fluctuates between, on the one hand, psychic and ideological investment in the fiction and ruptures in the fictional frame, and on the other, an assumption of distance, a refusal to believe (in) it. However one must resist the temptation only to retrieve reflections of the real world from within the performance, to "establish a mechanical cause-and-effect link between the surface of collective life and dramatic experimentation."[7]

Ideological Structures

At the deepest and most secret level of performance, one can activate and draw close to the implicit values of a mise-en-scène, establishing the fundamental contradiction(s) on which it is founded, notably its value judgments and axiological oppositions such as: Good versus Evil, True versus False, Nature versus Culture. The importance this book accredits to the notion of *ideologeme* in a sociosemiotic framework will become apparent.

This model, inspired by Umberto Eco, is interactive; it requires us to try out all possible circuits and to follow the arrows linking the different boxes and the particular focus of their inquiry. In this way our understanding of mise-en-scène is constituted stone by stone, without the process of elaboration ever being fully realized—although it does take into account, as much as is possible, the range of data that is able to be formalized.

This circuit introduces the possibility of a "dramaturgy of the specta-tor"[8] that is concerned with all aspects of reception: perception, interpreta-tion, evaluation, memorization, cognition, production of affects. Never-theless certain crucial stages in the circuit still need to be completed, in particular the sociologically relevant boxes; these will be worked on in what follows. In other words, the model-spectator who sees, hears, understands, and appreciates everything, at every stage of the circuit, has to be con-fronted with the empirical spectator who invariably reacts within a given enunciatory context, which sociology will help us to outline.

Sociology of Performance

The Object of Sociology

Alongside this circuit of the reader or model-spectator, inspired by Eco, my intention is to propose a sociological approach (and subsequently an anthropological one) that regards mise-en-scène as end result and artistic product, and not exclusively (as is usually the case) in terms of elaborative processes, training, and rehearsals. In reality, mise-en-scène is understood as *performance* (in the English sense of the term): the arts of the stage, the media, rituals, and ceremonies, *cultural performances* of all kinds—in short, what Jean Duvignaud called *dramatizations:*

> Celebrations, court sessions, marriage proposals, funerals, political debates, etc. All of them are dramatizations that combine and oppose social roles that are difficult to escape.[9]

From the Individual to the Mass

Composed of individual (and often individualist) spectators, the audience becomes a body of thoughts and desires, and of a sensitive listening that latches on to the actors. It comprises a material body that is very difficult to examine and very easy to disturb: "Collective attention creates a magnetic field—if one breaks it, the theater action becomes derisory, absurd."[10] The presence of a single spectator can compromise this magnetic field: "Why does the presence of a particular spectator create an irresistible resistance to the performance of the play?" Jouvet wondered.[11] Similarly, the silence of an entire audience is felt by performers, producing another mystery: "In the theater, why and how does one unerringly appreciate the meaning of the silence the audience creates?"[12]

Study Frames for Sociological Analysis

Georges Gurvitch's old article on the sociology of the theater[13] nevertheless remains the most lucid and comprehensive program for research. This has been confirmed by the research undertaken over the past forty years, without Gurvitch's project ever having been fully realized. Therefore I will begin with "the different branches of theater sociology" he proposes.

Audiences
Gurvitch recommends that we "avoid using techniques that are too mechanical in this research; they do not enable us to account for the diversity of audiences, for their different degrees of cohesion, and for the importance of their possible transformations into groups in the true sense of the word."[14]

Empirical Sociology
Unfortunately the study of audiences has often been entrusted to an empirical sociology that amasses quantitative data on the socioprofessional origins of the audience, but forgets to make the connection with an aesthetic analysis of the performance in question, or simply offers theoretical approximations about reception by describing it, for example, as "interpretation through consciousness of effective stimuli."[15] However, recent surveys undertaken by the Ministry of Culture in France[16] elucidate quite effectively the conditions of reception and prepare the ground for performance analyses. In particular their findings concern

- The sociodemographic structure of the audience
- Factors in the choice of this particular performance
- Ticket prices: do they seem too high, or are they reasonable?
- Judgments heard about the particular production
- The type of spectator thought to be uninformed, a novice, ignorant, difficult, familiar, unconditional, initiated

Wouldn't it be illuminating to create a psychocritical portrait of the *spectator in a state of bewilderment?* The spectator as neophyte, theater lover, specialist, occasional viewer, obsessional participant, semiologist, and so on.

Logic of the Cultural Field

In order to organize the findings of an empirical sociology, one can, with Bourdieu's help, evaluate what "incorporated cultural capital"[17] spectators have at their disposal: intellectual capacities, but also cultural ones, academic qualifications—everything, that is, that helps them "legitimately" appropriate the cultural capital conveyed by a performance in such a way as to enable it to be received in a manner that reaffirms conflicts and hierarchies.

In a difficult mise-en-scène, one that is obscure or illegible to ordinary mortals, there is sometimes evidence of what Bourdieu has defined as a "field effect":

> Where one can no longer understand a work (and the value, in other words the belief, bestowed upon it) without knowing the history of the work's field of production—then that is where exegetes, commentators, interpreters, historians, semiologists, and other philologists find their existences justified, insofar as they are the only ones capable of rationalizing the work and of recognizing the value with which it is accredited.[18]

So the "legitimate" spectator, confronted with the director, like an exegete of the exegetes, is here the one who possesses the secret key to the text staged or the performance. Therefore, performance analysis requires an awareness of these mechanisms and a discernment of precisely where the message(s) of the mise-en-scène go—and for which groups they are intended.

Between the Empirical and the Theoretical: Shevtsova's Questionnaire

Inspired by Bourdieu's work, although developing her own sociology of the theater, Maria Shevtsova[19] elaborates a questionnaire for an Australian Italo-Anglophone audience, so as to sketch the sociocultural profile of the audience:

1. Social composition of the audience: ethnic group, sex, age, educational level attained, profession

2. Spectators' contact with Italy (it was a bilingual performance, in Italian and English)
3. Knowledge of and contact with Italo-Australian informational sources
4. Cultural level and knowledge of the arts
5. Other theaters visited
6. Interaction and evaluation of the two plays performed
7. Themes suggested for future productions by this group
8. Which audience was the theater company targeting—that of the restricted group to which you belong, or a wider audience?

The range of these questions requires cultural factors in the interpretative role of the spectator to be taken into account, something that has rarely occurred in the past—and something that takes us toward a sociology of performance.

Performance
The second branch of sociology is "the analysis of theatrical performance itself, as unfolding within a particular social frame."[20] The social frames of performances are the fictional ways in which society is represented by means of writing and the stage. The question is one of knowing how to differentiate this theatrical representation of the social from the "social" as a historian would define it; there is "sometimes a correspondence, sometimes even interpenetration between the two distinct frames; and sometimes there is contradiction."[21] All mimetic theories simplify and falsify this correspondence—the Marxist theory of reflection, for example; one should rather look for mediations[22] or ideologemes,[23] which are the trace of social contradiction in the work of fiction.

The notion of "possible world" as used by Umberto Eco will be reexamined from the perspectives of a sociology and an anthropology. In theater, the possible world is not only a world imagined by the author and the reader; it is also a real stage world with its own conventions, its tricks and materiality, a scenic world that borrows from our own, without being confused with it. It is from within the social and cultural context that one evaluates and interprets this stage reality.

Since this context—the social frame—evolves incessantly with ongoing history, our questions about a stage work will evolve in the same way; and our understanding of it will also vary to the same degree. This is the core problematic of the aesthetics of reception.

The Actors

The third branch constitutes "the study of the group of actors as a theater troupe, and in a wider sense as a profession."[24] This is relevant for performance analysis given that the conditions of an actor's training, his social status (star or extra?), the identity of the group (permanent company or intermittent work?), all have repercussions for the way of performing, and certain mannerisms or actors' effects have no justification other than as trademarks of the above.

At a deeper level, that of body technique (of more concern to anthropology than to sociology), actors are marked, almost stigmatized, by the performance technique they have "incorporated." Hence the analyst's interest in knowing, and if possible experiencing, this technique themselves. Therefore the body of the actor, present and past, will impress its mark on the performance, the dramatic text included. From this also stems Duvignaud's idea,

> to define the sociological role of the actor as that of a bearer of signs, but of signs privileged by the very fact that they are embodied. . . . Without the body of la Champmeslé, perhaps Racine would not have conceived of the female characters who occupy the central focus of his plays, characters who reach their fullest crystalline realization in the face of Phèdre.[25]

Relation of Plays to Social Structures

This concerns the relation between the fiction (textual or scenic) and the society within which it has been produced or is received. A comparison between the two cannot be avoided. Once again, one remains wary of assuming that reality leaves a direct, mimetic imprint in the theatrical production. In fact, it is the deformation that is truly pertinent and revelatory.

Take, for example, the leitmotif of "Moscow" in *The Three Sisters;* it also functions as an ideologeme, since it controls the meaning of the play, like a password that signifies all desires imaginable:

- In Stanislavsky's production at the Arts Theatre, "Moscow" designates a goal that is distant, but theoretically accessible, a petit-bourgeois ideal.
- In Langhoff's production (1994), Moscow is no longer even a possible outcome; it is the tragic figure of all failings and opportunities missed, the town of imperial carelessness, whether Communist or neocapitalist.

Social Functions of Theater

This fifth and final branch issues from the preceding one, insofar as it prompts us to compare the various possible functions of theater according to a society's state at a particular moment. For each *new* mise-en-scène, therefore, it is advisable to reflect interrogatively on the transformation of our understanding of a performance in terms of what we take the social function to be; analysis is utterly historical and ideological.

With regard to *The Three Sisters*, for example:

- For its first production at the Arts Theatre, rather than satirizing officialdom, the play compassionately ridiculed the provincial life of an intelligentsia in the process of losing all of its frames of reference; it was a warning shot directed at these three dreamers driven out by petit-bourgeois mediocrity.
- In Langhoff's production, any belief in art's influence on social life has completely disappeared, along with any compassion for pitiful creatures. So what has changed is the ironic, benevolent perspective on the characters.

To a great extent Gurvitch's project remains unrealized; nevertheless, he outlines with precision and elegance the branches of the sociological tree, with its roots in an anthropology—as indicated by sociologists from Gurvitch to Duvignaud, and as verified nowadays by theater anthropologists from Schechner to Barba. But first we need to make a short detour through financial issues.

Finances of the Production

Quantitative sociology will certainly include production costs in its statistics. There is no point in reiterating the fact that finances in theater, as elsewhere, constitute the very sinews of the battle. One can also see and analyze a performance through the lens of its cost(s): in terms of the funding subsidies it has received, the exorbitant expense of its scenography, the high wages of its stars, often directly proportional to their particular idiosyncrasies. A trained eye will know how to read the invisible price tags on all these luxury items; it will see money going up in smoke at every turn in the performance, at every financially ruinous deus ex machina; it will price the slightest gesture, for

the financial implication of choices leads to the inclusion of the economic dimension in the aesthetic project, rather than considering it as a
supplementary given that is always more or less constrictive, and in any
case external.[26]

According to Jouvet, "first of all, theater must be a business, a flourishing
commercial enterprise; this is the only way for it to be able to assert itself
and become indispensable in the field of art."[27]

Reevaluation of Ideological Analysis

Restricted to Marxist usage for a long period of time, nowadays ideology no
longer appears in the guise of false conscience or of a smokescreen intended
to maintain exploitative relations. Now it is back in service in the context of
a theory of spectatorial identification. Althusser has shown that a spectator's identification does not occur exclusively in relation to a psychology,
but also to an ideology, once it reaffirms his or her values.[28] Numerous
analyses confirm this hypothesis, and examine the ways in which a text or
performance even sacrifices the hero to a confirmation of the audience's
ideology:

> The audience is basically much more interested in reconfirming their
> own values than caring for the happiness of the character with whom
> they identify; the hero is willingly sacrificed for the sake of what gives a
> sense of orientation in the world. Freud himself indicates that the
> fulfilment of suppressed drives on stage is conducive to anxiety. If so,
> only identification with the value system can bring about total harmony
> in the spectator's psyche.[29]

The stage also becomes the linking site where psychological and historical
conflicts are settled as an *ideological transaction:*

> Performance can be most usefully described as an ideological transaction
> between a company of performers and the community of their audience.
> Ideology is the source of the collective ability of performers and audience
> to make more or less common sense of the signs used in performance,
> the means by which the aims and intentions of theatre companies con-
> nect with the responses and interpretations of their audiences. Thus, ide-

ology provides the framework within which companies encode and audiences decode the signifiers of performance.[30]

In concrete terms, it is not easy to describe this transaction (which in fact entails neither encoding or decoding); for we lack sufficiently subtle working processes and tools to be able to specify the ways in which it functions.

To this end, I suggest the notion of *ideologeme*, borrowed from Medvedev, Kristeva, and Jameson. An ideologeme is a textual and ideological unit that functions within a social, ideological, and discursive formation. It exists as a conceptual unit in the extratextual ideological field, and in the textual field in the form of narrative or thematic units.

Let us look at three examples:

- The reference to Moscow in *The Three Sisters*. Each character understands "Moscow" in his or her own way; empty of meaning, the word allows for ideas to be exchanged, without anything ever being pinned down. This results in an ideological construction, to which the mise-en-scène contributes substantially. This construction is based on the discourses of the time; once cited in the fiction of the play, it becomes a thematic and narrative leitmotif, and therefore a textual unit that underpins the architecture of the *fabula*/plot. The ideologeme *Moscow* is not a simple theme or refrain; it is the mode of a contradiction. *Moscow* is a proper noun/name, a geographical and cultural referent, but in the play it is also an empty signifier for an abstract ideal: what one desires without knowing its exact meaning, without being able—or wanting—to attain it. The ideologeme can be felt when one reads the text, and the mise-en-scène can choose whether to make it the pivotal axis of the performance or not. In this case, the debt with regard to the reading of the text remains important, without it being assured, however, that the mise-en-scène will successfully convey this ideologeme. Nevertheless, the ideologeme will be apparent in the mise-en-scène, if the production has consciously endeavored to represent it by means of stage indices.

- It is apparent in the example of Heiner Goebbels's production of *Oder die glücklose Landung,* performed at Nanterre in 1993. The mise-en-scène and the musical composition as a whole are founded upon an ideologeme—not the obvious one of the disastrous intrusion by white men into the forest of black man, but rather that of a peaceful, amused, and attentive coexistence between electroacoustic Western music and the voice or the African kora. This can be felt in the way the different moments for the different kinds of music can be heard, in the dialogue and reciprocal listening between the musicians. This ideologeme is revealing in terms of the type of interculturalism suggested by the director Heiner Goebbels; this is not a search for universal elements common to the different musical forms, and neither is it a multiculturalism in which each group withdraws and creates in its own separate space; it is an interculturalism in which each culture knows how to listen to the other without appropriating it, or being engulfed by it, by bringing artistic experiences into confrontation in the style of a game, rather than of a conflict.

- The example of *Marat/Sade,* in Peter Brook's mise-en-scène (see chapter 3).

The Aesthetics of Reception

By examining how poetic and novelistic works have been variously received over time, and the new horizons of expectation that have caused reception to vary, Hans-Robert Jauss[31] has proposed an aesthetics of reception; theater studies would benefit from drawing on Jauss's work.[32] In addition, it allows one to relocate, or even to recycle, from the point of view of the receiver (spectator and audience) quite a few theories that can be directly called upon by performance analysts.

Horizon of Expectation
A key notion for Jauss, the horizon of expectation is that of the audience at a particular moment, emerging from the state of society, the audience's knowledge of the theatrical genre, its interests at that time. The range of parameters is considerable, and their reconstitution always rather hypothetical. In describing the performance, therefore, one should endeavor to retrace the system of expectations by noting the influence they exert on what is perceived at that moment.

Typology of Codes
This relates to an old inheritance from the semiology of communication, from the time when it was thought that everything could be coded and decoded in terms of signals intentionally emitted by the director and aimed at the spectator. Of course one can always draw up a list of such codes, but a misunderstanding soon occurs if one imagines that the sum of these codes produces the global meaning of the performance. On the other hand,

there is great interest in grasping what De Marinis calls the "the theatrical system of prereceptive preconditions," which is "presupposed in the act of reception."[33]

Prereceptive Conditions
The "theatrical system of receptive preconditions" constitute the "structured complex of factors—cognitive, psychological or otherwise (intellectual, ideological, affective, material)—which influence the behaviour, cognitive or otherwise, of the theatre spectator, providing him with a specific competence and thus making him capable of doing what is required of him receptively."[34] By reconstituting this "competence," one equips oneself with the means to show what will be received from the performance. One starts from the real possibilities of the receiver, rather than constructing theories around a production that lends itself to all sorts of different interpretations.

The Aesthetic Experience
The aesthetic experience is placed at the center of a theoretical reflection on the aesthetic experience by taking the fullest possible account of the artistic preparation of the spectator, and her previous experiences. "From now on the point of view of the current interpreter is affected not only by the 'historical series' of preceding interpreters, but also by her own artistic experience."[35] It is a matter of formalizing this past experience, of describing it by comparing it with the current experience, of collating common points, and of evaluating the originality of the new experience. Finally, and this is a crucial point, this individual experience must also take into account the analysis of the work under consideration, its structure, and in particular the way in which it anticipates its future mode of reception.

Hermeneutics
In this way it rediscovers its power, for it "overcomes the positivist naïveté, inherent in the concept of data, through reflecting on the conditions of understanding."[36] Understanding also entails being disoriented, dumbfounded; it means betting on the meaning and accepting a phase of incomprehension.

Taste-Based Criticism
Performances are also evaluated according to criticism based on taste, an area that has been abandoned all too quickly to impressionism and subjec-

tivity, whereas in fact it has a significant role to play in description or analysis that aims at the greatest possible objectivity. Determining the taste(s) of an audience—beliefs, opinions, habits, ways of speaking, and so on.— would first need a very systematic and elaborated critical apparatus. For in this context we are dealing with the concrete spectator, and not with Eco's ideal or model spectator any longer; the difficulty is in conceiving of this spectator, no longer as a pure construction, but as an empirical whole capable of leading to generalizations.

Limits of a Theory of Reception
To what extent does one hope to determine the receiver? One must beware of a euphoria that tends to create the belief that one day an absolute knowledge of the receiver (or of the mechanisms of reception) will be possible, and that therefore bringing them into play will be sufficient to analyze the received work. Fortunately, there will always remain some play in the mechanics of reception, certain unforeseeable or indeterminate elements. (Positivists will console themselves by recalling that this unforeseeable play is programmed by the work, and that the text is "a tissue of blank spaces, of interstices to be filled; and the emitter foresaw that they would be filled, and has left them blank.")[37] The circuits, like those of Eco, remain open and able to be routed in all directions. This opening can cause fright and produce a "field effect," but it "re-positions spectators who are no longer outsiders looking in . . . but who, *together with* performers, make the meanings of performances."[38] Theory, like the practice of contemporary art, and of theater in particular, is going in precisely this direction, no longer opposing artist and spectator, practice and theory, art and discourse on art.

Our interest, therefore, is not to stake everything on reception, without enquiring about the production that generates this reception. Nor is it to make the receiver-spectator into an omniscient being (who will sort out the work in a flash), or into a suspect who must first be identified or identify herself.

So let us not believe that a formal statement of one's exact situation as spectator, of one's motives and desires, made in front of the police (even the aesthetic police), will elucidate the aesthetic object for ever. Is it necessary for the spectator—prime suspect of the production—first to confess? Like the distinguished American theorist who closes his excellent work on the *Theories of the Theatre* by admitting to the need to reposition himself constantly, which he considers a "challenge, if one is, like me, culturally positioned on the dominant side of all the traditional discourses—a white, middle-class, academic, heterosexual male."[39]

Must one really be politically correct to understand *correctly* the performance of our lives? Putting reception into a historical perspective, contextualizing the work, questioning our relation to the other—all are legitimate and urgent processes: but do they really require such public confessions from us?

More seriously, sociology is only effective if it is incessantly confronted with other disciplines, such as psychology, psychoanalysis, history, semiology, or anthropology.

The sociological approach is reductive if it limits the work of art to its technological aspects, its relations with the economic infrastructure or with the class struggle. On the other hand, it is illuminating if it studies the links that exist between the work and the mentalities, ideologies, and conceptions of an era, a class, a group of individuals, so as to discern their meanings.[40]

From Sociology to Anthropology

Current research tends to abandon sociological methodology, in its strict sense, so as to integrate it into a greater whole, often under the term *anthropology* nowadays, although it had already been envisaged under various names by pioneers such as Moreno, Duvignaud, Turner, and Schechner.

For Moreno, theater (psycho- and sociodrama) serves to transform the observer into a participant, thanks to "theater's ability to be utilized as a process for sociological investigation."[41]

For Duvignaud, dramatic ceremony is only one particular form of social ceremony: "To differing degrees, a political meeting, a mass, a family or community celebration are all dramatic acts."[42]

For Turner and Schechner, cultural performance is a social phenomenon one is entitled to interpret using the analytical methods of performance practices, in accordance with the universal formula rupture/crisis/restoration/reintegration or schism.

This dissolution of theater into "cultural performances"—the dilution of sociology into anthropology—is not an isolated phenomenon; it goes hand in hand with the evolution of theater practice from a sociological militancy (e.g., Brecht, Vilar) to an anthropological participation (e.g., Beck, Grotowski, Barba). A shift that perhaps Heiner Müller embodies best of all:

There is a shift of accent in the habitual understanding of the function of theater, or, to put it another way, it is no longer a matter of sociology, but of anthropology.[43]

A shift that is still far from being common currency in today's theater, since "texts are still not used as material, as body": in other words, not really treated as a corpus, a bodily technique of the kind with which ethnology would concern itself.

Sociology seems buried, or at least entrenched, in the borderless domain of anthropology, probably because it is felt to be a local product when nowadays the search is under way for a more universal vision, one that is less directly social and political. However, like Bourdieu, one could interrogate this "distinction between ethnology and sociology," which is a "false border. . . , a pure product of (colonial) history with no logical justification."[44]

In any case, we need to look to anthropology to bring together our hopes of understanding performance, to integrate and synthesize psychological and sociological perspectives, to ensure a continual exchange between psychoanalytic interiority and sociological exteriority, while at the same time taking the oxymoronic formula of a *vectorization of desire* at its word.

Therefore we need to imagine, not a happy Sisyphus, but a spectator situated at the center of concentric circles extending from the initial ripples of psychology and sociology right out to anthropology, where she is lost in conjectures related to the scenic object that unleashed this shock wave—and where "once the moment of glory has faded, silence has fallen, the curtain is down, normal life has returned," she finds herself inhabiting the "infinite extension of memory."[45]

10

The Anthropological Approach and Intercultural Analysis

The anthropological approach to performance analysis does not constitute just one more method to add to those already outlined in this book. Rather, it provides an overall perspective whereby everything discussed to this point might be integrated and moderated, in particular the functionalism of semiology and the often very technical methodology characteristic of Western performance analysis. Moreover, it responds to a desire not to limit this discussion to text-based theater, nor even to performances produced in the West, but to open up the full range of contemporary performance practices, whatever their cultural contexts. Ultimately, the anthropological method is plural, continually in the process of being elaborated; it brings together a variety of different approaches and cannot be reduced to a single viewpoint.

The following chapter sets out to demonstrate that the topology of any performance has methodological consequences in terms of its reception. The growing number of intercultural performances and the extreme diversity of their contexts require the invention of a relevant method of analysis, a revision of our all too categorical judgments of Western mise-en-scènes, and a reevaluation of these productions by comparing them with non-European traditions and the "mixed" products of a so-called interculturalism. On each occasion, one must adjust adapt one's perspective and method. The anthropological approach demands a comparative evaluation and a critical reassessment of existing methods of analysis. Just as a culture only really defines itself in relation to and in contrast with other cultures, a theater tradition and its methods of analysis only become meaningful in relation to others.

Adapting One's Gaze and Understanding

The Perspective of the Other

The primary question is to know whether it is possible to appreciate and analyze a performance that is "foreign" to us—foreign because of its geographical or cultural origin, or as a consequence of our ignorance of genres and contexts removed from our own cultural horizon. Furthermore, perhaps one should even measure the various degrees of possible distance from us and realize that they might not necessarily be obstacles to our appreciation. In fact, distance is constitutive of any gaze; by definition, any performance to be analyzed is removed from us, whether it is Balinese or from Normandy. The anthropological gaze, therefore, does not exclusively concern itself with exotic objects.

Strangeness is one form of alterity. But where is the other situated for the spectator? It may be the other culture, with which I have never before been confronted; but obviously it is also everything that is not me. Of course one might declare the other to be unknowable, which is quite a fashionable response at the moment.[1] However, one could also conceive of this question quite differently, like Antoine Vitez for example, who will lend us his words here:

> I don't like being told that there is no way for me to understand others, nor others me. This fashionable trend for making differences irreducible fills me with horror. So since I am a man, supposedly I should not be able to understand women at all, nor Africans because I'm a European. This literally drives me mad. If I have to think in this way, I will not be able to go on living.[2]

Nevertheless, to say that alterity is not inevitably irreducible is not to deny its existence, nor the necessity for considering it in a differentiated manner. In particular, difference may be one of social class, sex, or ethnicity. It is this last aspect that interests me here, in terms of trying to verify whether an anthropological perspective is equipped to carry out a differentiated analysis that will both do justice to the object described and enrich the vision of the theater anthropologist.

The Anthropological Perspective

In order to account for the ethnological dimension of a performance that is "foreign" to us, it is not sufficient simply to adopt an anthropological perspective; one must also specify the type of performance anthropology we intend to practice. The investigative methods of anthropology alternate between (1) a distanced study where the foreign culture is apprehended from the outside, and (2) an immersion within this culture, or, at the very least, a participant observation. Two ways of seeing things, both of which have their advantages and disadvantages; but both of them will radically change our perception of the performance and its very nature, so to speak. In what follows, these two "ways of seeing" are systematized simply to provide an expository overview.

External perspective

■ The external observer draws back, places herself outside her object of study, and aims to be objective and distanced in her conclusions. She does not get involved in the preparation of the performance, only sees it once, reacting immediately to its impact and adopting a position as to its meaning. She rejects the kind of fieldwork done by ethnologists, who live with the indigenous people in order to experience as close a contact as possible with their culture.

■ She always employs the same well-tried analytical grid, and rigorous but somewhat inflexible tools: a questionnaire, for example, or a series of measurements or technical characteristics. She always employs the same mode of segmenting the performance, breaking it down into familiar components.

■ Reception is very quick, but often rather mechanical. In applying a proven grid or terminology, reception soon

Internal perspective

■ The participant observer becomes immersed in the performance, and in what precedes it as well as what comes after it. She participates in the life of the theatrical and cultural group; she attends and is actively involved in training and rehearsals, contributes to aesthetic choices, and blends in with the rest of the group to such an extent that she risks disappearing in terms of her role as objective observer, and becoming "one of them."

■ She uses the grids and categories specific to the culture being studied. So for example, if she is to account for the music and dance in an African performance, she will only do so by taking care not to dissociate these two inextricably linked elements in African cultures, in both her analysis and her terminology.

■ Her first task involves an ethnomethodological reflection: instruments for describing the world, categories, and aspects slides, under its scientistic gloss, in the direction of universal judgments that no longer apprehend the local conditions of the performance.

■ This kind of rapid, immediate reception benefits from the technology available for notation and quantification; it tends to employ the latest scientific methods of investigation.

■ The external perspective remains attached to an ideology of authenticity; cultural productions infiltrated by elements foreign to their tradition are judged severely; attempts are made to separate the "authentic" from the "watered down"; and the defining criteria of the foreign culture are sought, so that they may be set in opposition to the observer's own culture more effectively, and affirm the distance that separates them.

■ The external perspective judges a foreign production according to the idea the observer forms of its identity and integrity; she possesses a sound technical knowledge of the culture but lacks sufficient sensitivity toward its actual identity.

conveyed by the language and culture are all examined to determine what they reveal or conceal about the object of study.

■ Reception is rather slow and approximate; it compares the ways in which the foreign culture and theater tradition conceive and organize their knowledge of the world, with the different ways in which an observer from another culture would proceed.

■ The internal perspective takes into account the fact that there are no "pure products," that performances are always more or less hybrid and creolized, and that non-European traditions respond ("write back")[3] by also using the culture of the (European) other for their own ends.

■ This approach relativizes the possibility of finding tools for a "correct" evaluation of intercultural work. Nothing is definit(iv)ely correct any more—and, by the way, correct for whom?

Which of these two perspectives should one adopt? The answer to this question can only ever be tactical and political, and in the end it will never be definitively cut-and-dried. Each perspective offers certain advantages, which encourages us to avoid dissociating these two ways of seeing. Nevertheless, given the fact that the external, "objective" perspective has been elaborated to a much greater degree, the second option will be chosen here:

that of the internal perspective afforded by a participant observer, as specifically adapted to intercultural theater. First, however, let us consider the example of a performance form that is completely "foreign" to most Westerners, in terms of its geographical origin and its performance style: the traditional Indian dance form Odissi, as it was reconstructed and practiced by Sanjukta Panigrahi in recent years, before her untimely death in 1997.[4]

An Example of Analysis: Odissi Dance

For those who are not specialists or connoisseurs of Odissi dance, for those unfamiliar with the circumstances of its restoration as a form, it is not possible to reconstruct the full range of its motifs and *mudras* (hand positions). Even if one were able to learn at first hand from the dancer herself the narrative organization of each pose, and of facial and manual expressions, one would be no better equipped to analyze the choreography, or at least not in the manner of a Western description of gestuality or performance technique. In fact the account would lack a knowledge of the underlying reasons informing gestures and, in particular, their aesthetic evaluation; furthermore, if this is not too much to ask, it would lack an understanding of the pleasure experienced in following this particular dance form and its music. However a number of other solutions, which are only partially satisfactory, are available to us.

Eugenio Barba's Theater Anthropology

Barba's theater anthropology looks beyond concrete gestures for preexpressive, universal principles that are not tied to given forms: principles that in-form the use of the body, such as the opposition of contrary impulses and actions, the laws of balance and imbalance, the virtue of omission, the contrast of strong and soft principles (*keras* and *manis* in the terminology of Balinese dance), and of the daily and the extradaily (*lokadharmi* and *natyadharmi* in Indian terminology). Theater anthropology of this kind (which should not be confused with cultural anthropology as applied to theater) suggests that the body of the performer (actor/dancer) is subjected to the same set of recurrent principles, and the spectator perceives these so-called preexpressive universals before all else. Descriptions afforded by this approach, however, remain rather summary, for the entire visible and expressive surface of the dance slips by unacknowledged in favor of the major principles of preexpressivity. This approach should thus be filled out through other approaches.

Systematic Fragmentary Observation
This approach entails one choosing to observe, for example, the behavior of particular bodily joints. In the case of Odissi, it would be instructive to focus one's attention on the dancer's ankles or knees and follow the variations in the ways they are used. One would try to determine their role in the management of energy, in the structuring of movement, and in the more or less constant ideogram they draw in space.

One might also observe the way in which the spectator's gaze is captivated by signs originating in turn in the hands, then the chest, then the face, and the ways in which the dancer continues the same narrative by varying the use of her body, and by shifting without any interruption or break from one segment of the body to another, and from one kind of signification to another. The dancer's art, therefore, consists of vectorizing her body by moving from one bodily site or source to another, thereby creating a dramaturgy of the body, and neutralizing or emphasizing a particular, precisely focused body part.

Aesthetic Experience
The notion of the preexpressive principles and of fragmentary observation should not deprive us of an *aesthetic experience* and evaluation of the object being analyzed; quite the contrary. An appreciation of rhythm, of those moments at which music and gesture coincide perfectly, the virtuosity and plastic complexity of the movement, the identification of primary emotions, through facial expressions in particular, all serve to sensitize the least expert spectators to the beauty of this form of dance; one has the impression of being able to follow the dancer in a complex and perfect arabesque. Nevertheless, despite the fact that a poor knowledge of context and codes will almost inevitably distort one's judgments, this does not invalidate the aesthetic experience. One needs to understand that aesthetic experience itself, from the perspective of Hindu culture, is not an end in itself, but that it is connected to a religious experience. When the dancer touches the ground with both hands before any performance, or when she places an offering of fruit and flowers in front of the altar, she gives her actions a rit-

ual and religious meaning that goes far beyond the visible artistic manifestation. Such actions contain a relationship to an alterity that is often missed by Western spectators; they feel excluded without an adequate understanding of the spiritual dimension, and of the fact that Hindu spirituality neither prevents nor contradicts corporeality and aesthetics.

These three "foreign" perspectives on Odissi dance—theater anthropology, systematic fragmentary observation and aesthetic experience—are still a long way from exhausting the object of their study; they offer no more than an initial approach, a first step toward analysis. In particular, it should be pointed out that the object of analysis has not yet been clearly circumscribed: is it a question of isolated gestures and movements, an ordered sequence of a unit indissociably conjoining mind and body, or of a "cultural performance," which is much more than an aesthetic product, and involves an entire culture? The dimensions and limits of an anthropological analysis, as well as those of its object, must be established; they do not coincide with those of a classical semiological analysis, for each culture imposes its own ways of segmenting the world, of breaking it down into its constituent components.

The Object of Anthropological Analysis

Cultural Performance

When considered from the point of view of its inscription in cultures, performance is much broader than it appears. It goes far beyond the boundaries of performance considered as a finished, ephemeral, and disposable product. Hence the necessity of resituating performance practices, whether Western mise-en-scènes, theatricalized rituals, or non-European traditional dances, in a wider and reconsidered cultural context. This context involves not only the preparation that precedes the performance and the reactions of its audience afterward; it also includes all of the sociocultural practices that "carry" the performance. The theater anthropologist's "fieldwork" would involve living among the group, in the widest sense, who conceived and prepared the performance, both before and during the preparatory rehearsals, and "infiltrating" the cultural milieu in which the performance occurs.

Performance is approached as a particular case within the much wider overall range of cultural practices/performances, which are themselves considered as a sort of "culture in action."[5] The list is open ended, but these cultural performances consist mainly of popular culture, ceremonies and rituals, everyday behavior in the most diverse of circumstances, performing arts; so they are not limited to the arts of the stage.

Therefore, "theater," and more generally "performance practices," are approached as part of a very broad cultural framework. A particular element, such as an acting style, is thus "considered as a specific process among those social actions normally studied by anthropologists":[6] highly complex social actions that one has to consider over and above their ludic, fictional, and aesthetic dimensions.

Culture in All Its Possible Forms

When our conception of performance is broadened in this way, it extends to an entire cultural environment that one must evoke briefly here, given our inability to reconstitute it entirely. Culture is not always where we expect to find it: in exteriority, the visible and measurable. It manifests itself just as much in techniques of the body (Mauss), in ways of thinking or narrating, as in the less "spectacular" dimensions of the auditory, the rhythmic, and the haptic—in short, in what Kirsten Hastrup, in the wake of the pioneering work of Condon, Sander, and Changeux, calls "incorporated knowledge."

As has been discussed elsewhere,[7] it is difficult to grasp the notion of cultural identity without elaborating a hypothesis on cultural exchange, and in particular the transfer between source culture and target culture, which occurs when a cultural form (such as a performance, for example) is transferred from one place to another. Using the typology proposed by Kirsten Hastrup, let us now consider four main types of cultural exchange, on both the global level of society and the local level of performance practices.

Cultural Relations

In examining the relationship between culture and tradition, Hastrup proposes four main types of cultural relation. It is our task to verify whether this schema is valid for cultural exchanges in theater, and whether there are four major types of theater practice that correspond to them.

Image	Relation	Strategy of Identification
1. 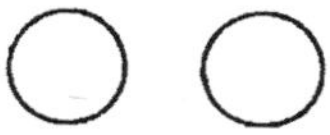 ⃝ ⃝ cultural islands	separation	contrast
2. 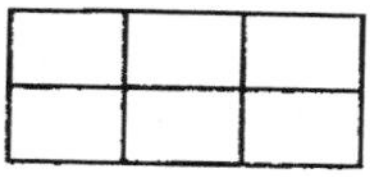 ⊞ cultural pluralism	contact	competition
3.  〜 cultural creolization	mixing	crossbreeding/ interweaving
4. 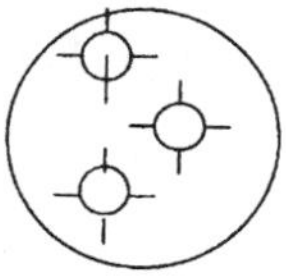 ⊘ multi-culturalism	absorption	fusion

Fig. 30. Culture/Tradition (Kirsten Hastrup, "Culture/Tradition," document circulated to International School of Theatre Anthropology participants in Londrina, Brazil, 1994).

1. *Cultural islands* also exist in theatrical life; for example, a performance of Japanese No and a Comédie Française production have nothing in common; neither is there necessarily a common denominator within the same cultural field, between commercial theater, for example, and the avant-garde.
2. *Cultural pluralism* occurs when a performance brings at least two products of different origins and styles into contact and competition with each other, all the while taking care that they come together as one performance with two or more voices, and not as two separate performances. We have already discussed a good example in Heiner Goebbels's *Oder die glücklose Landung*, a music theater production in which a white actor (who explores and describes the forest) and two black singer-musicians (who move freely around the space while singing) coexist in the same time-space. The explorer is supported by extensive technology, which produces sophisticated and powerful elec-

troacoustic music; the African griots play a kora and use their voices in a warm and human way. Two musical systems, two different relationships to space and time, two imaginaries thus engage in a symbolic competition, without either open conflict or enforced contact, as if it were an amicable joust, each trying to convince the other by only responding with their musical "weapons"; differences and similarities appear in their own terms, without ever synthesizing these different cultural voices into a "world music."

3. *Cultural creolization* implies a mixing of sources and traditions, and the production of a new culture, as in the case of Caribbean societies. Creolization is

> the brutal bringing into contact, in either insular or enclosed territories . . . of culturally distinct populations . . . who are called upon to invent new cultural schemes in order to be able to establish a relative cohabitation between them. These schemes result in a nonharmonious (and unfinished, thus nonreductive) mixture of the linguistic, religious, cultural, culinary, architectural, medical, etc. practices of the different peoples involved.[8]

The plays and productions of Derek Walcott, in particular *Dream on Monkey Mountain,* provide illustrations of such creolization on every level (African and European influences in the writing, thematic concerns, and acting style). One might also mention the "compilatory" performances of Were Were Liking that use all sorts of performance forms: puppets from Mali, Koteba and Didiga forms of intervention, Boloy dance, and so on.

4. *Multiculturalism* is an *interculturalism* in which each culture reflects the complexity and variety of an overall society, absorbing all influences without being overpowered by any one in particular: a meeting and absorption no longer conceived as a melting pot or crossroads, but rather as a confluence. This is the case in the Theatrum Mundi performances that Eugenio Barba produces after a week's work with ISTA (International School of Theatre Anthropology); selected examples from all of the different traditions involved (Balinese, Indian, Japanese, European) are performed to a wider audience, while great care is taken not to harm the integrity of these traditions.

So this very general typology can be applied to performance practices, and it provides an initial framework for more extensive analyses. These more specific analyses attempt to distinguish several different levels of legibility, levels that are closely linked to a specific use of signs and vectors. In order to demonstrate this, and examine how the spectator uses different kinds of legibility, let us take the example of Theatrum Mundi.

Levels and Itineraries of Legibility

Our thesis is that cultural legibility is the product of a construction resulting from an interconnected sequence of specific and partial legibilities: formal, narrative or antinarrative, ideological legibilities. One can establish this linkage using the typology of vectors, which constitute the theoretical frame of the present volume.

Displacement	Condensation
2. Connectors (narrative legibility) 3. Cutters (antinarrative legibility)	1. Accumulators (formal legibility) 4. Shifters (ideological legibility)

Schematically, one could describe Barba's Theatrum Mundi as a process that uses an accumulation (1) of forms, techniques. and materials, an accumulation that proceeds above all in a consistently linear manner, that is, through connections (2). Connection, and its resulting narrative legibility, also has recourse to ruptures (thematic, geographic, rhythmic) effected by means of cutters (3), and this gives the impression of a fragmented reading. Nevertheless, one's ultimate impression is of a performance that can be read by everybody, in accordance with a consensual ideology allowing everyone to shift (4) to a "standard" legibility in which everyone can be involved (ideology of quotas). The description of this itinerary is as much that of the genealogy of the performance itself, of the way in which it was constructed, as that of its final state, and of the way in which one can trace within it the four major vectorial operations, which underpin and organize the performance and form the link to the observer's interactivity.

Let us consider each of the steps of this itinerary of cultural legibility in turn, indicating in passing how the latter results from a discursive construction, given that any search for legibility, at each of the four levels, supports itself on ideological and discursive contradictions, which are very informative in terms of the connection between the theater work and social reality.

■ The accumulation of techniques and materials takes place in the reper-toire proposed by the Balinese, Indian, Japanese, and Danish artists, in terms of what seems to them either the most representative or the most appreciated by a Western audience. This first operation (and also first impression for the spectator) of an accumulation of riches creates from the outset a very abundant catalog and an open inventory of easily rec-ognizable forms, as if quoted with great formal respect, producing a reservoir and inexhaustible source of materials for all of the subsequent vectorial operations.

■ Materials selected and accumulated in this way are then placed one after the other (rather than alongside each other) as a sequence of separate moments, individual "acts" from which soloists emerge. The structural organization of the performance, this sequence of interventions, pre-serves the difference and integrity of each element or "act" in the revue. Barba makes no attempt to condense several heterogeneous traditions; he displaces certain improvisations throughout, but always in terms of a narrative thread that seems to concern the protagonists, and in terms of simple motifs: for example, the conflicting doctors with the newspaper; the formation of a couple (European/Balinese); the repeated action of sowing rice.

■ The plot very soon becomes more complex, and one moves to the third level, that of a fragmented or "mixed" narrative within which the het-erogeneity of styles and performing modes come to the fore; narrative legibility (2) is transformed into a sequence of ruptures in which cul-tural contrast, competition, and pluralism are clearly displayed.

■ Then, in spite of these ruptures and the heterogeneity of materials, one moves on to an ideological level where all is legible once more in terms of a baroque aesthetic of Theatrum Mundi; everything is now perfor-mance in terms of a generalized metaphorization, and every element resembles every other. The stage becomes the world—the metaphor of metaphors. Barba's elaboration of the performance suggests that it is sufficient to juxtapose this range of cultural fragments in order to repre-sent the world in all its diversity and chaos, while retaining the same universal(ist) principles. Theater anthropology pitches its tent in the uncertain terrain of the preexpressive.[9]

When viewed frontally from the auditorium, this also produces an impres-sion of a cultural "pudding," a *soft* postmodernity, a kind of fusional, beatific interculturalism that satisfies cultural institutions that are keen to locate "crossroads" between cultures (such as Korsväg at the Umea Festival

in Sweden). Theatrum Mundi does not propose a reworking and a creolization of traditional forms, in contrast with the restricted group work in
the course of ISTA gatherings, in which dancers are confronted with other
traditions, improvising in their own style while being influenced by their
"foreign" partners. Theatrum Mundi restricts itself to bringing the dancers
closer together *spatially*, allowing them to evolve to the same collectively
orchestrated music executed by the different groups.

Ideological legibility, the artistic consensus that results from the
processes of cultural legibility as a whole, corresponds absolutely to a multicultural (intercultural) aesthetic of *merging*,[10] that is, a bringing together
and meeting in which each tradition retains a certain autonomy, as in a
"federalist" model. Barba's mise-en-scène (or *mise en place*, rather: "placing" rather than "staging") confines itself to providing a particular brand of
"glue" between the different extracts, juxtaposing the various moments and
connecting them with the help of a musical leitmotif. In this sense, Theatrum Mundi reflects the dominant cultural model in Europe—that of a
multiculturalism within which all differences are invited to converge, while
preserving a certain autonomy, despite the rather contradictory catchword
merging, of meeting/fusion. Moreover, this multicultural model is justified
by the relative failure of the other three: beneficial isolation (category 1 in
Hastrup's schema above) is not feasible as it is incompatible with economic
globalization; the absolute contrast of competing contact (category 2)
entails conflict and hegemony; in spite of the recurrent praise for
hybridization, creolization (category 3) is rejected as an unproductive and
impure intermixing that is contrary to the ideology of authenticity. This
leaves the federative model (category 4), that of the great metropolises and
multicultural states within which any absolute choice between the cultural
"melting pot" of yesteryear and the ghettoization of communities is
resisted. Theatrum Mundi epitomizes wonderfully the successes and
naïvetés of cultural indecision of this kind. It is also symptomatic of a way
of thinking in which the concept of culture is currently inadequate to make
a connection between an anthropological approach and a political analysis
of the mechanisms of power; it is ill-equipped to understand the ideological and discursive construction of culture.

This constant reference to the cultural, which is undoubtedly the consequence of an ideology proclaiming that "everything is cultural," and of an
exclusively culturalist anthropology, is not without ambiguity. It is
explained by the appearance of a cultural politics that is interested in other

cultures, or in the cultural in all of its forms, in order to further neglect art in favor of cultural tourism; the latter is much more "spectacular" than art for the media, and less embarrassing for politicians.

However, should we go so far as to refuse all reference to culture in order to encourage the return of the individual art genius (as anthropology seems tempted to do)? Nothing is less certain. Let's leave the discussion with the disillusioned, albeit realistic remark of the anthropologist James Clifford: "Culture is a deeply compromised idea I cannot yet do without."[11] As we have just seen, cultural legibility is certainly very variable and is the result of a series of partial levels of legibility. But the objective of analysis remains to distinguish these different levels of legibility, and to reconstruct the itinerary and the vectors that bring us to an overall legibility of culture in the widest sense.

Person-Character and Body-Mind Relations in Different Cultures

To understand precisely the objective of the anthropological approach, one should go as far as to ask how the performers situate themselves in relation to themselves, their very being, and to the other, their character: that is, how they conceive of their "self." It is the task of the analysis of intercultural performance to observe the way in which each culture seems to conceive of the individual self according to a specific, relative, and conjunctural identity, an identity thus far removed from any notion of universal essence. In turn, this raises the question of the relationship between body and mind, which each culture regulates (i.e., thinks and imagines) in its own way.

To demonstrate this point, let us compare the artists brought together in Barba's Theatrum Mundi (in Londrina, Brazil, in 1994, and in part, in Umea, Sweden, in 1995) (fig. 31).

The entire body of the central figure is implicated, not as an indivisible whole, but as a series of elements—limbs, trunk, face—each of which can in turn be put to particular use. These units intervene without any trace of dualism, which would be evident if psychological or spiritual facial messages were contrasted with a solid, mechanical use of the body. Whereas in the Western dualist tradition, in psychological theater for example, the authenticity of the actor is defined in opposition to the exteriority of the acting style and the role, for the Indian dancer, on the contrary, the body-mind intervenes as a whole; facial expressions are only meaningful in rela-

Fig. 31. The Indian dancer from the Odissi tradition: Sanjukta Panigrahi. Theatrum Mundi, directed by Eugenio Barba, 1994. (Photograph
by Emidio Luisi/Fotograma.)

tion to the rest of the body. It is not the individual person who signifies the
character as a whole, but rather moments or fragments of body-mind that
relate to variable aspects of the character (who, in turn, imitates, narrates,
displays, and plays a role).

The Afro-Brazilian Dancer from the Orixa Tradition:
Augusto Omulu

The whole body of the dancer (on the right in fig. 31) is mobilized by the
dance; one can barely distinguish between the person and his role. The
shifts from rather vigorous (masculine) gestures to rather more gentle
(feminine) gestures is made without any obvious motivation or marked
intentionality. This results in the gesturally evident idea of a complementarity between the two modes; any action can be modulated by a different

Fig. 32. The Balinese dancer: Swasthi Widjaja Bandem. Theatrum
Mundi, directed by Eugenio Barba, 1994. (Photograph by Emidio
Luisi/Fotograma.)

key from each sex. There would be little sense in separating spirituality
from corporeality; each of them is continually converted into the other.

All parts of the dancer's body (on the right in fig. 32) are involved and
meaningful, in particular the eyes, arms and hands, chest, legs and feet. Each
area of the body is used as a means to, and a further stage in, a gestural, verbal, and musical narrative. This narrative is organized as a permanent transition from one "bodily zone" to another; the character is not represented by a
corporeal, psychically fixed self, but by a body-mind that is constantly evolving, reconstituting itself according to the needs of the narration.

In contrast to his colleagues, the Danish actor (on the left in fig. 33)
gives the impression of thinking before acting (which is not a compli-
ment). He prepares his actions internally, hence the initial slowness of his
movements; his head (in particular his forehead) seems to be the seat of
thought and decisions, which only implicate the rest of his body a few seconds later. This quite marked dualism seems to be dictated by a quasi-
Faustian search for "true" identity, with a marked difference between the
head and body, the top half and bottom half. The self is conceived as an
internal core that is "true," preexpressive and inalienable; it is maintained
by the actor despite constant changes of character. The underlying oppo-

Fig. 33. The Danish actor: Torgeir Wethal. Theatrum Mundi, directed by Eugenio Barba, 1994. (Photograph by Emidio Luisi/Fotograma.)

sition is that between authentic (being) and false (seeming), between the social role and the "true persona." The model of corporeality and the body-mind union that it presupposes seem very different from those of his Asian colleagues, despite the fact that ultimately the Western actor's objective is also to go beyond dualism.

It is only possible to compare these four artists who stem from such different traditions if we do not simply try to describe the "surface" of their gestures, so as to focus, beyond the preexpressive principles defined by Barba, on the different conceptions of self and of the body-mind union that lie at the heart of each cultural formation. This comparison of the *other*'s body-mind relationship requires the spectator-anthropologist to imagine the other body-mind (and the other culture) in experiencing the body of the other. Kirsten Hastrup's comment about the anthropologist is equally valid for the theater analyst:

It is only by using the entire self that one can take in what is perceived, and make sensations meaningful. One cannot practise culture (action implies presence) with the mind alone.[12]

Thus we come back to the idea of "performing a culture,"[13] as a means o defining the object of one's focus and coming to understand it, so as t access what Artaud was also in search of: "I must insist on this idea of a active culture, a kind of second wind growing within us like a new organ."[1]

If the object of an anthropological analysis of performance must be con stantly redefined and broadened in order for its cultural complexity to b grasped, we must rethink the existing methodology for analysis, by adapt ing classical "Western" semiology ("manufactured" in the West) to non Western traditions and intercultural productions.

Methodology for Anthropological Analysis

Ethnoscenology

It is time to introduce, and even constitute, a new notion: that o ethnoscenology, or the "study, in different cultures, of Organized Huma Performance Behaviors."[15] This discipline is concerned with cultural per formances and performance practices without imposing upon them th overly reductive model of Western theater (as do Burke, Turner, or Goff man). Ethnoscenological analysis goes back to the object described abov and combines it with the analytical method outlined hereafter. It favors a integrative and interactive perspective, since it is concerned with "th global aspect of expressive human manifestations, including their somatic physical, cognitive, emotional, and spiritual dimensions."[16] The first tas for ethnoscenological analysis will be to elaborate an ethnomethodolog that considers the means of adequately commenting upon/analyzing approaching a performance from another cultural sphere. Does the India artist have to use an Indian terminology to dismantle and describe a move ment? Should the Balinese dancer use (as she sometimes does) terms fron Western classical dance ("first position"), even if her aim is to help he Western students understand more clearly? And what would happen if sh applied a semiological grid to describe her traditional dance?

The method of analysis based on semiology lends itself to Western mise en-scènes insofar as it serves to clarify the mise-en-scène, to specify th relationship between different sign systems, and to deepen the study and organization of each of these systems. In true Cartesian style, it goes from the simple to the complex, systematizes description of the components, establishes a questionnaire relating to all elements of the production (or at least the greatest possible number), and concludes with the idea (rather old-fashioned nowadays) that the performance is a "language," a piece of "writing" controlled by an "author": the director. Moreover, this rationalization of meaning goes hand in hand with a certain mystical impressionism, given the fact that the West has not yet found a way to theorize such rhetorical and magical notions as presence, energy, *bios*, the real, and authenticity—all rather vague concepts, as if they were rationalism's unthinkable.

Shifting Questions

The analysis of non-Western or intercultural performance practices obliges us to reconsider all existing methods of analysis, and to shift the Western semiological perspective; the latter cannot remain purely functionalist, for it must try to come to grips with the other culture from the inside—and this invites the ethnoscenologist to make some excursions/incursions into the field of practice. But how can we modify the classical Western semiological perspective? To clarify things, the new priorities will be systematized and indications made as to what the main focus of this new perspective ought to be. It should be stressed that this is much more a question of changing attitudes and emphases than of replacing one method with another. Thus, in each case, the analysis will be concerned with one particular aspect rather than another. The *other* perspective is not built on the ruins of the former perspective, but rather on the fact of their complementarity. Furthermore, it should be noted that the criteria are not exclusively formal, but that they rely on fundamental considerations and involve an entire philosophy, even a metaphysics.

Theory of Cultural Exchanges

Lack of space here prevents us from returning to the model of cultural exchange for intercultural (in the strict sense of the term) mise-en-scène I have tried to outline elsewhere.[17] Let me simply point out that we find ourselves situated in an intercultural model and a perpetual and inevitable exchange between cultures. It is no longer very easy to distinguish what comes from a source culture and what reaches the target culture; it is as if each pole is already infiltrated by the other, and we cannot determine with any certainty a linear, unidirectional exchange between the pole of the source culture and that of the target culture. In order to describe exchanges between the poles, we would need an interactive model that does not simply observe how one culture (usually Western) appropriates another, but how *other* cultures also use aspects of Western culture for their own ends. (For example, one could show how mise-en-scènes of contemporary Indonesian texts are influenced by a Western genre or acting technique, and how they [re]organize this influence according to their own concrete, local needs.)[18]

The example chosen for this outline of the reevaluated principles for analysis of non-Western performance is that of the "archer drawing the bow," a sequence performed by the dancer from the Indian tradition of Odissi, Sanjukta Panigrahi. In addition to this particular case, what follows is of relevance to any intercultural performance, or indeed any performance practice other than the tradition of Western mise-en-scène centered around the unique and unifying thought of a director.

Readjustments in Anthropological Analysis

Parallel Series Rather Than Minimal Units
Instead of looking for minimal units, which are problematic to define, one focuses on series of signs in an entire sequence. In the bow-drawing sequence, for example, one can observe the constant position of the left hand and arm, which is holding the bow; the rest of the body is organized in relation to this constant, and the series of positions adopted by the right hand structures the narrative by itself: taking the arrow, flexing the bow, maintaining the correct position before the arrow is released. The right arm is supported and reinforced by the trunk, which is firmly rooted on the ground by feet that remain connected to the same spot, although they organize the movement and dynamic of the legs. For each of the mobilizable parts of the body (head, feet or torso, etc.), one might constitute a series of key positions, then compare the parallel series thus obtained. The sequence becomes meaningful once one is able to read the parallel gestural actions

within it, and to record its principal *articulations,* in both the literal and figurative meanings of the word.

Energy Rather Than Meaning

Often a sequence assumes no obvious meaning; it is neither possible nor very illuminating to translate a signifier into its corresponding signified, to meticulously decode isolated and static signs. On the other hand, the spectator is often sensitive to an expenditure of energy by the dancer, to a type of energy particular to the tradition being studied, or to energy changes within a series of movements, particularly when the variation occurs in accordance with the strong/soft polarity, as is the case in a large number of traditions. In the Odissi bow-drawing sequence, it would be useful to record moments of strong tension (which is quite easy given the consistent action of drawing the bow), and thus to note moments at which the strength and direction of the movement change radically. Describing energy involves showing in what ways it is specific to a dance form or an acting style (to the point that a dancer will retain its specificity even if she tries her hand at an entirely different form of dance). Furthermore, describing energy is informative in terms of the way in which the cultural context explains the use of a particular dance. Energy, that is always culture viewed from a certain perspective and concretized in a certain rhythm.

In less linear and specific examples, one might endeavor to reconstruct the flux and displacements of energy, to draw the trajectory of a physical action, and to follow the actor in what Barba calls "the dance of thought-in-action."[19] This recourse, or even return, to the notion of energy does not aim to replace a theater of signs (a Western semiology) with a theater of energies (like the one Lyotard called for), but rather to reconcile "Cartesian" semiology and "Artaudian" vectorization: in short, to experience the pulsional flux of the live event, but without moving outside the limits of a structured and localizable system.

Concrete Rather Than Abstract

The semiological search for meaning frequently leads to an exclusion of stage or corporeal materiality, for an abstract model records stage reality in an economical way by replacing material products with abstract signifying systems. The analyst is often tempted to reduce this materiality to an immaterial signified. In so doing, one loses the meaning of physical actions, and of *dramaturgy*—literally a sequence of "actions at work"[20] that struc-

Fig. 34. Sanjukta Panigrahi during a demonstration of the archer drawing the bow, as performed in Odissi dance. (Photograph by Nicola
Savarese.)

Fig. 35. The exchange of gazes in Theatrum Mundi. (Photograph by
Emidio Luisi/Fotograma.)

tures the story being recounted, forms the concrete line of the performance, and "works directly on the spectator's attention, on their understanding, their emotions, their kinaesthesia."[21] Here one can see culture
being inscribed and absorbed into the body of the actor and of the spectator, becoming an "incorporated knowledge"[22] for both parties. The Odissi
bow-drawing sequence offers us living proof, for the movement is literally
communicated in an aesthesic manner to the observer, as a simple, powerful, and assured physical action. Although it is invisible, the arrow
inevitably reaches its target, for it has been drawn, set in place, and fired by
means of visible, palpable microactions. Even if it were made of bamboo or
a laser beam, it would be no more concrete and present than this invisible
arrow fired effortlessly by the dancer's body.

Autonomy of Elements Rather Than Hierarchy
Of course, the entire body of the dancer is united in accomplishing this
fictive and, at the same time, concrete action; but each area of the body—

head, trunk, arms, legs—in turn takes center stage. The hierarchy between these different body parts is never fixed; each of them in turn is able to focus our attention and take its place at the heart of the gestural event. So each body part becomes the center of the movement of energy, as if, in a sort of "bodily democracy" (Trisha Brown), any part could, at any moment, become the "head of state."

In more general terms, this is valid for an entire performance that is not structured hierarchically from top to bottom, but remains subject to variations of intensity (and of *density*, as we will see). Certain attitudes, certain body parts, certain strong moments in the performance can become focal points, in Odissi dance as in other types of performance. In Odissi dance, gesture and music frequently converge in heightened moments, pauses, and syntheses, in which everything that has happened before that point suddenly assumes order and meaning.

Partial Perspectives Rather Than Centralization

The successive autonomy of the parts of a whole makes it impossible for a central perspective to be fixed. Within the heart of a production, one must be wary of homogenizing, unifying, and reconciling the different perspectives. For here there is a polyperspectivalism comparable to El Greco's painting *View of Toledo*, which Eisenstein used as an illustration of a global space bringing together specific spaces and perspectives, each of them coexisting alongside each other within the same frame. We should approach the analysis of the space and performance actions in this way, without starting from the idea that everything is necessarily organized around a vanishing point. The spectator must be able to locate partial perspectives, as well as, within what might otherwise pass as homogeneous, a sequence of shots conceived in the Eisensteinian way as a "montage of attractions."

We have already observed how the Odissi dancer subdivides her body and the body-mind union into zones that can be isolated, as if to further reveal the sophisticated mechanics of the linking of body parts and narrative episodes, and make them function more effectively. In an intercultural performance a fortiori, whether it is creolized or multicultural, it will be possible to compare different perspectives and evaluate a montage in large part realized by the spectator.

Differential Density Rather Than Homogeneity

A production is not always cut from the same cloth; it is not uniform in terms of its *density*. The notion of *thick description* comes from the anthropologist Clifford Geertz, who uses it to describe a given culture in a very precise way:

> The aim is to draw large conclusions from small, but very densely textured facts; to support broad assertions about the role of culture in the construction of collective life by engaging them exactly with complex specifics.[23]

The inspiration for this kind of analysis is in an anthropology that strives to conduct a detailed, *local* analysis and, at the same time, a *global* synthesis of the forces involved. The local is approached through microanalyses, movements or discourses, while the global becomes explicit in the general discourse of the mise-en-scène (if need be) or in the account of its major working principles.

In the case of the Odissi dance sequence, "thick" moments occur when there is a change of direction, a transfer of weight, an unleashing of energy, or a pause. In this particular instance, differences in thickness are not due to a cultural heterogeneity, but rather to a "respiration" and a differentiated distribution of energies.

In the case of more complex performances, which use all of the resources of Western mise-en-scène, analysis records those moments at which a number of series or units converge and intersect, thereby making their presence denser. It is the same for space: not every element of the performance has the same pertinence; there are dense zones, in which the slightest detail assumes importance, and neutralized zones, within which neither meaning nor energy seem to emerge. The same goes for plot: the key moments when conflicts are established or resolved are followed by more neutral moments. And also for actors: the zones of their bodies signify to varying degrees, or maybe their characteristics are attributed with a character that is more or less defined and individualized.

In the case of intercultural mise-en-scènes, one can clearly perceive different thicknesses if one is sensitive to the materials of diverse origins, particularly in terms of their cultural provenance and of the appropriate conditions to deal with them. The spectator must change her perspective constantly, and thus also her mode of analysis, but without definit(iv)ely identifying the sources and cultures.

Syncretism Rather Than Purity

Odissi dance does not display any visible characteristic of syncretism, in the sense of an amalgam of elements stemming from different cultures. Syncretism seems to be confined (although not necessarily so) to intercultural theater, in which several traditions or cultural fragments converge and coexist.

Remake Rather Than Describe?

Confronted with such difficulties in describing and evaluating the syncretism of cultures, would it not be simpler to ask the artist herself to talk about her art while reproducing it? When one asks Sanjukta Panigrahi to analyze the bow-drawing episode, she does so by going back to the principal physical attitudes, while commenting on them verbally, stopping to clarify a detail, identifying the motifs, poses, and transitions. This way of proceeding is also informative in terms of the manner of narrating, which is peculiar to each culture, with the examples she deems necessary and in accordance with her evaluation of the difficulties and originalities of her own actions. This work demonstration, halfway between reconstruction (which is impossible) and description (which dismembers), clearly reveals the difference between the thing and the word, between the stage action and the theoretical reflection. Furthermore, it is worth noting that this commentary/demonstration exercise is done exclusively by Sanjukta for the Westerners; it is carried out in English for a nonspecialist audience unfamiliar with Odissi as a whole, although nonetheless appreciative (let us at least acknowledge this openness of mind). In her school, with her own students, Sanjukta Panigrahi would proceed in an entirely different way. She would get them to do and redo the exercise, without commenting on its aims, her only concern being to transmit this dance physically. In the West, she agrees to our request, taking into account our desire for the rationalization and intellectual memorizing of information, our obsession with talking more than doing.

This indicates to some degree that analysis is not the only, "correct" method of recording and conveying a performance, all the more so if the aim is not to record a newly invented mise-en-scène, but to pass on a particular technical expertise to future generations, as is the case with Odissi dance.

Certain Western actors have also discovered the possibility of conserving and analyzing their past roles, going back to them or quoting them in the course of working demonstrations. This is how Iben Nagel Rasmussen proceeds, for example, as do other actresses from the Odin Teatret (Roberta Carreri, Julia Varley), or even Mike Pearson.[24] The latter has invented an entire system for bringing a past theater back to life, by proposing a response to it which not only re-members and analyzes it, but also re-creates and further evolves it.

Let us take one final example of this readjustment realized by the analyst, by considering the case of the German composer Heiner Goebbels who, at Nanterre in 1993, directed a production using fragments of texts by Joseph Conrad, Heiner Müller, and Francis Ponge, with African musicians playing the kora and singing.

Readjustments: The Example of Heiner Goebbels

Parallel Series Rather Than Minimal Units

Instead of insistently segmenting a few fragments of the performance into even smaller fragments, it would be more useful to draw up two paradigms through which the performance as a whole is articulated: on the one hand, the quest and arrival of the white man in the hostile milieu of the forest, which is in turn uncomfortable, frightening, or industrialized; and on the other, the musical promenade of the two African musicians who sing and play the kora. This double paradigm serves to bring all of the oppositions together: thematic, musical, and scenographic. It allows a systematic comparison, element by element and on every level: thematic, as well as stylistic, philosophical, and anthropological.

Energy Rather Than Meaning

Rather than trying to fully grasp the meaning of this double paradigm, one could measure the difference in energies emanating from the two kinds of music, and from the two different ways of using language and the voice. One is an electrical energy, since the electric guitar, the daxophone, and the synthesizers are all connected to the mains power supply; the other is a vocal energy that is "plugged in" to the body, but in fact constitutes it. One is a feverish, dissipated, irregular energy, based on an undefined research; the other is a contained, calm, resourceful energy. The energy of André Wilms (the white actor) is that of a mountain stream or waterfall, whereas the energy of the female singer (Sira Djeba) is that of a deep body of water, a powerful river flowing into the sea. Once this opposition is established, the exegetes are free to extend it to the ideological and political implications that underlie the play as a whole. The semantic oppositions are thus confirmed and reinforced.

Concrete Rather Than Abstract

Whether one approaches the performance on the level of the music, the use of the voice, or the scenography and its materials (sand, stone slabs, a forestlike polyester carpet), one notices an experimental, sensual use of materials, including the musical, vocal material that is produced live, in a playful way, and with no apparent motive other than to provide something immediate and agreeable for our consumption. However, abstraction, or meaning if one prefers, is never very far away; it is, as it must be, the inverse of the palpable, concrete side of signs. Thus the enormous cone, a gigantic hourglass or cement mixer that seems ready to empty its contents on to the still virgin forest, is inverted to take on the appearance of a hollow space, a camera obscura, a bellowslike camera that suggests both the trompe l'oeil of an illusionist stage space, and a mental space the explorer enters carrying a portable lamp. In the same way, the enormous Western machine churning out decibels also turns into its opposite; the warm voice of the female singer from Mali moves through the darkness and touches deep chords within us.

Autonomy of Elements Rather Than Hierarchy

The general structure of the mise-en-scène is at pains not to connect elements irreversibly, whether they be textual, scenographic, or musical. This is a real meeting/nonmeeting (a "merging" in Hastrup's sense). The progression of the performance seems to be conceived in a manner that clears the way for (instrumental) improvisation and juxtaposes signs and their vectors, rather than structuring them hierarchically. However, and this is the "thesis" of this mise-en-scène (for that is what it is, and a Western one at that), the two arts, of technology and the human voice, ultimately converge with each other, without either one needing to invade the other, yet still maintaining a constant competition between their very different energies. One might find this opposition between Western technology and untainted African nature somewhat banal, but one cannot deny that it is presented in a concrete and aleatory manner.

Partial Perspectives Rather Than Centralization

All of Goebbels's compositional work in the production consists of a kind of self-denial. He claims to create a collage of texts chosen for their assonance, whereas in fact all of these texts are connected through their complementary perspectives on colonialism; his aim is to provide an opportunity for the minimalist music of the African kora, although he organizes those moments at which it intervenes with great precision; he promotes an "interculturalism of equal arms," but in fact he suggests that the African forest will finish up as pole, mast, beam, board, and that the only trace of it to remain in place will be "the general idea" (a universal and abstract Western figure). In short, partial and autonomous perspectives are soon reassimilated within the transcendental, centralizing vision of Goebbels as creator. It would also be revealing to compare the French vision and the German vision of African culture, and to note differences in the performance's reception in Paris and Frankfurt.

Differential Density Rather Than Homogeneity

In the same way that the forest has a variable density, the performance gives the impression of moments of varying degrees of density and tension; first, through its very structure (technology/human voice), and subsequently through the alternation of the two paradigms and their quantitative imbalance, which is clearly inversely proportional to their qualitative difference. Thus, when silence settles around the minimalist composition of the kora or the griot's voice, these elements assume a remarkable prominence; here we find the kind of concrete and specific detail that reproduces on a local level that which the performance's structure suggests globally, with the additional factor of the concrete and aleatory materiality giving the "small, dense fact" an unprecedented authenticity, thereby facilitating a very "thick" description of the performance.

Syncretism Rather Than Purity

From then on, the notion of purity no longer has any meaning in this performance, at least in the sense of a monoculture or of a culture that is so strong that it has absorbed all others; for each musical culture keeps watch over its own identity, and is not the result of a hybridization. No syncretic music is produced; instead different musics are placed side by side, and are brought closer together, creating a confluence between components currently separated.

"Thickness" stems from the compression within a single motif of different elements accumulated to such an extent that it is no longer possible to disentangle them. Neither is it possible to establish their place of origin, or to reconstruct the network of their exchanges. The performance is naturally a collage, at times even a set of surreal images in which the force of the image lies in the incongruity of its components. The conjunction of goldfish and rabbit, the chance encounter of sewing machine and umbrella:

such is the logic of all mixed marriages in the sphere of interculturalism, over which the purist casts a dubious eye. In any performance, and a fortiori in any intercultural performance, one might assume that everything is already hybrid from the outset: a collage of techniques and a bric-a-brac of selected elements, a syncretic, creolized, Caribbean vision like Aimé Césaire's, in which "organic culture [has been] reconceived as inventive process or creolized 'interculture.'"[25] One should take care to distinguish between a collage of heterogeneous materials and an act of hybridization (or creolization) that creates a new product.

One might well expect just such a creolization in Barba's Theatrum Mundi, but instead we find a juxtaposition and a sequence of the "best moments" (for the Western spectator) of materials that are already familiar. The "aesthetic of quotas" (the democratic demand to represent traditions in a quantitatively egalitarian fashion) leads Barba to a montage not of *attractions,* but rather of *abstractions;* for the Western master of ceremonies feels obliged to essentialize the various cultural products, to select from them typical and recognizable aspects, and to avoid any interference between traditions, except in the comic interludes, which clearly serve to create a consensus among those audience members only too delighted to find out that that one can have fun anywhere . . .

Syncretism is most evident in contemporary Western mise-en-scène that, from the beginning, has been influenced, infiltrated, and regenerated by "other" practices and perspectives. Might one not suggest that current Western mise-en-scène is, in part, Chinese (alienation effect), Indian (union of body and mind), Balinese (in the wake of Artaud and his notion of bodily writing), or Japanese (antipsychological), and so on? The earlier conception of mise-en-scène as a centralizing mastery of meaning has now crumbled and, with it, the globalizing, purist pretensions of performance analysis. The same performance will be received differently by different groups; a theater work adapts itself to the gaze of the other and is infinitely remade; it often suggests specific cultural notations as much as universal ones and lends itself to being viewed as an exotic, consumable asset, or as a premeditated means of access to the culture of the other.

The Anthropological Gaze

The intercultural also exists within the intracultural. Isn't "French culture" thus the result of a series of particular cultures inherited from the past? Of course we must learn to respect cultures, but let us not forget that they are already heterogeneous constructions stemming from different cultural materials. Having gone back from analysis to practice, from the gaze to the object being observed, we also find ourselves back at our point of departure: the question of the usefulness of the anthropological approach in the domain of intercultural theater and of ethnoscenology.

But exactly what has changed since we started to mistrust the inevitable ethnocentricity of our perspective?

The anthropological approach seems imperative as soon as one is required to express an opinion about a performance that necessarily conveys cultural values other than our own. But it is just as useful for the analysis of our own traditions. Indeed it is neither possible nor desirable to strictly separate performances belonging to the culture(s) of the analyst from performances that are "foreign" to her, or intercultural. The anthropological perspective, close up and distanced at the same time, is the general rule, as is the performance open to cultural pluralism. One should therefore approach and analyze performances with a sense of relativity, adapting or even contradicting the analytical procedures usually used by Western semiology.

What then can anthropology or ethnoscenology bring to bear in performance analysis? Quite simply, they encourage us to shift our perspective toward the performance, which comes to seem like a "foreign body" (in the positive sense of the word): an-other "way of seeing," new and unconventional, but also a way of seeing that involves the whole *body*. Of course we cannot step outside our own culture, leaving its prejudices and inadequacies behind; but at least we know that our way of seeing is imbued with, as well as enriched by, all of our cultural experience.

A sudden suspicion: isn't the expression "Western semiology" in itself already ethnocentric? Not necessarily, if one considers the fact that the semiology of performance developed above all (to the best of our knowledge) in Europe and the United States, with the object of its focus (its target?) being Western mise-en-scènes. It is understandable, therefore, that its perspective should be partial and that it has to be adapted for other forms. This is what this volume has tried to initiate.

In the process of trying to develop this perspective, it soon became clear that it would involve an adaptation, a different gaze rather than a counter-methodology. The imbrication of cultures has been stressed repeatedly, particularly on the level of the frequently multicultural construction of performances, in both the *West* and the *rest* of the world. The observer should conceive of the performance object as both the same and the other. She need not be embarrassed by functionalist semiology, which has contributed a great deal to the elucidation of cultural products, a semiology whose rigor remains unequaled, and which seemed at a particular moment to be the dominant current in thinking. The observer should simply correct the deforming effects of a text-based theater and theory, or of the notion of a singular author creating performance. She should certainly go in the direction of the other, but she should not cover the ground on her own.

On the road to Damascus taken by the theater analyst charitably guided by the anthropologist, in short the route taken by the *ethnoscenologist* (if we have to give her a name), all sorts of pitfalls crop up, the least of which is perhaps that she may also disappear, body and soul, in the object of her research. Remember that the anthropologist, having left her own country in order to discover the other culture, "practises an all-consuming observation, after which nothing at all is left, apart from the definitive absorption—and this is a real risk—of the observer by the object of her observation."[26] The ethnoscenologist who abandons the assurance of her critical and semiological positions, in order to immerse herself in a performance and in the universe that produced it, runs a similar risk. Having set out to settle a banal question of epistemology or of performance analysis, she risks being transformed into a dramaturge, a director, even an actor; some destinies happen to be tragic! Of course, her participant observations help to abolish the frontiers between object and subject, between *I* and *you*, and to place her in the same situation as anthropological science, which is the only one "to make of the most intimate subjectivity a means of objective demonstration";[27] but in addition, she has lost her Western frames of reference, her confidence in an effective methodology for analysis, her belief in the social usefulness of her mission. Her disorientation is total, but salutary, for the "other" of analysis is the actual making of the performance; and what is this making if not an anticipation of its own reception, an analysis *avant la lettre* of what does not yet exist?

Ultimately, the anthropological perspective, both near and distanced at the same time, on intercultural theater will be of benefit to Western theory and practice. Indeed, it will force them to reconsider existing methods of analysis, to take note of cultural intermixing, and to take their place in a world that is richer and more complex than they ever imagined.[28]

Conclusions: Which Theories for Which Mise-en-scènes?

At the end of this lengthy exploration of methods of analyzing contemporary performance, it might seem rather strange to ask which theories we really need, and for which particular mise-en-scènes. Could it be a matter of there being too many theories for a standard theater product, or on the contrary too few for a plethora of forms that are not yet standardized in repertories? There is no easy answer, for it all depends on our perspective on theater work: do we think of it in terms of a general mise-en-scène needing a universal explanation, or a particular case requiring specific solutions?

No "general" mise-en-scène exists, and one must always specify the genre of mise-en-scène in which one is interested: a fact that does not facilitate the formulation of a single theory. Moreover this book has focused above all on Western mise-en-scène, an expression that in itself is pleonastic. For mise-en-scène, as a late-nineteenth-century invention, is localized in the West; and in addition it stems from a theater aesthetic particular to Europe, where "the expected pleasure of representation and simulacra that it demands is inseparable from the production of a meaning, from a reappropriation of the world, and from self-knowledge."[1]

This orientation, no less legitimate for being a matter of some delicacy, leads one to ask the question that has been skirted thus far: that of the aesthetic and ideological evaluation of mise-en-scène.

Evaluation of Mise-en-Scène

Evaluative Criteria

Often the criteria are not very explicit, and only rarely do they concern the pure artistic value of the stage production. So in fact one must determine what artistic elements the theatrical event has, and how they should be evaluated. It is equally important to appraise whether the work emerges from an authentic experience on the part of the artists concerned, whether it corresponds to the implicit discourse and expectations of a particular period, or whether the innovation it represents is superficial and banal. Pierre Gaudibert's remarks about the plastic arts are equally valid for theater:

> Nowadays, there is some confusion between the real innovation—that of languages and signs—that one finds in great creations, an innovation that modifies perception, as well as psychic and mental attitudes, and an avant-gardist impulse translated into superficial modifications that strive to be original and provocative.[2]

"Acceptable innovation" is one criterion that Western theater audiences readily latch on to, preoccupied as they are with discovering a technique or a new message, without their expectations and habits being overly mistreated. These expectations and cultural resistances can be augmented with so-called analytical resistances, which "stem from emotional and/or sexual blocks," resistances "triggered by works that bring into play sexuality, drives, phantasms (surrealism, for example), or by works that evoke the tragic, destruction, crisis, giving rise to anguish and despair."[3] In addition to overcoming such resistances, evaluation is concerned with the authenticity of a work, and with the human and artistic experience of those who have created it, at the risk of sinking back into the quicksands of the author's psychology.

Or perhaps into the discourse of style: the style of a mise-en-scène or of an artist (director, scenic designer, lighting designer, or actor). It is certainly possible to enumerate some characteristics that are peculiar to an artist or to a body of work; ultimately such characteristics constitute a trademark or a signature. However this is a very superficial notion of stylistics, quickly turning style into a "je ne sais quoi," which is only an initial typological approximation requiring immediate completion—as has been attempted here—by means of systematic and systemic analysis of the components of a mise-en-scène, its creative processes, and the results produced. Succumbing to stylistics of this kind can lead to something just as tempting, and every bit as bland: the normative criticism of "errors" in a mise-en-scène, the locating of its dysfunctional and incoherent aspects.

"Mistakes" in the Mise-en-Scène

Unexpected in a theory of mise-en-scène striving for objectivity and an avoidance of all value judgments, normative criticism of "mistakes" endeavors to call attention to a performance's incoherent and inconsistent elements in relation to a conductive through-line, to a comprehensive logic of the whole, to the mise-en-scène's implicit principles: in short, to what has sometimes been called the metatext or discourse of the mise-en-scène. So, for example, it might be a matter of establishing whether an actor remains faithful to an acting style, or whether the system of entrances and exits coheres with the scenographic choices made, or not. In other words, each new element in the proceedings will be examined in terms of its antecedents. Does it follow the logic of what precedes it, or does it in fact contradict previous dramaturgical and staging choices? Does it damage the overall schematic design of the piece, or does it open up a new and freely assumed perspective? Whatever steps outside the proposed framework can be perceived at times as an error in the mise-en-scène, at other times as keeping spectators' attention on the alert. Mise-en-scène is always located between chaos and redundancy, between the absence of a mappable order and an overly cumbersome systematicity. It is governed by two contradictory tendencies: the need for order and regularity, felt conjointly by both director and spectators; and the tendency to make the message more complex and engender its own self-organizing particularity. For contemporary mise-en-scène resembles a self-organizing system:

> In order for a system to have its own self-organizing particularities, its initial redundancy should have only a minimal value, since these particularities comprise an augmentation of complexity through destruction of redundancy.[4]

Therefore there is a real danger in establishing the metatext as an inflexible self-organizing principle, without the slightest deviation from the norm being permitted to open up the mise-en-scène to new or amplified possibilities of meaning. In short, "mistakes" can be voluntarily chosen and planned, intended to keep spectators attentive and alert; they are often the result of artistic or organizational decisions within the mise-en-scène.

So what could errors made by a director comprise? There is little point in endeavoring to list them, for such a list would be endless. The interest of these errors is in their ability to stimulate spectators' attention, keeping it on the alert, and to make their critical faculties more acute, despite the risk of boredom or of drifting away.

System of the Mise-en-Scène

In spite of a tendency to self-organization in contemporary mise-en-scène—in other words to the disappearance of any regularity—in other respects there is evidence of a return to the major principles of organization: to neo-Brechtian dramaturgical analysis,[5] for example, or to the synthetic understanding of simultaneous ensembles, to the metatext, or simply to the constitutive unity of the human spirit.

Dramaturgical Analysis

Historically and chronologically (the passage of text to stage), mise-en-scène has become, along with structuralism and semiology, a structural and systematic notion. Consequently it is natural to attempt to formalize a system for it, in particular through reference to dramaturgical choices—as in the heyday of Brechtianism when one established, in the blink of an eye, the action, the plot, the forms of space and time, the actants and their gestures. Although ideology is no longer what it was, enabling knowledge of the dramaturgical shaping of the plot's contradictions, it resurfaces once the focus is on referencing the options and dramaturgical framework of a performance; it allows the dramatic structure and its scenic shaping—that which in-forms its scenography—to be encapsulated in a glance.

Synthetic Understanding of Simultaneous Ensembles

It obeys the same logic of structuration in broad and clear ensembles. Our analytical experience of performance is always vertical and synthetic (and not purely linear and fragmentary); the spectator perceives all the elements of a mise-en-scène as temporal totalities, which coincide with and manifest themselves in synthetic scenic signs. In short, the spectator does not break up a performance into pieces, but employs broad spatiotemporal cross-sections within which meaning forms a coherent ensemble.

Metatext of the Mise-en-Scène

This notion remains useful for the systematic regrouping of the particular qualities of a performance, the sum of which forms a logical system. Remember that rather than being the director's particular property, the metatext is an evolutive structural system of use to the spectator for schematic guidance and synthesis.

Unity and Unicity of the Spirit

In short, it is the unity and unicity of the spirit that serves as conductive thread through a performance, despite the anarchic bombardment of signs. One could not express it better than Zeami, when he said that one must "conjoin the ten thousand means of expression through the unicity of the spirit"; "your spirit" must be "the thread by means of which, without the spectator's knowledge, you conjoin your 'ten thousand means of expression.'"[6]

In addition, as Zeami could have reminded us, neither mise-en-scène nor semiology constitute a catalog of signs, nor indeed a locksmith's provision of keys to dreams of all kinds; mise-en-scène and semiology are a gold string on which each of us can thread the pearls of the most disjointed and desultory of postmodernities. Is this because subject and author have staged a return? And should one be delighted by this?

Return of the Author and of Authority?

As soon as one talks of mise-en-scène, one quickly yields to the temptation of recentering theatrical activity in the director, making her the scenic author and authority, aesthetically and politically, of a performance. That was the idea of the very notion of mise-en-scène as it was elaborated a century ago by people like Craig, Stanislavsky, or Appia. However, this centralizing conception is attacked by a postmodern criticism of mise-en-scène; it reproaches mise-en-scène for arming itself with a dramaturgical analysis that is too rigid, for anchoring itself to an underscore that is too fixed, for submitting to the dictatorial whims of a demiartist, and, with this notion of stage language, for lapsing into a logocentrism with no interest in the stage except insofar as it is translatable into verbal signifieds.

Postmodern criticism mistrusts any notion of language, fearing that language could reintroduce a subject as its origin, which would erect a screen or filter between the spectator and the materiality of the theatrical signifiers. Such criticism advocates a direct relation to this materiality and to the corporeality of the actor; it requires the spectator's gaze to settle on, "the aspect of the nonintentional, the libidinal investment of events, the sensual materiality of all signifiers—which does not sanction turning aside from the corporeality of things, structures, and beings, thanks to which signification in theater appears."[7] Such a perspective—that of Lehmann, formerly that of Susan Sontag[8] and Barthes[9]—endeavors in this way to substitute an erotics for a semiology of art, reinstating the rights of desire and libidinal flux, for both actor and spectator. However, unless all that remains is to be an affirmative attitude of bliss *(jouissance)* of and in art, with no control over the unfolding of processes, one must reintroduce a meaning and direction to the erotic actions that the stage offers us for analysis. Which is what Lehmann does without hesitation:

> There is absolutely no question of privileging affect at the expense of concept; the concept must be able to receive within itself the reality of meanings, the seductiveness of what is, in the widest sense, erotic in the theatrical process.[10]

For our own part, this is what has been effected here in proposing the notion of *vectorization*, thereby attempting to provide for both concept and affect.

The question is of knowing whether this seductive concept represents a return of the subject and of her *authority*. In any case, it is more a matter of *authorization* than of *authoritarianism*.

So we are authorized in considering mise-en-scène not as work that is organic, coherent, and completed, but as a process gradually put in place, although in an episodic and unstable manner, a process within which one can still perceive the hypotheses, endeavors, and sketches of the director. Consequently mise-en-scène as end result (evidently still incomplete) is the place and the moment at which one can guess the way in which scenic materials have been structured, laminated, glued together, condensed, or displaced. For analysis, as much as for the production of the performance itself, it would be naive (and Hegelian, so to speak) to start from the principle of there being a structure that is organic, coherent, all-inclusive, a structure that can be broken up. It is well known that neither directors nor choreographers work according to the principles of universal harmony. Doesn't Pina Bausch, for example, state, "I don't work from beginning to end, but with small parts that slowly enlarge, combine with others, and grow toward the outside."[11] Analysis must take this into account, by avoiding the fixing of a performance into an aprioristic grid, and thereby failing to take into consideration the stage work's excrescences, manipulations, and irregularities. In this way, one will be able to remain wary of the absolute authority of the director who has purportedly foreseen everything and, at the same time, of the relative authority of the spectator whose gaze purportedly constitutes the work in its entirety. For a director's tasks are extremely varied nowadays.

Old and New Tasks of the Director

Master or Surveyor?
Two dangers seem to lie in wait for the director: that of being master of the stage *(maître en scène),* or that of being a simple surveyor *(métreur).* There have always been protests against the director's pretensions to rule over every aspect, and there is no lack of "angry men," such as Gillibert, to take offense at this:

> There must be no more "masters of the stage"; they kill the life truth of the work, that quality within it that makes it improbable, uncertain, but irresistible; they kill the life truth of the actor, who is not inventive any more, and no longer possesses emotional or imaginative abilities.[12]

In reaction to "mastery" of this kind, the director's role is often reduced to that of a simple surveyor: a subordinate entrusted with coordinating the movements of objects and actors, a site-foreman or storekeeper restricted to measuring distances, placements, or moves.

The director's role has changed a great deal since the classical conception of mise-en-scène as a harmonizing of materials, in the way that Copeau was able to define it in 1913:

> The outlining of a dramatic action. It is the ensemble of movements, gestures, and attitudes, the concordance of physiognomies, voices, and silences, the totality of the stage performance, emanating from a unique way of thinking that conceives, regulates, and harmonizes it.[13]

Therefore it is, as Meyerhold observes, "the widest specialization in the world . . . the theater of the actor, as well as the art of overall composition."[14] At the present time, directors tend to forgo their overall artistic responsibility in "favor" of a simple technical responsibility (surveyor, producer, showman—of dancing bears). The universal master of former times frequently delegates his or her power to various agents of mastery, those responsible for different components of the performance (sound, light, music, technology, etc.). Mise-en-scène has become decentralized and delegated; it no longer regroups nor composes anything; it limits itself to juxtaposing sounds, noises, images, bodies. In an antisemiological theater such as this, which Lyotard calls "energetic,"

> one makes the power relation (the hierarchy) impossible, and consequently, what also becomes impossible is the so-called domination of dramatist + director + choreographer + designer over the so-called signs, as well as over so-called spectators.[15]

This dehierarchizing makes any metatext, any commentary on the ensemble of signs, illegible or contradictory: henceforth no overall view, no general perspective seems to be in a position to report on the mise-en-scène. The difference from the classical position is that this illegibility (or invisibility) is definitive: one can no longer evaluate the mise-en-scène in the terms of a clear commentary set down in an easily legible metatext.

Visible Metatext or Ultraviolet Rays?
Previously, according to its classical conception—that of a Copeau, Stanislavsky, or Meyerhold—mise-en-scène was both implicit and, at the same time, perceptible to the attentive spectator, for "the ultraviolet rays of the principal idea of the performance must be invisible and penetrate the spectator in such a way that she doesn't notice them."[16] At the present time, the evidence is no longer even implicit, and the metatext no longer even tries to be discreet; it is either nonexistent, or contradictory and illegible.

Conceptual Mise-en-Scène
On the other hand, sometimes mise-en-scène is stressed and legible to such an extent that it becomes a critical commentary that in itself constitutes another separate work: the mise-en-scène is then "conceptual," in the sense of a "conceptual art." It takes itself to be of such intelligence that ultimately

it forgets it is mise-en-scène *of,* so as to be simply mise-en-scène, reflection in its pure state: no longer material for reflection, simply reflection as its only material.

Splintering
A writing that, in its fragmentation, has gone beyond the dramatic/epic alternative flies off into splinters—from the moment of the act of writing, and even more so from the intervention of the actor. Hence the difficulty of applying to it a unified language.

Whatever the strategy adopted by directors, it is rather difficult for the spectator to keep track of all the working processes in play in its formation and systematization. There is no surprise in the problems theory has in keeping up, nor that its scratching from the race is declared, even its immi-nent disappearance suggested. The immersion of readers, like spectators, into an era of suspicion, and of theoretical rejection, will be lasting. But is this really reasonable? What are the uses of theories, and of what do they dream? Do they facilitate analysis and appreciation of performances? Are they useful to practitioners? Becoming aware of the limits of analysis and of theory is not, however, a negative, disenchanted attitude: quite the con-trary!

Limits of Analysis, Limits of Theory

Reevaluation of Theory

Criticism of the Sign
A frequent argument employed to put one on one's guard against the difficulty of interpreting theater performance consists of stressing the impossibility of knowing whether a particular element of the acting or of the decor is (or is not) the sign of an intention expressed by the director. As soon as one adopts the point of view of an analysis of a performance, one chooses the perspective of its reception (and not of its production). Indeed it is always up to the spectators to make up their minds on this in terms of the overall performance. Not everything in the performance is reducible to a sign; there remain authentic moments, unforeseeable and unrepeatable events. How can one know whether the whiskey drunk by an actor is actu-ally whiskey after all, or whether the plaster cast covers a leg that is really

broken? Therefore, if everything can be a sign, and if nothing is absolutely certain, is it still useful to secure the services of semiology? Broadly speaking, this is Lyotard's argument:

> For the sign, Peirce used to say, is something which stands for something to somebody. To Hide, to Show: that is theatricality. The modernity of our *fin de siècle* consists of this: there is nothing to be replaced, no *lieutenancy* [*lieu-tenance:* "place-taking"/"taking-place"] is legitimate, or else all of them are; replacement, and therefore meaning, is itself only a substitute for displacement.[17]

Lyotard's thesis is valid for a unique, aleatory performance, such as a Cage event or a happening, but it is inapplicable as soon as a performance is given at least a second time, and its repetition necessitates foreshadowing the effects. Nevertheless, his argument has the merit of leaving mise-en-scène open as a reserve of materials and signs, as matter and spirit, signifier ready to signify. Moreover it is not a new argument, for Copeau had previously made it the touchstone of his aesthetic:

> We reject the empty old distinction, in an intellectual work, between what belongs to matter and what depends on spirit, between form and content. Similarly, we refuse to conceive of a factitious dissociation between art and professional craft.[18]

Criticism of Representation
Criticism of the sign leads to criticism of representation: Derrida, for example, rereading Artaud, directs such criticism at theater that continues to represent, instead of being life itself: "The theatre of cruelty is not a representation. It is life itself, in the extent to which life is unrepresentable."[19] This refusal to represent is sometimes claimed by actors (or more exactly *performers*) who do not perform any role (not even their own), yet remain present on stage, their performance no longer referring to anything other than itself.

The aesthetic of representation, which requires a community of themes or interests, gives way to an aesthetic of reception and of individual perception; receivers become the principal authority making judgments in terms of their tastes, life, and personal experience. In place of the represented work, they endeavor to substitute an erotics of art, an experience of sensoriality, in which everything is appreciated according to the pleasure taken in contemplation of the work. This "preexpressive" manner (as Barba would say) of enjoying theater distances us from signs and meaning, and pitches us into sensations of presence and of balance, which attempt to neutralize any intellectual aspect of theater experience. What emerges is an "energetic" criticism of semiology.

Energetic Criticism of Semiology
From the perspective of an "energetic theatre,"[20] criticism attempts to substitute the network of signs with the flux of impulses, the force of presence, the immediacy of the signifier and of scenic materiality. An energetic circuit is supposed to provoke displacements of affect and pulsional flux.

Instead of a static network of signs, I have suggested imagining a circuit in which meaning appears and is displaced in accordance with a "semiotization of desire" or "vectorization." This model reconciles a semiology of the perceptible with an energetics of displacements that are not visible. For example, space is not defined only in a representative manner—as a space already framed and put in perspective, a space to be filled—but rather as an energetic vector connected to its users, to their spatiotemporal coordinates, presence, energy, movements, and route through it. It is a question of holding to the oxymoronic notion of a "semiotization of desire"—of describing actor and spectator as objects inhabiting the space between semiotization and desemiotization, by keeping the energetic erotics of signifiers present for as long as possible. The attention we bring to bear on stage materiality is reinforced by a denial that reminds us incessantly that we are at the theater and that we perceive only forms and matter.

So the semiological model of the theatrical object caught in a network of signs with its own systems, connections, and regularities operates in relay with the vectorial model, a model that straddles a visual semiology and an energetics. Then, and only then, is it meaningful to talk of an "energetic charge," for the work as much as for its receiver, and one can reference this charge in one as much as in the other.

> In the work of art is inscribed an energetic charge, which arises from the creator's engagement; it is connected to their personal history, in the face of the society in which they are immersed and of their collective unconscious.[21]

In order for spectators to feel a similar shock, a similar discharge, this shock must be prepared by what they perceive; the spectators must also understand these impulses as signs and vectors, and not only as shock waves. Such is the aim of the "integrated semiology" that is being proposed here.

Reference Points for Integrated Semiology

Such recurrent criticisms of the sign, representation, and semiology are not without interest. They enable us to reevaluate a theory that is too statically modeled on a survey of abstract signs. One can propose central axes of reference in one's approach to mise-en-scène, and work theatrical representation as one works dreams ("dreamwork"): starting from major structural and structuring processes.

Let us return one last time to the model of vectors, inspired by Freud's *Interpretation of Dreams,* further developed by Jakobson and Lacan, adapted to the primary working processes of theatrical representation. Let us clarify the nature of its two main axes:

- The axis of *displacement,* or of *metonymy,* which replaces one element with another ("connector"), or breaks the chain's links so as to move on to something quite different ("cutter"): the axis of an aesthetic that is somewhat mimetic, realist, prosaic, linear, in which the stage is hewn from the external world with which it is consubstantial.
- The axis of *condensation,* or of *metaphor,* which accumulates and mixes elements (through "accumulators") or creates access to a quite different sphere (through "shifters"): the axis of an aesthetic that is somewhat nonrealist, symbolist, poetic, circular, and tabular, and in which the stage tends toward autonomy, condensing the world in a new reality closed in on itself.

Within this very general framework, one can examine the major axes according to which mise-en-scène works, and one can reference vectorial points of departure and outcomes, without necessarily deciding on the energetic forces that interconnect them. Vectorization remains open: not only does identification of the dominant vector at any particular moment remain difficult, but the link between connection, accumulation, rupture, and shifting remains to be established, and this is the very object of analysis and interpretation. Thus, at best this framework provides the conditions for all subsequent analysis. This has been verified in the analysis of "cultural legibility" in Eugenio Barba's Theatrum Mundi (chapter 10).

Conditions for Analysis

Dimensions

In the era of the video camera, remote control, and slow motion, the problem is no longer the ephemerality of performance, nor the exhaustive surveying and recording of all signs. Instead it is the choice of which signs to deem pertinent and noteworthy, and their hierarchization and vectorization. Nowadays one can find exhaustive critical works devoted to one mise-en-scène, even a second-rate one. The mass of informational and relentless technological detail might be intimidating to exegetes and nonspecialist spectators, all the more so given that recording technologies (video, computer and so on) are certainly capable of digitally encoding every aspect, but on condition that they take no interpretative risk.

Acceleration or Braking

Therefore, instead of accumulating and quantifying informational detail, I propose not only to articulate hypotheses on their vectorization, but also to concentrate on some aspects and to use a sort of mental remote control for acceleration, in order to perceive a mise-en-scène's lines of force. Acceleration (fast forward) can prevent the blocking of meaning, repair fragmentation, and release the lines of force. Deceleration (slow motion) can lead the spectator to a sort of illumination, a flash in which one is able to bring into relief all the pertinent factors in a sequence and to localize moments of recapitulative synthesis—moments variously called satori or Tao, propitious moment (Zeami), pregnant moment (Lessing), gestus (Brecht), or psychological gesture (Michael Chekhov).

These new conditions for analysis are not necessarily perceived as facilitating theory, but often on the contrary as an incitement to abandon theoretical debate, relativizing, even depreciating all analytical methods, calling into question the very possibility of theorizing stage work, and particularly so-called postmodern mise-en-scène. But need one be so hasty to exclude theory?

Against Postmodern Relativism

Difficulties of Description

Artists often reject theory, reproaching it for its inability to account for theatrical performance that is either unique and unrepeatable, or asemantic and closed in on itself. Barry Edwards and Geoffrey Smith, from the group Optik, for example, describe their performance *Tank* as an event that can be neither described nor foreseen:

> The performance event obviously cannot be "described," it's not a metaphor for "something else"; each performance generates its own evidence, its own history; but each performance is totally new.[22]

Even if each performance by Optik is indeed unique, in the same way as a happening or a ceremony that only takes place once, nothing prohibits describing and interpreting the event produced on that particular evening; ultimately it will still create meaning, even if it is in spite of itself, or as if fortuitously. Space, time, and action on stage necessarily inscribe themselves into history, our own history, once they are deployed to the knowledge of an audience. On the other hand, one cannot interpret the event as the response to a preordained text or intention. But who would still dream of doing that?

In the same way, nowadays who would dream of *decoding* a performance of this kind? Clearly a semiology of communication is of no usefulness in this context; given this, therefore, is it adequate to talk of *deconstructing* the performance? Now is an appropriate time to agree on some mutual understanding of this frequently employed word in postmodern criticism.

Limits of the Concept of Deconstruction

In the banal sense of the term, one talks of deconstruction when a mise-en-scène presents itself in a fragmented form, with no possibility of fixing a stable meaning, each fragment apparently in opposition with the others. When a mise-en-scène starts from a text, it can also deconstruct this text by opening it up to a multiplicity of contradictory meanings, proving the impossibility of a single correct reading being concretized in the performance.

In the technical sense of the term, that of Derrida and deconstructionism in philosophy, deconstruction applied to mise-en-scène could consist of finding a playful and interpretative disposition that "demonstrates" the impossibility of reading mise-en-scène by reducing it to one meaning, and that invents false trails and an entire strategy for unsettling and dismantling its own mechanisms, for quoting and parodying itself. Certain groups, such as Needcompany[23] or the Wooster Group,[24] have specialized in deconstructing their own aesthetics. There is always a moment at which the performance indicates how it is constructed (and therefore deconstructed), an element that at the same time discourages any referential allusion to the outside world. So it is not only the text that is deconstructed by the mise-en-scène (as is always the case to some degree, particularly when the actor critiques textual meaning in action); the entire mise-en-scène is contradicted and deconstructed by this very strategy.

In its banal version, deconstruction of the mise-en-scène can be constantly recycled; indeed the signification of the performance is never established, it is no more than a hypothesis at any particular moment—at best, the least unsatisfactory hypothesis continuously undone by new indices or as yet unexplored avenues.

Therefore any act of deconstruction is only provisional, in anticipation of those that will follow; and it is the spectator who decides in the final analysis on their succession. Consider for example the relationship between text and stage: even if the mise-en-scène attempts to contrive a space of neutrality between the dramatic text and the scenic configuration, the practice of the mise-en-scène soon fills this space in an "author-itarian" way; for it is the mise-en-scène as scenic writing and subject of the enunciation that decides, that creates meaning at the same time in the configuration and the dramatic text. Even if the director pretends not to want to assume a stable position with regard to the text, the mise-en-scène will suggest a connection between text and scenic configuration; if this connection manages to remain open, then the spectator will make a hypothesis of this openness and will assume that this connection is metaphoric, scenographic, or event-like (to take up Lehmann's categories again). Therefore there will necessarily be deconstruction of the text by the stage (or, if there is no text, of one stage system by another). In more general terms, the fundamental instability of mise-en-scène will readily produce the impression of self-deconstruction. Deconstruction occurs *en bloc,* so to speak, and not in the detail of analyses, nor in the plurality of its methods.

Methodological Pluralism Rather Than Eclecticism

For postmodern criticism resorts to an eclecticism (rather than a plurality) in the choice of its analytical methods; it prefers lucky dips to toolboxes. But what tools should be taken from the box? It would be tempting to reply:

any of them, provided that they are used systematically and not tossed around while they are in use! For example, we have already come across the following tools en route:

- *Structuralism* and *functionalism* offered us a semiology of stage systems, which remains an indispensable basis for all investigations. Let us remember that a semiology of mise-en-scène is not a matter of translating a performance's signifiers into linguistic signifieds (in other words, of verbalizing them). Rather the tendency is to base descriptions on the materiality of a performance, avoiding cutting it up according to the traditional categories and codes of bourgeois theater, thereby reestablishing these categories and codes.
- *Hermeneutics* have been reintroduced (although semiology arose in the 1960s as a means of moving beyond a subjective, raw art of interpretation). At present we encourage a hermeneutically controlled utilization of semiological instruments. This can clarify the constitutive processes of units, ensembles, syntax, itineraries, and (as we shall see later on) vectorizations between signs.
- The *historicity* of production and of reception have been brought into confrontation in order to lay the foundations for an aesthetics of reception.
- *Criticism of the sign* and of semiology, particularly Lyotard's, whether it results in an energetic theater or not, has the merit at least of sensitizing one to a fluctuation of energies and of lines of force in mise-en-scène. It enables access to the compromise of our "vectorization of desire," which in turn opens the way for a series of *theoretical oxymorons,* such as chaos theory, analysis of syntheses, blocks of isolated events, stage chronotopes.

The tension of these oxymorons protects us from an omnidirectional use of the most contradictory of theories; it is the guarantor of a necessary methodological plurality.

Paradigm Shift

A plurality of methods, nowadays widely accepted in performance analysis, seems to be on a par with a broadening of the favored paradigm of representation—visuality—toward paradigms of auditory perception, rhythm, and kinesthesia.

Through a reaction against literature and a literary conception of theater, performance semiology was founded on visuality, defining its units as signs of the visible made legible by means of a language of the stage.

In the wake of Vinaver's thoughts on mise-en-scène as "mise en trop,"[25] one is much more attentive to the rhythm of the text and to the orientations of auditive memory.

Furthermore, visuality and the auditory are not the only systems actively perceptive in the reception of a performance. In a way they are dependent upon the "entire muscular apparatus," as Jaques-Dalcroze demonstrated so effectively in his studies of rhythmics:

> Authentic perception of movement is not of a visual nature, it is of a muscular nature, and the living symphony of steps, gestures, and attitudes linked together is created and regulated not by the instrument of appreciation that is the eye, but by the instrument of creation that is the entire muscular apparatus.[26]

An analysis sensitive to muscular meaning describes the *kinesthetic* value (perception of movement), and more generally the *aesthesic* value, of a performance.

Sensitized in this way to the corporeality of performance, analysis draws considerably closer to a practice of sense and of the senses; one can then envisage theory and analysis from the point of view of the director's know-how.

Theory and Analysis from the Point of View of Practice

Distancing
In the course of rehearsals, the director tends to dissociate herself increasingly from the group (within) which her actors and collaborators negotiate, in order to place herself at a distance and to direct from the auditorium; in this way she prefigures her future audience and endows it with her perspective on the developing performance. Evidently all decisions on the mise-en-scène are influenced by her gaze, and by the analysis it presupposes: analysis determined by the signifying systems artists put in place (thus transversal analysis of the performance at a given moment), and analysis in terms of the rhythmic organization of time, and thus of the per-

formance's articulation, into different moments (longitudinal analysis). In elaborating a performance, the director has a sense of the division of work (between different, specialist trade groups) and of the segmentation of the performance. She knows how to articulate a scene in order for it to be legible, how to place key moments, rhythmic and dramaturgical turning points, how to prescribe breaks and pauses. In this way progressively the score and, for the actors, the underscore of the performance are set in place. This analytical structuration of the performance, these traces of its genesis, are still perceptible and able to be referenced in the finished product, like scars from former operations, or like the work's respiration. Some knowledge of practice is useful, even indispensable, to performance analysts; taking the end result as starting point, they can imagine what the preparatory dramaturgical work could have been, the decisions and chance occurrences that led to this end result. In turn, practice itself cannot dispense, if only as a first indication, with a theory for these various processes. One could even define mise-en-scène, as Juan Antonio Hormigón does, as "the coordinated articulation of dramaturgical work and technical-craft practice."[27] There is necessarily an element of dramaturgical work (even if it denies its own existence); it comprises the systematizing of practical actions realized in concrete terms by a "technical-craft practice."

Logic of Process, Logic of Result
Like practitioners, theorists are aware that performance analysis does not begin and end with one evening's show, that it must be interested in its preparation as well as its reception by the spectator. Carlos Tindemans perfectly encompasses the range of epistemological problems that confront analysis:

> The notion of performance analysis cannot limit itself to a phenomenological image of the scenic process; it must also cover the intentionality of the theater practitioners and the effect on spectators.[28]

Let us leave the notion of intentionality to one side, for it is unknowable and it does not prejudge the end result; instead we can distinguish three successive moments in the elaboration of a mise-en-scène:

(1)	(2)	(3)
Preparation of the performance	Phenomenological image of the	Effects on spectators

> scenic process
> (image of the preparatory
> process in the final
> performance)

However, this chronological succession is only apparent; it is an extreme simplification of the mechanisms in play at each moment and in each instance, artificially separating what should not really be separated.

Knowledge of a performance's preparatory process (1) has no interest, at least for analysis, unless it illuminates the phenomenon produced: the mise-en-scène (2).

The mise-en-scène will only be understood if one is able to evaluate the ways in which it touches and influences the spectator (3).

So the imbrication of all three moments and instances is at the crux of the problem. Description of one is of little interest without description of the other two. We locate ourselves in (3), we perceive (2), but in order to grasp it we must develop an idea of (1).

The difficulty is in dealing with the preparatory phase of a performance and at the same time the end result; the problem is one of knowing, to borrow Barba's terms again,[29] the logic of the process and the logic of the result. Evidently one should not confuse the perspectives of production and reception; but neither can one ignore the other side of the barricade. These two perspectives are those required by training institutions, in a clear-cut way: at universities, what is sought is the model, ideal spectator, excessively cultured and intelligent, knowing how to receive the finished performance; in drama schools, the perspective is that of future artists learning their craft, and thus concerned with technique and know-how, en route to producing their own performances and therefore engaged in creative process. This institutional opposition is baleful, and it blocks research that is both theoretical and practical.

Systemic Approach

Nevertheless, certain artists, such as Le Théâtre REPÈRE,[30] cover the entire cycle of production and reception. This group has elaborated a working method that enables the passage from rehearsals to performances without difficulty or rupture, and recycles performances by using them as starting points and raw materials for further work.

Resources are the starting point for research: spare material, scenes that have already been worked, particularly those that are triggers generating

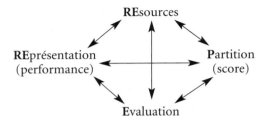

REsources

REprésentation
(performance)

Partition
(score)

Evaluation

themes and ideas. These resources are organized in the form of preestablished dispositions and an exploratory score that "allows the unconscious to access the conscious."[31] Evaluation authorizes critical reflection on the score; it reconstitutes a scenic metatext in which the principal options are already suggested. It leads to performance (*REprésentation*) that in turn could become material for a new cycle. So the "auto-corrective dynamic of creative systems" has been reconstituted by examining what options have been taken and when, what redundant material has been maintained, and what ambiguities (voluntary as well as involuntary) have been introduced.

This kind of cyclical orientation takes performance and its analysis out of their isolation, by showing the interaction and interdependence of process and end result. Analysis is no longer fixed at an ideal moment (that at which the spectators would purportedly understand everything); it is extended in duration and bases itself on data until now reserved for the creators and their penchant for secrecy.

In the same way, theatrical documentation is no longer exclusively the material trace of a performance, delivered after the event, constituting archival documents arising from the performance. It also includes preparatory materials, further enriching itself with knowledge of resources, intermediary scores, statements by those artists involved in the performance.

Evidently, when applied to contemporary mise-en-scène, theory and analysis have serious limitations; sometimes they give the impression of being impotent and mute in the face of the complex constructions of the postmodern. Nevertheless a pluralism of methods does not relativize the possibility of dealing with contemporary works. Far from surrendering before the complexity and sophistication of mise-en-scènes, theory can extend its domain into a sphere that seemed to reserved for artists alone: that of practice. The separation between doing and saying now finds itself challenged again, to the great joy of theorists. This major concession by practitioners to their less fortunate colleagues—theorists—opens up new research perspectives. If the hope of resolving the question of analysis quickly and definitively seems to grow ever fainter, on the other hand the prospect of a greater overall understanding of the creative processes of theater is perhaps no longer an empty mirage. In this respect, semiology—let us call it *integrated semiology*, locating itself at the intersection of theories and practices—can play a core role.

Integrated Semiology: At the Crossroad of Theories and Practices

A Theoretical Oxymoron for an Unlimited Stage Production

In the preceding pages, we have seen what semiology has borrowed and learned from poststructuralist theories (and the latter also owe a great deal to semiology). Preferring confrontation to compromise, I have chosen to connect contrary notions and thereby create oxymorons, as a site for productive contradiction

- Sign and energy
- Semiology and energetics
- Vector and desire
- Semiotization and desemiotization, etc.

Such oxymorons interrogate and destabilize the classical working methods of semiology, such as the location and reading of signs, the translation into signifieds, and so on. They suggest a movement beyond, or at least a reexamination, of other oppositions.

The opposition of diachrony and synchrony is one example, and not only through the performance being perceived as both process *and* end result. Performance analyses can also examine the ways in which a mise-en-scène is inscribed in history and history is inscribed in it, through successive layers or juxtaposed details. They can determine what stratifications history has already deposited on what seems a wholly present and actual contemporary object. Foucault's archaeology of knowledge, and the reevaluation it is currently undergoing, help us reference knowledges and discourses circulating in the detailed marquetry of a mise-en-scène.

The opposition between surface and depth, between discursive and actantial structures (in Greimas's terminology), is also contested: if only in the score/underscore coupling, which is based more on the difference between the visible and the invisible, the shown and the hidden, than on the notion of depth. In place of a binary model (depth/surface), I prefer a progressive ternary division for analysis, in the manner of Zeami:[32] skin, flesh, and bone, which correspond to "the three faculties of perception, the knowledge that comes from sight, from hearing, from the heart or spirit: sight corresponds with *skin*, hearing with *flesh*, and spirit with *bone*."[33] In terms of the voice, according to Zeami, vocal emission would be the *skin*, melodic modulations the *flesh*, and breath the *bone*. In terms of gesture and movement: "the general appearance is the *skin*, the patterned movements of dance are the *flesh*, the spirit of the dance is the *bone*." These metaphors remind us that psychology and contemporary linguistics also endeavor to bring together cognition and aesthetic perception; they assert that, in order to think of the most abstract things, we must have recourse to the imagination, and we must find a way of impregnating spirit with body, in Mark Johnson's sense in his book *The Body in the Mind*. As average rather than model spectators, we apprehend a performance with the body as much as the head, providing that we remain attentive to its materiality, and that we do not immediately translate sense perceptions into words or concepts.

This kind of oxymoron is particularly appropriate for avant-garde performances, which seem to go to great lengths to avoid linguistic or conceptual meaning; they immerse the spectator in a flood of sensations and perceptual impressions that unsettle and delight her, making her forget all desire to translate what is perceived into words or signifieds. Nevertheless, the necessity of maintaining a direction and vectorization means that one can never fully leave the domain of semiology, even if the performances of actors nowadays defy any controlling element in the mise-en-scène.

In fact it is as if the stranglehold of mise-en-scène has released its grip on the systems of signs, thereby losing all reason for its existence, becoming "performance," for instance: a "signifying practice" in which signs drift unmoored, as if an actor's performance resists the director's working strategies:

> If *mise en scène* is *mise en signe* (transposition into signs), then performing is displacing signs, instituting the movement of those signs, even their drift, in a defined space and time.[34]

Performing becomes a subversive activity displacing the certainty of a mise-en-scène's realized configuration and fixed metatext, notably its visual representation. Music emerges as the dominant analytical model, since it is a matter of evaluating rhythm, tempo, temporality, and the routes of vectors, both underlying and visible. Already perceptible in the work of many directors (Stanislavsky, Meyerhold, Pitoëff), reference to music becomes the dominant metaphor in the analysis of the progression of vectors (the actors' performance, forms, colors). Jaques-Dalcroze's rhythmics can be used once more, but as theoretical simulation rather than as an aesthetic; for it applies not only to music, but also to gestural systems, space, and diction. Nonetheless, the problem remains one of representing and describing this experience. We need to find a discipline capable of relating the experience without schematizing it, particularly so given the fact that there are several enunciators in play each complying with different logics.

Anthropology, a New Step for Semiology

Means of Narrating

The required discipline is none other than anthropology, since spectator-anthropologists must evaluate all aspects of an unknown experience that they can understand only by frequenting the performance, living with it at least for its duration. As in anthropology in the strict sense of the word, performance analysis must take into account the means of narrating and writing the object to be described. "Writing culture" requires cultural semiotics to observe how a culture or cultures are inscribed in the object described, and how writing itself imprints its mark on this object.[35]

Relativity of Perspective

Applied to performance practices, cultural semiotics and cultural anthropology provide new options for a semiology that has become either too general or too technical. Both are at pains not to make semiology's mistake; they avoid any hegemonic or totalizing/totalitarian pretension from the outset. They relativize all points of view on the society (or on the mise-en-scène) described ; for "there is no longer any place of overview (mountain-top) from which to map human ways of life, no Archimedian point from which to represent the world."[36] They are attentive to the way of recounting a performance, producing a description that is in fact a narrative. They consider social and cultural phenomena, in the same way as theater work, as processes and not (only) as final products. Making and performativity are integral parts of the work, and they become the focus of observation and analysis.

Interculturalism

The discourse of interculturalism is increasingly prominent today, both in our theaters and in daily life. In the same way as in the interculturalization of our lives, we have real difficulties recognizing and accounting for the range of cultural influences that come into play in contemporary mise-en-scène. Some people apprehend and categorize this mixing in terms of a postmodern relativism, a new melting pot, a "Coca-colonization" that scrambles and jams ways of proceeding, particularly social contradictions. At the present time anthropology is hailed as a new resource for, and a means of going beyond, sociology. Nevertheless, anthropological perspectives should not be established on the ruins of a sociological theory of exchange; neither should they paste the model of linguistic communication between transmitter and receiver on to a theory of cultural transfer; finally, they should not seek to regulate and explain social conflict in terms of cultural differences and a multicultural society. If anthropology asserts itself as an integrative model, then one can expect a great deal from it for performance analysis: in particular for understanding how diverse cultural influences shape a performance and, most remarkably, the bodies and behaviors of actors.

The application of cultural anthropology to theater readmits a theory of corporeity and of imagination. Both body and imaginary participate in reflecting on the whole, which enables us to avoid succumbing to a disembodied rationality. Anthropological perspectives provide the widest and most adequate framework for integrating and reevaluating the full range of knowledges that semiology, in alliance with psychoanalysis and sociology, has allowed to come to light. This takes us a long way from a postmodern despondency, but the pluralism of methods, the sophistication of analyses, the demands of rationality and *jouissance* can indeed make us feel dizzy . . .

To Conclude?

So which theories for which mise-en-scènes? Should one hope for a global model, a miraculous recipe that gathers up all the stakes and adapts itself to all kinds of performance? Evidently not!

And what about the performance analysis itself? Who will say whether it "works" or not? Perhaps quite simply it will succeed if an encounter between performance and spectator has occurred. Vinaver's words on textual analysis are also valid for performance analysis:

An analysis is successful, which makes it transmissible and thus useful, only to the degree that its author, combining affectivity and intelligence, has been engaged in his contact with the work; also to the degree that the writing of the commentary bears the mark of the event that the particular encounter between a reader and a text constitutes.[37]

Theories have followed the tendency to differentiate between performances, but nevertheless there remain certain core instances. There is always a time-lapse between theater practice and its theoretical articulation, as if theory takes some time to adapt to a new demand; the time-lapse is often about a decade. Brechtian theory, for example, still new and scandalous in the 1950s and 1960s, greatly inspired the semiology of the 1970s, but it is no longer appropriate for the decentered productions of the 1980s and 1990s. Or French theory (referred to as "poststructuralist" in Anglo-Saxon contexts), inspired by the work of Barthes, Derrida, Foucault, and Lacan; although there are few pertinent examples in French or European performance, poststructuralism is applicable to the American avant-garde ten years on: Robert Wilson, Richard Foreman, Robert Ashley, Merce Cunningham, Laurie Anderson. When theory comes back to France in the early 1990s, theater production has entered another phase: a time for restoration of the text and antitheoretical empiricism. At this moment, in order to resist the immaterialism of stage language (what Vinaver called "la mise en trop"), although already outmoded, mise-en-scène reintroduces the text; but now it postulates the text's irreducibility, its resistance to all "messe en scène" (High Mass on stage), hoping (naively) that it will hold its own on the stage, and will not be metaphorized by it.

However these successive waves of theory, desperately pursuing theatrical methods, should not sweep us away into listless skepticism or a free-floating postmodern relativism. In opposition to this drift, I prefer the apparent blockage of a paradoxical response, a theoretical oxymoron along the same lines as that of a *semiotization of desire*, the operative power of which we have been able to evaluate here.

In calling for new theories, more appropriate to the task and continually updated, performance practice also takes theory forward; and in return theory contributes to an improvement in the understanding we have of practice. In this way they feed (off) each other; out of this ongoing and generalized "intercannibalism" arises a revolution that is nowhere near its end.

As well as a permanent revolution in our performance analyses.

Notes

Introduction

1. Jean-Marie Pradier, "Ethnoscénologie: La profondeur des émergences," *L'Internationale de l'imaginaire* 5 (1996).

CHAPTER 1

1. Patrice Pavis, *Voix et images de la scène. Pour une sémiologie de la réception* (Lille: Presses Universitaires de Lille, 1985).
2. Marco De Marinis, *Semiotica del teatro* (Milan: Bompiani, 1982).
3. Roland Barthes, *Camera Lucida*, trans. Richard Howard (New York: Hill and Wang, 1981), 27.
4. Ibid., 26.
5. Richard Schechner, *Between Theater and Anthropology* (Philadelphia: University of Pennsylvania Press, 1985), 43.
6. Pavis, *Voix et images*, 250–94.
7. Tadeusz Kowzan, "Le signe au théâtre," *Diogène* 61 (1968), and *Sémiologie du théâtre* (Paris: Nathan, 1992); Patrice Pavis, *Problèmes de sémiologie théâtrale* (Montreal: Presses de l'Université de Québec, 1976); Anne Ubersfeld, *Lire le théâtre* (Paris: Éditions Sociales, 1977).
8. Michel Bernard, *L'Expressivité du corps*, 2d ed. (Paris: Seuil, 1995).
9. Helga Finter, "Théâtre expérimental et sémiologie du théâtre: La théâtralisation de la voix," in *Théâtralité, écriture et mise en scène*, ed. J. Féral (Montreal: Hurtubise, 1985).
10. Roland Barthes, *Leçon* (Paris, Seuil, 1978), 32. [English translation: "Inaugural Lecture, Collège de France," trans. Richard Howard, in *Selected Writings*, ed. Susan Sontag (London: Fontana, 1983), 471. Italics in original.]
11. Rodrigue Villeneuve, "Les îles incertaines. L'objet de la sémiotique théâtrale," *Protée* 17, no. 1 (1989): 25.
12. Charles S. Peirce, "Logic as Semiotic: The Theory of Signs," in *Philosophical Writings of Peirce*, ed. Justus Buchler (New York: Dover, 1955), 98–119.
13. To borrow the title of Mark Johnson's book, *The Body in the Mind: The Bodily Basis of Meaning, Imagination, and Reason* (Chicago: University of Chicago Press, 1987).
14. Pavis, *Problèmes de sémiologie théâtrale.*

15. Tadeusz Kowzan, "L'art du spectacle dans un système général des arts," *Études philosophiques*, January 1970.

16. Keir Elam, *The Semiotics of Theatre and Drama* (London: Methuen, 1980); Erika Fischer-Lichte, *Semiotik des Theaters* (Tübingen: Narr Verlag, 1983).

17. Jacques Derrida, "The Theater of Cruelty and the Closure of Representation," in *Writing and Difference*, trans. Alan Bass (London: Routledge, 1990), 232–50.

18. Jean-François Lyotard, "La dent, la paume," in *Des dispositifs pulsionnels* (Paris: UGE, 1973). [English translation: "The Tooth, the Palm," trans. Anne Knap and Michel Benamou, *Sub-stance* 15 (1976): 105–10.]

19. Ibid., 104. ["The Tooth, the Palm," 110.]

20. Quoted in Bert States, *Great Reckonings in Little Rooms: On the Phenomenology of Theater* (Berkeley and Los Angeles: University of California Press, 1985), 7

21. Hans-Thies Lehmann, "Die Inszenierung: Probleme ihrer Analyse," *Zeitschrift für Zemiotik* 11, no. 1 (1989): 48.

22. States, *Great Reckonings*, 7.

23. Villeneuve, "Les îles incertaines," 25.

24. Lehmann, "Die Inszenierung," 48.

25. Pavis, *Voix et images*.

26. Lehmann, "Die Inszenierung," 43.

27. Ibid., 44.

28. See Ivan Barko and Bruce Burgess, *La Dynamique des points de vue dans* texte du théâtre (Paris: Lettres Modernes, 1988).

29. See, for example, Youssef Haddad, *Art du conteur, art de l'acteur* (Louvain: Cahiers-théâtre, 1982); and Pepito Mateo, "Pepito Mateo, conteur?" *Dire* 15 (1990

30. See Tzvetan Todorov, *Théorie de la littérature. Textes des formalistes russe* (Paris: Seuil, 1965).

31. Anne-Françoise Benhamou, "Méandres d'un enseignement atypique, *Théâtre/Public* 82–83 (1988): 10.

32. Eugenio Barba, "Eurasian Theatre," *Drama Review* 32, no. 3 (T119) (1988 129.

33. Susan Foster, *Reading Dancing* (Berkeley and Los Angeles: University California Press, 1988), 58.

34. Pavis, *Voix et images*, 281–97.

35. Henri Schoenmakers, ed., *Performance Theory* (Utrecht: Instituut voor Theaterwetenschap, 1986); and Wilmar Sauter, *New Directions in Audience Research* (Utrecht: Instituut voor Theaterwetenschap, 1988).

36. Patrice Pavis, *Theatre at the Crossroads of Culture*, trans. Loren Kruger (London: Routledge, 1992).

37. Notably that of Maurice Merleau-Ponty, *The Phenomenology of Perception* trans. Colin Smith) (London: Routledge and Kegan Paul, 1962). For an application of phenomenology to theater, see States, *Great Reckonings;* Marvin Carlson, *Theories of the Theatre* (Ithaca, N.Y.: Cornell University Press, 1984); and Stanton Garner, *Bodied Spaces: Phenomenology and Performance in Contemporary Drama* (Ithaca, N.Y.: Cornell University Press, 1994).

38. Carlos Tindemans, "L'analyse de la représentation théâtrale. Quelque

réflexions méthodologiques," in *Théâtre de toujours, d'Aristote à Kalisky, Hommage à Paul Delsemme* (Brussels: Éd. de l'Université, 1983), 53.

39. Ibid., 55.

40. Maurice Merleau-Ponty, "Eye and Mind," trans. Carleton Dallery, in *The Primacy of Perception*, ed. James M. Edie (Evanston, Ill.: Northwestern University Press, 1964), 160.

CHAPTER 2

1. Eugenio Barba, *The Paper Canoe: A Guide to Theatre Anthropology*, trans. Richard Fowler (London: Routledge, 1995), 12.

2. I am borrowing Jean-François Lyotard's word, in the title of his book *Discours, figure* (Paris: Klincksieck, 1971).

3. Yves Reuter, *Introduction à l'analyse du roman* (Paris: Bordas, 1991), 102.

4. Jean-Michel Adam, *Le Texte descriptif* (Paris: Nathan, 1989), 8–9.

5. Ibid., 105.

6. Ubersfeld's and Helbo's questionnaires are reproduced in André Helbo et al., *Théâtre: Modes d'approche* (Paris: Méridiens-Klincksiek, 1987).

7. Patrice Pavis, "Questions sur une questionnaire pour une analyse de spectacles," in *Voix et images*. [English translation: "Theatre Analysis: Some Questions and a Questionnaire," trans. Susan Bassnett, *New Theatre Quarterly* 1, no. 2 (1985): 208–12.]

8. Pavis, "Questions sur une questionnaire," 318–24.

9. Villeneuve, "Les îles incertaines," 28.

10. Roger Pic and Chantal Meyer-Plantureux, *Bertolt Brecht et le Berliner Ensemble à Paris* (Paris: Arte éditions et Marval, 1995).

11. Mike Pearson, "Theatre/Archaeology," *Drama Review* 38, no. 4 (T144) (1994): 134.

12. Ibid., 133.

13. Barba, *The Paper Canoe*, 36.

14. Pearson, "Theatre/Archaeology," 139.

15. Hans Belting, *L'histoire de l'art est-elle finie?* (Nîmes: Éd. Jacqueline Chambon, 1989), 47.

16. Sigmund Freud, *Civilization and Its Discontents*, trans. Joan Riviere (London: Hogarth Press, 1939), 51, 53.

17. Sally Jane Norman, "L'image et le corps dans l'art vivant," presentation at the "collège iconique," *Les cahiers* 3 (1994).

18. Edmond Couchot and Hélène Tramus, "Le geste et le calcul," *Protée* 21, no. 3 (1993): 41.

19. Ibid., 44.

20. See, for example, Patrice Pavis, "Théâtre et média," in Helbo et al., *Théâtre*, 33–63.

21. Jürgen Müller, "Intermedialität als Provokation der Medianwissenschaft," *Eikon* 4 (1992): 18–19.

22. Jürgen Müller, "Le labyrinthe médiatique du film," *Mots/Images/Sons*, Col-

loque international de Rouen, March 1989 (Rouen: Presses Universitaires, 1990), 145.

23. Uwe Richterich, *Die Sehnsucht zu sehen. Der filmisch Blick* (Frankfurt am Main: Peter Lang, 1993), 43.

24. Étienne Decroux, *Paroles sur le mime* (Paris: Gallimard, 1963), 72. [English translation: *Words on Mime*, trans. Mark Piper (Claremont, Calif.: Pomona College Theatre Department, 1985).]

25. [Translator's note: cf.: "In the *secousse,* force-in-place is generated by tensing the muscles and then releasing them in a powerful and quick movement. Like a note held on the violin, the *fondu* involves continual slow movement at constant velocity with a constant degree of muscular tension. . . . Decroux illustrates the combination of *secousse* and *fondu* with the image of a fish which first darts and then glides." Deidre Sklar, "Étienne Decroux's Promethean Mime," in *Acting (Re)Considered: Theories and Practices,* ed. Phillip B. Zarrilli (London: Routledge, 1995), 111–13.]

26. Patrice Pavis, "Film est un Film," *Protée* 19, no. 3 (1991).

27. The German title, *Oder die glücklose Landung,* suggests that the arrival is "un-fortunate" *(glück-los),* i.e., unsuccessful.

28. In this section we have not considered electronic means of recording and understanding performance, nor the various different systems of notation. For further details, see Pavis, *Voix et images,* 145–69.

CHAPTER 3

1. For an excellent historical overview, see Robert Abirached, "Les jeux de l'être et du paraître," in *Le Théâtre* (Paris: Bordas, 1980).

2. For a critique of presence in theories of the actor, particularly in Eugenio Barba's work, see Patrice Pavis, "Un canoë à la dérive?" *Théâtre/Public* 126 (1995).

3. Lee Strasberg, *A Dream of Passion: The Development of the Method* (London: Bloomsbury, 1988), 177.

4. Jacques Lecoq, ed., *Le Théâtre du geste* (Paris: Bordas, 1987), 20.

5. Antoine Vitez, *Le Théâtre des idées* (Paris: Gallimard, 1991), 144.

6. Michel Bernard, "Quelques réflexions sur le jeu de l'acteur contemporain," *Bulletin de psychologie* 38, no. 370 (1986).

7. Bernard Dort, *La Représentation émancipée* (Arles: Actes Sud, 1988).

8. Eugenio Barba and Nicola Savarese, *A Dictionary of Theatre Anthropology: The Secret Art of the Performer* (London: Routledge, 1991), 54–67.

9. In both senses of the English word: both effecting actions, and performing as an actor.

10. Jacques Cosnier, introduction to "Signes et gestes" issue of *Protée* 20, no. 2 (1992): 38.

11. Jacques Cosnier and A. Brossard, *La Communication non verbale* (Paris: Delachaux and Niestlé, 1984), 9.

12. The choice of performances has been partially determined by the possibility readers have of referring to the examples analyzed. In certain cases, such as here,

this has led us to focus on theater filmed for cinema or television. Evidently such recordings of theater should not blind us to theater itself, nor to the variety of performance practices under consideration here.

[Translator's note: The English translation of Molière's *L'Avare* that is used in the following section is by John Wood: *The Miser* (London: Penguin, 1953), 139–43.]

13. B. Rimé, "Communication verbale et non verbale," in *Grand dictionnaire de la psychologie* (Paris: Larousse, 1991).

14. Deixis is the inscription of the word in the concrete, spatiotemporal situation.

15. Lecoq, *Le Théâtre du geste,* 21.

16. Cosnier, introduction, 36.

17. Rimé, "Communication verbale et non verbale," 148.

18. Valère Novarina, "Pour Luis de Funès," *Le Théâtre des paroles* (Paris: POL, 1989), 115.

19. Marcel Jousse, *L'Anthropologie du geste* (Paris: Gallimard, 1974), 54.

20. Walter Benjamin, *Versuche über Brecht* (Frankfurt am Main: Suhrkamp, 1931), 27. [English translation: "What Is Epic Theatre?" in *Understanding Brecht,* trans. Anna Bostock (London: NLB, 1977), 19.]

21. Klaus Scherer in Cosnier and Brossard, *La Communication non verbale,* 29.

22. Rimé, "Communication verbale et non verbale," 443.

23. Lecoq, *Le Théâtre du geste,* 102.

24. Jean-Claude Schmid, *La Raison des gestes dans l'occident mediéval* (Paris: Gallimard, 1990), 30.

25. Jean-François Lyotard, *Discours, figure.* [Translator's note: A section of Lyotard's French text, pertinent to the following section, has been translated into English; see "The Dream-Work Does Not Think," trans. Mary Lydon, in *The Lyotard Reader,* ed. Andrew Benjamin (Oxford: Blackwell, 1989), 19–55.]

26. Lyotard, "The Tooth, the Palm," 110.

27. Freud named these processes, respectively, *Verdichtung, Verschiebung, Rücksicht auf Darstellbarkeit,* and *sekundäre Bearbeitung.* See Sigmund Freud, *The Interpretation of Dreams,* Penguin Freud Library, vol. 4 (London, 1983). We are pleased to note the similarity of Michel Corvin's position: "Everything in theater . . . is substitution, displacement, gap, compensatory omission, stand-in, in other words, metaphor and metonymy. . . . Everything in theater is figure—in the double sense of concrete appearance and rhetorical play—everything there makes signs." *Dictionnaire encyclopédique du théâtre* (Paris: Bordas, 1991), 821.

28. Lyotard, *Discours, figure,* 278.

29. Lyotard, "The Tooth, the Palm," 105.

30. Ibid.

31. Lyotard, *Discours, figure,* 218.

32. In the sense of *darstellungsfähig,* in the German text: "able to be represented."

33. Lyotard, "The Tooth, the Palm," 105.

34. Ibid., 106.

35. Ibid., 107.

36. Gélinas, in "Mime contemporain et dramaturgie. Résultats de la première

étape du projet de recherche dramaturgique impulsé à partir de la Fédération européenne de mime," ed. Philippe Henry, Paris, 1993, distributed photocopy.

37. Ibid.

38. Henry, *Mime contemporain et dramaturgie*, 21.

39. Constantin Stanislavski, *Die Arbeit des Schauspielers an sich selbst*, vol. 2 (Berlin: Das Europaïsche Buch, 1988), 319.

40. Peter Brook, "À la source du jeu," in *Le Corps en jeu*, ed. Odette Aslan (Paris: CNRS, 1993), 302.

41. Johnson, *Body in the Mind*, xiv, 25.

42. Ibid., xiv, 4, 205.

43. John Martin, *The Modern Dance* (New York: Dance Horizons, 1966), 60.

44. Eugenio Barba, "La fiction de la réalité," in Aslan, *Le Corps en jeu*, 253.

45. Jousse, *L'Anthropologie du geste*, 55.

46. Darko Suvin, "The Performance Text as Audience-Stage Dialog, Inducing a Possible World," *Versus* 42 (1985): 15–16. Italics in original.

47. Otto Fenichel, "On Acting," *Psychoanalytic Quarterly* 15 (1946); original in *Aufsätze*, vol. 2 (Frankfurt am Main: Ulstein, 1985), 398.

48. States, *Great Reckonings*, 142. Italics in original.

49. Ibid., 138.

50. Decroux, *Paroles sur le mime*, 105.

51. Peter Weiss's play, first published in 1964, is based on historical events; it portrays how Sade produced historical performances with the "patients" of Charenton—in this instance, to quote Weiss's full title, *The Persecution and Assassination of Jean-Paul Marat as Performed by the Inmates of the Asylum of Charenton under the Direction of the Marquis de Sade*.

52. David Richard Jones, *Great Directors at Work* (Berkeley and Los Angeles: University of California Press, 1986).

53. Peter Brook, *The Shifting Point* (New York: Harper and Row, 1987), 189–90.

54. Peter Brook, "À propos du *Roi Lear* et de *Marat-Sade*," *Cahiers Théâtre Louvain* 46 (1981): 20.

55. Charles Marowitz, in relation to Peter Brook's production of *King Lear* quoted by Jones, *Great Directors at Work*, 237.

56. André Bazin, "Théâtre et cinéma," *Esprit*, June–August 1951, 171. Reprinted in *Qu'est-ce que le cinéma?* (Paris: Éd. du Cerf, 1975).

57. Ibid., 98.

58. Norman Bryson contrasts the *gaze* with the *glance*. See Norman Bryson "The Gaze and the Glance," in *Vision and Painting: The Logic of the Gaze* (London Macmillan, 1983).

59. Jacques Lacan, "Les quatre concepts fondamentaux de la psychanalyse," *Séminaire*, book 11 (Paris: Seuil, 1973), 107.

60. Brook, *The Shifting Point*, 48.

61. Christian Metz and Marc Vernet, "Entretien," *Iris* 10 (1990).

62. Quoted in Michel Mourlet, *Sur un art ignoré* (Paris: La Table Ronde, 1965) 51.

63. For further discussion of the notion of ideologemes, see chapter 9 below and Pavis, *Voix et images*.

64. Roland Barthes, *Camera Lucida*, trans. Richard Howard (New York: Hill and Wang, 1981), 47.

65. Decroux, *Paroles sur le mime*, 66. ["Words on Mime," 47.]

66. Ibid. ["Words on Mime," 48.]

67. Laurence Louppe, in Hubert Godard and L. Louppe, "Le déséquilibre fondateur," *Art Press*, special issue, 1992, 138. [For an English translation, see "Singular, Moving Geographies," trans. David Williams, *Writings on Dance*, "The French Issue," 15 (winter 1996): 12–21.]

CHAPTER 4

1. Guy Cornut, *La Voix* (Paris: Presses Universitaires de France, "Que sais-je?" 1983).

2. Michel Bernardy, "La métamorphose du verbe par l'acteur," *Change* 29 (December 1976): 201.

3. Michel Bernardy, *Le Jeu verbal, ou traité de diction française à l'usage de l'honnête homme* (Paris: Éditions de l'Aube, 1988), 200.

4. Nicole Scotto di Carlo, "La Voix chantée," *La Recherche* 235 (September 1991): 1025.

5. Antonin Artaud, *Le Théâtre et son double* (Paris: Gallimard, 1964), 54. [English translation: "Production and Metaphysics," in *The Theatre and Its Double*, trans. Victor Corti (London: John Calder, 1970), 27.]

6. E.g., treated by a piece of technology such as harmonizers or vocoders, as in the work of Laurie Anderson.

7. Denis Vasse, *L'Ombilic et la voix* (Paris: Seuil, 1974).

8. Antonin Artaud, quoted by Cornut, *La Voix*, 54.

9. Roland Barthes, "The Grain of the Voice," in *Image Music Text*, trans. Stephen Heath (London: Fontana, 1977), 188.

10. Marie-France Castarède, *La Voix et ses sortilèges* (Paris: Les Belles Lettres, 1987), 153.

11. Daniel Charles, "Thèses sur la voix," in "La voix, l'écoute," special issue of *Traverses* 20 (1980): 5. Italics in the original.

12. Fischer-Lichte, *Semiotik des Theaters*, 1:40.

13. Ibid.

14. Barthes, *Leçon*, 31–32. ["Inaugural Lecture," 470–71.]

15. Antonin Artaud, *Le Théâtre et son double*, 189. [English translation: "The Theatre of Cruelty: Second Manifesto," in *Theatre and Its Double*, 83.]

16. Roland Barthes, *Essais critiques* (Paris: Seuil, 1964), 42. [English translation: "Baudelaire's Theater," in *Critical Essays*, trans. Richard Howard (Evanston, Ill.: Northwestern University Press, 1972), 26.]

17. Tran Van Khê, "Techniques vocales dans les théâtres d'Asie oriental," *Encylopedia universalis*, vol. 18, "Voix," 1988.

18. Manuel Garcia-Martinez, "Réflexions sur la perception du rythme au théâtre," doctoral thesis, University of Paris VIII, 1995.

19. Ibid., 194.

20. See below, chapter 7. The author would like to thank Nicole Scotto di Carlo for comments on vocal technique.

21. Nicolas Frize, "La musique au théâtre," in *Une esthétique de l'ambiguïté*, ed. J. Pigeon (Lyon: Les Cahiers du Soleil Debout, 1993), 54. Italics in the original.

22. Richard Wagner, quoted by Adolphe Appia, *Oeuvres complètes*, vol. 1 (Lausanne: L'Age d'homme, 1983), 13.

23. See, for example, the productions of G. Aperghis and H. Goebbels.

24. For analysis of this performance, please refer to chapters 2 and 10 of this volume.

25. Gerhard Kubik, "Verstehen in afrikanischen Musikkulturen," in *Musik in Afrika*, ed. A. Simon (Berlin: Museum für Völkerkunde, 1983), 315.

26. Ibid., 316–17.

27. Ibid., 322. Italics in the original.

28. Ibid.

29. Castarède, *La Voix et ses sortilèges*, 90.

30. Jindrich Honzl, "La mobilité du signe théâtral," *Travail théâtral* 4 (1971) 6–20.

31. Vsevolod Meyerhold, *Écrits sur le théâtre*, vol. 4 (Lausanne: L'Age d'homme 1992), 325.

32. Garcia-Martinez, "Réflexions sur la perception," 66.

33. Meyerhold, *Écrits sur le théâtre*, 331.

34. Julia Kristeva, *La Révolution du langage poétique* (Paris: Seuil, 1974), 212, 217 Italics in the original.

35. Garcia-Martinez, "Réflexions sur la perception," 4.

CHAPTER 5

1. Merleau-Ponty, *The Phenomenology of Perception.*

2. Sami-Ali, *L'Espace imaginaire* (Paris: Gallimard, 1974), 241.

3. In particular, two books by Denis Bablet: *Le Décor de théâtre de 1870 à 191* (Paris: CNRS, 1965); and *Les Révolutions scéniques au XXème siècle* (Paris: Sociét Internationale d'Art, 1975).

4. Antonin Artaud, *Le Théâtre et son double*, 53. [English translation: "Production and Metaphysics," in *Theatre and Its Double*, 27.]

5. Edward Hall, *The Hidden Dimension* (New York: Doubleday, 1966).

6. Suvin, "Performance Text," 15–16. Italics in the original.

7. In Stanton Garner's sense of the term as used in his book *Bodied Spaces.*

8. Jacques Copeau, *Appels*, Registres 1 (Paris: Gallimard, 1974), 199.

9. Pearson, "Theatre/Archaeology," 151.

10. See Michael Chekhov, *To the Actor: On the Technique of Acting* (New York Harper and Row, 1953).

11. Garcia-Martinez, "Réflexions sur la perception," 3.

12. Pierre Boulez, *Penser la musique aujourd'hui* (Paris: Gallimard, 1987), 62–63

13. Émile Benveniste, *Problèmes de linguistique générale*, vol. 2 (Paris: Gallimard 1974), 83.

14. Mikhail Bakhtin, *The Dialogic Imagination: Four Essays*, ed. Michael Holquist, trans. Caryl Emerson and Michael Holquist (Austin: University of Texas Press, 1981), 84.

15. Michael Chekhov, *L'Imagination créatrice de l'acteur* (Paris: Pygmalion, 1995). [English translation: *On the Technique of Acting* (New York: Harper, 1991)]. [Translator's note: For further accounts of Chekhov's psychological gesture, see his *To the Actor*, 63–84; and Deirdre Hurst Du Prey, ed., *Michael Chekhov: Lessons for the Professional Actor* (New York: Performing Arts Journal Publications, 1985), 105–19.]

16. Honzl, "La mobilié du signe théâtral."

17. M. Honegger, *Dictionnaire de la musique* (Paris: Bordas, 1976), 820.

18. Garcia-Martinez, "Réflexions sur la perception," 20.

19. Guido Hiss, *Korrespondenzen* (Tübingen: Niemeyer, 1988).

20. Guido Hiss, "Freiräume für die Phantasie," *TheaterZeitSchrift* 35 (1994): 28.

21. Pearson, "Theatre/Archaeology," 150.

22. Sigmund Freud, "The Unconscious," trans. Cecil M. Baines, in *Collected Papers*, vol. 4, *Papers on Metapsychology* (London: Hogarth Press, 1953), 119, quoted in Sami-Ali, *L'Espace imaginaire*, 240.

23. Sami-Ali, *L'Espace imaginaire*, 240.

24. Ibid., 242.

CHAPTER 6

1. Maria Shevtsova, *Theatre and Cultural Interaction* (Sydney: Sydney Studies, 1993), 118.

2. Roland Barthes, "Les maladies du costume de théâtre," *Essais critiques*, 61. [English translation: "The Diseases of Costume," in *Critical Essays*, 49.]

3. Ibid., 53–54. ["The Diseases of Costume," 43.]

4. Giorgio Strehler quoted in Georges Banu, *Le Costume de théâtre dans la mise en scène contemporaine* (Paris: CNDP, 1981), 11.

5. Quoted in Banu, *Le Costume de théâtre*, 23.

6. Roland Barthes, *Le Système de la mode* (Paris: Seuil, 1967). [English translation: *The Fashion System*, trans. Matthew Ward and Richard Howard (New York: Hill and Wang, 1974).]

7. Marcel Mauss, *Sociologie et anthropologie* (Paris: Presses Universitaires de France, 1950), 365. [English translation: "Techniques of the Body," in *Incorporations*, ed. Jonathan Crary and Sanford Kwinter (New York: Zone Books, 1992), 455.]

8. Quoted in Dominique Paquet, *Alchimie du maquillage* (Paris: Chiron, 1989), 96.

9. François Delsarte, *Une Anthologie* (Paris: La Villette–IMEC, 1992).

10. Named after the painter who used flowers and fruit to construct human faces and figures.

11. Luc Boucris, *L'Espace en scène* (Paris: Librairie Théâtrale, 1993).

12. Jean Baudrillard, *The System of Objects*, trans. James Benedict (London: Verso, 1996).

13. Dominique Paquet, "Pour un théâtre de fragrances," *Comédie-Française: Les Cahiers* 17 (1995).

14. Jean-Louis Barrault, *Le Phénomène théâtral*, Zaharoff Lecture for 1961 (Oxford: Clarendon Press, 1961), 21.

CHAPTER 7

1. Michel Vinaver, *Écritures dramatiques* (Arles: Actes Sud, 1993), 896.

2. Ubersfeld, *Lire le théâtre*.

3. Alessandro Serpieri, *Come comunica il teatro: Dal testo alla scena* (Milan: Il Formichiere, 1977).

4. Erika Fischer-Lichte, *Das Drama und seine Inszenierung* (Tübingen: Niemeyer, 1985), x.

5. Elam, *Semiotics of Theatre*, 208.

6. Horst Turk, *Soziale und theatralische Konventionen als Problem des Dramas und der Übersetzung* (Tübingen: Narr Verlag, 1989).

7. Lehmann, "Die Inszenierung."

8. Heiner Müller, *Gesammelte Irrtümer* (Frankfurt am Main: Verlag der Autoren, 1986), 18. [French translation: *Erreurs choisies* (Paris: l'Arche, 1988).]

9. Vinaver, *Écritures dramatiques*, 893.

10. For an example from the theater of Marivaux, see Patrice Pavis, *Marivaux à l'épreuve de la scène* (Paris: Publications de la Sorbonne, 1986).

11. Vinaver, *Écritures dramatiques*, 893.

12. Jacqueline Martin and Willmar Sauter, eds., *Understanding Theatre* (Stockholm: Almquist and Wiksell International, 1995), 21.

13. Jacques Copeau, "Un essai de rénovation dramatique," in *Appels*, 29–30.

14. Lehmann, "Die Inszenierung."

15. Peter Brook, *Travail théâtral* 18 (1975): 87.

16. Robert Abirached, *Le Théâtre et le Prince, 1981–1991* (Paris: Plon, 1992), 166.

17. A term used by Chekhov in *L'Imagination créatrice de l'acteur*. [English translation: *On the Technique of Acting* (New York: Harper, 1991).]

18. Pierre Fédida, *Le Corps, le texte et la scène* (Paris: Delarge, 1983).

19. Vinaver, *Écritures dramatiques*, 896.

20. Decroux, *Paroles sur le mime*, 54.

21. Ibid., 56.

22. Ibid., 165.

23. Fédida, *Le Corps, le texte*, 252.

24. Hiss, *Korrespondenzen*.

25. Michel Corvin, *Molière et ses metteurs en scène* (Lyon: Presses Universitaires, 1985).

26. Michel Chion, *L'Audio-vision* (Paris: Nathan, 1990), 55.

27. Tatiana Slama-Cazacu, "Réflexion sur la dyade terminologique 'lisible/visible,'" in *Approches de l'opéra*, ed. André Helbo (Paris: Didier, 1986), 242.

28. Simon Thorpe, "L'oeil, le cerveau et l'image," in *Le Téléspectateur face à la publicité*, ed. Jean-Marie Pradier (Paris: Nathan, 1989), 59.

29. Lyotard, *Discours, figure.*
30. Dort, *La Représentation émancipée,* 173.
31. In fact, we are tempted to contradict totally the four primary principles of Vinaver's method:

1. It starts with the specific character of theatrical writing.
2. At the same time, it connects theatrical writing with any writing whatsoever, with writing in general; it inserts itself into the field of literature, while continually affirming its singularity.
3. It makes direct and immediate contact with the very life of the text, without requiring any previous knowledge: e.g., historical, linguistic, semiological; theatrical or literary; or cultural in general.
4. It does not presuppose adherence to a "theory," nor the acquisition of a "metalanguage."

Our counterproposals would be as follows:

1. It starts with an acknowledgment of the fact that there is nothing specific about writing for the stage.
2. It connects theatrical writing not only to other types of writing, but to all artistic practices.
3. One is never in direct contact with the text, but with the knowledge we have of it; this knowledge feeds on and is nurtured by all possible knowledges.
4. Without a theory and a metalanguage, at best it can only hope to access an illusion of something; this illusion would be self-defining without producing any new knowledge.

32. Eric da Silva, quoted in Philippe Prunot, "Emballage, mode d'emploi," *Théâtre/Public* 121 (1995): 21.

CHAPTER 8

1. Garner, *Bodied Spaces,* 26.
2. Éliane Vurpillot, "Gestalttheorie," *Grand dictionnaire de la psychologie* (Paris: Larousse, 1991), 326.
3. Tindemans, "L'analyse de la représentation théâtrale," 52.
4. Garcia-Martinez, "Réflexions sur la perception," 3.
5. Tindemans, "L'analyse de la représentation théâtrale," 55.
6. Chion, *L'Audio-vision,* 16.
7. See figure 21.
8. Pierre Gaudibert, "Entrevue," in *Peuples et cultures* (Grenoble: Presses Universitaires, 1982), 12.
9. Artaud, *Le Théâtre et son double,* 182. [English translation: "Fourth Letter on

Language," in *Collected Works,* trans. Victor Corti, vol. 4 (London: Calder and Boyars, 1974), 92.]

10. Sigmund Freud, "The Moses of Michelangelo," in *Art and Literature,* Penguin Freud Library, vol. 14 (London, 1985), 254.

11. Gaudibert, "Entrevue," 11.

12. Garner, *Bodied Spaces,* 49.

13. Sigmund Freud, "Psychopathic Characters on the Stage," in *Art and Literature,* 122.

14. Ibid.

15. Hans-Robert Jauss, *Ästhetische Erfahrung und literarische Hermeneutik* (Munich: Fink, 1977).

16. David Le Breton, "Le corps en scène," *L'Internationale de l'imaginaire* 2 (1994): 37.

17. Jacques Lacan, *Écrits,* vol. 1 (Paris: Seuil, 1966), 94.

18. Gaudibert, "Entrevue," 20.

19. Artaud, *Le Théâtre et son double,* 162. [English translation: "First Letter on Language," in *Collected Works,* 82.]

20. The name of a Spanish dancer Kazuo Ohno saw in Tokyo when he was very young, whose dance he endeavors to reconstruct in his performance.

21. Elizabeth Grosz, *Volatile Bodies: Toward a Corporeal Feminism* (Sydney: Allen and Unwin, 1994), 19, 22.

22. Élie Konigson, "Le spectateur et son ombre," in Aslan, *Le Corps en jeu,* 187.

23. Le Breton, "Le corps en scène," 41.

24. Ibid., 10.

25. Jean-Marie Pradier, *La Scène et la fabrique des corps* (Bordeaux: Presses Universitaires de Bordeaux, 1997).

26. Eugenio Barba, "Le corps crédible," in Aslan, *Le Corps en jeu,* 253.

27. Peter Brook, *Le Diable, c'est l'ennui* (Paris: ANRAT/Actes Sud Papier, 1992). [English translation: "The Slyness of Boredom," in *There Are No Secrets: Thoughts on Acting and Theatre* (London: Methuen, 1993).]

28. Peter Brook, *The Empty Space* (London: Penguin, 1968), 12–13.

29. Giorgio Strehler, interview in *Le Nouvel Observateur* 723 (1978).

30. In particular see André Green, "L'Interprétation psychanalytique des productions culturelles et des oeuvres d'arts," in *Critique sociologique et critique psychanalytique* (Brussels: Editions de l'Institut de Sociologie, 1970), 28.

31. Jean-François Lyotard, "Psychanalyse et peinture," *Encyclopedia Universalis* (Paris, 1985).

32. André Green, *Un Oeil en trop* (Paris: Minuit, 1969), 11. For some discussion of primary and secondary processes, see "Processes of Stage Work" below.

33. Ibid., 41.

34. Sigmund Freud, *Gesammelte Werke,* vol. 10, 172.

35. Freud, "The Moses of Michelangelo," 253–54.

36. Freud, *Gesammelte Werke,* vol. II/III, 27.

37. Sigmund Freud, *Essais de psychanalyse* (Paris: Payor), 189.

38. Please refer to the earlier discussion of *Terzirek,* with photographs, in chapter 3 above.

39. Robert Musil, *L'Homme sans qualités,* vol. 2 (Paris: Seuil, 1982), 218. [English translation: *The Man without Qualities,* trans. Eithne Wilkins and Ernst Kaiser, vol. 3 (London: Secker and Warburg, 1960), 225.]

40. Ibid.

41. Géza Roheim, *Origine et fonction de la culture* (Paris: Gallimard, 1972), 12.

42. Green, "L'Interprétation psychanalytique," 36.

CHAPTER 9

1. Belting, *L'histoire de l'art est-elle finie?* 32.

2. Umberto Eco, *Lector in fabula* (Paris: Grasset, 1979), 88.

3. A term used by Stanislavsky to designate the range of factors defining the context of a character's dramatic situation.

4. Eco, *Lector in fabula,* 94.

5. Ibid., 130.

6. Ibid., 50.

7. Jean Duvignaud, *L'Acteur. Esquisse d'une sociologie du comédien* (Paris: Gallimard, 1965), 37.

8. Marco De Marinis, "Dramaturgy of the Spectator," *Drama Review* 31, no. 2 (1987): 100–113.

9. Jean Duvignaud and Jean-Pierre Faye, "Débat sur la sociologie du théâtre," *Cahiers internationaux de sociologie* 11 (1966): 104.

10. Antoine Vitez, *Écrits sur le théâtre,* vol. 1, *L'École* (Paris: POL, 1994), 123.

11. Louis Jouvet, *Réflexions du comédien* (Paris: Librairie théâtrale, 1941), 32.

12. Ibid., 34.

13. Georges Gurvitch, "Sociologie du théâtre," *Lettres nouvelles* no. 35 (1956).

14. Ibid., 202.

15. Anne-Marie Gourdon, *Théâtre, public, réception* (Paris: CNRS, 1982), 128.

16. Jean-Michel Guy and Lucien Mironer, *Les Publics du théâtre* (Paris: La documentation française, 1988).

17. Pierre Bourdieu, *Questions de sociologie* (Paris: Éditions de Minuit, 1986), 78.

18. Ibid., 117.

19. Shevtsova, *Theatre and Cultural Interaction.*

20. Gurvitch, "Sociologie du théâtre," 202.

21. Ibid.

22. Lucien Goldmann, *Le Dieu caché* (Paris: Gallimard, 1955).

23. For further discussion of ideologemes, please see Pavel Medvedev, *Die formale Methode in der Literaturwissenschaft* (1928) (Stuttgart: Metzler, 1976); and Fredric Jameson, *The Political Unconscious* (London: Methuen, 1981).

24. Gurvitch, "Sociologie du théâtre," 203.

25. Duvignaud and Faye, "Débat sur la sociologie du théâtre," 104.

26. Boucris, *L'Espace en scène,* 58.

27. Jouvet, *Réflexions du comédien,* 42.

28. Louis Althusser, "Notes sur un théâtre matérialiste," in *Pour Marx* (Paris: Maspéro, 1965).

29. Eli Rozik, "Towards a Methodology of Play Analysis: A Theatrical Approach," *Assaph* 6 (1990): 63.

30. Baz Kershaw, *The Politics of Performance* (London: Routledge, 1993), 16.

31. Hans Robert Jauss, *Pour une esthétique de la réception.* (Paris: Gallimard, 1978).

32. For an application of Jauss's work to theater, see Pavis, *Voix et images,* 233–93.

33. Marco De Marinis, "Sociologie," in André Helbo et al., *Théâtre,* 88.

34. Marco De Marinis, "Cognitive Processes in Performance Comprehension: Frames Theory and Theatrical Competence," in *Altro Polo: Performance: From Product to Process,* ed. Tim Fitzpatrick (Sydney: University of Sydney, 1989), 175.

35. Belting, *L'histoire de l'art est-elle finie?* 45.

36. Ibid., 32.

37. Eco, *Lector in fabula,* 63.

38. Shevtsova, *Theatre and Cultural Interaction,* 10.

39. Carlson, *Theories of the Theatre,* 540.

40. Gaudibert, "Entrevue," 15.

41. Gurvitch, "Sociologie du théâtre," 196.

42. Duvignaud, *L'Acteur,* 6.

43. Heiner Müller and Robert Weihmann, "Gleichzeitigkeit und Repräsentation," in *Postmoderne-globale Differenz,* ed. R. Weihmann and H.-V. Gumbrecht (Frankfurt am Main: Suhrkamp, 1991), 193.

44. Pierre Bourdieu, "La sociologie est-elle une science?" *La Recherche* 112 (1980): 742.

45. Copeau, *Appels,* 144.

CHAPTER 10

1. This results from a recognition of minorities of all kinds; groups tend to define themselves by excluding "others," and by refusing them the right to become members of the group, or even to include and accept them.

2. Antoine Vitez, "Je n'aime pas. . . ," *Pandora's Box* 11 (1983): 10.

3. In the sense in which formerly or recently colonized countries sometimes "write back" using the colonizers' own (linguistic) weapons. For further details, see Bill Ashcroft, Gareth Griffiths, and Helen Tiffin, eds., *The Empire Writes Back: Theory and Practice in Post-colonial Literatures* (London: Routledge, 1989).

4. For further details, see the photographs and studies devoted to Sanjukta Panigrahi's work in Barba and Savarese, *Dictionary of Theatre Anthropology.*

5. John McAloon, *Rite, Drama, Festival, Spectacle* (Philadelphia: Institute for the Study of Human Issues, 1984), 8.

6. Kirsten Hastrup, "Incorporated Knowledge," *Mime Journal* (1995): 1.

7. Pavis, *Theatre at the Crossroads.*

8. Jean Bernabé, Patrick Chamoiseau, and Raphaël Confiant, *Éloge de la créolité* (Paris: Gallimard, 1992), 31.

9. For a critique of the preexpressive, see Pavis, "Un canoé à la dérive?"

10. Kirsten Hastrup's term, in category no. 4, for "confluence, fusion."

11. James Clifford, *The Predicament of Culture* (Cambridge: Harvard University Press, 1988), 10.

12. Kirsten Hastrup, "Reflections on ISTA," paper distributed at International School of Theatre Anthropology, 1996, 13.

13. In the English sense, i.e., of accomplishing an action and a culture, or realizing them rather than imitating them.

14. Artaud, *Le Théâtre et son double*, 10–11. [English translation: "Theatre and Culture," in *Collected Works*, 2.]

15. Jean-Marie Pradier, "Ethnoscénologie, manifeste," *Théâtre/Public* 124 (1995).

16. Ibid.

17. Pavis, *Theatre at the Crossroads*.

18. For further discussion of this particular topic, see Marianne König, *Theater als Lebenweise—Theater als Ethnologie. Der indonesische Regisseur Boedi S. Otong* (Tübingen: Narr Verlag, 1997).

19. Barba, "Eurasian Theatre," 129.

20. Eugenio Barba and Nicola Saverse, "Dramaturgy," in *Dictionary of Theatre Anthropology*, 68.

21. Ibid.

22. The title of an article by Kirsten Hastrup, "Incorporated Knowledge," 4.

23. Clifford Geertz, *The Interpretation of Cultures: Selected Essays* (New York: Basic Books, 1973), 28.

24. Pearson, "Theatre/Archaeology."

25. Clifford, *The Predicament of Culture*, 15.

26. Claude Lévi-Strauss, *Anthropologie structurale*, vol. 2 (Paris: Plon, 1973), 25.

27. Ibid.

28. An outline of this area of study has been published in French in the journal *L'Internationale de l'imaginaire* 5 (1996) ("La scène et la terre. Questions d'éthnoscénologie"). This volume reprints papers given at the very first ethnoscenology colloquium, coordinated by Jean-Marie Pradier, at UNESCO and at La Maison des Cultures du Monde (directed by Chérif Khaznadar).

CONCLUSIONS

1. Abirached, *Le Théâtre et le Prince*, 157.

2. Pierre Gaudibert, "Conversation sur l'oeuvre d'art," *Peuples et Culture*, 22.

3. Ibid., 11.

4. Henri Atlan, *Entre le cristal et la fumée. Essai sur l'organisation du vivant* (Paris: Seuil, 1978), 52.

5. Cf. Juan Antonio Hormigón, *Trabajo dramaturgico y puesta en escena* (Madrid: Publicaciones de la Asociación de escena en España, 1991).

6. Zeami, *La Tradition secrète du Nô* (Paris: Gallimard, 1960), 130–31.

7. Lehmann, "Die Inszenierung," 48.

8. Susan Sontag, *Against Interpretation* (New York: Dell, 1967).

9. Roland Barthes, *The Pleasure of the Text,* trans. Richard Miller (New York: Hill and Wang, 1975).

10. Lehmann, "Die Inszenierung," 48.

11. Pina Bausch, "Gesprech mit Pina Bausch," 1987, archives of the Wuppertal Tanztheater.

12. Jean Gillibert, *Les Illusiades* (Paris: Clancier-Guénaud, 1983), 310.

13. Copeau, "Un essai de rénovation dramatique," 29–30.

14. Meyerhold, *Écrits sur le théâtre,* 344.

15. Lyotard, "The Tooth, the Palm," 109.

16. Meyerhold, *Écrits sur le théâtre,* 339.

17. Lyotard, "The Tooth, the Palm," 105.

18. Copeau, *Appels,* 102.

19. Derrida, "The Theater of Cruelty," 234.

20. The expression is Lyotard's, in "La dent, la paume." See also Godard and Louppe, "Le déséquilibre fondateur." ["Singular, Moving Geographies".]

21. Gaudibert, "Entrevue," 11.

22. Barry Edwards and Geoffrey Smith, "Theatre Statement," program for Diskurs, European festival of student theater, Giessen, 1993, 90–100.

23. A Dutch group that deconstructs universal classics.

24. An American group that grew out of Richard Schechner's Performance Garage, inspired by intercultural deconstruction.

25. Michel Vinaver, "La mise en trop," *Théâtre/Public* 82–83 (1988). [Translator's note: Vinaver's expression "mise en trop," which critiques certain mise-en-scènes as excessive and redundantly illustrative, puns on the title of Molière's *Le Misanthrope.*]

26. Émile Jaques-Dalcroze, *Le Rhythme, la Musique et l'Éducation* (Lausanne: Foetisch Frères, 1919), 140.

27. Hormigón, *Trabajo dramaturgico,* 63.

28. Tindemans, "L'analyse de la représentation théâtrale," 45.

29. Barba, *The Paper Canoe.*

30. Irène Roy, "Schématisation du parcours créateur au théâtre," *Protée* 21, no. 2, p. 87.

31. Ibid.

32. Zeami, *La Tradition secrète du Nô,* 146.

33. Ibid., 147.

34. Dort, *La Représentation émancipée,* 182.

35. James Clifford and George Marcus, eds., *Writing Culture: The Poetics and Politics of Ethnography* (Berkeley and Los Angeles: University of California Press, 1986).

36. Ibid., 22.

37. Vinaver, *Écritures dramatiques,* 11.

Bibliography

Abirached, Robert. "Les jeux de l'être et du paraître." In *Le Théâtre*, ed. D. Couty and A. Rey. Paris: Bordas, 1980.

———. *Le Théâtre et le Prince, 1981–1991*. Paris: Plon, 1992.

Adam, Jean-Michel. *Le Texte descriptif*. Paris: Nathan, 1989.

Althusser, Louis. "Notes sur un théâtre matérialiste." In *Pour Marx*. Paris: Maspéro, 1965.

Appia, Adolphe. *Oeuvres complètes*. Vol. 1. Lausanne: L'Age d'homme, 1983.

Artaud, Antonin. *Collected Works*. Trans. Victor Corti. Vol. 4. London: Calder and Boyars, 1974.

———. *Le Théâtre et son double*. Paris: Gallimard, 1964. Trans. Victor Corti as *The Theatre and Its Double* (London: John Calder, 1970).

Ashcroft, Bill, Gareth Griffiths, and Helen Tiffin, eds. *The Empire Writes Back: Theory and Practice in Post-colonial Literatures*. London: Routledge, 1989.

Atlan, Henri. *Entre le cristal et la fumée. Essai sur l'organisation du vivant*. Paris: Seuil, 1978.

Bablet, Denis. *Le Décor de théâtre de 1870 à 1914*. Paris: CNRS, 1965.

———. *Les Révolutions scéniques au XXème siècle*. Paris: Société Internationale d'Art, 1975.

Bakhtin, Mikhail. *The Dialogic Imagination: Four Essays*. Trans. Caryl Emerson and Michael Holquist. Ed. Michael Holquist. Austin: University of Texas Press, 1981.

Banu, Georges. *Le Costume de théâtre dans la mise en scène contemporaine*. Paris: CNDP, 1981.

Barba, Eugenio. "Eurasian Theatre." *Drama Review* 32, no. 3 (T119) (1988).

———. "La fiction de dualité." In *Le Corps en jeu*, ed. Odette Aslan. Paris: CNRS, 1993.

———. *The Floating Islands*. Holstebro: Odin Teatret Vorlag, 1983.

———. *The Paper Canoe: A Guide to Theatre Anthropology*. Trans. Richard Fowler. London: Routledge, 1995.

Barba, Eugenio, and Nicola Savarese. *A Dictionary of Theatre Anthropology: The Secret Art of the Performer*. London: Routledge, 1991.

Barko, Ivan, and Bruce Burgess. *La Dynamique des points de vue dans le texte du théâtre*. Paris: Lettres Modernes, 1988.

Barrault, Jean-Louis. *Le Phénomène Théâtral*. Zaharoff Lecture for 1961. Oxford: Clarendon Press, 1961.

Barthes, Roland. *Camera Lucida*. Trans. Richard Howard. London: Fontana, 1984.

————. *Essais critiques.* Paris: Seuil, 1964. Trans. Richard Howard as *Critical Essays* (Evanston, Ill.: Northwestern University Press, 1972).

————. "The Grain of the Voice." *Image Music Text.* Trans. Stephen Heath. London: Fontana, 1977.

————. *Leçon.* Paris: Seuil, 1978. Trans. Richard Howard as "Inaugural Lecture, Collège de France," in *Barthes: Selected Writings,* ed. Susan Sontag (London: Fontana, 1983).

————. *The Pleasure of the Text.* Trans. Richard Miller. New York: Hill and Wang, 1975.

————. *Le Système de la mode.* Paris: Seuil, 1967. Trans. Matthew Ward and Richard Howard as *The Fashion System* (New York: Hill and Wang, 1974).

Baudrillard, Jean. *The System of Objects.* Trans. James Benedict. London: Verso, 1996.

Bausch, Pina. "Gesprech mit Pina Bausch." Archives of the Wuppertal Tanztheater, 1987.

Bazin, André. "Théâtre et cinéma." *Esprit,* June–August 1951. Reprinted in *Qu'est-ce que le cinéma?* (Paris: Éd. du Cerf, 1975).

Belting, Hans. *L'histoire de l'art est-elle finie?* Nîmes: Éd. Jacqueline Chambon, 1989.

Benhamou, Anne-Françoise. "Méandres d'un enseignement atypique." *Théâtre/Public* 82–83 (1988).

Benjamin, Walter. *Versuche über Brecht.* Frankfurt am Main: Suhrkamp, 1931. Trans. Anna Bostock as *Understanding Brecht* (London: New Left Books, 1977).

Benveniste, Émile. *Problèmes de linguistique générale.* Vol. 2. Paris: Gallimard, 1974.

Bernabé, Jean, Patrick Chamoiseau, and Raphaël Confiant. *Éloge de la créolité.* Paris: Gallimard, 1992.

Bernard, Michel. *L'Expressivité du corps.* 2d ed. Paris, Seuil, 1995.

————. "Quelques réflexions sur le jeu de l'acteur contemporain." *Bulletin de psychologie* 38, no. 370 (1986).

Bernardy, Michel. *Le Jeu verbal, ou traité de diction française à l'usage de l'honnête homme.* Paris: Éditions de l'Aube, 1988.

————. "La métamorphose du verbe par l'acteur." *Change* 29 (December 1976).

Boucris, Luc. *L'Espace en scène.* Paris: Librairie Théâtrale, 1993.

Boulez, Pierre. *Penser la musique aujourd'hui.* Paris: Gallimard, 1987.

Bourdieu, Pierre. *Questions de sociologie.* Paris: Éditions de Minuit, 1986.

————. "La sociologie est-elle une science?" *La Recherche* 112 (1980).

Brook, Peter. "À la source du jeu." In *Le Corps en jeu,* ed. Odette Aslan. Paris: CNRS, 1993.

————. "À propos du *Roi Lear* et de *Marat-Sade.*" *Cahiers Théâtre Louvain* 46 (1981).

————. *Le Diable, c'est l'ennui.* Paris: ANRAT/Actes Sud Papier, 1992. Trans. as "The Slyness of Boredom," in *There Are No Secrets: Thoughts on Acting and Theatre* (London: Methuen, 1993).

————. *The Empty Space.* London: Penguin, 1968.

————. *The Shifting Point.* New York: Harper and Row, 1987.

————. *Travail théâtral* 18 (1975).

Bryson, Norman. "The Gaze and the Glance." *Vision and Painting: The Logic of the Gaze.* London: Macmillan, 1983.

Burke, Kenneth. *A Grammar of Motives.* Englewood Cliffs, N.J.: Prentice-Hall, 1945.

Carlo, Nicole Scotto di. "La Voix chantée." *La Recherche* 235 (September 1991).

Carlson, Marvin. *Theories of the Theatre.* Ithaca, N.Y.: Cornell University Press, 1993.

Castarède, Marie-France. *La Voix et ses sortilèges.* Paris: Les Belles Lettres, 1987.

Charles, Daniel. "Thèses sur la voix." In "La voix, l'écoute," special issue of *Traverses* 20 (1980).

Chekhov, Michael. *To the Actor: On the Technique of Acting* (New York: Harper and Row, 1953).

————. *L'imagination créatrice de l'acteur.* Paris: Pygmalion, 1995.

Chion, Michel. *L'Audio-vision.* Paris: Nathan, 1990.

Clifford, James. *The Predicament of Culture.* Cambridge: Harvard University Press, 1988.

Clifford, James, and George Marcus, eds. *Writing Culture: The Poetics and Politics of Ethnography.* Berkeley and Los Angeles: University of California Press, 1986.

Cole, Toby, and H. K. Chinoy. *Actors on Acting.* New York: Crown, 1970.

Copeau, Jacques. *Appels.* Registres 1. Paris: Gallimard, 1974.

Cornut, Guy. *La Voix.* Paris: Presses Universitaires de France, "Que sais-je?" 1983.

Corvin, Michel. *Dictionnaire encyclopédique du théâtre.* Paris: Bordas, 1991.

————. *Molière et ses metteurs en scène aujourd'hui.* Lyon: Presses Universitaires, 1985.

Cosnier, Jacques. Introduction to "Signes et gestes," special edition of *Protée* 20, no. 2 (1992).

Cosnier, Jacques, and A. Brossard. *La Communication non verbale.* Paris: Delachaux and Niestlé, 1984.

Couchot, Edmond, and Hélène Tramus. "Le geste et le calcul." *Protée* 21, no. 3 (1993).

Decroux, Étienne. *Paroles sur le mime.* Paris: Gallimard, 1963. Trans. Mark Piper as *Words on Mime* (Claremont, Calif.: Pomona College Theatre Department, 1985).

Delsarte, François. *Une Anthologie.* Paris: La Villette–IMEC, 1992.

Derrida, Jacques. "The Theater of Cruelty and the Closure of Representation." In *Writing and Difference,* trans. Alan Bass. London: Routledge, 1990.

Dort, Bernard. *Lecture de Brecht.* Paris: Seuil, 1960.

————. *La Représentation émancipée.* Arles: Actes Sud, 1988.

Duvignaud, Jean. *L'Acteur. Esquisse d'une sociologie du comédien.* Paris: Gallimard, 1965.

Duvignaud, Jean, and Jean-Pierre Faye. "Débat sur la sociologie du théâtre." *Cahiers internationaux de sociologie* 11 (1966).

Eco, Umberto. *Lector in fabula.* Paris: Grasset, 1979.

Elam, Keir. *The Semiotics of Theatre and Drama.* London: Methuen, 1980.

Fédida, Pierre. *Le Corps, le Texte et la Scène.* Paris: Delarge, 1983.

Fenichel, Otto. "On Acting." *Psychoanalytic Quarterly* 15 (1946). Original in *Aufsätze,* vol. 2 (Frankfurt am Main: Ulstein, 1985).

Finter, Helga. "Théâtre expérimental et sémiologie du théâtre: La théâtralisation de la voix." In *Théâtralité, écriture et mise en scène,* ed. J. Féral. Montreal: Hurtubise, 1985.

Fischer-Lichte, Erika. *Das Drama und seine Inszenierung.* Tübingen: Niemeyer, 1985.

————. *Semiotik des Theaters.* Tübingen: Narr Verlag, 1983.

————. "Die Zeichensprache des Theaters." In *Theaterwissenschaft heute. Eine Einführung,* ed. R. Möhrmann. Berlin: D. Reimer Verlag, 1990.

Foster, Susan. *Reading Dancing.* Berkeley and Los Angeles: University of California Press, 1988.

Freud, Sigmund. *Art and Literature.* Trans. James Strachey. Penguin Freud Library, vol. 14. London, 1985.

————. *Civilization and Its Discontents.* Trans. Joan Riviere. London: Hogarth Press, 1939.

————. *Essais de psychanalyse appliquée.* Paris: Gallimard, 1976.

————. *The Interpretation of Dreams.* Trans. James Trachey. Penguin Freud Library, vol. 4. London, 1983.

————. "Psychopathic Characters on Stage." In *A Case of Hysteria, Three Essays on Sexuality, and Other Works,* trans. James Strachey, Standard Edition, vol. 7. London: Hogarth Press, 1953.

————. *Die Traumdeutung, Studienausgabe.* Vol. 2. Frankfurt am main: Fischer, 1972.

————. "The Unconscious." Trans. Cecil M. Baines. In *Collected Papers,* vol. 4, *Papers on Metapsychology.* London: Hogarth Press, 1953.

Frize, Nicolas. "La musique au théâtre." In *Une esthétique de l'ambiguïté,* ed. J. Pigeon. Lyon: Les Cahiers du Soleil Debout, 1993.

Garcia-Martinez, Manuel. "Réflexions sur la perception du rythme au théâtre." Doctoral thesis, University of Paris VIII, 1995.

Garner, Stanton B. *Bodied Spaces: Phenomenology and Performance in Contemporary Drama.* Ithaca, N.Y.: Cornell University Press, 1994.

Gaudibert, Pierre. "Entrevue." In *Peuples et cultures.* Grenoble: Presses Universitaires, 1982.

Geertz, Clifford. *The Interpretation of Cultures: Selected Essays.* New York: Basic Books, 1973.

Gil, José. "Le corps abstrait." In *La Dance, naissance d'un mouvement de pensée ou le complexe de Cunningham.* Paris: Armand Colin, 1989.

Gillibert, Jean. *Les Illusiades.* Paris: Clancier-Guénaud, 1983.

Goffman, Erving. *The Presentation of Self in Everyday Life.* New York: Doubleday, 1959.

Goldmann, Lucien. *Le Dieu caché.* Paris: Gallimard, 1955.

Gourdon, Anne-Marie. *Théâtre, public, réception.* Paris: CNRS, 1982.

Green, André. "L'Interprétation psychanalytique des productions culturelles et des oeuvres d'arts." In *Critique sociologique et critique psychanalytique.* Brussels: Éditions de l'Institut de Sociologie, 1970.

————. *Un Oeil en trop.* Paris: Minuit, 1969.

Grosz, Elizabeth. *Volatile Bodies: Toward a Corporeal Feminism.* Sydney: Allen and Unwin, 1994.

Gurvitch, Georges. "Sociologie du théâtre." *Lettres nouvelles* 35 (1956).

Guy, Jean-Michel, and Lucien Mironer. *Les Publics du théâtre.* Paris: La documentation française, 1988.

Haddad, Youssef. *Art du conteur, art de l'acteur.* Louvain: Cahiers-théâtre, 1982.

Hall, Edward. *The Hidden Dimension.* New York: Doubleday, 1966.

Hastrup, Kirsten. "Incorporated Knowledge." *Mime Journal* (1995).

———. "Reflections on ISTA." Paper distributed at International School of Theatre Anthropology, 1996.

Helbo, André, et al. *Théâtre: Modes d'approche.* Paris: Méridiens-Klincksiek, 1987.

Henry, Philippe, ed. "Mime contemporain et dramaturgie. Résultats de la première étape du projet de recherche dramaturgique impulsé à partir de la Fédération européenne de mime." Paris, 1993. Photocopy.

Hiss, Guido. "Freiräume für die Phantasie." *TheaterZeitSchrift* 35 (1994).

———. *Korrespondenzen.* Tübingen: Niemeyer, 1988.

Honzl, Jindrich. "La mobilité du signe théâtral." *Travail théâtral* 4 (1971): 6–20.

Hormigón, Juan Antonio. *Trabajo dramaturgico y puesta en escena.* Madrid: Publicaciones de la Asociación de escena en España, 1991.

Hurst Du Prey, Deirdre, ed. *Michael Chekhov: Lessons for the Professional Actor.* New York: Performing Arts Journal Publications, 1985.

Ingarden, Roman. *Das literarische Kunstwerk.* Tübingen: Niemeyer, 1931.

Jaques-Dalcroze, Émile. *Le Rhythme, la Musique et l'Éducation.* Lausanne: Foetisch Frères, 1919.

Jameson, Fredric. *The Political Unconscious.* London: Methuen, 1981.

Jauss, Hans-Robert. *Ästhetische Erfahrung und literarische Hermeneutik.* Munich: Fink, 1977.

Johnson, Mark. *The Body in the Mind: The Bodily Basis of Meaning, Imagination, and Reason.* Chicago: University of Chicago Press, 1987.

Jones, David Richard. *Great Directors at Work.* Berkeley and Los Angeles: University of California Press, 1986.

Jousse, Marcel. *L'Anthropologie du geste.* Paris: Gallimard, 1974.

Jouvet, Louis. *Réflexions du comédien.* Paris: Librairie théâtrale, 1941.

Kershaw, Baz. *The Politics of Performance.* London: Routledge, 1993.

König, Marianne. "Modernes Theater in Indonesien." Ph.D. diss., University of Berne, 1995.

Konigson, Élie. "Le spectateur et son ombre." In *Le Corps en jeu,* ed. Odette Aslan. Paris: CNRS, 1993.

Kowzan, Tadeusz. "L'art du spectacle dans un système général des arts." *Études philosophiques,* January 1970.

———. *Sémiologie du théâtre.* Paris: Nathan, 1992.

———. "Le signe au théâtre." *Diogène* 61 (1968).

Kristeva, Julia. *La Révolution du langage poétique.* Paris: Seuil, 1974.

Kubik, Gerhard. "Verstehen in afrikanischen Musikkulturen." In *Musik in Afrika,* ed. A. Simon. Berlin: Museum für Völkerkunde, 1983.

Lacan, Jacques. *Écrits.* Vol. 1. Paris: Seuil, 1966.

————. "Les quatre concepts fondamentaux de la psychanalyse." *Séminaire*, book 11. Paris: Seuil, 1973.

Le Breton, David. "Le corps en scène." *L'Internationale de l'imaginaire* 2 (1994).

Lecoq, Jacques, ed. *Le Théâtre du geste*. Paris: Bordas, 1987.

Lehmann, Hans-Thies. "Die Inszenierung: Probleme ihrer Analyse." *Zeitschrift für Zemiotik* 11, no. 1 (1989).

Lévi-Strauss, Claude. *Anthropologie structurale*. Vol. 2. Paris: Plon, 1973.

Louppe, Laurence. "Le déséquilibre fondateur." *Art Press*, special issue, 1992. Trans. David Williams as "Singular, Moving Geographies," *Writings on Dance* 15 (winter 1996).

Lyotard, Jean-François. "La dent, la paume." *Des dispositifs pulsionnels*. Paris: UGE, 1973. Trans. Anne Knap and Michel Benamou as "The Tooth, the Palm," *Substance* 15 (1976): 105–10.

————. *Discours, figure*. Paris: Klincksieck, 1971.

————. "Psychanalyse et peinture." *Encyclopedia Universalis*. Paris, 1985.

Marinis, Marco De. "Cognitive Processes in Performance Comprehension: Frames Theory and Theatrical Competence." In *Altro Polo: Performance: From Product to Process*, ed. Tim Fitzpatrick (Sydney: University of Sydney, 1989).

————. "Dramaturgy of the Spectator." *Drama Review* 31, no. 2 (1987).

————. *Semiotica del teatro*. Milan: Bompiani, 1982.

Martin, Jacqueline, and Willmar Sauter, eds. *Understanding Theatre*. Stockholm: Almquist and Wiksell International, 1995.

Martin, John. *The Modern Dance*. New York: Dance Horizons, 1966.

Mateo, Pepito. "Pepito Mateo, conteur?" *Dire* 15 (1990).

Mauss, Marcel. *Sociologie et anthropologie*. Paris: Presses Universitaires de France, 1950. Trans. as "Techniques of the Body," in *Incorporations*, ed. Jonathan Crary and Sanford Kwinter (New York: Zone Books, 1992).

McAloon, John. *Rite, Drama, Festival, Spectacle*. Philadelphia: Institute for the Study of Human Issues, 1984.

Medvedev, Pavel. *Die formale Methode in der Literaturwissenschaft*. Stuttgart: Metzler, (1928) 1976.

Merleau-Ponty, Maurice. "Eye and Mind." Trans. Carleton Dallery in *The Primacy of Perception*, ed. James M. Edie. Evanston, Ill.: Northwestern University Press, 1964.

————. *The Phenomenology of Perception*. Trans. Colin Smith. London: Routledge and Kegan Paul, 1962.

Metz, Christian, and Marc Vernet. "Entretien." *Iris* 10 (1990).

Meyerhold, Vsevolod. *Écrits sur le théâtre*. Vol. 4. Lausanne: L'Age d'homme, 1992.

Mourlet, Michel. *Sur un art ignoré*. Paris: La Table Ronde, 1965.

Müller, Heiner. *Gesammelte Irrtümer*. Frankfurt am Main: Verlag der Autoren, 1986. Trans. as *Erreurs choisies* (Paris: l'Arche, 1988).

Müller, Heiner, and Robert Weihmann. "Gleichzeitigkeit und Repräsentation." In *Postmoderne-globale Differenz*, ed. R. Weihmann and H.-V. Gumbrecht. Frankfurt am Main: Suhrkamp, 1991.

Müller, Jürgen. "Intermedialität als Provokation der Medianwissenschaft." *Eikon* 4 (1992).

———. "Le labyrinthe médiatique du film." In *Mots/Images/Sons*. Colloque international de Rouen, March 1989. Rouen: Presses Universitaires, 1990.

Musil, Robert. *L'Homme sans qualités*. Vol. 2. Paris: Seuil, 1982.

Norman, Sally Jane. "L'image et le corps dans l'art vivant." Presentation at the "collège iconique," *Les cahiers* 3 (1994).

Novarina, Valère. "Pour Luis de Funès." *Le Théâtre des paroles*. Paris: POL, 1989.

Paquet, Dominique. *Alchimie du maquillage*. Paris: Chiron, 1989.

———. "Pour un théâtre de fragrances." *Comédie-Française: Les Cahiers* 17 (1995).

Paul, Arno. "Theater als Kommunikationsproze." In *Theaterwissenschaft im deutschsprachigen Raum*. Darmstadt: Wissenschaftliche Buchgemeinschaft, 1981.

Pavis, Patrice. "Un canoë à la dérive?" *Théâtre/Public* 126 (1995).

———. *Dictionnaire du théâtre*. 1987; Paris: Dunod, 1996.

———. "Film est un film." *Protée* 19, no. 3 (1991).

———. *Marivaux à l'épreuve de la scène*. Paris: Publications de la Sorbonne, 1986.

———. *Problèmes de sémiologie théâtrale*. Montreal: Presses de l'Université de Québec, 1976.

———. "Theatre Analysis: Some Questions and a Questionnaire." Trans. Susan Bassnett. *New Theatre Quarterly* 1, no. 2 (1985).

———. *Theatre at the Crossroads of Culture*. Trans. Loren Kruger. London: Routledge, 1992.

———. *Le Théâtre contemporain*. Paris: Natahn, 2002.

———. *Vers une théorie de la pratique théâtrale*. Lille: Septentrion, 2000.

———. *Voix et images de la scène. Pour une sémiologie de la réception*. Lille: Presses Universitaires de Lille, 1985.

Pavis, Patrice, ed. *La Dramaturgie de l'actrice*. Bouffonneries, nos. 97–99, 1999.

Pearson, Mike. "Theatre/Archaeology." *Drama Review* 38, no. 4 (T144) (1994).

Peirce, Charles S. "Logic as Semiotic: The Theory of Signs." In *Philosophical Writings of Peirce*, ed. Justus Buchler. New York, Dover, 1955.

Pic, Roger, and Chantal Meyer-Planttureux. *Bertolt Brecht et le Berliner Ensemble à Paris*. Paris: Arte éditions et Marval, 1995.

Pradier, Jean-Marie. "Ethnoscénologie: La profondeur des émergences." *L'Internationale de l'imaginaire* 5 (1996).

———. "Ethnoscénologie, manifeste." *Théâtre/Public* 124 (1995).

———. *La Scène et la fabrique des corps*. Bordeaux: Presses Universitaires de Bordeaux, 1997.

Prunot, Philippe. "Emballage, mode d'emploi." *Théâtre/Public* 121 (1995).

Reuter, Yves. *Introduction à l'analyse du roman*. Paris: Bordas, 1991.

Richterich, Uwe. *Die Sehnsucht zu sehen. Der filmisch Blick*. Frankfurt am Main: Peter Lang, 1993.

Rimé, B. "Communication verbale et non verbale." *Grand dictionnaire de la psychologie*. Paris: Larousse, 1991.

Roheim, Géza. *Origine et fonction de la culture*. Paris: Gallimard, 1972.

Roy, Irène. "Schématisation du parcours créateur au théâtre." *Protée* 21, no. 2.

Rozik, Eli. "Towards a Methodology of Play Analysis: A Theatrical Approach." *Assaph* no. 6 (1990).

Sami-Ali. *L'Espace imaginaire*. Paris: Gallimard, 1974.

Sauter, Wilmar. *New Directions in Audience Research.* Utrecht: Instituut voor Theaterwetenschap, 1988.

"La scène et la terre. Questions d'"éthnoscénologie." Special issue of *L'Internationale de l'imaginaire* 5 (1996).

Schechner, Richard. *Between Theater and Anthropology.* Philadelphia: University of Pennsylvania Press, 1985.

Schmid, Jean-Claude. *La Raison des gestes dans l'occident mediéval.* Paris: Gallimard, 1990.

Schoenmakers, Henri, ed. *Performance Theory.* Utrecht: Instituut voor Theaterwetenschap, 1986.

Serpieri, Alessandro. *Come comunica il teatro: Dal testo alla scena.* Milan: Il Formichiere, 1977.

Shevtsova, Maria. *Theatre and Cultural Interaction.* Sydney: Sydney Studies, 1993.

Sklar, Deidre. "Étienne Decroux's Promethean mime." In *Acting (Re)Considered: Theories and Practices,* ed. Phillip B. Zarrilli. London: Routledge, 1995.

Slama-Cazacu, Tatiana. "Réflexion sur la dyade terminologique 'Lisible/visible.'" In *Approches de l'opéra,* ed. André Helbo. Paris: Didier, 1986.

Sontag, Susan. *Against Interpretation.* New York: Dell, 1967.

Stanislavsky, Constantin. *Die Arbeit des Schauspielers an sich selbst.* Berlin: Das Europaïsche Buch, vol. 2, 1988.

States, Bert. *Great Reckonings in Little Rooms: On the Phenomenology of Theater.* Berkeley and Los Angeles: University of California Press, 1985.

Strasberg, Lee. *A Dream of Passion: The Development of the Method.* London: Bloomsbury, 1988.

Strehler, Giorgio. Interview in *Le Nouvel Observateur* 723 (1978).

Suvin, Darko. "The Performance Text as Audience-Stage Dialog, Inducing a Possible World." *Versus* 42 (1985).

Thorpe, Simon. "L'oeil, le cerveau et l'image." In *Le Téléspectateur face à la publicité,* ed. Jean-Marie Pradier. Nathan: Paris, 1989.

Tindemans, Carlos. "L'analyse de la représentation théâtrale. Quelques réflexions méthodologiques." In *Théâtre de toujours, d'Aristote à Kalisky, Hommage à Paul Delsemme.* Brussels: Éd. de l'Université, 1983.

Todorov, Tzvetan. *Théorie de la littérature. Textes des formalistes russes.* Paris: Seuil, 1965.

Turk, Horst. *Soziale und theatralische Konventionen als Problem des Dramas und der Übersetzung.* Tübingen: Narr Verlag, 1989.

Turner, Victor. *Dramas, Fields and Metaphors.* Ithaca, N.Y.: Cornell University Press, 1974.

———. *From Ritual to Theatre.* New York: Performing Arts Journal Press, 1977.

Ubersfeld, Anne. *L'École du spectateur.* Paris: Éditions Sociales, 1981.

———. *Lire le théâtre.* Paris: Éditions Sociales, 1977.

Van Khé, Tran. "Techniques vocales dans les théâtres d'Asie oriental." *Encyclopedia universalis,* vol. 18, "Voix," 1988.

Vasse, Denis. *L'Ombilic et la voix.* Paris: Seuil, 1974.

Villeneuve, Rodrigue. "Les îles incertaines. L'objet de la sémiotique théâtrale." *Protée* 17, no. 1 (1989).

Vinaver, Michel. *Écritures dramatiques.* Arles: Actes Sud, 1993.
———. "La mise en trop." *Théâtre/Public* 82–83 (1988).
Vitez, Antoine. "Je n'aime pas. . . ." *Pandora's Box* 11 (1983).
———. *Le Théâtre des idées.* Paris: Gallimard, 1991.
———. *Écrits sur le théâtre.* Vol. 1, *L'École.* Paris: POL, 1994.
Vurpillot, Éliane. "Gestaltthéorie." *Grand dictionnaire de la psychologie.* Paris: Larousse, 1991.
Zeami. *La Tradition secrète du Nô.* Paris: Gallimard, 1960. Trans. J. Thomas Rimer and Yamazaki Masakazu as *On the Art of the No Drama: The Major Treatises of Zeami* (Princeton: Princeton University Press, 1984).

Index